THE
30ROCK
BOOK

THE
30ROCK
BOOK

Inside the Iconic Show,
from Blerg to EGOT

MIKE ROE

Abrams Press, New York

To Kristiana, my spectacular wife.
Thank you for being the Liz to my Criss
(and thankfully not a Hazel).

Contents

INTRODUCTION

Seven Seasons of
Super-Specific Weirdness

30 Rock was the show that made *Saturday Night Live* head writer Tina Fey a bona fide star. It was always a ratings underdog, but one that fought its way into the hearts of viewers season after season. Coming on the air after the end of *Friends*, the show embodied an idea that was revolutionary at the time: it was better to be funny than to make an audience swoon or to tie characters up in romantic entanglements.

What set *30 Rock* apart, besides Tina Fey's distinctive view on the world, was the show's obsession with hyper-specific jokes—from Liz Lemon's much-memed "night cheese" to cutaway music video earworms proclaiming, "It's Never Too Late for Now." In the comedy world, those are often called one- or two-percenters—the jokes that will only work for 1 or 2 percent of the people out there, but for that audience, the jokes *really* work. When you're in that group, you feel like there's a show that's finally talking to you, just you, for a moment—that 2 percent was enough to earn the show seven seasons and numerous awards.

But with *30 Rock*, it wasn't just the type of jokes, it was the pace. The show never paused to wait for you to catch up. It would continue throwing jokes at you so fast that even if you missed what a few of them were going for, you'd still be laughing from the one before that.

It's an approach to comedy that wasn't usually done in sitcoms, which had traditionally been shot with a multiple-camera setup, filmed before a live audience. Those shows had to make sure their setups and punchlines were so super clear that every member of the audience could catch them, then pause for extended laughter, the kind that makes people feel like they aren't alone. *The Simpsons*, since it was animated and had no studio audience or laugh track, was able to fit in more jokes—but it took mainstream TV a long time to catch on to the possibilities dropping the laugh track could bring.

Where *30 Rock*'s contemporary *The Office* used the lack of an audience to allow awkwardness to hang in the air, *30 Rock* pulled you in. This was not a lie back and enjoy yourself show—this was a "you better sit on the front of your couch or you will miss twelve amazing jokes that you never saw coming" show. *30 Rock* was part of a generation of single-camera sitcoms that popularized a denser joke format, and it was the most packed of them all.

The show would let Fey deliver commentary about her time on *SNL*, network execs, and everything else she had to deal with as a creative person in comedy at a major TV network. Liz Lemon became the ultra-relatable nerd who'd won at life, the underdog who blossomed and finally achieved everything she wanted. She was someone who got ahead because she worked hard and cared a lot about what she was doing. It reflected Tina's intense drive, and her awkwardness made all those viewers who'd felt just as awkward over the years—which is basically everyone— latch onto her.

This book is about how *30 Rock* survived tough competition and a changing network TV landscape year after year, the true stories and behind-the-scenes battles that often turned into plotlines, and how it found its voice while becoming a critical favorite and beloved cult classic. It will explore the castings that almost were, and glimpse awkward and heartfelt moments between cast and crew, drawn together in their quest to create top-notch comedy. It tells the story of *30 Rock* primarily based on nearly fifty interviews I conducted with members of the show's cast, guest stars, writers, directors, producers, and crew, as well as TV critics, personal assistants, and more, as I investigated what was behind the jokes that made me laugh so hard my face hurt. My extensive research also includes material from archival interviews I conducted with members of the *30 Rock* family, DVD commentary, books, and other published interviews. I used to write and perform sketch comedy at several Los Angeles theaters, so I apply my own experience with writing jokes to examine how next-level the team behind *30 Rock* really was. And I'll be sharing stories throughout in the words of those who lived it so that you can feel what it was like to be a part of that moment. (Some quotes have been edited for conciseness and/or clarity.)

Congratulations! You're about to take a tour through *30 Rock*. I'm your Kenneth the Page (but moderately more self-aware and less likely to tell you you're condemned to eternal hellfire).

Ready? Let's go.

Creating the *30 Rock* Pilot

In 2002, Tina Fey was looking for a new project. She'd made a name as the first woman to become head writer of *Saturday Night Live*, as well as the first woman to anchor *Weekend Update* since the early eighties. She was proving all the idiots who said that women aren't funny wrong by writing jokes ten times funnier than those of her male colleagues, leading an *SNL* renaissance.

But while she was well liked by comedy fans, Fey wasn't quite a star yet. She hadn't made her impact outside of late-night comedy, just beginning to develop the script that would become the feature comedy *Mean Girls*, and she was working to figure out how to graduate out of *SNL* to her own projects. This was during the era where she said herself how bad she was in sketches on *SNL*, including saying so *in* an actual *SNL* sketch, long before her breakout performance as Sarah Palin in 2008.

> **Daisy Gardner (writer):** One thing that's really hard to remember in an era of *Fleabag, Broad City*, shows with funny women in them: Networks didn't take a chance on funny female leads, written and directed by funny female leads. Like, that was Tina.

SNL creator and executive producer Lorne Michaels, the behind-the-scenes Yoda to generations of late-night talent, suggested Fey develop a sitcom with NBC. As with the show's other talent, her contract included Michaels and his Broadway Video production company being involved in the show's development. Then-president of NBC Entertainment Jeff Zucker was also encouraging Fey to do a sitcom, convincing her that this was the right move and convincing Lorne Michaels that she was the next great voice in comedy. Tina signed a contract in 2003 that required her to develop a project for the network.

After a few months of working on ideas, she was set to make her pitch to NBC exec Kevin Reilly. Reilly had developed shows for NBC in the eighties and nineties including *Saved by the Bell*, *Law & Order*, and *ER*. He'd left the network but continued to develop for them, including shepherding *NewsRadio* to air, as well as *The Sopranos* at HBO.

Reilly was back at NBC, but it was a time of decline for the network, with NBC in fourth place behind ABC, CBS, and Fox. Longtime hits including *Friends* and *Frasier* were wrapping up, with decades of Thursday-night Must See TV comedy dominance fading. The network responsible for *Cheers*, *Seinfeld*, and *Will & Grace* was desperate for another hit.

Fey came to him with her big idea: a show about a cable news producer working with a right-wing host, à la Fox News ratings champ/blowhard Bill O'Reilly. And she wanted the part to be played by liberal actor/activist Alec Baldwin, who'd proven his comedic performance chops through years of guest hosting on *SNL*.

Reilly said thanks, but no thanks. Fey was told that she should write something inspired by working on *SNL*, since her original pitch had just taken her own experiences and put a light veneer over them anyway.

At the same time, she'd been working with Michaels on the movie *Mean Girls*, which went on to be a huge hit and offered a look at what Fey's voice would sound like outside of *SNL*. The movie, which debuted in spring 2004, took the feminist ideas that had often been part of Fey's work on *Weekend Update* and put them in a fictional world that fans continue to quote.

Fey reluctantly went back to work on her project, writing a new version of the *30 Rock* pilot episode. The new direction wasn't lighting a creative fire for her, but she was inspired when her husband, composer Jeff Richmond, suggested keeping that conservative Alec Baldwin character. She realized that, in a faux showbiz show, she could add her former *SNL* castmate Tracy Morgan and create a triangle of different viewpoints going at each other—and the earliest version of *30 Rock* was born, which would ultimately take its name from the site of the iconic NBC studio that houses *SNL* itself. Richmond would continue to collaborate with Fey on the show, providing the score and serving as an executive producer.

NBCUniversal Television and Lorne Michaels's Broadway Video officially announced that they were shooting a pilot for the *Untitled Tina Fey Project* in early 2005, with Michaels attached as an executive producer. Tina Fey had worked hard getting her pilot off the ground, writing it by herself before any other writers were brought in. That's the standard model for a TV show—the original creator crafts the pilot script before hopefully getting the network to agree to actually film it. There's a lot riding on those pilots, with the network deciding whether the show will get to be a whole series based on how the pilot turns out.

Someone else also had the idea to do a show going behind the scenes at a *Saturday Night Live*–style late-night show: Aaron Sorkin. The high-profile playwright, screenwriter, and TV showrunner had created a highly rated, all-time classic with *The West Wing* for NBC. Now he wanted to do a drama about what goes into making a late-night sketch comedy show. Sorkin always loved getting into what makes a TV show tick—he'd previously created the critically acclaimed *Sports Night* about a *SportsCenter*-like cable show and would later go on to create *The Newsroom* for HBO, centered on the cable news world.

Don Scardino (director): Aaron is one of these guys, when *The West Wing* started, he would get everybody together when the show went live out on the air. It didn't matter that it was already in the can or anything—he would say, "We're on TV!" It's that kind of love for this business. So I know that his heart was in the right place—he wanted [*Studio 60*] to, like he did with *West Wing*, capture the backstage inner workings of that show.

Sorkin's new faux late-night show—originally titled *Studio 7 on the Sunset Strip*, before ultimately having its title number bumped up to *Studio 60*—prompted controversy behind the scenes from the beginning, with Tina Fey and Lorne Michaels less-than-excited to have Sorkin moving in on their turf. He was seen as an outsider not just to late-night, but to NBC, as he was developing the show for outside production company Warner Bros.

Bradley Whitford (*Studio 60* actor): I loved *30 Rock*.

Tina Fey (Liz Lemon): That god damn *Studio 60* almost killed us.

Whitford ran into Tina Fey at a Television Critics Association event.

Bradley Whitford: I love Tina Fey. I was just saying, "Oh my god. Good luck!" She's pointing at me, and she's like "What? Are you kidding? It's you guys. It's *you* guys."

Speculation at the time indicated that NBC surely wouldn't pick up both shows about late-night TV. Alec Baldwin said he'd be stunned if NBC picked up both of them.

Alec Baldwin (Jack Donaghy): And ours has the tougher task, as a comedy, because if it's not funny, that's it. Whereas a drama can start off as a hard-hitting medical show about real issues, and before you count to three it's about who's fucking who.

When NBC broke with expectations and put both shows on the schedule, *30 Rock* quickly looked like the dark horse between these two competing programs. How could two shows about the same thing on the same network both be hits? It was a ready-made battle to the death. NBC was playing the parent who knew they weren't supposed to say who their favorite child was, even if everyone else knew who the favorite child was.

> **Kevin Reilly (NBC executive):** I saw the problem coming from a mile away. But these are very particular artists, who write what they care about.

The network had a relationship to rebuild with Aaron Sorkin and needed to keep him from leaving for the competition. They also had a star in the making with Tina Fey, whom they'd been grooming for bigger things, as well as a relationship both cozy and successful with *SNL* ruler Lorne Michaels. Reilly told Michaels in advance that the network was picking up *Studio 60*, trying to reassure him that the new show wouldn't be a copy of *SNL*.

As the shows were being developed, Aaron Sorkin and director/executive producer Thomas Schlamme asked Lorne Michaels to let them come watch *SNL* being filmed for a week to learn more about how the show worked. Lorne declined.

> **Adam Bernstein (director):** Among the inside circle of the *SNL* crowd, there was a lot of displeasure over *Studio 60* and how it was borrowing from the same territory. But obviously, *30 Rock* ended up having a life.

Whitford said that he and the rest of the *Studio 60* team didn't feel that same sense of competition with *30 Rock*. They had been hopeful, thinking this could be opening up a new type of show with room for more than one version.

> **Bradley Whitford:** We were embarrassed, because we felt a little misinterpreted. I remember going, "There's a lot of law shows. There's a lot of cop shows." I didn't like being in that position, that they thought we were cocky bastards. We heard that they thought we were full of shit or something.

> **Don Scardino:** I love Aaron, but (*as Don gives a thumbs-down*) suck it! (*laughs*)

30 Rock was the latest in a long line of projects from former *SNL* stars, and seemed unlikely to become a smash hit for the network. *Studio 60* came from a man still considered to be one of the best writers in television, not to mention writing *A Few Good Men* and *The American President*. This was his triumphant return to TV, and NBC proved excited to welcome him back even after he left *The West Wing* at the end of its fourth season and dealt with a somewhat public drug problem.

And while not as directly as *30 Rock* pulled from Tina's life, *Studio 60* was built on Aaron Sorkin's experiences. He was even working with some of the same cast members who'd made *The West Wing* so beloved. He had his own juicy real-world drama, with Matthew Perry as an avatar of his fired TV genius dealing with a drug problem, Perry's character in a relationship with a religious star that mirrored Sorkin's own with actress/singer Kristin Chenoweth.

Bradley Whitford: The shooting schedule on *The West Wing* was notoriously brutal, and I was exhausted. Everybody was telling me that Aaron had written this amazing script. I didn't want to read it because I didn't want to be in the position where I would want to do it, or feel actor-desperate about it and put Aaron in that position, again, because he had given me the part of a lifetime in Josh [Lyman on *The West Wing*].

He said, "Have you read it?" I said, "No, because I know I'm going to like it." He said, "It really feels like your voice. Will you read it?" I read it, and I loved it.

I had a complicated conversation with my family about it. I thought to myself, *Well, this is what you do. You're a horse at a racetrack. You love this, you know it's going to be an intense commitment, but you have this writer at the top of his game.*

Don Scardino: We were the bastard child. *Studio 60* . . . (*whistles*) after all of Aaron's successes, was the Big Kahuna. We were both on NBC. And we were just going to be the crappy one.

Robert Carlock (co-showrunner): We moved to New York, having a lot of confidence that we could do a really funny and good show, but thinking, just from an actuarial standpoint that, especially with *Studio 60* out there and having billboards in Times Square and on Sunset Boulevard, that we would be back in Los Angeles before too long.

Nate Corddry (*Studio 60* actor): We never considered them to be an opponent. We were sure they would last maybe half a season, just as a favor to Lorne and Tina. *Saturday Night Live* was so successful that NBC was like "OK, we'll give you this half-hour show, but really, we're investing in Aaron Sorkin." I did not expect *30 Rock* to have any kind of legs.

Scott Adsit had to audition for the part of Pete Hornberger on *30 Rock*, even though he was friends with Tina and a longtime improv collaborator. He was also auditioning at the same time for *Studio 60* and had to make a choice.

Scott Adsit (Pete Hornberger): I couldn't sign the contract on both. So I had to decide which show to go with: The show about *SNL* with Aaron Sorkin, the guy who's winning Emmys and created *The West Wing*, or the show about *SNL* by the head writer of *SNL*, who some people are aware of, some aren't.

John Riggi (writer/director): Everybody loved Tina, but it was such an unknown quantity. Whereas [*Studio 60*] was Sorkin, this big buzzy show, Judd Hirsch was on—there were a lot of big names on that. We didn't really have anybody. Even Alec, at the time, was in a bit of a holding pattern.

Scott Adsit: The surefire bet was Aaron Sorkin. But I went with Tina, just because I'd rather spend a day with Tina than Aaron Sorkin. At that point, anyway.

Fey's scrappy project continued to move forward. Tracy Morgan had met Tina Fey a couple seasons into working on *SNL*. He felt that she heard his comedic voice, writing to that on the show and creating classic sketches that let him be his funniest. Morgan's recurring sketches ranged from "Brian Fellow's Safari Planet"—where he played the enthusiastic animal show host who doesn't know anything about animals, constantly states his own name, and hallucinates the animals ridiculing him—to *Astronaut Jones*, where he plays an astronaut who happens to act just like Tracy Morgan, hitting on lady aliens.

Tracy Morgan (Tracy Jordan): I got a call from Tina. She was like, she's doing this TV show, and she wanted me to play this character that was similar to me, the person, Tracy Morgan. I was on board from day one.

Lorne Michaels (executive producer): She knew how well she played off him and with him, and she knew how to write for him. He lived an outsized life, at *SNL* and obviously back in the early days of *30 Rock* as well.

Much of Tracy's character is based off of who he really is—though he has at times disputed just how much comes from his life, sometimes even refusing to acknowledge that the character was based on him. According to Tracy, the character was based more on show business outrageousness from other performers. Tracy saw what he was doing as a role, not just being himself on camera.

Tracy Morgan's former assistant: He once made me drive him around New York City in a Porsche, or some kind of car that costs more than me, and made me keep the roof down. It was November in New York City. He'd just had a new sound system installed and was blasting Michael Jackson and Prince while driving through Times Square, then getting very pleased when people recognized him—but also a little perturbed.

It was two and a half years after the call with Tina before they started shooting *30 Rock*, according to Morgan. After seven years on *SNL*—a standard contract for *SNL* stars, who have historically been required to stay with the show for at least seven seasons if the show wants them there—Morgan left to star in his own sitcom. But *The Tracy Morgan Show* failed to take off, getting canceled after a single season. He had other small roles during this time, including voicing a dog named Woof on a TV series called *Where My Dogs At?*

Kevin Ladson (prop master): When I met Tracy, he came to me in a very humble manner and said, "I've been out of work a while, and it sure is good to be back to work." I said, "Listen, I hear you. Anytime I get to work and have fun, that's gravy."

Meanwhile, Alec Baldwin had been a high-level actor for decades. He'd started out in soap operas before bigger roles in movies like *Beetlejuice*, ultimately breaking out as a star in *The Hunt for Red October*. He created an all-time memorable role in *Glengarry Glen Ross* with just minutes of screen time, delivering the famous "coffee is for closers" monologue. He brought a gravitas to everything he did, but had proven his strength in comedy hosting *Saturday Night Live*, with classic sketches like the faux public radio show seen in "Schweddy Balls" (co-written by Robert Carlock).

As much as Fey wanted Baldwin, he didn't necessarily think making a television show was the best use of his time. When he was approached in 2006 about doing TV, it was something that he'd never wanted. He was a film and theater actor before the rise of streaming, when the world still turned its nose up at the smaller screen. But he also didn't mind the potential paycheck.

Nathan Lane (Eddie Donaghy): He kept saying, "I need to do a series." I said, "I know—when one of them works, it's like winning the lottery. So I wish you luck. I've not had that good fortune."

Matthew Broderick ("Cooter Burger"/James Riley): When Alec was gonna be doing it, he was complaining bitterly. I think he wasn't sure.

Adam Bernstein: Alec Baldwin ended up being pivotal to the show, but they never really had him. When we did the pilot, he was just a guest star—he wasn't committed to being on the show full-time.

Baldwin eventually agreed to do the pilot, but all he would commit to if the pilot was eventually picked up by the network was six episodes a season, for up to six seasons.

Once the pilot was ready to move into production, a number of directors were in contention to direct the episode. The show went with Adam Bernstein, who'd directed sitcom pilots for *Scrubs* and oddball cult favorites like *Strangers with Candy* and *The Adventures of Pete and Pete*, while also having experience working on the police procedural *Homicide: Life on the Street*.

Adam Bernstein: I didn't have any preexisting relationship with Tina or the *SNL* people. Maybe they had some interest in me because, with half-hour comedy pilots, they're usually multi-camera or single-camera—and directors tend to get pigeonholed.

It's hard for a director to move from one list to the other, but Bernstein was one of the rare directors on both, thanks to the variety of projects he did early in his career. Still, he wasn't the only one up for the gig.

Paul Feig (director): I was directing a lot of television, and I don't know if they were gonna hire me, but I had been sent the pilot script to consider. I thought it was really funny—I've always been a fan of Tina Fey's. But I didn't pursue it.

It was before television developed a rep for being home to the best storytelling, where you could go in-depth with a character over eight or ten episodes of tightly written TV. That meant that getting together the best team possible for the pilot was a tough mission for the New York–based production.

Bernstein brought a number of crew members he'd worked with before to the show, while producer Jerry Kupfer was hard at work putting the rest of the team together. He'd previously worked with Bernstein and some of the others on the eccentric Nickelodeon classic *The Adventures of Pete and Pete*. One of Kupfer's key hires: prop master Kevin Ladson.

Kevin Ladson: People in my union only wanted to do feature films. I could hardly get a crew. I had misfits, ne'er-do-wells—I'd take anybody I could get.

It's a problem that got better after the pilot, but the show still gave more inexperienced crewmembers a chance. Cinematographer Vanja Černjul had done just one TV show, *Ugly Betty*, and had never shot on an actual soundstage before. When he got the interview for *30 Rock*, he didn't expect to get it and even left the country to work on a movie in Europe. But when he got the call for *30 Rock*, he rushed back to the States. Michael Trim had a similar story.

Michael Trim (cinematographer): I started doing TV because my commercial career had died, because all the people I worked with in commercials either retired or had heart attacks all at once.

The pilot was set to start filming in summer 2005, in between seasons of *SNL*. But Fey got pregnant with her first child, delaying the shoot until January 2006.

While Tina, Tracy, and Alec became the core of the show, the original cast had one other key element: Fey's longtime real-life friend and *SNL* co-star Rachel Dratch, who originated the role of *The Girlie Show* star Jenna. If you don't remember her playing the part, that's OK—the original version of the pilot, which filmed with Dratch, never aired.

While that pilot was similar to the one that eventually aired, large portions of it were reshot before it premiered. The original version of the show relied more heavily on the show-within-a-show's sketches. NBC even planned to put full versions of the sketches up online, announcing that publicly, but it never ended up happening. That version also relied more heavily on the relationship between Liz and Jenna. When you watch them in their original scenes together, you can feel that genuine connection. Instead of the Actress-with-a-capital-A vibe Jane Krakowski later brought, you see Dratch's Jenna amazed and excited to be a part of this show. She's relatable, without the hilarious entitlement that Krakowski embodied. Dratch's Jenna even had a different last name to fit the original star, playing Jenna DeCarlo.

> **Scott Adsit:** That was just like coming home, because Tina and Rachel and I were like siblings for a long time. Dratch is someone you can totally put all of your trust into, as a person and as a performer.

But test audiences didn't respond to Dratch. Notes from the writers' room brought together after that pilot detail the reaction:

> Some changes—due to testing. Negative responses to the show within the show. The only time we see the show—it's bombing. We don't see Rachel be funny, we only see her screw up. People didn't believe Rachel as the star of her own show. Like to find someone else to play the actress in The Girlie Show.

> **Rachel Dratch (original Jenna):** After we shot the pilot, I got a call from my agent. "They're going in a different direction."

> **Michael Trim:** Rachel was incredible. I could not believe when I heard that they got rid of Rachel. Who knows what goes on there?

> **Doug Abel (editor):** Her style of comedy doesn't seem totally grounded in reality. She's a bit of a broad comedian. Is 30 Rock this gritty New York thing, or is it this more-goofy pretend television world? Things didn't quite mesh.

Fey had originally managed to cast her show with real-life friends like Dratch and Adsit, as SNL co-star Tracy Morgan and Alec Baldwin brought the star power. Now her plan was falling apart, with the fate of the show hanging in the balance. The network agreed to pick up the show as a series only after Dratch was replaced with Jane Krakowski. She was brought in with the network's eyes on her being more of a fit as a sitcom star, someone with decades of TV experience, including five years on the Fox dramedy Ally McBeal.

> **Andrew Guest (writers' assistant):** Tina's hand was forced. The character, Jenna Maroney, fulfills all the criteria that the testing was looking for in terms of somebody you believe was starring in the show, and having a much stronger comedic voice.

> **Doug Abel:** Jane Krakowski, she's great, but I really love Rachel Dratch. I was bummed when I learned that she wasn't going to be part of it, and it just

seemed cheesy. Corporate came down like "No, we want somebody who's a big blonde lady."

Alan Sepinwall (TV critic): It's a shame that they had to get rid of Dratch. If you look at that pilot versus the one with Krakowski, Jenna is almost instantly much more of a cartoon figure than Dratch's character was.

With Krakowski sliding in, the writers looked at giving the character less time, with a greater emphasis put on the show being a three-hander focused on Liz, Tracy, and Jack. That was thanks in part to notes from NBC—network executives saw that trio as the heart of the show.

Dratch was shifted into a new role. She was no longer the star but would instead recur on the series throughout its first season.

Rachel Dratch: I thought it could be fun to be a *Where's Waldo?* character. I felt way more comfortable doing these kinds of parts than playing Jenna, a diva type who, in the pilot, sort of tries to seduce Alec Baldwin. No one needs to see me try to seduce.

Lorne Michaels: Both Tina and I obviously adore Rachel, and we wanted to find a way in which we could go to her strength.

It was thought Dratch was best when deep in character, closer to what she did in sketch comedy. She was committed to the show for six episodes, and the writers brainstormed different options they could use her for, like Jack's ex-wife, the mail boy, or Liz's therapist. She didn't end up getting the ex-wife role—that went to Isabella Rossellini—but she played a new version of the pilot's cat wrangler and would go on to play a wide variety of weirdos, including a particularly threatening take on Elizabeth Taylor.

Jesse Thorn (public radio host): Immediately, the show was too specific and too weird, right from the beginning. The second they decided that their ousted cast member was going to come on in a variety of characters as a Cat Lady or whatever, it was too weird to be *The Mary Tyler Moore Show.*

The writers were told that there was no obligation to use Dratch, but to fit her in only if it really worked in the context of the episode. While Dratch accepted it at the time, after she left *30 Rock* at the end of the season, she found getting another break as an actress incredibly difficult. No one else was offering her lead roles, or even wacky friend roles.

Dratch wrote in her book *Girl Walks into a Bar* that she didn't have a big talk with Tina about her feelings on being replaced but was confident that Tina fought for her.

Rachel Dratch: I've never known Tina to be the kind of gal who'd be into putting some Shawn Colvin on the iPod, pulling out an afghan and two mugs of hot cocoa, patting the couch, and saying, "Hey, girlfriend, c'mon over here and let's share our feelings. Mmmm. That's good cocoa."

There were other adjustments from that pilot, like a re-casting of the actress who played Liz's assistant Cerie. Writers' room notes indicate that she was meant to be a take on "tall, blonde, entitled girls who don't care about their job terribly—have had everything handed to them." They were thinking of a woman a generation removed from Tina Fey, a millennial who could serve as a foil for her, with the role inspired by someone who'd worked the reception desk at the real *SNL*.

But Dratch's smaller role is the one that most radically shifts the show's dynamics.

Rachel Dratch: Because I still had a part on the show, I was in the unique situation of being there for the reshoot of the pilot I had shot a few months earlier. To her credit, Jane made things much easier early on when we were in the makeup room. She stated outright, "This is awkward," and I agreed and that was that.

Andrew Guest: *But,* the thing that was always a struggle was, did you *believe* that [Jane Krakowski as Jenna] and Liz really went back? And had a strong friendship? They just didn't seem like people who would be close. Who would hang. As opposed to Rachel Dratch, who if she had stayed there, you would have believed the idea that Tina and Rachel's show was being ruined—which was the idea in the original conception of the pilot. You believe, because these people, you get their dynamic.

While Liz's relationship with the new Jenna didn't always make sense, it evolved into depicting an often-one-sided friendship in a relatable way. It also set a new path for the Jenna character.

Alan Sepinwall: The Dratch character was a bit of a sad sack. Not quite Debbie Downer, but she felt more tethered to the real world, whereas Jenna was inherently ridiculous. In general, the show was best when it was inherently ridiculous.

Judah Friedlander (Frank Rossitano): I like how Jenna and Liz are friends and they go way back, even though Jenna is constantly pissing Liz off. I think everyone has a friend like that.

There was a long labor to get there, but after three years of development, the *30 Rock* placenta was finally leading to a little TV baby. With the new cast in place, the network was ready to move ahead.

Behind the scenes, Tina was getting an assist from friends as she embarked on her first scripted series. With this being Fey's first time in charge of a show, the network was looking to do what it often does with first-time creators: pair them with someone with more experience, someone who can help the more inexperienced writer with what goes into a network sitcom, as well as helping them to manage the staff.

> **Andrew Guest:** When we were shooting that pilot, the two writers who came to help Tina out during production were Robert Carlock and Mike Schur. It wasn't necessarily going to be Carlock who was working on the show—they were both just helping their friend out. They'd both written for her on *Weekend Update*, and watching their dynamic between the two of them was really interesting.
>
> But I have a memory of JoAnn Alfano, who was at Broadway Video and was one of our first EPs [executive producers], turning to somebody else and being like "We need to lock down either Robert Carlock or Mike Schur if this thing goes, to run it." I think about what the show would have been if Mike Schur had done the job, as opposed to Robert. I've now worked on a show that was created by Mike Schur, and I know what his sensibility is like, and what Robert's is like. *30 Rock* could have been something very different.

While the show was pulling elements from *Mary Tyler Moore* and its empowered female TV producer, it actually has more in common stylistically with legendary TV writer Norman Lear's shows—prioritizing comedy writing and social issues over deep character moments.

> **Emily VanDerWerff (TV critic):** The best shows tend to be those that can blend both types of storytelling, as *Mary Tyler Moore* and *All in the Family* could. *30 Rock* is a good example of the best of those shows, but it's very influenced by the "jokes at all cost" thing. Honestly, you look at *Saturday Night Live,* and that show began in an era when Norman Lear was King Shit. Those early seasons especially are so heavily influenced by his work, I don't see how it couldn't trickle down into the things made by people who used to work on *Saturday Night Live.*
>
> **Jesse Thorn:** Right from the beginning, it was clear that *30 Rock* had failed at its primary objective, which was to make *The Mary Tyler Moore Show*. I read the script for *30 Rock* before it was on TV, and thought, *Wow! They're really trying to make Tina Fey into Mary Tyler Moore. I wonder if that works?* Mary Tyler Moore is basically the greatest comic actress in television history.

Beyond *SNL*, Carlock brought experience from writing for NBC's now-departed golden goose, with several years as a writer on *Friends*, as well as being a co–executive producer on *Friends* spinoff *Joey*. Of course, Carlock could also get weird—he began his career writing for the short-lived but beloved by comedy nerds sketch program, *The Dana Carvey Show,* renowned for an opening sketch that ended with Bill Clinton breastfeeding puppies.

Meanwhile, Schur had yet to make as high-profile a name for himself. He'd recently come off of working on *Weekend Update* and was a writer for HBO's *The Comeback*, before going on to rise through the ranks of *The Office*, co-creating *Parks and Recreation* and *Brooklyn Nine-Nine*, and creating *The Good Place*.

Daisy Gardner: What people don't realize about Robert Carlock is—because he looks so upper-crust and he's New England WASP, Harvard-y and very regal almost—he can be the funniest, goofiest. If we had a conference call, he and Tina could do a bit after the call where they created ten different characters and the conference call just kept going. You would cry laughing.

After the filming of the original pilot, the show locked down Carlock as Tina Fey's joke-crafting teammate for seven seasons—and, it turns out, beyond. They've continued to create shows together since *30 Rock* went off the air, their instincts gelling with one another.

Andrew Guest: They believed in themselves—they had Lorne there behind them on those first few notes calls backing them up and believing in them. There was a certain cachet, and a certain coolness about the show, from day one of pre-production.

Don Scardino: They're both workhorses. Their brains are fever-pitched. They're constantly thinking and working. Their sense of humor, their funny bone— particularly their satirical, political, cultural skew—is very well matched.

The decision was also made early on to shoot *30 Rock* on film. Digital cameras were still in their early years of being used in television.

Michael Trim: Shooting Tina could be tricky—my biggest concern was making sure that she looked good. Digital is not nice to women, and in the first few years, it took a while for digital to get better.

Tom Houghton (cinematographer): We did a quick test on digital—at the time, it wasn't pleasant to look at.

Tina Fey: If we shot on high-def video it would go faster, but we would look like the zombie backup dancers in *Thriller*.

Despite all the work that went into its creation, Tina Fey doesn't like the *30 Rock* pilot. Blasphemy, I know. She described it as "awkward" and "sweaty," and said that there was no reason to go back and watch it. Like most creative people, she's being a bit hard on herself—but you can see that it hasn't yet become The Show that people know and love.

Doug Abel: To be honest, I didn't think it was really going to work when I first saw it. I thought, *This is all over the map, and some of it's very broad, and some of it's very heady*. It was a little hard to wrap our head around.

It's also Frankensteined together from the original pilot shoot, and another months later.

Doug Abel: There were some really bumpy things that probably didn't make sense. There was a big scene toward the end in the studio, and it was just a mess. They didn't have enough time to shoot it properly, cover it properly. From a production point of view, it was difficult to pull it all together. They didn't quite have time to build up a set properly and get enough extras, and it felt a little low rent. Before it was delivered, they made some aggressive cuts to it just to get it to be more spunky.

Plus, on a personal level for Fey, the pilot that aired represents not being able to live her dream of starring in the show alongside her longtime friend, and the tough decisions that pushed her out. Still, the seeds for what the show would eventually become are all there.

Andrew Guest: I still have all my notes, and day one, so much of the show is there in the notes. Robert had never run a sitcom before—neither had Tina. For whatever reason, they walked in, they knew this was going to be a great show, and that they were going to have the level of comedy that they wanted.

The *30 Rock* pilot opens with a scene that sets the tone for the show, introducing our hero in her quest for happiness that we'd follow for the next seven years. Her do-or-die mission in that original first scene: getting a hot dog.

We meet Tina Fey's Liz Lemon impatiently waiting at a New York street hot dog stand. A man comes up from the other direction to order, claiming there are two separate lines. Liz is *not* having this, calling out this interloper for what she sees as a deep injustice—but people start splitting off from the actual line to follow this guy.

Liz's answer: buying all the hot dogs and "giving them to the *good* people," the ones who stayed in the original line.

She ends up with a moral victory while everyone who got in line behind the other guy gets mad at Liz. It's one of the many pyrrhic victories that she would "win" over the course of the show.

Liz serves as Tina's alter ego, a less personally fulfilled version of her life. She gets to be Liz Lemon, bringing some Lois Lane alliteration to her character, complete with Lois spunk. An earlier version of the script had her as "Lisa Lemon," but Tina switched it up and used her own middle name, Elizabeth. While the real Tina Fey studied theater in college, Liz studied theater *tech*, because she's an even deeper nerd than the real Tina.

Jon Haller (writers' assistant): Liz Lemon, she's the Mary Tyler Moore of that time. It was just a perfect storm of Tina's talent, Robert's talent, and the cast. But Tina as that character—you hear TV pitches constantly, and it's like "Liz

Lemon meets this, Liz Lemon meets that." She created this comedic centerpiece for those years.

Tina Fey: It's sort of based on me and all of the lady writers that worked at *SNL* when I first started there.

Adam Bernstein: She was mostly trying to concentrate on her performance, at least on the pilot. It was a nice collaboration—she very much wanted to depend on the director, because she couldn't watch herself act.

The opening leads into a music montage intro, a song exclaiming "That's her!" as Liz plays Hot Dog Robin Hood throughout Manhattan. She's mostly met by confusion and rejection of the processed meat treat. A homeless man she hands a hot dog to throws it back at her—he was played by an actual New York City homeless luminary known as Radioman, who carries a radio around his neck and was known for showing up on film sets and keeping track of everything filming around the city.

The show would build a tradition of recurring characters, including multiple recurring homeless characters—Radioman (under the name "Moonvest"), as well as two played by *30 Rock* writers, Jack Burditt and Hannibal Buress.

That opening music pays tribute to the show's Mary Tyler Moore inspirations, a different theme for Liz than the rest of the series. The show would often tip its hat to *The Mary Tyler Moore Show* and both shows' fundamental question: Can a working woman have it all?

Jeff Richmond's score gives the show a jaunty vibe, with cues that kept the momentum during the perfect comic timing of an entrance, a reaction, waiting for a look. But it took time for the music to fully gel with the show.

Doug Abel: Tina's husband was doing the music at the time. Bless his heart. He got to be very, very good at it, but at the time, maybe we'd use some of his stuff and some library music. I thought, *Wow, this guy is not quite qualified to be doing this quite yet*. It seemed like a hot mess.

That original opening song pivots—it turns out the song isn't about Liz, but about "Pam, the Overly-Confident Morbidly Obese Woman," a sketch from Liz's late-night comedy show. The character's played by Jenna Maroney (portrayed by Jane Krakowski), wearing a fat suit and surrounded by dancers.

Yes, the show basically opens with fat-shaming. It was 2006. Pop culture was even more insensitive, and not every joke has aged well, despite the fact that the show isn't that old. It can even come off as cruel, with jokes that would be career-enders fifteen years later.

Of course, the "Pam" sketch is also *meant* to be an obviously hacky joke. But the level of acceptance for making fun of a group, even within a joke that's taking a shot at that kind of comedy, has also changed over the years. That comedic sensibility led to greater criticism when Fey moved on to *Unbreakable Kimmy Schmidt* after *30 Rock* wrapped, along with more of a critical look back at *30 Rock* itself—especially following the death of George Floyd and the greater rise of the Black Lives Matter movement.

The show-within-a-show became known as *TGS* throughout its run, but it started as *The Girlie Show* (after being named *Fright Night Bits* in an earlier draft of the pilot), with Jenna as its ego-tastic star and her best pal Liz as its head writer. The show had a conversation with feminism and feminist tropes throughout its run.

The show's writers often went back to the pilot for inspiration, taking the threads laid out here and pulling them out to their most extreme logical conclusions.

The most important part of that show DNA was the relationship between Liz and Jack Donaghy. Baldwin quickly slid into the role of the classy, charismatic network suit that Fey had written, the character drawing inspiration from Fey's own relationship with Lorne Michaels.

There's a lot of pressure on any art with a handsome male lead opposite a beautiful woman to have the two get together eventually, but *30 Rock* tries to throw as much cold water on that as possible, as often as it can. It's a mentor–mentee relationship. Jack's early lines to Liz aren't sexual—his big early evaluation of Liz is when he tells her, "You have the boldness of a much younger woman."

When we first see Jack, he literally kicks the door down in his still-under-construction office, introducing himself to Liz and Pete after his predecessor dies. That's the kind of male aggression that pours out of Jack's veins, while Liz has to get ahead using her brains and wit—and occasionally stealing a move or two from Jack.

Pilot director Adam Bernstein originally had an even more dramatic entrance planned for Jack.

Michael Trim: Adam had this idea of Alec coming down on a crane—that's how he would be introduced. This impressed me in a lot of ways, it was a pretty cool shot. When he was talking to Alec about it, Alec's like "No, that's not my thing."

For whatever reason, that wasn't working for him. I'm like "Oh my god," I had never seen that shot before. But the more impressive thing was watching Adam, who was like "Oh, OK." Ten minutes later, we were in the office set, and he came up with the idea of Alec kicking the door down.

The show's endless mocking of NBC and its corporate parents starts early, with Jack's position as the "Vice President of East Coast Television and Microwave Oven Programming." His big claim to fame is the development of "the Trivection oven" for parent company GE.

The show made it sound absurd, but it's actually a *real thing* that GE sold. GE even ran ads during the show for the oven to remind viewers that, hey, here's a thing you can actually go buy.

Tina Fey: I was trolling GE's website when I was writing, trying to figure out where this guy's area of expertise was. I found that oven in there, and I liked it. There was no GE product integration—it was all done without their knowledge.

Judah Friedlander: Doing *30 Rock* over the years, I've probably learned more about microwave ovens than I ever planned on learning.

As Jack put it, he's the one who came up with "the third heat." It's a running gag, with Tracy showing up on live television in the climax and proclaiming, "I'm the third heat!" to widespread applause.

The original version of the pilot had been shot near the beginning of the year, before they went back in the fall and started doing the reshoots, along with filming more episodes of the series itself.

Adam Bernstein: When Liz is talking to Jack at that lectern with the sketch in the background, if you look carefully at the shots, Alec Baldwin's head and his face actually change between cuts. His hair is a different color and he's a different weight—he changes between one sentence and another.

Jon Hamm (Dr. Drew Baird): I actually auditioned for the role of Jack Donaghy. It was way early in the process. So somewhere on tape, there exists me talking about three kinds of heat.

Jack having connections with Republican D.C. politicians is also established early. It's what birthed everything from him dating former secretary of state Condoleezza Rice to developing a "gay bomb" with Dick Cheney.

He's described in notes from day one of the writers' room:

Play Alec as a staunch, well-informed Republican – has more info than you so you can't win the argument. – Alec doesn't want his character to be an idiot – take the most pragmatic part of conservative attitude – Alec secretly has a box of "Honeymooners" tapes so that he can learn about his job, he wants to do it well.

Like many great pilots, the show is built around characters who either act as opposites or closely mirror specific traits of our heroes. It lets the show explore our leads in greater depth. Liz faces her boss-opposite in Jack—they're both bosses, but Jack is all alpha while Liz brings a different energy to the job. You get Writer Liz vs. Actress Jenna, absurd comedian Tracy against the straitlaced Black Harvard grad "Toofer," Kenneth the lowly page somehow besting uber-lord Jack and earning his admiration through Kenneth's simplicity.

While Baldwin brought such a great dynamic to the show, he only had limited time windows on the pilot—a few hours over a couple of days. One of director Adam Bernstein's biggest contributions that lasted throughout the series was the use of handheld camera shots for most of the show, which also helped with filming Baldwin as quickly as possible. Bernstein brought the idea from his time directing an episode of the original *Law & Order*.

Adam Bernstein: There was a camera operator on that who I thought was astonishing, because it was always in his hand—he wasn't using any special Steadicam. He was able to just hold the camera, but have it seem fluid and seamless. He was this wizard of handheld work.

The one agenda I had going into [the *30 Rock* pilot] was to give the show a flavor of realism—I didn't want it to be cartoony. That handheld camera, even if you're not doing it like a documentary, it denotes in a subtle way to the audience that what they're watching is actually happening.

Given the eventual direction of basically all of the characters, Bernstein didn't exactly get his wish with avoiding cartoonishness. But there was always an element holding them down-to-earth, and that definitive camera style was part of that.

Don Scardino: I'd done tons of *Law & Orders* over the years, and [Adam] said, when he got the job for the pilot, he thought the backstage world of an *SNL* is so fraught—and it's live, and it's happening. He thought using the handheld style on a comedy maybe hadn't been done.

Adam Bernstein: Our agenda was, we're going to shoot this comedy half-hour, but we wanted to shoot it like *Law & Order*. I actually recruited Pete Agliata, who was the [camera] operator from *Law & Order*, to work on the pilot.

Peter Agliata (camera operator): With handheld, you have to see stuff coming. You get to read an actor well and you know what they're going to do. You can see it in their eyes. You can see when this is the performance they're feeling and you're not going to get it again.

[But] I had sworn off television because the hours were just too demanding. Then Adam called with this. I thought, It's Tina Fey, it's got all these perfect elements, and it's just a pilot. I do a pilot, and then I'm on to something else.

Adam Bernstein: He ended up staying on almost the whole run, years after I was there.

When we first meet Tracy Jordan, he's being brought in by Jack to goose *The Girlie Show*'s lackluster ratings. You can see parts of the character referencing everyone from Eddie Murphy to Tyler Perry, as well as the real Tracy Morgan's public persona. The first clip we see of Tracy features him in his underwear running down the street with a lightsaber, yelling "I am a Jedi" in a moment reminiscent of that time Martin Lawrence ran down the street in his underwear. Tracy also had a different name in an earlier draft of the pilot—Lawrence—but the show followed in the tradition of Tony Danza and named the character after Tracy.

While Tracy's initially an antagonist to Liz and Jenna, he's so hilarious and likable that you never feel too bad about the problems he puts Liz through. He's quickly seen in a flashback as an old woman in Tracy Jordan's *Honky Grandma Be Trippin'*, à la Tyler Perry's Madea.

After meeting Liz at a fancy Italian restaurant—where he bugs out over being recommended pumpkin ravioli—Tracy relocates their meeting to a diner in Harlem. He follows this up by dragging Liz to a strip club, a moment that would be echoed in the series' surprisingly emotional finale. And it's all happening between the dress rehearsal and the show that night.

> **Linda Mendoza (director):** There is no way in hell the head writer would have left between dress and air. Because between dress and air, all hell is breaking loose. They're reordering sketches, they're cutting. It is insanity. (*laughs*)

Of course, that hell is the lives of the *TGS* staff for years to come. And we continue to find out that *TGS* isn't a very good show, so perhaps its head writer's constant absence is part of the problem.

Alongside Tracy comes a giant entourage—when the show was picked up, only two of those members would stay: Grizz and Dot Com, who started as extras.

> **Adam Bernstein:** We had to create a posse for Tracy's character, so we brought in a bunch of guys. I hired those guys, then it turned out they were actually friends with Tracy.

> **Tracy Morgan:** I met Grizz, he was a bouncer at a strip club—big guy, beautiful heart.

> **Grizz Chapman (Warren "Grizz" Griswold):** We always had conversations about doing something together, but it was really nothing serious. Then he went on to do *Saturday Night Live*. At that time, I was a bodyguard. Eventually, I went for the *30 Rock* audition, and I got it—but he didn't know I got the job until the day we started filming—he was like "Oh, OK!" We already had a relationship, so that's why it really comes across well on camera.

And the actor who played Dot Com, Kevin Brown, had been Tracy Morgan's first comedy manager back in the early 1990s. Grizz and Dot Com played the calm counterweights to Tracy's manic energy. And sometimes literal weights—Grizz's role in Tracy's entourage includes sitting on him to calm him down.

Liz calls out a recurring theme in the pilot that would be revisited throughout the show's run: how society pits white women and Black men against each other. The exploration followed Fey's look at how society pits women against one another in *Mean Girls*. How the show handled race would be controversial at times—including using blackface in service of its satire, in episodes that were ultimately removed from streaming services in 2020—but the show's POV seemed to be that the real enemy is the system. The writers always wanted the show to be about race, gender, and class in the workplace, according to notes from the writers' room.

Tracy tells Liz that "this show is our chance to break the shackles 'cause the white dudes want to see us fail." He almost gets it—though when Liz asks which white dudes he's talking about, his list includes Jack Donaghy, General Electric, George Bush, and "Karl Robe." Tracy adds, "Affirmative action was designed to keep women and minorities in competition with each other to distract us while white dudes inject AIDS into our chicken nuggets. That's a metaphor." OK, so maybe Tracy doesn't quite get it.

Director Don Scardino compared directing Tracy to directing a Little Rascals film—you make faces, Tracy would copy them.

> **Don Scardino:** Tracy loved line readings—Tracy would love you to stand off camera and say, "Say it this way," "No try *this* way." It made him play and be funny, and it took some of the onus off him having to come up with it.

> **John Riggi:** I have such a soft spot in my heart for that guy. He literally would say to me, "Just tell me how to say it, John Riggi." I would go, "Tray, I don't want to do that." And he's like "No, it's OK. You are not going to hurt my feelings. Let's get it exactly the way you want it."

> He didn't have much of an ego. He's just a really funny dude who's kind of crazy and out there. He's also smart enough to know that he comes off as a little crazy and to push that persona really hard, because he knows people like it.

We learn early on that Liz and Jenna moved to New York City together after coming up in the Chicago improv comedy scene. Aside from working on this late-night show, it's the most obvious connection between Liz and real-life Tina Fey. The cast itself is filled with improv powerhouses. Beyond Dratch in her now-reduced role, it includes Scott Adsit, another old friend from Tina's Chicago days. Fey, Dratch, and Adsit were all in the same Second City theater company. There are even photos from Fey's and Adsit's Second City revues up on the walls of their characters' offices.

> **Jack McBrayer (Kenneth Parcell):** Tina has employed approximately forty-eight percent of anyone who's ever been just through the doors of Second City on episodes of *30 Rock*. Not only performers, but also audience members and people who just stopped in to ask for directions.

Scott Adsit: We would improvise at the beginning of the scene and quite often after the last line of dialogue. Ad-libbing, you do it all the time, but the shows are so tightly written, and they're always overwritten by about seven minutes, so we'd have to cut that down. That means killing your babies, the jokes that they'd work on for months. So the idea that the improvised dialogue might survive was rare.

Adam Bernstein: [*The Office* and *Parks and Recreation*] were much looser in their style. They're carefully scripted, but there's also a ton of improv in those.

Scott Adsit: The fact that Tina and I had worked together so much, and Dratch, there was a freedom in that. We were very playful with each other. There's a part where I punch her in the boob or something, and she was like "Just do it, just do it." I have the freedom to punch Tina Fey in the boob, because we've got such a long history. I don't recommend it to anyone else.

Fey said that it was well within the boundaries of their friendship.

There was one problem with Jack being such a key part of the show from the beginning: Alec Baldwin hadn't signed his contract to keep doing the show yet. As NBC prepared for the annual upfronts presentations, where networks pitch their new shows to advertisers in the spring before they premiere, Baldwin was still officially just a guest star.

SNL and *30 Rock* producer Marci Klein, also a close friend of Baldwin's, took it upon herself to get him to commit to every episode. She had to compromise, getting him to agree to do the first half of the season. If the show was later picked up for a full season—a decision often made by networks after seeing ratings on the early episodes—he wasn't obligated to appear in any of the later episodes. And he would shoot only three days a week, which could make the show complicated to schedule.

Chris George (location manager): For the run of the show, Alec's deal was that he basically did not work Mondays or Fridays. Anytime Jack Donaghy was in the show, we had to shoot it between Tuesday and Thursday.

That meant a lot of scenes with Jack in his office, or the *TGS* studio, since they could quickly grab those without having to take Alec out to another location. When they did venture out, they had to keep it within ten or fifteen minutes of Silvercup Studios most of the time.

Andrew Guest: Alec was our wild card. Up until the eleventh hour before the upfronts, he hadn't signed his contract. And when they finally got him, we only had him for a guaranteed thirteen episodes.

NBC pushed *Studio 60* at its upfronts hard. The network hailed the show as one that would help the network reclaim its throne in the network TV world, and when it came time to talk with local TV affiliates, there were 150 people lined up to see them before the show had even aired. Everyone wanted a photo with the cast, especially Matthew Perry. Meanwhile, the casts of *The Office* and *30 Rock* were both nearby, and no one cared.

While the network was clearly favoring *Studio 60* in development, that also meant that—along with most of the television executives being based far away on the West Coast—*30 Rock* was protected from too much interference.

> **Lorne Michaels:** There wasn't that much at risk. There was a big, important show on this same topic, and I think all the energy went into that. They were very nice, and supportive, and encouraging, but with very low expectations. When there's low expectations, they don't come by that often.

With Carlock as the co-leader of *30 Rock*, his hard-edged, hard-joke sensibility won out over Schur's gentle love for character. It was a tighter match with Tina's personal style and gave the show the off-the-wall sensibility it's remembered for.

> **Andrew Guest:** Mike Schur has a phrase he uses called "invisible weekenders." Where these jokes that are super attractive in a writers' room, and that you want to do, slowly chip away at the reality of a character. And then you can't use them in the same way.
>
> On a certain hand, Mike Schur was right. But on another hand, I could not think of a funnier show than *30 Rock*. The jokes were so worth it. You don't give a shit if the characters don't make sense, or you don't believe them, or the storyline gets abandoned and who cares what it was about anyway. Because it was about comedy. And there is a level of satire there, too—a certain sharpness from Robert and Tina that you don't get from Mike. Mike is wholesome, Middle America, and he's got more of a hangout vibe on his shows. You love the characters, and you love watching them hang out with each other, but it doesn't have some of the bite.
>
> They're both going to hate me now.

While Carlock was locked in, pilot director Adam Bernstein directed five episodes that first season—but also saw his role diminish over time, leaving the show after that first year. During his time with the show, he helped lay the groundwork and create the visual language that the show would become known for. It was all in collaboration with the showrunners, because as opposed to film, the writer gets the last word in television.

> **Adam Bernstein:** What always happens, when you're a pilot director, you're playing this midwife role. The writer has had this idea for the show, they've been nurturing it, they've written the script, and they've survived all the notes,

all the different iterations—and finally, the network says they're going to make their show. So they have not only a huge amount of history with this material, but all this pressure, right? Because now it's like "Oh, this could be the next seven years of my life if it goes well."

You end up having a really close collaboration with the writer when you're making the pilot, because you're helping them realize this thing that they've been working on for so long. You're talking about everything—the casting, the locations, what it's going to look like, music. But then, once the show goes to the series, they don't need you quite as much. I'm not saying that in a bitter way, I'm just saying it in a practical way.

It was the first time Fey and Carlock had done single-camera comedy, and Bernstein feels his role with the pilot was to help them get their sea legs. It was unclear if the retooled pilot episode would be a success once it hit the airwaves—either with critics or, more importantly, viewers.

Kevin Ladson: I don't know if people thought that it was going to fly. I said, "Listen, if I'm laughing, that means the script is funny." I let my father read it, because my father's my good luck charm. If he likes it, then it's going to be a success. He says, "Well, I really liked this." So I went back to work saying that my father said it's going to be a success. No one could really care less what I was saying—'til they won the Emmy.

SEASON 1
(2006–07)

30 Rock vs. Studio 60

Studio 60 got a jump on the competition, with its pilot premiering September 18, 2006, almost a month before *30 Rock*. The pilot tells the story of a Lorne Michaels–esque producer of a sketch comedy show—*Studio 60 on the Sunset Strip*—who gets fed up with network interference after not being allowed to air a sketch called "Crazy Christians." The fictional NBS network's standards department finds it too offensive. Executive producer Wes Mendell, played by Judd Hirsch, goes on live TV and rails against the trite, anti-intellectual strain of pop culture—including on his own show, thanks to the network. He challenges viewers to turn off their televisions. The network's brand-new president has to fire him.

That opening rant is a trope Sorkin would use again in *The Newsroom* on HBO, that time with a fictional anchor going off about the way news has been produced. It also seemed like Sorkin exorcising his feelings following *The West Wing* and leaving that show after its fourth season.

The new network president decides to hire two talents who left the show in a previous creative struggle: comedy writer Matt Albie and director Danny Tripp, played by Matthew Perry and Bradley Whitford. The characters also served as Sorkin's alter egos, with Tripp returning to the show because he can't get a bond that will let him direct a movie due to a positive drug test. And Albie acts as the voice for writers everywhere, struggling with the pressure to write something truly great.

The shows even each had their own corporate executive named "Jack," with the *Studio 60* version played by Steven Weber. One of the big distinguishing traits: *Studio 60* was set in LA, separating it from *SNL*, while *30 Rock* was true New York all the way through. *Studio 60* also takes place on a fictional TV network, whereas *30 Rock* explicitly emphasizes that it's on NBC and makes fun of its home network constantly.

Studio 60 was slotted on Monday nights at ten P.M., the later evening prestige time slot following *Deal or No Deal*, a breakout hit for NBC at the time. Critics raved over the Sorkin show's pilot episode.

Nate Corddry: During production, we were thrilled. The pilot, I think, is stunning. It's brilliantly directed, and written, and performed.

Andrew Guest: The amount of fun the writers had watching *Studio 60*, because it was a *great* pilot. And the question was always, where do you take this show after that?

Bradley Whitford: All of that shit backfires, because there was this huge expectation for the show. If the pilot of *Studio 60* was the first thing Aaron ever wrote, it would have been a firestorm of discovery and adulation.

Nate Corddry: You start making assumptions. It made the suffering all that more acute when things started to fall apart, and you slowly realize, *Oh shit, this is not going to go the way that I had imagined.* Then you carry that with you for the remainder of your career.

Despite the critics excusing wit instead of laughs early on, viewership numbers were a concern. That pilot episode drew 13.4 million viewers, enough for it to finish second in its time slot. But it was behind CBS's *CSI: Miami*, which brought in 17.6 million viewers. And both that and its other competition, *Supernanny*, would add viewers over the course of the hour—*Studio 60*'s viewership dropped, losing 2.5 million viewers, indicating a failure for the show to grab and hold on to its audience.

Bradley Whitford: It was very clear, with this big buildup—when the first numbers came in, I joked with Matt, "We're dead men walking." The way publicity works, our show was set up—if we are not a massive network, award-winning, moneymaking machine for the better part of a decade for NBC, then we're a failure.

It felt like the show was collapsing under the weight of its expectations, and Whitford thinks that *30 Rock* had an advantage as the underdog.

Bradley Whitford: The older I get, I swear to God, [*30 Rock*'s position] is a much better position to come into this with. In my experience on *The West Wing*, there was no publicity [ahead of time]. There was no expectation for it.

[For *Studio 60*,] there was a three-story photograph of me draped on the Kodak building, and we went to take a picture of it. I looked at me three stories high and thought, *That's not a good place to be.*

SNL's Lorne Michaels noted that the very premise of the *Studio 60* pilot, set off by the show not being allowed to do a sketch about Christians, was off-base.

> **Lorne Michaels:** Since we do sketches about Christians all the time, I guess [Sorkin's] going for a bigger set of issues, his characteristic subject being power and its responsibilities. But is this a new insight, that networks are not to be trusted? The reality is that the network isn't that powerful anymore—talent is.

30 Rock had an advantage when it came to a lesson *Studio 60* hadn't learned: Don't do sketches.

> **Tina Fey:** In the very, very beginning, I thought, *Ooh, and maybe sometimes we could see the show*. But a half hour of comedy is about 21.5 minutes these days, and that's a very short amount of time to tell stories. So immediately, the first thing to go would be your idea of stopping for three minutes to do a sketch in the middle that doesn't forward things.

> **Doug Abel:** You really had no idea what [*TGS*] actually was. It was like some imaginary show. But that's the best.

> **Tina Fey:** We talked in our writers' room, saying the best template for the amount we see in the workplace really is *The Mary Tyler Moore Show*, where you cared about these people and you heard their stories, but you never saw the news and you didn't talk about the making of the news very much.

In fact, the *30 Rock* writers were directed by the network not to do sketches. It was a choice designed to help *Studio 60* out, giving Aaron Sorkin his own playground when it came to showing what was on the show itself.

> **Andrew Guest:** That really saved us. Watching a drama writer try to write comedy is amazing. Because Aaron Sorkin is the best ever at writing characters, particularly fathers, or father figures, or somebody making profoundly reverent speeches. And having reverence for things, for institutions—like comedy. But comedy is irreverent. The whole idea is that you don't take it seriously, and you don't take yourself seriously.

> **Jesse Thorn:** The great thing about there not being sketches on *30 Rock* is that it lets them make the joke that *TGS* is just barely good enough to stay on the air.

> **John Riggi:** Aaron's a great writer, but he'd never worked on a live variety or comedy show like *SNL*. So there was a level of inauthenticity that was baked into the show that we were able to avoid—because Tina had lived it, had been there, and knew exactly what it was like.

Bradley Whitford: When you set something in *Saturday Night Live*, you're talking about the funniest people in the world. When you're doing *The West Wing*, the arena is C-SPAN.

When you're watching the government function and you get wit, it's a gift. When you're watching what are supposed to be the funniest people in the world and you get wit, it pisses you off.

30 Rock premiered on October 11, 2006, kicking off Wednesday nights at eight. It brought in just 8.1 million viewers its first week out, third in its time slot and behind any episode of *Studio 60* to date—then dropped to 5.7 million viewers in its second week.

While they weren't bringing in the kind of numbers the network would have liked, the show was largely a critical success, with reviewers praising the pilot in particular. But the threat of cancellation was always hanging over the heads of Fey, Carlock, and the rest of the show's cast and crew.

Some of the other early episodes didn't get as warm a reception from critics—or audiences—as the show worked to find its rhythm. But you can also see the world getting built out quickly in those early shows, as the writers threw everything at the wall and saw what would stick. You can also see them realizing which bits of the original formula weren't going to work. The original idea was for a deep ensemble of *The Girlie Show* performers, but not showing sketches meant less of a need for that.

One of the victims of that shift in focus was Lonny Ross, who played Josh. The show seemed to forget he existed at times, never finding exactly the slot to put him into. His role has been compared to what Jimmy Fallon did when he was on *SNL*, being the young goofball who can do impressions. Ross was a fan of Fallon, mimicking his impressions as he worked on his own.

Ross ran into a roadblock just before *30 Rock* was about to start filming: jury duty.

Lonny Ross (Josh Girard): I was panicked. I was afraid to be unavailable, and my excuse to get out of it was so unbelievable even to me. I went down to the court to explain, with a straight face, how I was about to start filming on the new Tina Fey show, *30 Rock*. The woman working there said she knew about the show—she had been seeing commercials. And I got excused.

As the show focused more on the craziness of behind-the-scenes life, Tracy and Jenna's antics began to loom larger than Josh's solid impressions. They were embracing backstage instead of what was on *TGS*. But Josh also offered many of the show's more grounded storylines, along with showing you more of what goes into being a sketch comedy performer.

As *30 Rock* found its footing, *Studio 60* was struggling. Its ratings were steeply declining from week to week, the critics were increasingly unfavorable, and the show didn't seem to be able to deliver on the idea of a show that was allegedly saving sketch comedy. *Studio 60*'s sketches weren't so-bad-they're-funny like *30 Rock* did with its intentionally bad sketches that were seen in brief glances. Instead, *Studio 60*'s attempts at sketch comedy were in a muddy middle ground.

Nate Corddry: Aaron is super fucking funny, but he isn't a sketch writer. [Sketch show *Kids in the Hall*'s] Mark McKinney was around to help him write sketches, but that all disappeared, because I don't think he was really willing to allow other writers to come in and write a lot of content for the show.

Bradley Whitford: There's a real difficult creative problem you have to solve when you're going to have people who are playing brilliant writers and producers saying, "This doesn't work, and *this* is fucking brilliant." If that isn't brilliant, you're just putting way, way, way, way, way too much pressure on it.

Nate Corddry: Every time we did sketches, I always felt, *Oh fuck.*

Andrew Guest (writers' assistant): Aaron Sorkin sent a bottle of champagne and some flowers to Tina's office in one of our first weeks, just congratulating her on her pickup—and she was like "Fuck that guy." (*laughs*)

When *30 Rock* showed the actual sketches being performed on the fictional *TGS*, the point was the absurdity of how over-the-top bad and/or juvenile they were, like the pilot opening with a hack sketch making fun of a woman's weight and confidence—baking in a lowbrow approach from the jump.

Daisy Gardner: I was at the wedding rehearsal dinner for Dave Mandel and Becky Whitney, seated next to Al Franken. At the time, Al was a senator. Al realized I was on *30 Rock*, and he asked me if I could get a beloved sketch he'd written at *SNL* into the *TGS* bits. It was called "Fart Doctor." "Fart Doctor" featured an amazing genius of a doctor who was talked up by everyone else before he appeared—"He's a genius. Top in his field! I've never seen anything like it!" Then the genius doctor appears and examines the patient. While onlookers watch with bated breath, the doctor asks the patient to fart. He sniffs the fart, closes his eyes, and triumphantly declares, "Consumption!" or "Diphtheria!" or what have you.

I brought this request back to Tina and Rob. They both shouted, "No!" "Fart Doctor" was a sketch that was notorious for being over ten minutes long. Tina went on, "*Absolutely not.* If he wants 'Fart Doctor' to appear on the show, he can come to a table read and watch it die like we all did." Apparently, Al Franken would just turn in "Fart Doctor" [at *SNL*] and then leave. Then the rest of the cast and writers would have to soldier on through a ten-minute sketch about farts that never ended while laughter died around it.

"Fart Doctor" made it into *TGS* shortly thereafter.

30 Rock gave you "Fart Doctor," while *Studio 60* delivered sketches with a deep, esoteric point that played into the episode's themes but weren't often particularly funny. Or were funny with an asterisk—*Ah, yes, I appreciate the point they are making here,* you might think, but you probably wouldn't laugh. *30 Rock* kept the focus on what was happening behind the curtain.

Alan Sepinwall: [*TGS*'s] "Fart Doctor" takes away any of the pressure that ultimately crushed *Studio 60*, which was those sketches were not funny.

Jesse Thorn: The second that the premise is that the show is popular or good, it has to constantly deliver that. Even *Saturday Night Live* can't do that, and *Saturday Night Live is* popular and good. Sketch comedy is a sloppy mess, especially when you're doing it on a weekly basis—that's the whole point. That's what's fun about it—you see what works.

Don Scardino: When you saw the show-within-a-show on *Studio 60*, it wasn't really funny. [Sorkin] didn't hire writers for the table who came out of that *SNL* world. But when you looked at our show, you realized, these people came *right* out of *SNL*—everybody involved—and they knew what it's really like to be backstage at that show. To write for that show. So the [*TGS*] writers' room—even though we always called them The Writers Who Never Talk, because frequently they were paid as extras and didn't have lines—the writers' room rang true. They were modeled, usually, after real people.

Aaron captured the dynamics of interpersonal relationships very well in that show, like he always does, but the world of it—you thought, *This is the funniest show on TV? How come I'm not getting it?*

Studio 60 eventually figured out that the sketches weren't its strong suit, switching to a tactic that *30 Rock* made use of throughout its time: putting characters in ridiculous costumes (man-size lobster, anyone?) but not showing the sketch itself, leaving it to your imagination/your assumption that yes, if they say it's funny, it's funny in the story. But critics were quick to turn on *Studio 60* for both the failure of its sketch comedy and taking itself too self-seriously. Sorkin fans were used to that approach to the working lives of politics, but while the writer of this book (hi! *waves*) may have deeply loved *Studio 60*, an appreciation for the inner lives of comedy writers wasn't as widely held.

Nate Corddry: I was backstage at the UCB, it was a packed room—they didn't know I was there. Someone was talking about how self-important and ridiculous it was. I was like "Oh shit. I don't see this at all."

Every time the new script pages arrived, it was like Christmas. Then to see that my own personal tastes are not the tastes of my comedy nerd friends, that was a shock. I wish it hadn't been. It's made me a little bit more judgmental of the work that I make now.

Corddry pointed to a particular *Studio 60* exchange that comedy fans have torn apart, but which he couldn't see the humor in at the time. His character, Tom Jeter, takes offense to his mom calling what he does "skits," replying, "We don't do skits, Mom. Skits are when the football players dress up as the cheerleaders and think it's wit. Sketches are when some of the best minds in comedy come together and put together a national comedy show that's watched and talked about by millions of people." He goes on to tell his dad that they're standing in "the Paris Opera House of American television," to which his dad responds, "That's swell, Tom, but your brother is standing in the middle of Afghanistan!"

Jesse Thorn: Despite some great performances on *Studio 60*, it was obvious which was the better show. It's just that the profound, intense middlebrowness of Aaron Sorkin conflicted with a subject matter that he just didn't understand, and didn't get what was interesting about.

Bradley Whitford: All of this, nobody has a fucking clue what they're doing. What's frustrating to me as somebody who's been lucky enough to be a television actor for this long is, leave these fucking things on or don't do them at all, because if they're any good, they need to find themselves.

If you think of all the shows that you and I love, none of them were conventionally developed. If anybody thought *The Sopranos* was going to be any good, [creator] David Chase wouldn't have been near it. You never would have met James Gandolfini. Bryan Cranston [on *Breaking Bad*], never in a million fucking years. He should have, but the network would have ruined it.

What those shows get to do is arrive with a strikingly original vision that can get you through the writers and actors understanding where this thing is going to go.

30 Rock brought more of that freshness and did it from the perspective of someone who authentically understood sketch comedy and late-night television from lived experience. One of the strengths *30 Rock* developed is that it had a cast full of characters who could carry their own storylines, with actors capable of delivering performances that held viewers' attention beyond just the top few stars. Even characters relegated to background status at first, like Kenneth, would go on to be central, beloved figures on the series.

The show had an absurdist quality that let it lead audiences in a million different directions. It was a joke machine, while also always keeping social commentary at the front of its storytelling.

Andrew Guest: There's a certain cynicism [with Robert's writing], but also a desire to craft a joke that nobody else can craft. That is a testament to Tina as well, who had the same style.

Judah Friedlander: This is a very fast-talking show. In a movie, they pretty much never tell you to talk faster, but in TV, they pretty much tell you that every day. "That was great, say it faster."

That style came about because the writers were always trying to pack so many jokes into every episode. While Tina Fey was responsible for writing the first couple episodes, she worked with co-showrunner Robert Carlock to assemble a team after the show was picked up.

Andrew Guest: They were killers when it comes to comedy, both of them. And they hired amazing writers.

Adam Bernstein: Once a head writer's show goes to series, what they really desperately need are writers. Because now the daunting task is to produce enough good scripts under incredible time pressure—to keep the bar of the material that high under all these deadlines. And then, a director is useful, and they're helping to execute stuff, but it's not the same relationship in series that you have during a pilot.

Peter Agliata: Any show would've cut off an arm to have one of those people in the room. They had eight writers deep, and then assistant writers who moved up to be writers who were just as smart and funny and talented.

Daisy Gardner: I was obsessed with the pilot of *30 Rock*. I was like "Oh my god, I love this so much. I would kill to work on this show." Back when it was still in script form and they hadn't shot it or anything.

A few months later, Gardner was among the writers who made it through to getting screened by Tina Fey.

Daisy Gardner: Rachel Dratch was also on the phone, walking with her. Tina said, "Look, we're just talking to you to make sure you're not a psycho. And at three A.M., you just want to like the people you see in the halls." And the next thing I knew I was moving out to New York.

While there were some New Yorkers, much of the writing staff was moving out from working in TV out in Los Angeles, or from the Second City improv world in Chicago.

They didn't have their own offices at first, working out of Lorne Michaels's Midtown Manhattan offices. They were next to David Letterman's soundstage, working above the old Studio 54.

> **Daisy Gardner:** Everybody tried to figure out the city together. Because none of us knew New York, Tina and Jeff, her husband, would take people out, host a dinner at this lovely seafood place in the Upper West Side, and just try to help us. Because we're all in these crappy apartments.
>
> I moved from place to place all over the city. I would get a sublet someplace, I was in Hell's Kitchen for a while—honestly, coming together and figuring out New York, and figuring out what *SNL* was to Rob and Tina, was part of the experience.
>
> Kay Cannon, her husband at the time [*SNL*'s Jason Sudeikis] had no sense of smell. So he got them an apartment above a Burger King that just reeked, and she was so grossed out. It was just full of rats. She would turn on a light, throw something down the hallway, and yell, "Rat, rat, rat, rat, rat!"

Kay Cannon came out of the Upright Citizens Brigade comedy theater world, ultimately going on to write the *Pitch Perfect* movies and becoming a director in her own right. She made cameos in *30 Rock* bit parts like the wife in ten-second-long sitcom *Makin' It Happen!* and a human table during the Ludachristmas party. Cannon would end up being credited with the second-highest number of episodes written behind Tina Fey herself.

> **Jon Haller (writers' assistant):** Kay Cannon stood out to me because she was always bright and peppy. While we were working until eleven o'clock at night, she was also writing *Pitch Perfect*. So, when somebody's able to create that much comedy from nine A.M. to eleven at night, and then go off and write that? That's what Tina showed people: "I'm a force of nature, what can *you* do?"
>
> **Daisy Gardner:** John Riggi had an artist's loft in SoHo, with giant lips everywhere. But he was also like "This is not really my aesthetic in this apartment."
>
> **John Riggi:** I was living in New York for the first time. New York was like going to some amazing amusement park. If I could live my life the way I live it and do the work I do, I think about moving back there all the time, because it got under my skin so much that I miss it tremendously.

John Riggi spent a career fascinated with what goes on behind the scenes. He came from stand-up comedy to work on HBO's legendary *The Larry Sanders Show*—another show about a show. He'd go on to other shows digging into the real world behind what's being presented to the public, from *The Naked Truth* to *The Comeback*.

> **John Riggi:** The essence of show business is we decide what people will see. As a director, when you frame a shot, you decide what's going to be in the frame.

We have the control to show what we want and hide what we don't want. And the idea of the things that we don't want to be seen coming out, spurting out from the sides, seems funny to me.

He'd met with *The West Wing* about coming in to add some comedy to that show and was also offered an executive producer position with *Ugly Betty*. Despite his flashier options, he didn't end up on either of those. (Given how fantastical the world of *Ugly Betty* was, when one particularly absurd Liz plan goes awry, her only response is "This would work on *Ugly Betty*.")

John Riggi: I had one more appointment, and that was what at the time was called *The Untitled Tina Fey Project*. I went and saw that and really, really wanted to do it. Everyone on my team—my manager, my agent—was saying, "Boy, *Ugly Betty* has got a lot of heat on it," and "You really should go with *Ugly Betty*." I was like "With all due respect, I would rather do this Tina Fey show."

He joined with *30 Rock* only having a guaranteed thirteen episodes—fewer than *Ugly Betty*. Riggi became one of the show's key writers, going on to be a prolific director for the show and work with Fey and Carlock on other projects. Riggi's mission was to always make audiences feel like these characters are real people talking to you.

John Riggi: I've never been in a writers' room where we wrote that many jokes per page, ever. We were a joke machine. I like that, but I also tried to infuse some heart into it, too. That's what I do—I try to find a little bit of humanity in things and not kill the comedy by doing that. It's surgical in nature, almost, to pull that off—but when you can do it, it's really great.

Daisy Gardner: Riggi was always the one who was like "I have no doubt that this will be funny. What I think we always have to work out and watch out for is, is there a real relationship between Jack and Liz, and what is the dynamic of it this episode?"

Donald Glover, before starring on *Community*, becoming a superstar rapper as Childish Gambino, creating *Atlanta*, or appearing in the *Star Wars* franchise, landed a job writing on the first season of *30 Rock*. It happened when Tina Fey's manager David Miner, who was also an executive producer on *30 Rock*, reached out to him after seeing videos from his sketch comedy group online. Glover was a fan of Tina Fey and was intimidated when he first started working on the show.

Donald Glover (writer): But then you hear her tell a couple fart jokes, and you're like "Oh, she's human."

Daisy Gardner: He was already a super-hot sketch writer, famous in the New York comedy scene. We were just walking around Rockefeller Center one day, and people would yell out lines from his sketches that he'd done at NYU.

Donald Glover: Being a woman writer, I think [Tina] realizes, not every joke should be written by a white dude from Harvard.

Still, Fey has frequently noted that she put into practice a lesson she learned from *Saturday Night Live* while building her show: The idea that the ideal writers' room staff is a mix of Harvard grads and improv performers.

Each episode started in the writers' room, with the team coming up with what would happen, known as "breaking the story." The way a writers' room works is that you have a showrunner in charge of running the room, with different levels of writers pitching their own ideas. Carlock being there as Fey's co-showrunner was meant to help her with her first TV show, as well as being a reality of the fact that as the star, she couldn't spend all her time in the writers' room.

Chris George (location manager): Carlock was more involved in the scouting and the selecting of locations than Tina herself. She was always either on camera or in the writers' room. He was more of a presence in the production, the logistics of making the show.

Tracey Wigfield (writer): We have a big whiteboard where we write all the ideas we come up with—ideas from packets we write, and ideas we come up with in the room. There's just hundreds of ideas written in tiny serial-killer scrawl by Robert Carlock. Sometimes when we need a story, we'll pick from that list.

Wigfield described working on *30 Rock* as a graduate school for TV writing.

Daisy Gardner: It was learning how to not compromise and how to say, "OK, this is good. It could be better. What is the smart take on this? This is the thing you would expect. How do you twist it? How do you subvert it? How do you make it funny? How do you make it something no one's ever seen before?" And when you're being asked those questions all day long by your boss, you start to think that way.

That ethos carried through to every part of the production, including guest directors like Dennie Gordon.

Dennie Gordon (director): You have to try several different ways. You know it's funny, but how could it possibly be funnier? Is it the cutaway to the deadpan look? And you can never really stop. You have to always be looking at "What else, what else, what else?"

When the writers started, they would work at *Saturday Night Live*'s Studio 8H in the actual 30 Rockefeller Center when that show was on hiatus and the *SNL* writers weren't occupying their offices.

Daisy Gardner: I loved being in that space, going in those old crappy elevators that broke down all the time. But then, when you're walking through Studio

8H, you see the pictures on the walls of the performers. It's just silence, with no one there, and you're with all the ghosts of the people that worked on the show.

The writers are helped by a writers' assistant, who takes notes on everything that's said so that the writers can refer back to it later—either while brainstorming or when working on the actual scripts.

Jon Haller: It was hard, because my job was to keep track of everything and write down the hilarious things that were coming out of everybody at every possible minute. And Robert Carlock speaks fast—his mind works at a faster RPM, as well as Tina's. But that incites everybody to be as smart and as funny. It is the hardest I've ever laughed in my life, in that room.

Don Scardino: [Tina] thinks faster than anybody I know—except maybe Baldwin, who thinks faster than anybody.

Andrew Guest: From Season 1, I was doing my best to do a great job as writers' assistant and show that I was talented as a writer. I asked Robert Carlock to read some of my work, and I did everything I could to make myself indispensable.

Jon Haller: The writers' assistant, you are a stenographer, you are an archivist. In pre-production, at the beginning of the season, there was one room where all the writers were together, coming up with as many stories for the season as possible. And then once you got things going, there were usually two rooms. The writers' assistant would be in one room, and the script coordinator would be with the other room, writing what everybody is saying, archiving all the stories as far as where they're all ending up.

Other writers would take over when Tina and Robert weren't available to run the rooms.

Jon Haller: The sub-captains were John Riggi, Ron Weiner, and Matt Hubbard. Sometimes Jack Burditt. When Robert or Tina wasn't in one of those rooms, somebody else would be co-running that and trying to get a story going. But everything would then be taken to Robert, and then Tina, so everybody's DNA was all over everything by the time it made it to air.

The writers' assistant would also help to communicate between departments, particularly the craft departments—letting everyone know the props, sets, art, and costumes that they'd need.

Jon Haller: You have a joke about a robot, you need to let Props know, "We're going to need a robot." Assistants are basically helping the writers and the showrunner keep everything on the rails.

Fey brought together a writers' room known for its long hours and commitment to perfectly crafted jokes. You'd write all day, then often head back to Tina's place to keep writing as she cared for her child—then come back to do it again bright and early the next day.

John Riggi: The thing about *30 Rock* is, once you went in to *30 Rock*, your life was *30 Rock*. You didn't think about anything else. You just worked on the show, and to craft that show took a lot of work and a lot of effort. It took up your life—at least for me, I didn't really think about too much else.

Jon Haller: The "no assholes" policy that Tina has [meant] it was just this super diverse, super smart, and super polite room. I've worked in rooms since where it's just a locker room, where people are shouting over each other to be heard, and here you apologized if you interrupted somebody.

Diversity at the time meant that there were several white women, in addition to the white men. While there was encouragement for everyone to fire on all cylinders, it was also a room where the competition could be fierce. That was an attitude carried over from Fey and Carlock's experience on *SNL*.

Andrew Guest: Both Robert and Tina come from the Lorne Michaels school of "what you have is really special already." Anybody who's there is so lucky to be there. And it's your job to not only dampen their creativity—because people will want to come up with lots of extra ideas, and you have to squash all that. But also, you never make them feel comfortable.

Writers got fired a lot. No one would ever have a conversation with them beforehand about how they were doing, and it was a lot of pressure on the writers to deliver, and to deliver to the standard that Robert and Tina somehow already had set up.

A lot of writers' rooms, there's small talk that leads to a half joke, then somebody adds to it. This was not that type of environment. When you pitched a joke, you pitched the full joke. And if you didn't, it didn't go anywhere. You weren't looking for help, or to have somebody finish your thought for you.

We would sit in silence. We would work on one joke for hours. I would be typing all the versions of the joke onto the page, and we would wait for Robert to have decided we were there. And sometimes that meant we would just sit there. If he wasn't satisfied with the joke, we fucking were *there*.

Daisy Gardner: *30 Rock* is a show where people have toiled on those jokes 'til four A.M. You've all been sitting there, someone pitching a joke, then someone topping it, and then someone topping it. So, you can always say, "It was a joke that got to the joke that got to the joke." Everybody contributed in some way to that final thing that appears on the screen.

Andrew Guest: We would work, particularly in Season 1, until ten o'clock at night at Silvercup. Then a small group would go back to Tina's apartment, where her newborn daughter was being put down. She would come sit out in the living room, and the baby monitor would be there. At a certain point, Tina would fall asleep, and the rest of us would work typically 'til about four in the morning, almost every night.

So I think that's why the jokes were so good.

Especially as *30 Rock* progressed later into the season, more of the show would be getting group-written late into the night.

Daisy Gardner: One thing that sounded so glamorous about *30 Rock* or *SNL* is, if the subway wasn't running 'cause you were there that late, it would be like "We got you a special car," and it would be a black town car. But we learned to just hate those cars. Because they were always driven by messed-up drivers on meth who would drive you to New Jersey.

There was one night where it was two or three in the morning, and Matt Hubbard realized they were going the wrong way through the tunnel back to New York. And he was like "Wait, there's headlights coming at us. We're going the wrong way in the fucking tunnel."

The scripts would always be punched up by all the writers no matter what, pushing each joke to be as funny as it could get, along with notes from other powers-that-be—ranging from network executives to Lorne Michaels.

John Riggi: Our scripts were always fat, and there was no way we were going to shoot all of that. That was the biggest problem—you get your episode back, and it wasn't uncommon for your running time to be thirty-six minutes, and you've got to cut ten minutes out of it.

Jon Haller: One of my weird jobs was, we would write scripts that would come in around thirty-five pages. And that would be after honing and rewriting, and even then, so many jokes would have to be cut for the edit, which ended up being around twenty-two minutes. At one point, Carlock was wondering about all those lost jokes. I was like "Oh, I could find them, come up with a file of all the cut jokes that were written and filmed but never aired." That took me quite a few months, and it ended up being a four hundred-page document of the cut jokes of *30 Rock*.

30 Rock is like *Arrested Development*, where structurally you were telling five stories, sometimes six, seven at a time. So the fourth and fifth story would be so much more reduced, and sometimes an entire story would get lost so that you could have a Liz or Jack story in full. It was mostly any of the fat around the scenes, but any of the fat of a *30 Rock* script is delicious, hilarious, and genius fat.

After being written, the show goes to a table read with the cast reading the script out loud. It's meant to help figure out what works when it's actually being performed, versus something that might have just seemed funny on the page or in the writers' room—part of the continuing process of crafting impeccable comedy television.

> **Daisy Gardner:** *30 Rock* was the first table read I went to where, if a joke didn't work but Tina and Rob believed in it, it would stay in. Normally you do a table read, and if something's flat, it's taken out and you immediately replace it with something else. But if it was something Tina believed in, she would say, "No, I know this is funny."
>
> And she was always right. It was weird—there were no missteps. She and Rob have great instincts, and they trusted those instincts. Maybe she would take out other things that got mild laughs and try to make them ten times better—you would spend the night rewriting something else and bringing it up a zillion times, and that would support the original thing they were trying to do.

Each episode would be shot in about a week, though the director and other parts of the staff are doing prep before shooting begins. The writers also act as producers, though with Tina Fey as the star of the show, she was always able to provide a writer's perspective on set. The show would shoot long hours, with days running about fourteen hours for the actors at times. Fey would be in the writers' room herself before they started shooting, but once production started, she'd be addressing questions from the wee hours of the morning in the makeup chair until after they wrapped each night. The show would sometimes get behind and it would take more than a week to film an episode, or they'd be shooting parts of multiple episodes at once. They would also sometimes deploy multiple crews to film simultaneously to help make their schedule. The season as a whole shot for about seven months, though there are hiatuses within that time frame.

Despite trimming the scripts, they'd still shoot more than they could use. Shooting scripts came in around twenty-eight minutes, so several minutes of solid jokes still needed to be cut in the editing room to get it down to a twenty-one-minute, thirty-second airtime.

> **Ken Eluto (editor):** It was a struggle to get some episodes to length. There were times we asked, or more accurately *begged*, for another five or ten seconds. We very rarely cut full scenes—we mostly got an episode to time by lifting dialogue and picking up the pace as we went.

To get the show there, there were multiple levels of edits, along with notes from producers as everyone worked together to craft each episode.

Ken Eluto: The director usually gets two days to work with the editor after their cut is complete. The cut then gets turned over to the producers. *30 Rock* used a lot of the same directors for different episodes, so you'd usually have a good rapport with them from working together in the past.

Initially we'd get notes in writing from the show's executive producers, and sometimes from some writers. Obviously, Tina's and Robert Carlock's notes were given the most weight. Lorne Michaels would also weigh in through Tina and Robert, especially in the early seasons.

The editors would use temp music in the cuts, and our library of score grew fast over the seasons. Jeff Richmond, the composer and executive producer, would come in to rework music selections and placement, as well as make editing suggestions.

Doug Abel: I'm pretty isolated. I'm in a dark windowless room. Because the neighborhood didn't have much to offer, Tina and Carlock would often bring in lunch. You really felt you're sequestered there. I guess the production office had windows, but we didn't.

They would come in and just giggle as we'd watch cuts or takes about some line they wrote for Tracy just to really mess with him, knowing that they would get a funny delivery because it's custom-built to be funny coming out of his mouth.

Ken Eluto: As we got closer to sending cuts to the network, Tina, Robert, and Jeff could come into the edit room to watch cuts and make any final decisions before [the edited cut] went out. Then, after getting notes from the studio and network, which had a few passes, they'd also come in for the final lock of the episode.

Doug Abel: What you're dealing with is there's going to be some scenes, some actors, something that just didn't work, or didn't land. Or frankly, Alec Baldwin was in a bad mood that day. In a situation like that, you're trying to get the subpar scenes to work—then there's going to be fabulous scenes. Sometimes you can amazingly fix it in the edit, or by doing a quick pickup, and you can work around it. Alec was the one cast member, when he did come to look at a cut, I had to leave the room. There was definitely an aura. I know he was fussy, gave people shit.

Once we get past the pilot, the show continues to portray what happens as Tracy's energy infects Liz's show. It's already tight from the beginning, but the pace keeps increasing once the characters are all set up. The show also moves away from being about specific goings-on of the show-within-a-show, and more about the lives of the people who make that show. Tracy started as the crazy one, the one with the most absurd backstory. Tracy Morgan had the comedic skills to make whatever weird detail they wanted to add to Tracy Jordan's life, whatever odd thing they wanted him to say, completely work.

> **Daisy Gardner:** Even in those first few weeks, we knew how special it was. I can't explain how cool that is. It's the only time I've ever felt that for a show that's starting up, where you're like "Oh, this is going to be a jewel. This will outlast everything, and this will be great." We had nothing to back that up, but we all felt that.

Another thing that set *30 Rock* apart from the competition was not only the New York City setting, but also the fact that the show was actually shot there and had a cast and crew filled with people who considered themselves New Yorkers. That's why the show was opening with jokes about the city's infamous developer Donald Trump even in its first season, such as Liz trying to get the writers to pay attention to her instead of leering over Cerie by saying that they need to change a Trump joke in the show—and as Liz realizes she's being ignored, she adds that it's because Trump was eaten by a lion, aboard the International Space Station. Perhaps some New Yorker wish fulfillment? *30 Rock* always makes clear that the city is dirty, grimy, and filled with rats, but that it's also the greatest place on earth in the minds of the people behind the show.

> **Don Scardino:** If *30 Rock* had been anywhere else, it wouldn't have been *30 Rock*. You can shoot Toronto for New York, god knows I've shot LA for New York in various places. But New York has that energy.

> **Matthew Broderick:** I think it's great that it had all those New York actors, because I'm one.

They would take advantage of shooting at the actual 30 Rockefeller Center when they could, including scenes at the building's famed Wollman Skating Rink. Filming there could be a challenge, especially because *30 Rock*'s Monday through Friday schedule meant they couldn't film on weekends when it was less busy. Location Manager Chris George had to work to maintain a relationship with the company that owns and manages their namesake—though the first time they went to shoot there, the property management company didn't charge them anything.

> **Chris George:** When it came time to talk about what the fee would be, they just said, "Oh, don't even worry about it. You're called *30 Rock*, and you're going to come here. We'll just work it out. It's you guys." Then, after that first time, they realized how many trucks and campers, and crew, and background, and craft service, and cable, and lights, and PAs redirecting traffic, pedestrians, vehicles, everything. They changed their tune.

It became a running joke between Jerry Kupfer and me. He would say, "What's with these prices? Don't they know if it weren't for our show nobody would ever go to Rockefeller Center?"

The show tried to use other New York locations to their advantage, along with the weather you can't get out in Los Angeles.

Don Scardino: We were shooting a restaurant on the Upper West Side, and a blizzard had kicked up. Being battle-hardened New York crew, we all showed up and got started a little late in the restaurant. But because of the snowstorm, the producer said to me, is there anything else we can shoot? I said, "Well, we have that scene of Liz hailing a taxi—let's go out and hail a taxi on Amsterdam Avenue, with the snow coming down, and it'll look so cool!"

Tina was game, and we run out—took the camera handheld, and snow was just swirling and whirling. She flagged a real taxi down, and we're filming it. She gets in, drives off, and makes the guy come back. It was great.

Then, when we went to cut the episode together, I said, "Where's the shot? Where's that great shot?" And he says, "We have to reshoot it." "Why?" Well, because the scene that followed, we had already shot in the studio—it was in Jack Donaghy's office.

They'd already shot that scene with Alec against a sunny sky, and since Liz was on the phone with him and they were cutting back and forth, it just wasn't going to work to include it. With Baldwin's limited shooting schedule, it was Fey's side that had to change.

Of course, New York weather brought other problems.

Dennie Gordon: We weren't able to go in and out of the front door of the actual 30 Rock that we very much wanted to use because it was so cold that gigantic icicles were falling from the building. They were like these death ice knives that were falling on the ground. We had to hurry up and get our work done before noon when they were going to start melting even more and dropping on our heads.

While the show took advantage of shooting in Manhattan when possible, their home base was the stages at Silvercup Studios in Long Island City. They went into Manhattan for exteriors and tried to shoot there a couple days a week (where, as Jane Krakowski put it, they would pretend to know people from the *Today Show*). The view out Jack's office is, sadly, a backdrop, with camera angles carefully chosen to make sure it never looks *too* fake.

Teresa Mastropierro (production designer): He looked out his window quite often. That got a little scary for the art department, because they would go stand awfully close to the backdrop, which we would just bite our nails thinking, *Oh gosh, if the camera gets too close, you're going to notice it's fake*. He's the actor and that's where he wants to stand.

Production designer Keith Raywood, who was also the production designer for *SNL*, had spent the summer at Silvercup building the show's sets. The only one that was built for the pilot was Jack's office, with the rest shot on location, so now it was time to build out everything else. That included Tina's office, the writers' offices, the studio, the hallway that leads to the studio, dressing rooms, and more.

> **Keith Raywood (production designer):** I had to build NBC. I would go measure the windows [at the actual 30 Rock], and draw the windows. I would measure the radiators, which are very unusual radiators. Everything was exactly as I saw it.
>
> It was just making it so it was shootable for a sitcom. So ceilings had to be able to come up and down, walls had to be able to be pulled out to bring in camera and shoot certain angles.

Raywood even ordered the real 30 Rock's actual red carpeting, with the gold NBC peacock on it, through the building's management company. The similarities caused some strange mixing of realities at times, like when Raywood saw Lorne leaning against the wall in the hallway, just like he would outside the real *SNL* stage. Marci Klein walked down the hall, turned, saw the door to what used to be her real-life office, and opened it—to find nothing but brick.

> **Keith Raywood:** It was like *The Twilight Zone*. Imagine your real life becomes a studio set.

A photographer was brought in to shoot the backdrops that would hang outside the windows on the show, including shooting outside of where Jack's office would be. Raywood took a little extra care with making things extra *Twilight Zone* for Tina Fey. He went to the office Tina had used while head writer at *SNL* and photographed it to make sure that Liz Lemon would have the exact same view that Tina had—Fey appreciated the inside joke.

Production designer Teresa Mastropierro, who took over when Raywood left, would further refine the show's spaces. That included finding reasons for characters other than the writers to end up in the writers' room—so Mastropierro helped design an attached kitchen area so that the *TGS* cast might come by to grab a coffee.

> **Teresa Mastropierro:** I would look at a lot of research, then close the book on that. The things that stuck out in my mind would be the things that were iconic, and that makes the set a bit funnier, because they were tropes.

With sets built, we get more glimpses of what the show will become in **episode 2, "The Aftermath."** *The Girlie Show* officially becomes *TGS with Tracy Jordan*, helping to fuel Jenna's paranoia about being replaced as the show's star, as well as giving it its own *SNL*-esque nickname. *30 Rock* replaces the opening musical number from the pilot with actual opening credits, which remained largely unchanged throughout the show's run. New series regulars didn't get added, and characters who may not have always had the largest roles (sorry, Pete and Frank) still got to hold on to their places in the opening.

The second episode is where we really start seeing the cutaways that were one of the show's hallmarks—someone mentioning an absurd idea, then cutting away to show you that no, that's not *just* a passing reference, here's the fully realized version of what they were talking about, but only for about five seconds. Animated series *Family Guy* became known for perhaps taking this concept the furthest, but *30 Rock* would do these jokes while somehow maintaining just enough real-world groundedness to make you feel connected to these characters and care about their relationships. The stakes of their lives could at times be ridiculous, but they were real to these people, and that's what made them real to you.

Liz starts on the road to being mentored by Jack, with the show taking us with Liz into Jack's completed, post-renovations office for the first time. Keith Raywood wanted to give him a corporate office fit for a microwave executive, all cold mahogany and inlaid steel. Liz spends much of the first season in particular being put in the position of management against her show colleagues, who she's always treated as friends. But Jack's guidance is more subtle at first—lessons in the course of business, rather than the formal mentor–mentee relationship that they eventually reached. As Alec Baldwin became more committed to the show, the writers felt more confident letting the weight of the show shift to Jack. That dynamic starts to replace the drama around what's happening in the writers' room, or on air with any particular episode of *TGS*.

30 Rock eventually became less about Tracy and Jack causing problems for Liz, and more about Liz's personal life and how that relates to her relationship with Jack. The show's writers chose not to make Liz a working mom, helping to differentiate her from her real-life counterpart.

Tina Fey: It left her a little more open for stories. And also my husband, Jeff, who is a producer on the show, made it very clear that if I made him a character on the show, and made jokes about him, he would kill me.

Andrew Guest: The problem with Liz as a character is she's got what she wants. Tina was very adamant that she didn't want Liz to be wanting a baby—I mean, they got there later. Or, it wasn't about a guy—it wasn't like you were worrying about this date going well or not. And the truth is she had the thing she wanted from the beginning—she had the show, and that's what she cared about most. So it was hard to put stakes in. Going into it, we thought that it would be like "Oh my god, Tracy and Alec are making life miserable and difficult to do her job." Which was what the pilot delivered on, and what the first few episodes were about. But at a certain point, as an audience member, you don't care about that.

While they may seem to be coming from opposite places, Jack ultimately proves to be the only one who really, truly gets Liz Lemon.

The show continued to deal with race. It pushed the envelope, at times making decisions that were ill-informed and which some of those involved have expressed regret about. But it was also at times ahead of the curve in actually trying to say something through comedy about race in America and in television. The writers combine that with the way the show takes on the corporate side of NBC in "The Aftermath," with NBC promoting Tracy on *TGS* by promising to "bring the Black back to NBC."

We also get to see Tracy, who grew up underprivileged, getting one up on Toofer in the writers' room. Tracy calls him "Theo Huxtable" and asks how he's doing. When Toofer says that he's doing good, Tracy corrects the Harvard grad's grammar, telling him, "Superman does good; you're doing well. You need to study your grammar, son." With that mic drop, Tracy exits.

The episode also includes a bit that perfectly summarizes who Tracy Jordan is: He invites the entire cast to party on his yacht. Except, by the end, we learn that this is *not* his yacht and that Tracy is, as usual, a completely absurd man.

Adam Bernstein: The concept was Tracy was throwing a party. Everyone showed up, and they found out at a certain point in the party that it's not actually his apartment. I pitched, "Oh, let's put it on a boat!" Because I thought the boat was so much more bling-y. We found some insane yacht that was in Jersey City—it was designed and decorated like someone's brownstone. If you went inside, it was all wood paneling. It ended up being a lot of pressure to get everything shot, because we were depending on daylight. And the spaces ended up being so small, I ended up really hating myself for coming up with the idea of a boat.

Scott Adsit: I didn't know [Jane Krakowski] at all—I hadn't seen *Ally McBeal* and I didn't know Broadway well enough to know who she was. There was a scene where we're all on Tracy's yacht, and she starts singing. After a take, I run over and say, "Wow! You're a good singer!" And she kind of gave me a side glance, like "Uhhh, yyyyeah I am." But in the best way.

There's a brief tease here of a Tracy/Jenna love interest, but just like with Jack and Liz, that was very much not what this show was about. This was a show about a workplace, and people being friends, and mentors, and connected—but that didn't mean that they had to wind up in each other's beds.

That also meant that Liz was often alone. Her relatable loneliness is symbolized by her choking multiple times in **episode 3, "Blind Date,"** realizing that she could die with no one there to help her—and that no one would find her body. Hold on, I think I just made *myself* too sad writing that.

Jack tries setting Liz up on a blind date—and initially assumes she's a lesbian. But the woman he sets her up with is actually pretty great, and even Liz has to doubt her own heterosexuality given how strong a pick Jack makes. The episode was written by an openly gay member of the show's writing room, John Riggi. He didn't feel that the story specifically resonated with him as a gay man, but that perspective may have helped to fuel the casual, natural way that the relationship is approached in the episode.

John Riggi: We did try to be aware of things, but we were also—there was a sense of irreverence, like everything's up for grabs on *30 Rock*. We lived in that. So they would for sure turn to me for that stuff, but we didn't really do a whole lot of gay storylines.

This episode is also where Kenneth's storyline kicks off. While he doesn't always have the most central storylines, he may have the biggest arc. In the third episode, Jack tries playing poker with Kenneth but can't read the thickheaded page's tells. By the end of their competition, Jack declares that "in five years we'll all either be working for him or be dead by his hand."

The writers worked over the years figuring out how to make that prophecy come true. Kenneth rises to new opportunities while always longing for his beloved role as a page, but those seeds of Kenneth being something more than what we see start early.

Tracy bonds with Kenneth early on as a kindred spirit—someone who everyone else may see as dumb, but they're actually the ones with the greatest potential.

Scott Adsit: The writers must approach him like "What would Appalachian Jesus do?"

This was the kind of discovery that you see happen as the show takes its first few episodes to find its pacing. They aren't yet making use of the full power a single-camera sitcom has to deliver more jokes when there's no live audience. The editing's rhythms still feel at times like what Tina Fey did with *SNL*, leaving space for you to laugh rather than coming at you like pulses of electricity. But as everyone becomes more at home with one another, you can feel the performers fighting to get their lines out on top of one another, and the rhythm the show became known for settles in.

The show starts to dive deeper into Jack's character in episodes 4 and 5, with Baldwin moving closer to being at the center of the show. In **episode 4, "Jack the Writer,"** the show starts to develop Jack's deep, emotional need for power at General Electric. He is a true believer, espousing the importance of famed management philosophy Six Sigma, championed by real-life GE head Jack Welch. We also see more of Jack's Republican ties, including a 2006 Jeb Bush mention long before Jeb ran for president (and became a "please clap" meme).

The series continues to build the background of the world—some of the characterizations start out broad, but many of them are refined as the show continues. The writers leer over Cerie early on, but *30 Rock* made a statement about this kind of behavior, with Liz calling for Cerie to wear more-appropriate work attire. The *TGS* writers are largely upset, with Pete in particular growing frustrated and declaring that leering at Cerie is one of the few things he has in life.

Katrina Bowden first auditioned for the Cerie role in the original version of the pilot when she was just sixteen years old, but they felt like she was too young at the time. When they went looking for someone to replace the original actress, though, they brought in Bowden when she was still just seventeen. She'd just finished high school and had plans to go to college, but ended up working on *30 Rock* instead.

Pete was supposed to be Liz's good friend and advisor, but he also comes off as a creep at times.

> **Scott Adsit:** Early on, they were writing him a bit like they were still looking for him. Where he was a fool, and then he was the wise man. They found a nice balance between the two. He gives good advice to Liz, can't counsel himself. I was a little wary about making him *really* pathetic, and horny, in a foolish way. I mentioned that to Robert a couple times, and he agreed. We steered him away from being just a bald joke so that he is a richer character, not just a collection of the worst traits in a man.

> **Jesse Thorn:** As crazy as *30 Rock* is, and it's totally bonkers, every joke is character-driven. If you think of Pete, what's Scott Adsit on that call sheet? Seventh or something. And Pete is so clear, what's funny about him is so funny, and it's also more than most sitcoms would give the seventh person on the call sheet, even if it was a *great* sitcom. He gets as much as Norm gets on *Cheers*, and Norm is fourth or fifth on *Cheers*, and *Cheers* is the other best show ever.

At the same time, Tracy sends Kenneth on a mission in this episode to pick up an illegal exotic fish, offering him the sage advice he wishes he would have received when he was Kenneth's age: "Live every week like it's Shark Week." It created one of the biggest problems for the crew during Season 1: Tracy's aquarium, which was filled with real fish, and needed to be cared for at the show's Long Island studios.

Kevin Ladson: Keeping those fish alive in Silvercup Studios was a problem. It was a freshwater tank, [but] even with a freshwater tank, the upkeep and the maintenance—what happens when we're on Christmas break? We come back and all the fish are dead.

And [here's] where Kenneth goes to Chinatown and gets this exotic fish. Now this was not only an exotic fish, it was a dangerous spine-paralyzing fish that cost $600. So now this fish is part of the show. This fish kept dying, so I said to my one assistant, "You are in charge of keeping this fish alive." And the fish kept dying still. So one of the electricians came up with a great idea: "Why don't you just make it a tank with an iguana?"

Got rid of the fish and we got a great-looking fake iguana and put him in the tank. Iguanas hardly move, so it was perfect.

Tracy Morgan lived up to some of his character's own traits—including that love for exotic fish.

Kevin Ladson: We had built the tank [for his fish on the show]. So Tracy comes to me on a personal level. He says, "Kevin, I want you to come over to my house, and I want you to build a fish tank for me. I'm gonna have sharks and octopuses." I said, "Well, Tracy, I can do a design, but I think you're going to need some sort of engineer that's gonna need to figure out the pounds per square inch and all that." Now, I didn't have a conversation with him after that. The next news I heard was that his fish tank exploded, and his apartment had flooded the apartment down below. I said, "Man, it's a good thing [I didn't make that]—I wouldn't want that on my head."

Tracy Morgan's former assistant: It was a 24/7 role, and he would call me at four o'clock in the morning, anything that popped into his head—as mundane as, can you remember to change the clocks for daylight savings, to he needed a giant Pacific octopus.

I found him the only captive giant Pacific octopus outside of an aquarium. I had to pay a guy about a hundred grand to go out on a boat and scuba for one. Then I managed to track down the original "Thriller" jacket for him. I can't even begin to tell you the price on that.

I learned that you can kind of find anything you want. With this octopus, I called all his exotic fish guys, and they all told me to get lost, 'cause they said it was impossible. It just taught me to never go to a boss with "no," or I was gonna get shouted at pretty severely.

This episode also played with the *Studio 60* comparisons, featuring one of Sorkin's trademark "walk-and-talks." The technique is used to make a show feel exciting even when two characters are just having a long back-and-forth, delivering explanatory dialogue—so on *30 Rock*, they have a walk-and-talk where they end up making a complete circle.

While the show may have been finding its creative voice and diving deeper into character, episode 4 drew just 4.6 million viewers.

> **Andrew Guest:** Without Lorne, we would have gotten canceled. We started with twenty good years on Wednesday nights. There was a day we came in, and it was our third airing, and we were told we had to hit a number—and we didn't. We were all sitting around waiting to get the call that we were canceled. Lorne pulled some strings, and we got another week. Without that, that would have been the end of the show. We were always barely getting by.

The writers anxiously waited for the ratings to come in, celebrating when they hit their numbers and were able to stay on the air. Looking back, though, those ratings that were just barely keeping them on TV are better than almost any network show on the air today.

NBC moved the show to Thursdays at nine thirty P.M., trying to see if it could find an audience elsewhere on the schedule. The show may not have had the power to lead NBC's attempt to do comedy on Wednesday nights, but it was getting a new shot in the warm home of Thursday nights for the network as part of the network's new "Comedy Night Done Right" campaign. While not what they once were, it was still a solid night for the network—though it was also closing the night rather than opening it, helping to ease the pressure on the newer show to perform.

> **Robert Carlock:** You were sick to your stomach every Friday morning. Well, we were on about twenty different nights. They actually added days to the week to make sure we could move more. On Glurnsday you would wake up and know that email was coming. There were tenths of a point between getting a congratulatory phone call and feeling like "Oh boy, we're not getting it done here."

> **Kevin Ladson:** [*30 Rock*] was a show that nobody believed in. My father and I were its biggest supporters, and my father would tell all of his senior citizen buddies, "You have to watch *30 Rock* on Thursdays. It's a funny show, and my son is working on it." He's in rural South Carolina wearing a *30 Rock* T-shirt.

> **Andrew Guest:** If Lorne hadn't been there, it would have gotten watered down like much of network television. And some of the jokes that felt like one-percenters would have been noted, and we would have been forced to change. It was interesting working there, and working in New York City at the time. All

my friends were like "Oh my god, you work on *30 Rock*! It's the most popular show!" And I was like "No! It's going to get canceled! Every week, we're gonna get canceled." There was this disconnect.

Don Scardino: You [pay attention to the ratings], because you know that your fate hangs in the balance, and you want the show to do well. We were doing better in the cities than we were doing in the heartland, and we understood that. *30 Rock*, for its low comedy, fart-joke type value, was also a very layered show. A lot of people would say to me, "I have to DVR it and watch it two or three times because I miss so many jokes, and I realize there are so many things happening."

That disconnect continued, with the big-city, elite elements of the show seeming to keep it from connecting with a broader audience. These weren't working-class heroes—Kenneth serves as a representative of being both poor and from the South, and those elements are constantly ridiculed throughout the run of the show. Yet there was still an affection for Kenneth that blossomed over the years. The audience that did buy into the show was a crowd with more money on average than viewers of other programs, which meant it could still make a profit without the viewership numbers the network wanted.

Andrew Guest: Robert would always say, "Obviously, Universal's making money on this show. We wouldn't be continuing to do it if there wasn't some way to monetize it." That was when, historically, the advertisers were really interested in the type of viewer that was watching *30 Rock*, because it skewed more afflu-ent. So you could charge more for your commercials, and you could advertise certain things. But you watch a new show premiere now to a 0.7, and they're like "It's a hit!"

That may be a slight exaggeration, but a 0.7 rating (0.7 percent of all households with televisions) is still enough fifteen years later to keep your show in the top one hundred. Meanwhile, *30 Rock* was hitting a 1.6 rating but facing possible cancellation.

Dennie Gordon: It was never a luxurious schedule. The show was never funded completely enough for us to be able to do what we wanted to do. If we were clever in the way we scheduled the day, then we were able to steal time. You're always leaving a scene going, "Ugh, I wish I could have done that." We fought to have enough time to find the gold.

There's disagreement on when the first season finally clicked, or whether it ever actu-ally did. Early on, and to some extent throughout much of the first season, the show has a more cinematic feel.

The first episode on Thursdays was **episode 5, "Jack-Tor,"** which is one of the episodes frequently mentioned for when things began to settle into the *30 Rock* we know and love. Along with the time slot change, NBC also tried to goose "Jack-Tor's" ratings by delivering a "supersized" episode, running in a forty-minute block.

The show follows up Jack's efforts at writing with him getting put in the position of acting on *TGS*. *30 Rock* explores early on the idea of Jack as a writer or an actor, and we quickly see these are among the only talents Jack *doesn't* have. It's particularly strong when he tries acting and Jonathan quickly informs Liz that there's a video she needs to see—and we see the secret ill-fated industrial film Jack recorded for GE where he takes dozens of takes to get anything usable, unable to hold a coffee cup and handle props on the same line, or even just walk over to a chart. Acting makes him so self-conscious that he can't figure out what to do with his arms and starts walking like a robot—unsure of what to do with his hands, he holds two coffee mugs.

> **Don Scardino:** It was scripted that he can't remember his lines, and he's having trouble—but so much of it was Alec playing. When we finally reveal, [Jonathan] comes in with the tape and says, "Don't let him go out there live, he can't remember lines," and he plays all the outtakes—that was just Alec saying, "Well let me try this! Let me try that! Let me fall down! Oh, the bird at the window!"

> **Doug Abel:** There was a lot of editing back and forth with that. That little video, with something like that, once you see it for the first time, it stops being funny. There's a danger of sucking the soul out of it by having too many people lay their hands on it—I felt like we were on the cusp of it, [but] that ended up being quite funny.

This was director Don Scardino's first episode.

> **Don Scardino:** I wasn't a producer yet, I'm just a gun-for-hire. When we did "Jack-Tor," as someone who grew up acting and on a soap opera—live television when I first started—I've always been a huge fan of and in love with backstage. So I was always saying to them, "Can I take this scene and put it behind the flats instead of out in the open like you've got it?" Or in the hallway—"Can I take this one—I want to shoot it through the prop cage as they come around." Just creating the world of it.

Don met Tina behind the scenes—and failed a quick quiz.

> **Don Scardino:** She said to me, "You don't remember me, do you?" I said, "Uh oh, why? Did we date, what?" She said, "No no no, I was on the props crew of *A Few Good Men* when you brought it to the University of Virginia on your way back to Broadway."

Scardino had directed Aaron Sorkin's *A Few Good Men* on stage before it became a movie. Fey said it was all right that he didn't remember—she looked different, and most of her work on the play was walking the star's dog. Scardino would go on to be a key figure in the show's evolution, directing numerous episodes over the show's run and becoming a producing director, guiding whichever director was coming in for an episode. That included lessons on how to handle Alec Baldwin and let him deliver his best performances.

Don Scardino: I would say to the directors, "Let him play. Just roll the camera. Ask him if he wants another—he'll come up with great stuff." As long as you don't tighten up and think, *I've got to make the day, and I can't let him improv or play.* Alec loved to turn the camera on and just say, "Run, man. I'll do ten versions of that line. Ready? Here we go."

The episode was inspired by an early viral video, "Winnebago Man." The video spread thanks to the extreme response seen in outtakes of a Winnebago salesman who struggles to get his dialogue and prop work down, swearing constantly as he screws up take after take. According to John Riggi, the writers' room was obsessed with him.

Daisy Gardner: It just becomes *King Lear*—a Shakespearean tragedy of how much he can't remember his lines or play to the camera, and it would make us die laughing. So that's what we wanted Jack to experience.

But while Jack was made to look the fool, it all paid off in the growth of Jack and Liz's relationship.

John Riggi: There was a little tiny moment in that episode when Liz was walking home and she walked through the *TGS* studio. Jack was lying on the stage on his back. He looked at her, and he said, "I can't do it, Lemon. I don't know how to do it. And I've never . . ." The idea was, this is a guy who never says, "I don't know how to do something." And Tina looked at him in this great moment and said, "Yeah, I know."

We went on with the comedy, but that little benchmark right there makes me feel something slightly different that I would never normally feel if it was just joke after joke. My theory is that people invest a little bit more. They start to feel like these people, as corny as it sounds, are real characters as opposed to just joke delivery systems.

Andrew Guest: A lot of people realized, when that episode happened and you saw vulnerability from Jack, that there was more there. The dynamic between the two of them was powerful. The thing that had a lot of weight for both Robert and Tina was their feelings about Lorne, particularly Tina's feelings. This was a way to address some of those feelings about him—a person who, on certain levels, you really disagree with, and their lifestyle is bananas. They live in a different rarefied world, and they think that everyone does. That's a lot of his comedy— thinking *Why didn't you buy a house yet, Liz? You should have sixteen-foot ceilings.*

Lorne Michaels: I always say, get an apartment so that when you come home at night, you go, "Who lives here? Somebody great must live here. Oh, I live here!" Because you work really hard.

Alec Baldwin: Jack is modeled on kind of a generic GE executive. A lot of Jack is based on Lorne Michaels. In terms of aiming for success with as little guilt as possible, Lorne is the model. Lorne lives the life I wish I was living.

Tom Houghton: [Jack]'s duplicitous. He's new school and old school at the same time. They really are just interested in the bottom line, and NBC was just one of the many, many instruments they had to make money. It's all just a factory. It's not the aspirational thing, why we went into the business—not the magic part.

30 Rock takes one of its biggest swings at GE and, by extension, then–GE subsidiary NBC, in "Jack-Tor." After hearing the inane faux GE tagline, "Imagining the future today," Jack pushes the idea of product integration. He asks for positive mentions, or "pos-mens" of GE products on *TGS*.

While he does this, everyone talks endlessly about how great Snapple is, delivering an *Inception* of product placement. It culminates with Cerie looking straight at the camera with a come-hither look, declaring that she dates guys who drink Snapple. The scene was such a hit that Bowden would go on to be hit on by men using only drinking Snapple as a pickup line. Later in the episode, a guy in a Snapple suit walks out of the elevator, with nothing more said about it.

Andrew Guest: There was a need to do some product integration on the show because we were struggling and trying to earn our worth. Tina and Robert were able to think of a way to do it, and wink at it, in a way that you had the Snapple Man there, and it worked. And it was funnier than *not* doing a commercial, somehow.

It was a technique that started to be increasingly used by shows "on the bubble"—those whose positions were uncertain, in a Schrödinger's cat box with their future life or death unknown. Both NBC's *Community* and *Chuck* benefited from a partnership with Subway sandwiches.

Robert Carlock (writer/co-showrunner): Most of the product mentions on the show—ninety-nine percent of them—are just us going after a joke that's funnier with the specificity. I always enjoy a company that likes a joke. Because on more than one occasion, we would have people who were really excited about doing product placement, and then bail once they saw what we'd written—our gentle meta-comedy.

While Jack is hard at work memorizing his lines, Tracy is busy not bothering to learn his. The show may not always portray Tracy as the smartest, but it makes clear that he's not as dumb as others judge him to be at times, either. When Tracy doesn't bother learning his lines, Liz and Jenna jump to the conclusion that it's actually because he can't read. Liz is hesitant to assume this about Tracy, but has to admit it might just be true. Tracy ends up using this to his advantage to get more time off work, claiming he needs time to learn to read.

Of course, the real Tracy Morgan was reluctant to learn his lines in advance, too.

Tracy Morgan: Ain't it crazy that I never read the script—[producer Jerry Kupfer] just gives me my sides? Everybody says I don't do it—I do my takes in three or four takes, man.

Don Scardino: Tracy is a child. He's a playful, grown-up child. And the more you play with him, the funnier he is, and the more he likes it. He doesn't have a process other than not to learn his lines—that's his process. He'll respond to things like "Do it like Barry White."

Ultimately, it turns out that of course Tracy Jordan knows how to read—Liz catches him reading a newspaper. It ends up as a subversion of a Black stereotype—while also coming dangerously close to another one with the depiction of Tracy as lazy. Tracy cops to his real reason for going along with Liz and Jenna's racist assumption, with the show ultimately calling out that the belief is related to Liz's own white guilt.

Alan Sepinwall: Race has been kind of an Achilles' heel for Fey and Carlock, with both this show and *Unbreakable Kimmy Schmidt*. Sometimes they do really, really smart stuff with it, like [this episode]. Other times, the minority characters on her shows veer really, really close to caricature, and it's more through the strength of the performers than the writing that allows it to rise above that.

While Tracy Morgan at times wanted to distance the real him from the fictional him, there were definitely points where they matched up.

Tracy Morgan: During this time, I was going through some hard times with my DUIs and stuff, so I just didn't want art to start imitating life, and life imitating art. Because this guy Tracy Jordan seems always to be getting in trouble, and at the same time Tracy Morgan was getting in trouble. But I guess it gets bumpy for everybody sometimes, and nobody's immune. I got through it.

This episode includes the seeds of what would become the Pranksmen, a group with Toofer and Frank at its core. The show had so much amazing talent that it often had trouble finding storylines for everyone, so there were some surprising pairings—like these two writers working together to pull pranks. In this episode, they use their scheming to make Jenna think she might lose her job.

And while Jenna and Tracy started out at odds earlier on, their rivalry quickly fizzles. There are even moments in these early episodes where it feels like they might go for Jenna and Tracy as a couple, but that never fully materializes. Instead of enemies, they more often become teammates in absurdity, their individual crazy multiplying that of the other. It lets them each get to even more ludicrous places.

The show starts to capitalize more on Jane Krakowski's Broadway background. While we see Jenna singing from the beginning, it becomes clear with the new casting that she's more of a multi-threat performer than necessarily being known for her skills as a comedienne. She delivers the club-thumper "Muffin Top" in "Jack-Tor," challenging everyone to resist being sexually attracted to . . . the fat spilling over her waistband.

> **Scott Adsit:** At first, she was a little intimidated by all of these comedy people. She'd done comedy all of her life, but these were high-density comedy people whose whole lives were centered around comedy. And she was afraid she wouldn't fit in. But she proved herself wrong immediately.

The lyrics for Jenna's hit were written by Dave Finkel and Daisy Gardner—and Donald Glover.

> **Daisy Gardner:** I love that Donald is responsible for both "Muffin Top" and "This Is America."

The show was drawing more viewers in its new time slot, with the sixth season of medical comedy *Scrubs* as its lead-in. The two programs ended up being a more natural pairing, each offering its own farcical take on the workplace comedy. "Jack-Tor" pulled in 5.2 million viewers, and the next episode would draw 6 million. But the cast and crew still didn't know their fate—whether the show would get picked up for a full season with an order of an additional nine episodes. *Studio 60* had gotten its back-nine order in early November.

> **John Riggi:** It was getting close to Christmas, and we still hadn't heard about our pickup. I said, "Somebody go out and get us some Christmas cookies and some champagne or something, because this might be it." We just didn't know. And I think we went on our Christmas break hiatus not knowing if we were gonna get the back nine.

> **Nate Corddry:** On the set, people would start whispering on Tuesday mornings, "Did you see the ratings?" The first big move is a pickup of the back nine. We were waiting a little bit longer than everyone expected. I was like "Oh jeez." Then we get a full season, but it was sort of tentative.

30 Rock was filming one of their more absurd episodes at the time, "Black Tie" with guest star Paul Reubens (aka Pee-wee Herman). As Fey noted in her book *Bossypants*, they weren't trying to be a cult hit—they wanted to be *Home Improvement*. They kept trying to adjust the show to make it that, but it never quite worked.

Tina Fey: By ["Black Tie"] *30 Rock* had really found its voice, and it was the voice of a crazy person. The episode ended up being called "Black Tie," but while we were shooting it, we referred to it as "Goodbye, America."

Episode 6, "Jack Meets Dennis," delves into Liz's first big love interest: Dennis Duffy (Dean Winters), the douche-bro loser whose big claim to fame is being the Beeper King of New York. He likes to claim that beepers are going to come back, because technology is cyclical. (It isn't.)

Adam Bernstein: I knew Dean Winters from *Oz*—Dean played the head of the Irish mob. What was amazing was, on that show, he's just playing a badass criminal. Then he came in for *30 Rock*, and of course they're bringing in all these funny guys—comedians, people that had done a lot of comedy. Dean came in, and he just fucking blew everyone else out of the water. He was *so* funny. He played it so straight, and he knew exactly where all the funny was.

He starts as her ex, and Liz is quickly pulled back into his web, taking him back when he's the only one who remembers her birthday. In his own strange way, he cares. But he's really, really bad at it.

Dennis plays an inverse of Liz. He owns the confidence she hasn't fully embraced, with none of the brains. Their whole relationship is Dennis negging Liz—his loving nickname for her is "Dummy," despite Liz being a successful woman who works as the head writer of a TV show making her living with her quick wit. It's the dynamic Liz fights all around her, continually unappreciated and unable to really triumph. When she tries to dress up and show a different side of herself, her good friend Pete tells her that she looks like a fancy prostitute.

Being able to see how wrong Dennis is for her is one of the earliest signs we get that Jack might be a legitimately great mentor, not just an opposing force for Liz. But Liz rejects Jack's efforts to guide her. Liz does end up fighting back against the powerful pull of an ex, kicking Dennis out just two episodes after he moves in.

Tina Fey is widely acknowledged to be a beautiful actress, but the show's characters take shots at Liz's looks at every turn. It makes you root for her that much more. She may have significant career success, but she's still struggling with self-esteem problems like so many of us. Jack might compliment her eyes, but enthusiastically describe them as being like "black shark's eyes." When she puts on a dress, Frank's response is to say, "I just threw up in my mouth" (a phrase that hadn't yet been driven into the ground). Jack scolds her, "Don't be cute, Lemon—you're too old for that."

And in an eerie moment, the show manages to predict a real-world event. After a bad rehearsal, Pete hopes that breaking news overtakes them, and asks how Gerald

Ford's health is. Former President Ford would die less than a month after the episode aired. *cue Twilight Zone music*

Following better numbers on a new night, *30 Rock* received a reprieve after the sixth episode aired. NBC announced it was picking up the back nine episodes of the season in early December, bringing it to a full twenty-one episodes.

Adam Bernstein: There was a lot of celebration when it got its back-nine pickup—it wasn't the shoo-in for anything. A lot of it had to do with Alec Baldwin committing to the back nine.

Kevin Ladson: Tina Fey's father came on to the set and made the announcement.

Don Scardino: Suddenly you realize, oh, they're picking up the back nine. With *30 Rock*, it came late. And now you're scrambling.

Andrew Guest: We wouldn't have survived if it had been a few years earlier and we were competing with *Friends* to stay on the air. We weren't that show. And even more so, when I got to *Community*, it was a time when Kevin Reilly was gone from NBC, and we were allowed to do creatively crazy shit.

Daisy Gardner: Network television was fracturing, and there hasn't been the one big show that grabs everybody. We were lucky, because even though it was "a niche show," it found its audience, and its audience knew what it was and loved it.

Another episode that's often credited as where *30 Rock* showed what it could be was **episode 7, "Tracy Does Conan."** The show puts more hard left-turns in Tracy's dialogue in this episode as it pushes to ever-more-preposterous heights.

Tina Fey: We needed to jump the shark immediately. We became basically a SeaWorld show about how many sharks one could jump.

Andrew Guest: Tracy was one of the easiest and most fun [characters to write for], because you could do anything. For me, there was a moment in Season 1 that crystallized what the show was. I ended up meeting with [Dave] Finkel and [Brett] Baer when they were running *New Girl*, and I went in for a writers' meeting. I was like "I remember when we figured out what the show was." And they were like "Ah, episode 5, 'Jack-Tor,'" when we had the scene between Tracy and between Jack and Liz." I was like "*No*. I actually thought it was 'Tracy Does Conan.'"

That moment early on where the tone really started to gel: Jack was preparing a speech about GE head Jack Welch, which he asks Lemon to help him punch up. One of his own pitches was that Welch has such great management skills, Welch's grape juice was named after him, because of the way he squeezes the juice out of his workers' "mind grapes."

Andrew Guest: He's trying to write, and he's terrible at writing jokes. Then we got to [the next] scene where Tracy is sitting with the writers, trying to come up with material for going on *Conan*. Somebody pitched, "Hmm . . . what's on my mind grapes?" And it doesn't make any sense! It defies any kind of logic, and it never gets explained—this was a stupid phrase that Jack had come up with in [the previous] scene. The fact that we knew that an audience would enjoy that connection, and that more importantly, Robert and Tina wanted to follow the joke as opposed to maintaining the reality . . . The jokes were more important than anything else on that show. A joke trumped everything. It trumped character, it trumped the story. But to me, when the show, in that first season, was willing to bend reality for a joke, I was like "Now this show can go fucking anywhere if the joke leads them there."

Alan Sepinwall: I was expecting a slightly more tethered-to-reality workplace comedy and was not prepared for just how ridiculous the show wanted to be and became.

Chris George: We would always do a combination production meeting and readthrough. It would be Tina, Robert, [the director], and all the department heads. Sometimes we wouldn't even have seen the script before we would go through it. I remember laughing uncontrollably alone in a room of forty other people, and Adam Bernstein pausing and saying, in his very high school teacher way, "Mr. George, is there something you'd like to share with the rest of us?" I just held up the script and said, "This shit's hilarious." Then everybody laughed.

While the show would eventually turn its focus to Don Geiss as the faux GE exec they'd build plotlines about, the early episodes featured more of Jack Welch. Welch was also an influence on the Donaghy character himself. Editor Doug Abel had the chance to attend a charity event at Welch's Manhattan home.

Doug Abel: It was just amazing meeting him. It's like "I've met your doppelgänger in comedic form."

Early on in the episode, Jenna gets bumped from promoting *TGS* on *Conan* in favor of Tracy because he's a movie star. Even though the last time he was on the show, he pretended to be a robot and tried to stab Conan. Liz tries to find a way to get Jenna on the show instead of Tracy, asking her if she has a movie that she could promote, which she responds to with the first mention of *The Rural Juror*. Which we see is, for some reason, directed by Casey Affleck in 2006—long before he would become a director in his own right, but likely a commentary on this movie being the bargain basement version of a movie directed by his brother, Ben. No one else has any idea what Jenna's saying so fast with all the R's making for a tongue-twister of a title, but also know better than to ever possibly question anything Jenna says because it would cause some instantaneous *drama*.

Andrew Guest: We were looking up Alec Baldwin's credits in the writers' room. A lot of the writers were so excited about writing for Alec, and we were just pulling his IMDb up, and we saw *The Juror*.

Tina Fey: I said, "You know what two words I cannot pronounce properly?"

Andrew Guest: Somebody had a hard time saying the word "juror," and somebody said "rural juror"—and that was it. Then you have a whole storyline.

Tina Fey: We wanted to hurry up and get it on the air before someone else did. As if someone else would stumble on such a random joke.

The Rural Juror returned a few weeks later in its own self-titled episode. The legacy of this ridiculous movie goes all the way to the series finale, when we finally get what we've all been waiting for: a song from the *Rural Juror* musical. But the movie doesn't score Jenna a spot on Conan's show.

This episode features the introduction of another character who at times makes Tracy look like the sane, reasonable one by comparison: Dr. Leo Spaceman (Chris Parnell).

Daisy Gardner: We were talking about the moment when Tracy freaks out and Liz is asking him who his doctor is. Dave Finkel yelled, "Dr. Spaceman!" Then Matt Hubbard looked up quietly and said, "It's 'Spa-che-man.'"

But Tracy is happy to just pronounce it like "spaceman."

Andrew Guest: [Parnell's] delivery and tone is just unbelievable, and he is somehow crazier than Tracy, but in the most subdued way.

John Riggi: The Spaceman line of reality is always very difficult to figure out, because we would write jokes and then say, is that—? Oh, he can't say *that*. But then Parnell says it, and it seems funny, and we're on board.

Alan Sepinwall: Dr. Spaceman is not someone who could exist on many shows in the history of television, but he fit in perfectly there.

He's like the next level of *The Simpsons*' Dr. Nick Riviera, but instead of being a con man who's bad at his job, he has this blithe, white guy confidence that everything he's doing is completely correct. He'll confidently say, "I've always said humans need more animal blood. It keeps the spine straight." Plus, he's also more than happy to write you a prescription for anything, or just hand you pills—"Some reds? Yellows? Just got some purples in from Peru"—while giving you drugs that probably aren't FDA-approved.

Meanwhile, making this time on Conan's show even worse, Tracy is having some issues with his medication—thanks a lot, Dr. Spaceman—leading to this episode's

Rachel Dratch cameo as the strange "Blue Dude" that Tracy keeps seeing everywhere, pushing him to bug out. As well as bust into a Chewbacca cry of pain, inspired by Morgan being a huge sci-fi fan and doing that Chewbacca noise on set.

Adam Bernstein: That was the best episode I did. I love the moment where Jack McBrayer, he gets sent to Duane Reade to get Tracy's medication, and then he gets to the corner and there's a Duane Reade on every corner.

When Tracy eventually gets on the show, his appearance goes moderately more successfully than the time with the attempted stabbing, as he simply dances . . . and dances . . . and dances for way too long as the band plays him on, refusing to take a seat. But when he finally sits down, he instantly falls asleep, leaving Conan to toss to commercial.

Adam Bernstein: The *SNL* floor was on six, and *Conan* was on eight. We were shooting all of Conan's stuff on his floor, where he did his show. We were moving pretty fast, and I was running down the hallway, and I kind of plowed through Lorne Michaels. That was an "oops" moment.

While Liz had been planning to break up with Dennis, he gets a reprieve at the end of this episode when she gets home and finds that he got her a cheeseburger—one thoughtful gesture after a terrible day. With Dennis back together with Liz at this point in the show, we see more of how *30 Rock* would plant little details and let them grow. We learn that she dated Conan, which seems both a little absurd and also totally on point for being who a high-level comedy writer and TV showrunner would have dated.

We learn a key, character-defining fact about Jack here: that he's the kind of guy who wears a tuxedo after six P.M. Liz had thought that the speech he was giving was tonight, but no, that's not the reason why Jack was wearing a tuxedo. He's still got plenty of time before the speech. But as Jack puts it, "It's after six—what am I, a farmer?"

Alec Baldwin: Jack Donaghy is Lorne, first and foremost. "What am I, a farmer?" That *is* Lorne. I think he said that. Lorne's got a tuxedo in the glove compartment of his car. Lorne is a person who seduces you into thinking that if you take his advice and play your cards right, you're going to end up with his life.

Daisy Gardner: To me, Rob [Carlock] is always—you know where Jack Donaghy shows up wearing a tuxedo? That [joke] is just right from Rob's mouth, and perfectly encapsulates who Rob is.

Pete also gets a look at an alternate life. He jokingly puts on a wig while playing around with Liz backstage, but Jack looks at him and earnestly tells him how much younger it makes him look. Jack eventually insists that Pete wear it, and we get to look at the alternate world where Pete is the suave, debonair guy who he perhaps longed to be deep down. But Liz eventually tears the wig off him and cuts him down to size, because Pete is never, ever, over seven seasons, allowed to truly succeed.

A bonus to watch for in this episode: Aubrey Plaza as an NBC page, as in these pre–*Parks and Recreation* days, she was an actual NBC page—who was given the opportunity to play one on TV. Also, on the way to fulfilling that prophecy about someday ruling us all, Kenneth interviews himself on the Conan set during the end-of-episode tag, followed by Kenneth clogging in what Tracy Morgan told Jack McBrayer was a star-making moment.

While Liz was too tired and thankful to dump Dennis in the previous episode, she finally leaves him behind in **episode 8, "The Break-Up."** Liz tries moving on, looking to find a new guy with Jenna as her wingwoman. But while guys want to buy her drinks, Liz is more interested in an order of mozzarella sticks. Liz starts to consider getting back together with Dennis, especially after he brings her an early Christmas present—but then she spots him on *Dateline* spin-off *To Catch a Predator*. Uh-oh.

In a moment where Toofer got the chance to shine as an individual, he calls out Tracy for cross-dressing on the show, arguing that it's demeaning to Black people. Toofer tells him that the reason Tracy acting foolish bothers him is "there are racist people in this world, and when they see you act like a fool, they assume we're all fools." In *30 Rock*'s world, there's also a whole other level of Black television that white people don't know about. Toofer says they never would have done drag on *Black Frasier*.

Josh ends up finding success with his own female character, frustrating Tracy—who then challenges Toofer's Blackness, using the N word. Toofer tries using the word himself, but his own more uptight delivery leads to even Tracy finding the term offensive. Toofer ultimately ends up conceding that Tracy in drag as *The View* co-host Star Jones is, in fact, pretty funny.

It's more of the pushing the envelope that the show would continue to do throughout its history, as well as one of the rare storylines based on divisions within a minority culture, rather than everything being presented against white culture as the norm. It's also about who gets to claim an authentic Black experience—the question of whether Toofer's experience is any less valid because he came from a different upbringing than Tracy did. The show would keep wrestling with this throughout.

Keith Powell: This industry has not always been kind to smart, young Black men. And there is so much stereotyping, and so much people wanting to put you into a box of their own making, because it feels easier for them, and it's safer for them.

Ira Madison III (critic, TV writer): Toofer was like a college-educated yuppie Black, and Tracy was really just sort of like Tracy Morgan. It felt so much like him, so that character, also being paired with Jenna, it didn't seem like they were making the dumb Black character.

SNL wouldn't get to ending Black cast members cross-dressing until after the end of *30 Rock*, when Kerry Washington appeared on the show and mocked the lack of representation of Black women—shortly after *SNL* star Kenan Thompson said he would no longer cross-dress to play Black women when the show didn't have a Black woman cast member. Morgan had done characters in drag on *SNL*, and would continue doing so here, including an episode later this season paying off with him embodying Oprah.

We continue to get hints here that Jack is dating then–Secretary of State Condoleezza Rice—or, as Jack coyly describes her, a "high-ranking African American member of the Bush administration." She isn't shown (at least during their relationship), but Jack has to deal with jealousy after seeing Vladimir Putin touch her back. Jack runs into Dennis, who encourages Jack to play hard to get. So we get two break-ups in this episode, as Jack ends things with Condi, and the Jack/Dennis dynamic gets flipped with Jack finding wisdom in what this dummy thinks.

Episode 9, "The Baby Show," has the show going head-on at the traditional idea of women wanting to be mothers, and whether having a baby is an essential part of happiness or success. While it would have been easy to focus on Cerie's sexuality, the show chooses to have her be the one in a seemingly happy, stable relationship. She announces that she's engaged to a billionaire shipping heir, with a goal of being a "young, hot mom," which prompts Liz to think about starting a family herself. It's a storyline that would come back off and on, ultimately paying off at the end of the series. The episode let Liz go through her emotions about children—something close to Tina Fey's heart as a new mother at the time—while not having it take over her life, always of lower importance to her than what she really cared about: her show.

At this point in the season, *30 Rock* was already getting nominated for awards— albeit the less prestigious People's Choice Award. Members of the cast and crew flew out to Los Angeles for the show, as they were nominated for favorite new TV comedy. But they lost to *The Class.* "What is *The Class*," you say? Why, it was a short-lived CBS comedy canceled just two months after the awards show. But the *30 Rock* team didn't let it spoil the fun, with Morgan, Bowden, and more cast and crew heading out to party at the Saddle Ranch on the Sunset Strip, including riding the bull.

In **episode 10, "The Rural Juror,"** Jenna's poorly named film finally comes out—a legal drama about a Southern lawyer that goes by the name of Constance Justice, starring Jenna, and based on a novel by John Grisham's lesser-known brother, Kevin. But the *TGS* crew remains unsure exactly what she's saying thanks to the easily mumbled words filled with R's. And Liz discovers upon viewing it that the film is, in fact, terrible. But the writers watch it and fall in love with it, and Liz is forced to concede that she was jealous of Jenna's success.

This was the first episode credited to *30 Rock* writer Matt Hubbard.

Daisy Gardner: Matt Hubbard was the quietest genius. He would just say nothing, say nothing, say nothing—and then say the funniest, most outrageous, genius weird thing you'd ever heard.

The episode was also Beth McCarthy-Miller's first episode directing, a longtime collaborator with Tina as a director on *SNL* who started transitioning into episodic TV.

Beth McCarthy-Miller (director): It was an absolute thrill and an honor for Tina to trust me with her show when it was brand-new. When I went in there, I wanted to make sure that I got great performances from Tina. I just knew with my familiarity with her, she would be comfortable on set.

It takes a few episodes for everyone to figure out who their characters are, and Jane really blossomed in that episode. Everybody got into a groove, and the writers started figuring out the rhythms of all the characters and how they interact with each other.

Tracy showed growth here, too—while he was usually used to parody Black comedians, or his own persona, there's also a streak of George Foreman running through him. That includes here, where he endorses the Tracy Jordan Meat Machine.

As the show continued to build behind the scenes, Grizz and Dot Com started getting bigger features, despite being some of the most inexperienced actors on the show.

Grizz Chapman: It was a situation where you go from sixth grade straight to college. I didn't ask too many questions in the beginning, because I was just paying attention. Then throughout the years, I started asking more and more, because it became [clear] that I was in this. I did a lot [of] questioning of the cameramen, because eventually I wanted to start directing my own stuff.

They were giants with a soft, sensitive side.

Grizz Chapman: That's being true to life. I'm really more mild-mannered. I talk, but I'm on the quiet side—I'm more of an observer. Some of the jokes were like, I spent all the money on WorldCom—those one-liners showed the testament of who I was. I could have minimal lines, but I could have really big funny from those lines.

The episode also shows a soft spot for adult contemporary music, which would continue over the course of the series with a guest spot from Michael Bublé, multiple references to Christopher Cross, and more. Tracy offers Jack a mix tape, asking, "You like Phil Collins?" Jack's response: "I've got two ears and a heart, don't I?"

Episode 11, "The Head and the Hair," features Liz and Jenna competing for the attention of an intelligent coworker they nickname "the Head" and a handsome dude with a great head of hair they call "the Hair."

John Riggi: "The Head and the Hair" was literally based upon these two guys. My mom had a restaurant in Cincinnati, Ohio, where I grew up. And every once in a while we'd run out of milk or something, and there was a little store next door. I'd have to go over to buy something for our restaurant. There were two guys who worked there.

Me and another waitress that worked at my mom's restaurant, we started calling them "the Head" and "the Hair." Because one was really, really handsome—the Hair. And the other one had a giant head—the Head. So you'd tell a story like that [in the room], that would seem like a funny idea, then maybe you'd get a story [for the show] out of it.

Daisy Gardner: It's one of those weird things where you feel like you contribute a lot to a certain episode, then that's not the episode you end up writing. I felt a connection to that one, because I had told a story about getting asked out by the popular guy in high school, and how weird it was. What that feeling is, as kind of a comedy nerd, and the popular guy is paying attention to you.

But this isn't the beginning of a new Liz-mance—she finds a photo of her great-aunt in the Hair's apartment and realizes they're related.

Tracy realizes in this episode that his autobiography is due to the publisher the next day. Tracy, your fellow procrastinating writers feel your pain. Thankfully, he can task the *TGS* writers with ghostwriting it all in one day, until they finish and he remembers that the publisher had rejected him.

Jack and Kenneth switch places for "Bottoms Up" day, another peek at the possibility of Kenneth one day running NBC. This episode also features the first appearance of famed angry tennis star John McEnroe, who would go on to frequently recur on the show.

Episode 12, "Black Tie," is one of the best episodes at cutting off any sexual tension between Jack and Liz at the pass. Jack invites Liz to a fancy dinner hosted by a prince. But when she asks him whether or not it's a date, Jack bursts into laughter, the idea so alien to him and opposite of the kind of women that he dates. They tease it once more near the end as Jack takes Liz home to her apartment, with Liz thinking this might be a moment . . . and then realizing it was just Jack taking off her necklace that he'd loaned her for the occasion.

> **Tina Fey:** Alec had said before, "We should have a pact that none of the characters on the show can sleep with each other" because I do think then if it's characters who are in that core family, you get stuck in this Sam and Diane [from *Cheers*] thing playing out.

> **Alec Baldwin:** Once they cross that line, all the tension goes out of those relationships.

> **Don Scardino:** In the first season, it was always like "Oh, is this going to become a romance with the two of them?" They knew that was never going to be the thing, but it was speculated about in the press, and people thought about it. Because we knew that once you did that, ech—that would be over.

When Baldwin first met Fey, he had asked *SNL* talent coordinator Marci Klein if Tina was single—at which time Klein pointed to Tina's husband, Jeff Richmond, off to the side. While Baldwin was initially dismissive of Richmond, wondering what she saw in him, he later developed respect and appreciation for Richmond and his talent.

This episode featured Pee-wee Herman himself, Paul Reubens, as Prince Gerhardt Hapsburg, the eccentric and incredibly inbred prince who is also the last of the Hapsburg royal line. The character was partly inspired by the real-life *Habs*burg royal line, particularly the last monarch of that family, Carlos II—known for his distinctive jaw as a result of royal inbreeding, along with various health issues. Reubens first introduced himself to Tina Fey after seeing *Mean Girls* on an airplane and being blown away.

> **Paul Reubens (Prince Gerhardt Hapsburg):** I got off the plane, I called *SNL* and said, "Tina Fey, please." They put me through to her voicemail. So I left her this long, rambly, profusely complimentary, but one hundred percent heartfelt message, going like "You don't know me, but I just got off a plane—I saw your movie. I felt like I had to tell you how great it was, and congratulations on making a movie and have it come out so great."

He got a call back inviting him to a benefit Tina was doing at a comedy club, where they met in person. Not long after that, he got the call inviting him to be on *30 Rock*.

> **Paul Reubens:** I'm terrible at the auditioning process. If somebody calls me in and thinks I'm right for something, they almost always don't think the same thing when I'm finished. This was an offer—they were like "Do you want to do it? Here's the script." And I was like "Oh my god. Absolutely."

Reubens was familiar with the show early on, thanks to the well-publicized rivalry with *Studio 60*.

Paul Reubens: To see something that was a misfire, and then to see something else that was the absolute opposite—that was totally on the money, but was really the underdog of the two projects—was fascinating in every way to me.

Reubens's prince was one of the most visibly off-putting characters in the entire run of the show, straight out of a David Lynch movie. He has a single ivory hand (actually a ceramic prop), tiny legs on his royal wheelchair, and the waxy complexion of a zombie.

Don Scardino: I think he came up with the ceramic hand. He also came up with "How about I just occasionally *shout* my lines?" All of that creativity—when you have guest stars of the caliber that we were fortunate to get all the time, they come in with great ideas.

Paul Reubens: So many people assume that I had a lot to do with writing that, with the creation of that character, but I literally had nothing to do with it. It was something that was so simpatico to me that my friends have all gone, "Wow, God, you guys, what a great collaboration." And I always go, "It wasn't a collaboration." She wrote that. I don't know if she thought of me when she was writing it, but it certainly seemed like something I would have written. I would take any credit anybody wanted to give me for one iota of that character.

Along with his strangeness, he also seems to be warmhearted, a romantic, and you start to root for him just like you root for all the rest of *30 Rock*'s misfit toys. He falls in love with Jenna, which he expresses by telling her to dance for him. He threw out different styles of dance for her to do, which was all improvised on Reubens's part, as were Krakowski's dances.

The prince's legs were puppeteered on strings by prop master Kevin Ladson, just out of range of the camera. Reubens was delighted when he first saw the rig, thinking it was ingenious.

Paul Reubens: I got into it for the first time and everybody laughed really hard, myself included. They called Tina over and a producer or two, and a writer, and a gang of people came and looked at me in that rig and went, "Oh my god, it's even funnier than what was in my mind."

Kevin Ladson: It was Paul Reubens who first gave me my break on *Pee-wee's Playhouse* in 1986. So in 2006, I heard he was coming to be the prince, and— well, I really started getting nervous. I said, "You know, I haven't seen him in twenty years, and I never got a chance to thank him for helping me get in the business." He came to the show to get fitted for the chair and said, "Do I know you?" I said, "Yeah, you gave me my start, and I just wanted to thank you. Because I'm here now because of you."

It wasn't until I got up on my ten-foot ladder to manipulate the legs in the scene, it hit me—there was a rush—because it was the same thing I was doing on his show, on *Pee-wee's Playhouse*. I come down off the ladder and Don Scardino says, "You OK?" I say, "Give me a second." Because it all came back full circle for me then.

And the big cake—I called up Bruce's Bakery, and I said, "Listen, I need a big cake that looks majestic." We were shooting the day after the Thanksgiving holiday. He said, "I can't do it." I said, "What do you mean you can't do it? I need a big cake for Pee-wee." Couldn't sell it. So I ended up making a fake cake out of Styrofoam, which was the same technique that I used on *Pee-wee's Playhouse*.

Paul Reubens: It always strikes me when people go, "I don't know if you'd remember me," and it's somebody you remember so vividly. But he's in that category. I was like "Are you kidding me? Of course I remember you."

Kevin Ladson: I would sit with Paul Reubens during lunch, and we would talk and reminisce—so that episode meant a lot to me, because it was the first season. I said, "OK, I'm working with a bunch of nice people. I'll stay."

Ladson gave Reubens that ivory hand, which he still has to this day.

Will Forte played the prince's attendant, and his delightful weirdness ended up making him one of the few actors to be cast in two separate roles on the same show. He returned several seasons later as Jenna's boyfriend Paul. Forte and Reubens bonded on set that day, with both being veterans of the Groundlings comedy troupe.

Nathan Lane: I read it, and it was very funny. But I was in the midst of doing this rather challenging play. I couldn't really focus on taking a day or two and doing this thing.

I was also at a point where I was feeling "Oh, I can't do another one of these flamboyantly silly characters. I need to play a human being." So I said no, and then they came back again. I said I'd like to play a character who doesn't die, who might actually come back. I'd love to have a scene with Alec—I love Alec. So, I turned it down.

And then, of course, they all cite this episode as the turning point for the show. They felt like they were on the bubble. They didn't know whether they would come back. But much like the Chinese restaurant episode in *Seinfeld* where everything seemed to come together, this was the episode they thought they had finally found the voice of the show. They loved this character. Paul Reubens wound up doing it. He's brilliant and absolutely hilarious in it, and then I totally regretted not doing it.

Reubens insisted on shooting an alternate ending, with the prince potentially living on—but Fey felt that the prince's death (due to drinking champagne as he experiences a moment of happiness with Jenna, knowing he'll be unable to metabolize the grapes) helped give the episode's storylines higher stakes.

> **Paul Reubens:** It was completely self-serving in every way that I wanted to live, and that I asked them to do it like that, because I did think it would be so much fun to come back to be on another episode. I pitched everything, believe me, to live. Not only in the scene, but I kept saying stuff like "I could come back as the identical twin. I could come back as a cousin. I can come back as somebody, playing a different character but something very similar."

The party also features Jack's ex-wife, Bianca, played by Isabella Rossellini. She's a match for the upscale world that Jack plays in. When she thinks there's even a possibility that Liz may be a rival for Jack's affections, Bianca engages in a knockdown fight with Liz, tearing at her dress and showing that she's still at least a little in love.

> **Tina Fey:** Isabella Rossellini, very much committing to beating the crap out of me. She was a little scary.

The show increasingly incorporated "whip-pans," where the camera turns so fast the scene blurs, to get in and out of quick cutaways—often for flashbacks or fantasy sequences.

> **Teresa Mastropierro:** Instinctively, we allowed those to be a little more absurd because they were quick. If you're going to whip-pan into a ten-second scene, you don't have time for subtlety.

Cameraman Peter Agliata was a master of those whip-pans. Most of the time.

> **Peter Agliata:** Isabella Rossellini's just the most beautiful woman you've ever laid eyes on. A demeanor and poise and intelligence that's really hard to explain. She had that rock-solid certainty, without ego.
>
> She was saying something and I was supposed to whip [the camera] off her. We see what she's referring to in the past, then I'm supposed to whip back. The first time we shot the scene and it came and went, Don [Scardino] came in the room. He's like "You didn't whip." I was like "I didn't?" "No, you didn't whip." I'm like "What is that? Right. Yes, I've got to whip."
>
> We did a second take, I didn't whip. Five lines after she said her cue line to whip, I was like "Wait a minute. That— [*laughs*] I was supposed to whip." That's all I could think about as we were shooting. That happened four times in a row. I'd never missed one. Don's like "What the hell's going on? Do you need us to cue you?" I said, I literally, I just couldn't whip off of Isabella Rossellini, she was mesmerizing.

But neither is the right woman for Jack—while he may think he wants high society, it ends up being a very different kind of woman that makes him happy. And he wouldn't get there until the series finale.

The episode was shot at Brooklyn's Grand Prospect Hall, an elaborate banquet hall. The schedule was tight, with Alec Baldwin's contract making him available only Tuesday through Thursday at the time.

Chris George: It was only maybe a month or two into the actual production of the show. I was still a new, inexperienced location manager. It had to be shot in the window between Thanksgiving and Christmas. I needed not only the right-looking perfect location for that episode, but I needed a window of time where we could basically own the entire place for five days, because we needed at least a day to prep it, three days to shoot it, a day to restore it.

I only had a team of two other people. We were looking and looking. Everybody would say, "I can give you a day, I can give you thirty-six hours, maybe this Tuesday, but you have to leave it and then come back Thursday. We have Christmas parties, we have corporate events." It's the holidays.

I had TV on one night while I was sweating over this, biting my nails and racking my brain. There was a place in Brooklyn. It was an older married couple who owned the place—you could look it up on YouTube. The commercial comes on and it's just these long shots of gold staircases. At the end of the commercial after they're talking about what they can do for your wedding or your bar mitz-vah, it's this couple who own the place on the grand staircase saying, "Grand Prospect Hall, we make your dreams come true."

I left a message that moment. They called me the next morning and said, "Yes, the week you're looking for, we don't have anything scheduled. Come see it." Immediately we jumped in the scout van and went over there. Everybody looked at me as soon as we walked in like "This is perfect." I just collapsed into a chair.

Paul Reubens: That location blew me away. It was phenomenal. I mean, still to this day, I just was like "Well, I could stay here forever, in this location." I literally would have moved a bed in there and lived there for the rest of my life.

Doug Abel: That was a nightmare to shoot. They ended up having to go back and do a lot of pickup shots, because it was logistically really difficult. That one stood out as being really fun to edit because it was grandiose and a bit more epic-feeling.

Reubens still keeps in touch with both cast and crew from his *30 Rock* appearance.

Paul Reubens: I have a very, very large database. I keep track of people. If I put in "30 Rock," fifty-two names come up. The first one, and I guess they're in alphabetical order, is Alec Baldwin.

He was also officially a *30 Rock* fan, watching the series until it went off the air.

This was director Don Scardino's second episode directing the show, on the way to becoming the show's longtime, most prolific director.

Don Scardino: In the first season, I was only slated to do one—that was "Jack-Tor." It went so well that they said, "We have some holes open in the back nine," so we can do one or two more—and I ended up doing two or three more.

Up next: the first-ever *30 Rock* Valentine's Day episode! In **episode 13, "Up All Night,"** you can see that the characters still have a way to grow. While coping with his divorce from Bianca, made official on Valentine's Day (ouch), Jack picks up a prostitute played by Rachel Dratch. It doesn't fit with the kinder, gentler version of Jack that we get in later seasons, though perhaps his emotional turmoil is part of that transition.

Tracy tries to enjoy a night role-playing with his wife, Angie (Sherri Shepherd), but gets interrupted by Jack. This was Shepherd's first appearance on the show, shortly before she was hired as a host on *The View*, but she still made time to come back for a total of eleven episodes over the run of *30 Rock*. She replaced Sharon Wilkins, who played Angie briefly in "Jack the Writer." Shepherd brings a new, brassy energy to the character, grounding Tracy's character and laying the groundwork for Tracy as a secret family man.

Ira Madison III: I can see problematic areas of Toofer or Tracy, but those characters never really offended me. I always felt more offended by the portrayals of Black women on the show—they tended to be very loud, abrasive. Angie is a hilarious character because Sherri Shepherd was able to make her feel really three-dimensional, but it's unfortunate that every Black woman on *30 Rock* defaulted to be a bit like Angie.

Angie's character starts a bit underwritten, but as the show continues to write to Shepherd's strengths, she grows into something better.

The episode ends with the introduction of Liz's first major non-sleazy love interest. She accidentally gets flowers meant for a "Liz *Lemler*," discovering that they're from a cute lawyer who works in the 30 Rock building named Floyd (Jason Sudeikis). Sudeikis was already a breakout star on *Saturday Night Live*, though this was one of his first ventures outside the sketch comedy world. Another Second City alumnus, he'd started with *SNL* as a writer who'd occasionally appear in sketches before moving to the actual cast in 2005.

This episode also includes one of the show's experiments with different pairings early on. A fun one that stuck for a bit was storylines putting Kenneth with Cerie. They each have an optimistic obliviousness to life—Kenneth from a position of country bumpkin, Cerie from the privilege of the rich and beautiful. McBrayer and Bowden remain real-life friends to this day.

It was at this time that NBC announced that *Studio 60*—already set for a midseason hiatus—would be going on hiatus a week early. The announcement came after it delivered its lowest ratings yet, with 6.39 million viewers the episode before the announcement. And it dipped further to 6.1 million for the final show before their hiatus.

In **episode 14, "The C Word,"** writer Lutz calls Liz the C word, which makes her reconsider how she's been as a boss. When someone called her that word in real life, Tina Fey said, she didn't know how to respond.

> **Tina Fey:** That C word thing actually did happen. I was furious, and I had this weird reaction where I kept saying, "You can't say that! My parents love me!"

While promoting her 2015 movie *Sisters*, Tina Fey revealed on *The Howard Stern Show* that *SNL* writer Colin Quinn was the one who called her that word, while she was *SNL*'s head writer. He was also her predecessor as anchor on *SNL*'s *Weekend Update* and left the show the year after she became head writer.

> **Tina Fey:** I was trying to help him with a show he was working on, and I think his anxiety about the writing of the show spilled over.

Fey didn't know why Quinn said it, but she did make up with him at *SNL*'s fortieth anniversary show in 2015. She asked him multiple times to be on *30 Rock*, but he always declined.

Lutz, played by actual *Saturday Night Live* writer John Lutz, joins Tracy as one of *30 Rock*'s few characters who use part of their real names in the show.

> **John Lutz (J.D. Lutz):** In the pilot, [Tina] said hey, do you want to be an extra in the writers' room? And that might become a character. I was like, of *course* I want to do that.

Little did Lutz know that his character would become one who everyone, largely inexplicably, hates. It could originate with his brief appearance here, insulting Liz, but the moment isn't referenced again. It's likely the meanest thing he does over the course of the entire show, but his character karmically suffers for it throughout the run of the series.

> **Aaron Sorkin (*Studio 60* creator):** There's a writers' Darwinism that takes place. If you give somebody a line early on—and I'm not talking about making a

meal out of it, if it just clicks somehow—then you want to give them two lines, and suddenly a character starts to happen. And over time, they're fully part of your show, the way Lutz [was].

The episode also includes Jack trying to use Tracy at a celebrity golf tournament to bond with GE CEO Don Geiss (Rip Torn), but Tracy realizes he's being brought along to be the funny Black guy. He starts using the opportunity to speak truth to power, calling out Geiss for not hiring enough Black people and ruining Jack's efforts to schmooze. Jack fires back by telling Tracy that it's this kind of thing that ruined his movie career in the first place. It's an uncomfortable power dynamic, with the lesson seeming to be that the Black man needs to play along to succeed. Tracy makes up for embarrassing Jack by giving an emotional speech to Geiss about his daughter's battle with diabetes—he has no daughter, but it works, and gets Jack and Tracy an invite to Martha's Vineyard.

Kenneth continues his brief run as a romantic, this time with fellow page Grace Park (Charlyne Yi). They kiss, but Kenneth's duties as a page must always come first, pulling him back and leading to him forgetting all about her.

Episode 15, "Hard Ball," lets you see Jack at his corporate mostness, bringing the full weight of his power down on Josh while negotiating a new contract. Liz wants to see Josh crushed after discovering that he's been negotiating with another show, despite the opportunities Liz has given him. Jack uses it as he continues to try bringing Liz under his wing, telling her that he wants to teach her something. He adds a *Dangerous Minds* reference, offering, "I would like to be Michelle Pfeiffer to your angry Black kid who learns that poetry is just another way to rap."

Your author has never been good at negotiating. Jack Donaghy makes me want to be a better negotiator. He does the thing that people who love negotiating have told me that I should do: treat it like a game. It will help you get that raise, it will help you get a better price on that used car, and it will help you become a corporate titan.

He has several great negotiations over the course of the show, but this one really pops. Since Liz doesn't quite get how the whole manager/employee thing works yet, she sees Josh as a friend—and spills the beans about why the show sees him as valuable and doesn't want to let him go.

Jack uses a multi-pronged strategy to make the negotiation a game:

1. He creates a whole separate office "negotiation set." He pulls out his office's negotiation decorations like the rest of us pull out Christmas lights. It includes comically low chairs to make his opponents have to look up at Jack's dominance, and chairs so high that Liz's feet can't even touch the ground on the other side.

Lonny Ross: I walked onto the Jack Donaghy office set for the first negotiation scene in "Hard Ball" and saw they switched out the chairs. So Tina's and Alec's chairs were up really high, and my and David Alan Basche's (Josh's agent) were really low. When David and I sat in them for the first time in rehearsal and practically sunk to the floor, it got solid laughs from the crew, and it was like "That works."

2. He plays mind games. Jack starts a negotiation from a place of one dollar, and goes lower from there. Josh tries talking his agent into taking that deal. For Jack, the whole negotiation is mental chess. He wants to take out your queen—saving the company money is just gravy.

3. He treats his opponent ultimately with respect. Josh had another deal on the table from *The Daily Show*, but Jack's already used his corporate power (in *30 Rock*'s world, conferred on him by NBC's parent company GE's parent company, the Sheinhardt Wig Company) to get that offer revoked. Jack bullies Josh into re-signing to the same terms as his previous contract, and Liz loses her mind over Jack not humiliating Josh even more. She calls for him to "do more stuff," then forces Josh to do the Worm. Even Jack is taken aback by these tactics—Liz doesn't get it. As fun as it is to watch your opponents humiliated via full-body ground dance à la The Worm, Jack always cares about the bigger game of negotiation.

Lonny Ross: It was incredibly fun being from New York, filming in New York, and getting recognized once the show started airing. Early on, when I wasn't really prepared for it, I was in the New York Public Library looking for a book, and a woman approached me and in hushed tones leaned in and said, "Do the worm."

But you can get a little presumptuous about getting recognized after it happens a few times. I remember in the Village, I could tell someone was approaching me, and I was like "Here we go, another satisfied customer . . ." And it was a person asking if I had change for the bus.

Tracy invites Kenneth to join his entourage and their regular activities, such as playing *Halo* and harmonizing.

Grizz Chapman: Me, Tracy, and Dot Com sitting there singing—on set, Tracy would just break out in song, out of nowhere.

But Kenneth blows up their spot, revealing what yes-men both Grizz and Dot Com are. Tracy declares that he loves the cornbread he's eating so much, he wants to "take it behind the middle school and get it pregnant." He later says that he loves the video game *Halo* so much that he wants to take *it* behind the middle school and get it pregnant. As Grizz and Dot Com laugh, Kenneth calls out that it's the same joke he said earlier. To which Tracy responds that he keeps his material fresh—so fresh that he wants to take it behind the middle school and get it pregnant.

Tracy fires Grizz and Dot Com after Kenneth makes him realize they've been letting him win at everything, but Dot Com and Grizz ultimately save Tracy from a mob in the end, the protesters incensed by repeated offensive comments from Jenna. These included Jenna screwing up in a televised interview and asking, if the president is so serious about the war on terror, why doesn't he hunt down and capture "Barack Obama" before he strikes again? She then adds that she plans to vote for Osama in 2008.

> **Jane Krakowski:** [Jenna's] and Tracy's characters are so self-absorbed and unaware of the world around them that it gives them so much freedom to be wrong. In a sense, I think we all forgive her for these absolutely ridiculous things she says. She is quite racist. She doesn't understand what is happening in the world. She thinks things that are bad are good. She hears compliments when they are insults. It gives you so much freedom to get to play the most wrong side of the choice.

Jenna consistently makes horrifically offensive choices, out of a combination of cluelessness and privilege. It's not that she has strong political opinions most of the time, it's that she can't be bothered to actually care about politics. Of course, as *TGS* tries to present her as the all-American girl to make up for her comments, someone probably should have noticed in advance that the fiery pinwheels behind her on stage look like swastikas when they're not spinning.

Grizz, Dot Com, and Tracy have their *Bodyguard* moment together as they carry Tracy away from the crowd and reunite as the OG entourage. Lorne Michaels described it on the DVD commentary as "oddly moving." Which is often how this show gets to you—being moving when you don't expect it, making you feel something at a surprising moment with heart amid the silliness.

In **episode 16, "The Source Awards,"** Liz goes on a date with Tracy's business manager, Steven Black (Wayne Brady), before finding out that he's kind of terrible. But as Black implies that she's uninterested in him because of his race, she keeps dating him thanks to her white guilt.

Jack gets rapper Ridikolous (LL Cool J) to endorse his terrible-tasting Donaghy Estates wine, with the wine becoming a sponsor of the Source Awards. Jack tries to get Tracy to host the show, making up with Ridikolous after Tracy previously wouldn't let the rapper into one of his parties, but Tracy's afraid he might get shot.

> **Daisy Gardner:** LL Cool J was there, Ghostface Killah was there, and Jack McBrayer in the middle of it just started improvising. We got it the way it was

on the page, but then there was just a version where he runs up to LL Cool J and goes, "Got your nose!" and steals his nose. And LL Cool J turns to his entourage and is like "Go get my nose back."

But Liz ends up being the one who shoots someone, taking Tracy's gun . . . and accidentally shooting her date in the butt. He thinks it's because he was grabbing something from her purse, nailing down in his mind that she's a racist.

As episode director Don Scardino pointed out, the show was often targeting the white response to Black culture.

Don Scardino: The last thing Tina is, is racist. The very, very last thing. And she wrote to that—I mean, we satirized the hip-hop culture, but we also satirized the white liberal culture as it relates to hip-hop culture, and every culture for that matter. It takes liberals to task as much as it takes anybody else to task.

The show was willing to take risks. Though a writers' room with a lack of diversity, featuring mostly white writers, would sometimes lead to the show stepping into blind spots that could have been avoided while keeping all of the comedy.

Emily VanDerWerff (critic): If you want to do ensemble comedy and have an ensemble that reflects the world as we live in it, you are inevitably going to have diversity that is not reflected behind the scenes. This is not a way to say Tina Fey and Robert Carlock are let off the hook. They should have done more to have a diverse writers' room, but especially when your cast starts to get as large as the *30 Rock* cast, with as many recurring characters and regulars who were in one or two scenes per episode.

You have a writers' room that stays pretty fixed at probably twelve-ish people. A lot of those people are going to carry over from season to season. The problem is a lot of those people who carry over are going to be white. The structural problems within the industry that make that happen need to be solved, and *30 Rock* is not absolved of contributing to those.

You get to a point where you're like "Oh, all of these people have a history with the show, and we know they're good writers and we don't have to train them. We're just going to keep hiring them." That's how Hollywood continues to be so white and straight and cis and male, despite groundbreakers like Tina Fey who are, at least, not male. White and straight and cis, but . . .

Daisy Gardner: [2020] was a watershed year for everyone, where it was all of a sudden, there's no more excuses. Either you have a diverse room or you don't. But I think [*30 Rock*] was a product of its time. It was weird [at the time] to have even two women writers in a comedy room. Usually the proportion was like ten guys, one or two women. So, having three women on staff in Season 1 of *30 Rock* was an improvement. And writers who are people of color have faced even more barriers. There was always one or two diverse writers, which was the case of every show I have worked on. The year I was there, it was Donald Glover, which is hilarious to think of. There's this star. I mean, he's a legend. He's a genius, and he can just do anything.

One of the writers said, "Do you know how many Black writers I've worked with in TV?" The other writer who was standing there with me was like "No, how many Black writers have you worked with in rooms over the years?" And he was like "One, and it's Donald." Which is bananas, when you think of all the talent that's just out there.

Andrew Guest: Our first week of pre-production, Donald Glover got hired. He came in and sat there, and it might have been the very first day—but he had to leave a little early to go to his other job. Which was being an RA at his dorm at NYU. He was still an RA when he got *30 Rock*.

Daisy Gardner: Now that Twitter exists, you see comedians, and you see comic voices, and you read people you wouldn't have found otherwise. There's no excuse to not have a diverse room when you know there are these genius joke writers out there. It's so silly to me that it was like "Well, I guess there's only one writer." And like, yes, it's Lando Calrissian. It's Childish Gambino, it's—one of the most talented people of all time is there.

That's how talented you had to be to break into a writers' room as a Black dude. The most mediocre white guys could get into any room, but to be a Black writer in a white comedy room, you had to be a man who now has Grammys and is a movie star. In Season 1, Donald Glover was the funniest, best dude in the writers' room, but it's crazy that it took a writer of color being a budding genius to make it through the network comedy hiring process.

The guest-star-filled **episode 17, "The Fighting Irish,"** tells us a lot about where Jack comes from. It's a family of Irish stereotypes, con men, and alcoholics constantly ready to start a fight. The guest stars include Jack's brother Eddie (Nathan Lane after passing on the prince in "Black Tie"), sisters Katherine Catherine (Molly Shannon) and Patricia (Siobhan Fallon Hogan), and brother-in-law (Boris McGiver).

Alec Baldwin: Nathan Lane's my brother, Molly Shannon's my sister, Brian Murray was my dad, and Elaine Stritch is my mom. Which pretty much explains why I'm so F'd up—why I'm so desperate.

Nathan Lane: It's always tricky [coming in as a guest star]. You're entering into a machine that's running at full speed, and they all have relationships, so you feel like the outsider.

Eddie shows up, and after a brief physical altercation, tells Jack that their dad's dead. The rest of the family joins to mourn—but eventually Jack's dad Jimmy (Brian Murray) shows up, telling Jack that his brother Eddie died. Jack realizes that he's being conned by both sides, with Eddie asking *TGS*'s staff to make checks out to Chicago All Saints Hospital—and that they should just use the initials. It leads to a full Donaghy family fist fight.

> **Dennie Gordon:** Alec and I had a lot of fun trying to figure out how to do that, and I don't know that he'd ever done a fight this way before. I said, "Please don't hurt him, but just fight with the cameraman." That sequence where he's looking right into the lens wrestling, they hadn't done that before on the show. That's a classic example of being able to do something fresh and fun, and bringing something to the party [as an episodic director]. Comedy is harder—it's like a sweater, you unravel it at your peril.

> **Nathan Lane:** The funniest thing to me is when they get into the big fight, and they all have fist names—*names* for their *fists*. Sandra Day O'Connor and Bono—very funny.

Jack puts up his dukes, introducing them as St. Patrick and St. Michael. His father responds with some older Irish references, fists named Tip O'Neill and Bobby Sands. Eddie finally adds his, Bono and Sandra Day O'Connor, which Jack declares to be the stupidest fist names he's ever heard.

The episode includes Jack again pushing Liz to make cutbacks. She has to cut 10 percent of her staff. Liz lets her feelings for Floyd get in the way, firing his girl-friend Liz Lemler from the accounting department—and then she just starts firing anyone who questions her decisions, the power of clearing the way to Floyd's heart going to her head. Jack ultimately hires everyone back, noting that the network needs accountants since their goal is to make money and, presumably, be able to count it. But he also subtly helps Liz by transferring Liz Lemler to a new job at GE HQ in Connecticut.

> **Dennie Gordon:** If you've got Jason and Tina, just get out of their way. There's not much you have to do, but isn't it nice in comedy to let things just breathe a little bit?

Tracy spends the episode trying to find the right religion. It lets the show dig in deeper on its characters, explaining the type of church each of them would belong to: Liz declaring that she pretty much just does whatever Oprah tells her to do, Jenna explaining that Kabbalah "mixes the fun part of Judaism with magic," and Jack's family with their Irish Catholicism.

In the real world at the time, Alec Baldwin had made headlines for all the wrong reasons—a profanity-laden voicemail berating his then-eleven-year-old daughter Ireland, with TMZ releasing the message.

> **Dennie Gordon:** When I was doing the show, it was the height of the scandal around Alec and the phone call he had made to his daughter. Press was trying to get in on the set, trying to get to people. It was a rather unfortunate, tense time, because who knew the truth of what had occurred—but this recording was out there. It was really hurtful to Alec and really hurtful to the family. It was taking up a lot of his attention—it was definitely in the air on the episode.

Baldwin said that he'd made a mistake and that it was a dark moment, later telling *Playboy* that he'd considered suicide over the voicemail. While *30 Rock* often incorporated stars' real-life issues in some way into the show, the writers declined to do so here. Fey told the press that she thought he would have a sense of humor about it, but that making fun of it on *SNL* seemed like a more natural outlet than finding an allegory in the world of *30 Rock*. Baldwin would go on *The View* shortly after the controversy and say that he was planning to quit the show—but NBC ended up denying the request, holding him to his contract.

Episode 18, "Fireworks," was another expanded-length episode, coming just after an episode of *The Office*—the next several episodes would air at nine rather than nine thirty, flipping spots with *Scrubs* as *30 Rock* became the show with the momentum. *30 Rock* was also officially renewed for its second season just before this episode.

We meet Devon Banks (Will Arnett), perhaps Jack's greatest antagonist over the course of the show. He matched Jack's intensity, with Arnett using his GMC truck-commercial voice to have regular deep-voice-offs with Baldwin. While Jack was the embodiment of old-school East Coast, Banks was from Los Angeles.

> **Beth McCarthy-Miller:** Oh my god, he's so funny as that character, and Tina had that genius line: "Why don't you do it [lowers voice] talking like *this* guy?"

> **Lonny Ross:** I remember when Will Arnett came in for Devon Banks, and watching him *destroy* at the table read.

Baldwin's own quiet talking throughout the series was a pain for the sound and editing departments.

> **Doug Abel:** From a post-production point of view, he's an actor who whispers. The sound guys were good at just creeping in on him when they needed to, then you have to always boost it in post. He whispers his way through takes, then will get really big all of a sudden and blow your ears off.

Banks's Achilles' heel was having a lustful crush on Kenneth. Arnett and McBrayer knew each other from the improv comedy world, as he'd done improv with Arnett's then-wife Amy Poehler. They'd also worked together on *Arrested Development* (McBrayer played a waiter), and that intimacy seems to have come in handy here. The two get very close to one another, with Arnett in a robe that leaves little to the imagination. As Banks notes, he hemmed it himself.

When asked if the storyline bothered him at the time, Jack McBrayer told *Time Out*, "When you're in the hands of someone like Tina Fey, I don't care if they make me eat crap from a homeless man's butt. I'm like, I'll do it. Put it on paper and I'll do it, Tina Fey."

Liz worries when she discovers that Floyd's the kind of guy who she sees going to church on a Tuesday—but upon following him, discovers that he's in Alcoholics Anonymous. She uses the opportunity to steal his secrets, and they start dating. It's a habit that reflects a little of the real Tina Fey.

> **Don Scardino:** Tina Fey is someone who, be careful what you say, because she's listening at the keyhole of everything. And frequently what people said or what they did made its way onto the page, so it had the ring of truth.

> **Jon Haller:** That room was like a vacuum for anything strange and weird that was happening in someone's life.

This episode features a perfect example of *30 Rock*'s prescience, always five steps ahead. They make fun of the trend toward quick online content (on your phone, which was wild at the time), with the faux show *Makin' It Happen*. The joke is that the episodes are around two seconds. The trend at the time was toward "mobisodes" for your cell phone, back when cell phone screens were tiny and no one had that much of a data plan. Writers Kay Cannon and Dave Finkel played the stereotypical sitcom couple in this nano-program.

The big fireworks finale, with Jack asserting that TV needs to be bigger and ends up shooting off fireworks in Midtown Manhattan . . . in a stunt that resembles a terrorist attack to those not in the know . . . was based on a real incident at an NBC network anniversary show produced by Lorne Michaels. Which took place less than a year after 9/11 and ended with Tina Fey and Beth McCarthy-Miller telling stars not to panic.

> **Beth McCarthy-Miller:** Tina and I were laughing so hard when we were making that episode, because, when we did that NBC seventy-fifth anniversary, we got special permission to blow off fireworks. And Tina and I kept saying in the meetings, "You sure we want to do this? I don't really know if it's such a great idea."

[And they said,] "No, no, no, we want to do this." And then the day of the show, I'm like "Maybe we should make an announcement to the crowd that we're doing fireworks." [They said,] "No, no, no, it's gonna be fine." I will never forget going down to the party after, because as we were shooting it, it literally looked like the GE building was being attacked by terrorists. And we're like "OK, this is happening."

Daisy Gardner: The whole city freaked out.

Beth McCarthy-Miller: Some people left a little early and went down to the party in Rockefeller Center, out where the skating rink is. I got out of the elevator, Jennifer Aniston was standing there, and she was like "Why didn't you tell us there were going to be fireworks?" I'm like "I'm sorry. They wouldn't let me." She was like "There was smoke billowing in the building. Everyone thought the place was on fire."

Daisy Gardner: It would make us laugh constantly to think about how not a good idea it was, and it was like "OK, then this has to go in the show." So there's a whole episode written with: How do we get that footage in? How do we write to this? And what's the situation where this could possibly be happening? How does Jack Donaghy decide that they need fireworks over Rockefeller Center?

The "Fireworks" episode is the first time I've seen, OK, there's one big set-piece and one big joke, and we have to write a whole story that supports it. Because normally you start from the point of view of "OK, what's the story? Someone's feeling insecure about the bridal shower. And then a joke that could happen here is this." As opposed to "This is the funniest thing. We have to emotionally find a path that gets us there."

After discovering in "Fireworks" that he was related to Thomas Jefferson, **episode 19, "Corporate Crush,"** sees Tracy decide to develop a movie about Jefferson where he plays all the parts. He insists on it being a serious drama and demands Liz give him all the resources of the show "for no more than three weeks" in order to make a fake trailer for the movie, but Liz shoots him down. Tracy declares that Liz is his Alexander Hamilton—leaving Liz with no idea what that meant, as this was many, many years before Lin-Manuel Miranda's *Hamilton*.

Tracy plays his fake trailer for GE head Don Geiss, but Geiss sadly doesn't go for it. The company wants a sequel to his movie about a large dog, *Fat Bitch*. It's a title the show clearly knew was offensive, but seems unlikely to have even been seen as being acceptable as a joke years later.

Tracy's solution to not being given approval for his historic epic: plans to produce *Jefferson* himself. Jordan apparently loved history, as he goes on to work on a Harriet Tubman film in *30 Rock*'s later seasons.

After the fireworks plan goes awry, Jack has his beloved microwave oven division taken away from him. It leads him to a post-Condoleezza rebound: the literally brittle Phoebe (Emily Mortimer). They meet at Christie's auction house, where Jack goes when he's feeling depressed. He asks for Liz's approval of the relationship, then quickly proposes to Phoebe.

> **Emily Mortimer (Phoebe):** It was amazing doing telly. I'd never done a sitcom before and it was so fast. You're given dialogue as you're walking onto the set and it's kind of hairy. There are ten people standing around watching the monitor and if they don't laugh, then instead of having another chance to do it, someone writes another line.

This was still the period when it seemed, at least to audiences, like Jack and Liz might eventually be a thing. And Jack's relationship with Phoebe didn't do much to dispel that notion. She suffered from "avian bone syndrome," meaning that her bones were hollow and Jack couldn't really touch her. The relationship felt inevitably doomed pretty early, as well as a mismatch between Phoebe's quiet, reserved uptightness and Jack's all-out machismo.

In **episode 20, "Cleveland,"** Liz and Floyd visit his hometown of Cleveland, which also turns out to be Floyd's odd dream city. Floyd starts looking to leave New York after losing out on a big promotion to Alan Garkel—a Black man in a wheelchair. The show jokes that there's no way that he as a white man will get chosen over Garkel, with the implication seeming to be that Garkel isn't getting ahead solely on merit but, instead, due to affirmative action. It's another joke that seems like the product of a majority-white writing staff.

The episode was directed by Paul Feig. After an unsuccessful film, he wasn't having much luck as a movie director at the time. But he had developed a prolific career as a TV director, directing episodes of *The Office*, *Freaks and Geeks*, and *Arrested Development* before later going on to direct movies like *Bridesmaids* and *Ghostbusters*.

> **Paul Feig:** When the show was up and running, I got a call asking if I wanted to do an episode. I love working in New York anyway, and I really love Tina. I got sent the pilot and a couple of episodes and thought it was really funny.

Feig was excited about the chance to work with Tina, and he ended up enjoying working with everyone. Well, almost everyone.

> **Paul Feig:** Alec is a little challenging. I loved working with Tracy Morgan. He was a blast, and such an interesting talent. And Jack McBrayer is just such a sweetheart. Alec was slightly less fun, but hugely talented and very, very funny. I had a connection to Alec Baldwin, because I'm good friends with Joe Mantegna,

and Joe's close with Alec. Joe said, "Oh yeah, my friend Alec's on there. Say hi." And it was ironic then that Alec turned out to be the least fun one to work with.

Chris George: There's something about his performances, even though he could be very temperamental at times, a somewhat difficult personality. He's who I still think of as the heart and soul of the show.

Feig credits those difficulties to it being the first season of the show. It's a time where nobody knows if they're on what's going to turn out to be the worst show in the world, a bomb that's absolutely hated, according to Feig.

Alec Baldwin: *30 Rock* was a work in progress in its first season, like many hit shows.

Feig had similar experience on other shows where some actors don't know if the series is going to be any good.

Paul Feig: There tends to be either an impatience with the writing, or a mistrust of the scripts. Or in Alec's case, he was like, I just want to get in and out. So, if you wanted to do something a little more elaborate—or not even elaborate, let's just say you wanted to do more than a few takes. But Alec is so brilliant, that two takes, you get something great. It's just as a director, then you go, "Ooh, try this," because I could maybe even make it ten percent greater, and he's just like "No, we got it."

Actors on the first season of a show are usually up for being more experimental—Feig said that he got that opportunity with Tina, who was still working to discover the show.

Whether you spell it blerg, blurg, blurgh, or blërg, the "Cleveland" episode also features the beginning of that catchphrase. The show drives it home a few times through repetition in the episode, giving birth to a phenomenon that would outlive the series itself for many viewers.

Paul Feig: It was my episode where "blerg" actually started. It was written in the script as "blerg." It was supposed to be like "blech." Then Tina, at the table read, just said it, kind of as a joke. When we got to set, I was like "Tina, you should just say it—say it as 'blerg' because it got a huge laugh. This is funnier than going 'blech!' or whatever." So it just became this thing. When I'd watch the show after that, I'd go, "Oh, I'm glad I at least had a little part in that."

You can substitute any swear word you want for "blerg." It's less specific than "frak," more specific than "smurf."

While Floyd gets excited about settling down in the midwestern city of Cleveland, Liz isn't ready to say goodbye to her dream New York City job for the sake of their relationship, even after a charming visit. The show used New York's Battery Park City to double for Cleveland and give it a midwestern feel.

Jason Sudeikis and Tina Fey sing a jazzy song about the city, composed by show songwriter Jeff Richmond. Feig tried to make Cleveland seem like a magical place, where a police officer asks Liz if she'd like to pet a real horse—she would—and someone actually lets her go first in a hot dog cart line, in comparison to the harsh reality of New York City seen both here and in the pilot.

Paul Feig: With the horse, that was my gag—oh, the horse should wink. I'm normally always trying to ground everything. So, if somebody gives you free rein of this heightened reality—especially her falling in love with Cleveland—it was a chance to go, oh, let's idealize this idea of Cleveland, where even the horse is magical and winks at you, versus [New York].

Daisy Gardner: The important thing about New York is, it is the most exciting city ever that just continually punches you in the face—which is why it's funny and why it's a great setting. I always think of that episode where it's springtime and Liz Lemon's walking down the street and she's like "I love New York in the spring!" and someone literally spits in her mouth. I think that was everybody's experience in New York.

Paul Feig: When we were trying to work out that gag, the prop department came to me with these whole rigs. The guy would have some hose next to his mouth. I just went, "Guys, we don't have to see it." I don't need to see a close-up of the spit going in her mouth. Just the idea of this very neutral shot as we walk down the street, and "Oh my god, that guy spit in my mouth," I think is ten times funnier than seeing the math of it all.

Daisy Gardner: [John Riggi's] catchphrase was "The city got to me." He loved working there so much, and then there were just days where the city would just get him—and get all of us.

Teresa Mastropierro: There are a lot of jokes about New York being so crazy and hard on people. There are always characters who just won't be broken down, whether it's Liz Lemon or Kimmy Schmidt. Setting them in a place that's hard on people helps tell that story.

Feig closed the episode with a re-creation of the famed finale shot from *The Godfather* with the door closing behind Jack, shutting Liz out. Feig had even brought the clip to set on an iPad to make sure he got it just right—if you line them up, it's almost an exact match.

Paul Feig: That was the thing that Alec lost patience with me on, because he was like "We're done." I was like "Well, no, I just need this specialty shot." And I think he interpreted that as me trying to be too fancy.

Feig wasn't the only one who had trouble with Baldwin over the years.

Doug Abel: Obviously, Adam [Bernstein] didn't stay on the show. I think Alec was part of the reason—they did not get along.

According to Abel, one of the rough moments between Baldwin and the director included Bernstein holding up his thumbs to frame a shot. Alec turned to him and said that, if he did that one more time, he was going to assault him. And he didn't say it with a smile on his face.

Doug Abel: Paul Feig is a fantastic director, and Alec was just refusing to do takes. He's a great actor. Mostly, he's mad at himself. Some days he was cranky, but you would see it—he'd be mad at himself for flubbing a line.

Floyd delivers a great embodiment of the idea that no, you can't have it all—career and companionship come to a head. Floyd ends up not being quite as warm and genuine in later seasons, helping to lead viewers away from feeling that these two were always meant to be together. But for the moment, he's nice. He's really nice.

Phoebe notes that she wants to be the Yoko Ono in Jack's life, seeing the way Yoko made John Lennon realize that he was better than the rest of the Beatles as a good thing. There's also a tease that Phoebe may not be the prim and proper Brit that she pretends to be, letting the accent drop in front of Liz for just a moment, though the show doesn't end up giving the moment much of a payoff in the rest of Phoebe's arc. Liz also spots her holding hands with an older man, putting into question her supposedly "hollow bones."

The series' first finale comes with **episode 21, "Hiatus,"** as Liz tries a long-distance relationship with Floyd that ultimately doesn't work out, Jack suffers a heart attack during sex with Phoebe while thinking about the fact that his mom (Elaine Stritch) doesn't like her, and Tracy on the run from the Black Crusaders—an elite group of Black celebrities who control everything.

The idea of the Black Crusaders was set up in the previous episode, inspired by a 2006 conspiracy theory about a group known as the "Dark Crusaders" who supposedly pushed Dave Chappelle to leave his Comedy Central show because they didn't like how it depicted Black people (it turned out to be a fake conspiracy theory, a hoax viral marketing plan for a T-shirt business).

The real and fake groups even share alleged members in common, include Bill Cosby. Before he was sent to prison, he'd made headlines for telling young Black men how to dress and how to behave. So *30 Rock* took that next level here, leading Tracy to get paranoid and flee. We spot Tracy in the background of a shot in Cleveland, but he eventually ends up going rural and staying with a member of Kenneth's family (played by guest star Sean Hayes).

The show landed Broadway legend Elaine Stritch to play Jack's mom, Colleen Donaghy. She's one of the few characters who can be Jack's kryptonite—the core wound he's still struggling with. Stritch brought a boldness, always taking it to Jack and never backing down from a confrontation. We learn early on that Jack stress eats when he thinks about her, particularly confronted with the idea of her possibly visiting. As we discover over the course of the show, she's also pretty racist. Quoting her out of context is difficult, since without Stritch's acting, the lines just sound . . . very, very wrong.

> **Tina Fey:** There are a lot of deeply racist characters on *30 Rock*, but that's only because I think there are a lot of deeply racist characters in the world.

It's always a delicate tightrope, with the show letting these bigoted ideas exist in the show while not endorsing them and pointing out that they come from idiots. The show sometimes feels like it could bring more of a critical lens to how it uses these moments, but the show's own problematic material comes more from a lack of perspective than from ill intent, and the writers were always trying to call out that real-world bigotry. It's the subtle, less obvious prejudice that can sometimes get a pass from the show.

Writer John Riggi was tasked with being the show's link to Stritch, thanks to his enthusiasm for going after her as a guest star and landing her for the role.

> **John Riggi:** We sent her the script, and she sent back this message that said she had a lot of notes. T. Fey looked at me and said, "Riggi, you're going." It was a Saturday. I got in the cab and went up to the Carlyle [Hotel]. She went through the script page-by-page in the tea room and gave me joke pitches, stuff she wanted to say different, all this other stuff. At the end I said, "Elaine, I want you to know, I'm one of the producers, but really Tina is going to be the one that's going to approve all this. I will take all this back. I will give them all your thoughts. But you need to know that there's a process here." And she was like "Uh-huh" and was not hearing it.

> **Jesse Thorn:** By the time Elaine Stritch was on *30 Rock*, she had fifty years of being Elaine Stritch and being perfect at it. So they basically just wrote to Elaine Stritch. They realized they had the perfect astringent old lady, who could make Alec Baldwin seem warm, at least in comparison.

> **Emily Mortimer:** At the last minute, she gave me this joke to say, but I didn't understand it—it was an American New York colloquialism. I didn't know what it was, but I was too scared of her by a million miles to say I don't know what

that joke is. So I couldn't deliver it, and I really failed. She got more and more angry. She turned on me—finally, she was like "Just do it! Can you not hear the rhythm of it?" I was like "No, say it again—how am I meant to say it?" She was like "Just say it as I fuckin' say it!"

Jack's heart attack ends up revealing his true feelings about Phoebe: the fact that she stresses him out more than she makes him feel good. As he lies in the hospital with Phoebe and Colleen at his side, Jack's heart monitor serves as an impromptu lie-detector test, beeping faster as he tries concealing the truth and gets agitated.

So the season ends with neither Liz nor Jack in a good position with their romantic relationships. The only relationship that seems to be getting stronger is their connection with one another, with Liz as Jack's emergency contact—not Phoebe. Dr. Spaceman suspects Jack may have scurvy, as he keeps asking for "Lemon."

Alec Baldwin: This is the foreshadowing of the next couple seasons. A constant string of failed relationships for me, failed marriages, engagements. Lemon, noncommittal boyfriends, putzes. Because we're not together, we're not in love with each other—we're in love with show business. Show business is our mate.

But because this is a sitcom, and characters can't learn *too* much, Jack's near-death realization is that he wishes he would have worked more. And it would take him another six seasons to learn the flaws in that mindset. It's a struggle that Tina seems to have dealt with as well—as a working mother, she would work late into the night while also trying to make her child a priority throughout her time working on the show. This episode also featured the last of Rachel Dratch's regular cameos as assorted weirdos, playing Liz's doctor here.

While it wasn't what the old friends had envisioned, with Dratch no longer a full cast member and the show not always finding a strong role for Adsit, there was still joy in these longtime improv pals getting to be on a TV show together.

Scott Adsit: The first year, when Dratch was there every episode, and Tina and Jack [McBrayer], we were all there as a family that had existed before this new family—it was like a dream. It was just constant elation that this was getting done. I got to move to New York, I got to play with my friends.

When you're at Second City, sometimes when you're not thinking what's going on immediately on stage and then your show, you're thinking about where this might lead you. This is exactly the kind of fantasy you have—that all of my friends who I work with now will be paid a lot of money to do it on a national level, and that's an incredible feeling.

With the season finale, the *30 Rock* staff had made it to the finish line—though with that second-season pickup, they were going to have to do it all over again before long.

The show ended the season with an average of 5.8 million viewers, right behind reality show *The Real Wedding Crashers* on NBC—just a couple years after *Friends* drew 22.8 million viewers on average for its final season, with the finale pulling in 52.5 million viewers. Viewership was down following the show's move to nine P.M., with the finale itself bringing in only 4.7 million viewers.

Meanwhile, *Studio 60* finished with an average of 8.5 million viewers an episode during its season, beating out *30 Rock*. But the added cost of a cast full of established stars, high-paid behind-the-scenes talent, and the higher production costs of an hourlong drama versus a half-hour sitcom—as well as the show's continued downward ratings slide throughout its run thus far—sealed that show's fate.

Nate Corddry: You tend to forget when you're there in the moment, working on a really complicated walk-and-talk, that you are just the moments between Mercedes and Burger King commercials. If they can't get a high enough rate for Carnival Cruise Line, the show's not going to run. It does not matter.

Steven Weber: I suspect that there were a lot of financial issues with the show, even though the actors did it for relatively low sums, for the possibility of working with Aaron Sorkin. Matthew Perry, who was by no means making what he made on *Friends*. For that matter, I wasn't making what I could've made. Everyone took "pay cuts," but they were relative to what anyone would have gotten. Everyone just said, "Fuck it. Let's do this."

NBC announced *Studio 60*'s cancellation during its advertiser presentations on May 11, 2007. The final six episodes of *Studio 60*'s season hadn't even aired yet, with the network dumping them in late May and June to the show's lowest ratings yet, ranging from 3.9 to 4.4 million viewers.

Still, those final episodes let Aaron Sorkin write in classic Aaron Sorkin fashion, telling stories that pulled in the broader issues that he deeply cared about. Those last few episodes focused on a brother of one of the *Studio 60* writers being in Afghanistan, culminating in a final episode, which Whitford directed.

Bradley Whitford: I killed it. But we knew that there was no way in hell they were going to pick us up. People at the readthrough were like "Oh, we're in Afghanistan now?"

I got into trouble, because we were doing prep. Tommy [Schlamme] said, "You haven't watched the show, have you?" I said, "Not since the pilot"—I don't like to watch [myself] in general. But I can tell you, I had watched every *30 Rock*. (*laughs*)

Whitford was glad to see Aaron Sorkin back to writing the way he wanted to write. At the same time, Whitford was drawn to *30 Rock*'s "unmitigated joyous comedy."

Andrew Guest: We all really wished that [*Studio 60*] had had more episodes and more seasons, because every night after it aired, when we came into the room the next day, we would pick apart this mess of a show that was trying to do a storyline about somebody in Iraq or whatever, and you're like "What the fuck is this?" Oh my god, [the sketch] "Science Schmience."

While *30 Rock* would continue to explore whether a woman could have it all, there was one woman on *30 Rock*'s Season 1 staff whose answer was "no." Writer Daisy Gardner was engaged to be married, and her partner had moved out to New York to be with her. But he told her, "You're working twelve to sixteen hours a day. And I haven't seen you, and we have a house in Los Angeles." So she agreed to move back to LA.

Daisy Gardner: I knew what that trade-off was, which is, you would never find another show like that. And for a while, I loved the show so much and I loved those guys so much that I'd turn on Season 2, and I'd be like "Oh, it's such a great episode. I can't watch it." 'Cause I missed it.

I enjoy [the show] and get such a kick out of it now. But at the time, making that choice was really painful and hard. It was the choice of either you have marriage and kids, which I have, or you have the show, and then all of that would have to come later. I don't think that's a decision the guys had to make, but that was a decision I had to make. Because I was a girl.

Figuring out if you can actually have kids is omnipresent, and it's a thing every female comedy writer I know has had to wrestle with. It was a hard choice, and it sucked.

The question of how a woman who doesn't have the same advantages as Liz Lemon can truly have it all never gets addressed in much depth on *30 Rock*, and it's a question that remains for women at many levels of society today.

That aside, *30 Rock* ended the season without much fanfare—but then the Emmy nominations hit.

SEASON 2
(2007–08)
The Strike

The second season started with *30 Rock* fresh off its first Emmy win, taking home Outstanding Comedy Series and taking down its NBC single-camera colleagues at *The Office*. The first season was nominated for a total of ten Emmy Awards—Elaine Stritch also won for her work as Jack's mom, Colleen, in "Hiatus." Tina and Alec were both nominated in the lead acting categories, while Tina and Robert Carlock each received individual writing nominations for "Tracy Does Conan" and "Jack-Tor," respectively.

> **Don Scardino:** The surprise to us was "Whoa, all these Emmy nominations!" It was like "Well, sure, but I mean, there aren't that many comedies, so all right." And then they go to that first-season Emmy Awards and win. I've got two somewhere. Even though we were not a ratings giant, we clearly were doing something right. And we certainly were an industry favorite. That validation was better than any number. We just felt, OK, we're scoring somewhere, and we're scoring with the people who matter.

As NBC executive Jeff Zucker noted during the show's run, if viewers loved *30 Rock* as much as the critics, it would have been that era's *Friends*—though it could have gone the other way, too.

While *30 Rock* wasn't necessarily a breakout hit, with ratings leaving much to be desired, the critical acclaim helped. But the actors would still sometimes get told by fans how much they loved them on *3rd Rock from the Sun*. Those awards helped give the network the confidence to continue investing in *30 Rock*, with the show being profitable enough and having enough potential to keep going. Still, the show would face real-life budget cuts and always had to figure out how to make episodes work within those constraints.

Alec Baldwin was honored with a Golden Globe and a SAG Award for his work on the show thus far. But despite that success, Baldwin still wasn't contractually obligated to stick around for every episode.

Andrew Guest: Ever year, Alec would be like "Welp, this has been really fun, but I can't wait to go do this indie movie I'm going to do while you guys are shooting the back nine." He would dangle it over Tina's and Robert's heads every year, then he would stay and do them.

Whether those desires to be a part-timer were ever genuine or just hardball negotiation, Alec kept doing the second half of the season, building on the dynamic set up in the pilot.

This season would begin and end with big acclaim, with Season 2 itself ending up nominated for seventeen Emmys—more than any comedy series in history at the time.

John Riggi: We would shoot on location and nobody would pay attention to us. Like *nobody*. Then we won the Emmy, and I remember going to shoot at 30 Rock outside on the plaza for the first time, and we had to put up stanchions and get crowd control. Because everybody wanted to see Alec. Everybody wanted to see Tina.

Todd Buonopane (Jeffrey Weinerslav): My theory is, they were making a show that wasn't getting good ratings, but it started winning awards, and NBC couldn't cancel it—and probably didn't even really understand a lot of the jokes. And they couldn't believe they were getting to make this show. They made fun of the network that they were on all the time, and everyone thought it was funny and was proud of it.

Kevin Ladson: Then all the people who didn't want to work with me on the pilot, my phone is ringing off the hook. "Oh yeah. I hear you . . . are you looking for anybody to work on *30 Rock*?"

Adam Bernstein: I got the Emmy because I was one of the producers. But because I'm not a good careerist, I wasn't really that aware that that was going on until I got the package.

Beyond personality conflicts, the show would have to grapple with the real-world turmoil of a strike by the Writers Guild of America (WGA), the union that represents television writers. It led to a shortened season with a long midseason hiatus, with the writers on strike from November 5, 2007, through February 12, 2008. One of the central reasons for the strike was how much writers get paid when their content is shown online, as the WGA had no agreement with producers over the use of online content. It's almost quaint to think about now—streaming wasn't nearly as big a part of the industry at the time. But the writers saw the foreshadowing in the business and knew that it was important to lock in higher payments now, before it was too late. And the producers knew they had to play hardball here, as the future of their profits depended on not giving the writers too much. Another key issue in negotiations: payments from DVD profits, which didn't end up being quite so key in the long run. But the fight over streaming was also because of DVDs, as at the peak of DVD sales, the writers weren't getting big payments. Now, they wanted to keep themselves from being in that position ever again.

Tina Fey came into the season wanting to make changes. She told the *Philadelphia Daily News* that she wanted to live in the world the show had created and explore the characters they have, as well as slowing down the rapid-fire feeling of the comedy. Still, the season ended up with guest appearances by everyone from Jerry Seinfeld and David Schwimmer to Carrie Fisher and Al Gore.

> **Jon Haller:** What Tina and Robert did with that, which I wish more shows would do, is you don't just have this great set of characters—you have this rich world. Every extra, every person you see in that universe has their own specific comedic point of view.
>
> Even the smallest line, it's amazing—in two words, you get this character. And then, once you get a Matt Damon or a Michael Sheen, you'd notice their comic wheelhouse—this is something that they can do, then you write to that. But they don't treat it as guest stars. It's treated as here's another person in this universe—how would we want to attract this person the most? Other comedies, everybody is there to support the main cast, and not necessarily flesh out an entire world.

Even with the constant guests, the storylines *did* still manage to dive deeper into the show's main characters and continue playing out the directions for each of them set up in Season 1. Those guest stars would have their own great moments while also heightening the drama (and comedy) in our weekly friends' lives.

While they had that awards win, there had been some real-life drama between seasons—after the first season wrapped, Tracy Morgan was fitted with an ankle bracelet due to multiple instances of drunk driving. His real-life struggles would continue to provide creative fuel for the show, with the writers able to process real life into comedy.

The writers were working as hard as ever. Fey and Carlock never took a breath, getting everything teed up before the rest of the writers started working.

Jon Haller: Over the hiatus, Tina and Robert would spitball ideas of where they wanted things to go. The writers would meet in June, then we would talk at the beginning of the season—here is the arc we see for Liz, here's the arc we see for Jack. What crazy shit will Tracy get into? What crazy shit will Jenna get into? Then as that goes along, it's just dictated by how much you fall in love with an actress that comes in.

Tami Sagher (writer): We got very little sleep. We would go sometimes until nine in the morning. We would go to Tina's apartment and write from there, because she was burning her candle at every end, as was Robert.

So we would work weekends . . . it was a very intensive show, hour-wise. But it was also super fun. The writers' room, it was all of us laughing really hard, even as we desperately wanted to go home and go to sleep.

It also set a standard of excellence. Tina and Robert—we worked these crazy hours, but nobody worked harder than from the top. It never felt like anybody was picking up the slack for anybody else. And as hard as we worked, every other department worked just as hard or harder, because they had to prepare stuff.

Jon Haller: There were times when something didn't work, then there would be a Saturday, and we would be at somebody's house. I mean, there were long hours. It is what it is. Part of that is that leftover *SNL* culture. The *SNL* writers worked so long, you think, *Oh, we have to be up late. We have to go over these things*. It was a combination of *SNL* culture, plus this desire for perfection.

Tina Fey had also used her break from the show after the first season to shoot the movie *Baby Mama* with her longtime friend and collaborator Amy Poehler. The movie was a moderate success when it came out the following spring, bringing in $64.4 million on a budget of $30 million. But it took Fey away from the writers' room for some time between seasons. Fey was balancing her multi-hyphenate position on *30 Rock* with a burgeoning movie career, along with raising her own young daughter, Alice—just shy of two years old at the time. Still, it let Fey act in something that she hadn't written herself, the first time she'd ever had someone offer to write something for her to star in.

Some of the same crew members that worked on *30 Rock* also worked on *Baby Mama*. Bellamy Forrest, who worked as an assistant director on both projects, found out she was pregnant the day before they started shooting *Baby Mama*.

Bellamy Forrest (assistant director): Tina was very generous, and she gave me a bunch of things that she had been gifted, like a very expensive stroller—I mean, I got so much stuff off of that movie for my baby.

In the ouroboros eating its tail meta/product placement nature of *30 Rock*, an ad for *Baby Mama* also pops up this season on a screen in the "Succession" episode. It was part of the ongoing need for corporate synergy and product placement to make *30 Rock* feel like it was earning its keep for its corporate parents.

Katrina Bowden (Cerie), Keith Powell (Toofer), and Lonny Ross (Josh) were all officially bumped up to starring roles this season, up from recurring characters before. They received juicier storylines, though none of them ever quite broke out enough to get arcs fully constructed around them.

After directing six episodes in the first season, Don Scardino was brought back for Season 2 as a producing director. He helped to both define and continue to build on the visual voice of the show.

> **John Riggi:** What Donnie was able to do was really bring a look. He's a big fan of comedy, so he was able to bring a visual sense that melded with the comedy for us and landed everything, and just made us more consistent.

> **Don Scardino:** After Season 1 ended, I got a call during the hiatus from Jerry Kupfer, one of the producers, saying that Adam Bernstein, the director/producer who had hired me, was moving on to something else. And they couldn't offer me the job yet of producer, but would I kind of unofficially be the producer and help not only direct episodes but also prep the other directors? So I said yes—then midway through that season, they gave me the producer job that Adam had vacated.

Scardino fell in love with the show-within-a-show elements of *30 Rock*.

> **Don Scardino:** If you ever go by *SNL*, like our set—which was modeled after the *SNL* set—the hallways are institutional, and then you go into the world of the show, and it's chaos. There are people pulling along gorillas on wheels, something for a sketch.

> **John Riggi:** Don came in, saw what he needed to do, started doing it, and added a huge positive element to the show. Conversely, if you weren't doing that, you'd find out soon enough that you weren't and you needed to get on track with what we were trying to do.

Scardino used his experience as an actor to provide a different perspective on directing, relating to the actors and knowing where they're coming from. He'd use his experience, both with the show and connecting with actors, to help the other directors that came in, briefing them on what they needed to know before getting to set.

> **Don Scardino:** You don't want someone sitting behind your shoulder going, "Don't you need a shot of this? Don't you know that?" I didn't want to encroach

too much on another director's territory. But what was valuable was knowing how all the actors work, our regular cast—knowing how Alec or Tracy liked to rehearse.

When I got there, I always felt that the show was from Liz's point of view, even if you're in another character's scene. In Liz's world, it's a kind of jangly place. We're frequently handheld, on the shoulder. Then sometimes when we were in either the studio or in Jack Donaghy's office, we'd go on the dolly. There'd be this measured feeling in the halls of Jack Donaghy, upstairs, the vaunted air of the upper reaches of Rockefeller Center.

We had a very aggressive schedule. These shows, sometimes they had seven pieces, fifty scenes—sometimes there'd just be a snippet of Jack or somebody in the past, or in a circus. While they remember, boom, you go to this little thing. Each one of those have to be lit, and shot, and set up. We had to find a way to shoot that would be fast. That handheld style helped us out there.

During his time with the show, Scardino directed thirty-eight episodes of *30 Rock*, more than any other director. He also always wanted to be helping the show's guest directors, serving as quality control with casting, locations, and everything else that goes into directing episodic TV—while also letting them put their own stamp on their episodes.

The rest of the crew also continued to evolve, including a shift in the editing team. Meg Reticker joined the show as an editor in the second season, staying through until the final year of the show. Editor Ken Eluto, who'd been on Season 1 as well, would go on to edit sixty-six episodes of the show—more than anyone else— while Reticker would edit the second most, editing fifty episodes of the show. For several years, they would edit *30 Rock* during the season, then use their hiatus to go edit on HBO's *Bored to Death*. The only other editor who even makes double digits was Doug Abel, who edited a total of twelve, but left after the second episode of Season 2.

The all-around strength of the team, both in front of and behind the camera, gives Season 2 an even greater confidence. The characters show real growth—at least as much as sitcom characters can grow.

Bradley Whitford: I would watch it and you'll see [Tina] find what works. By the second and third year, it's taking off. What I loved about it, it was just constantly sending things up in a way that they fully deserve to be sent up.

This season also began to feature more of Jonathan, with Jack's assistant getting more screen time and developing a *Simpsons* Smithers-esque deep affection for his boss.

30 Rock pays tribute to the history of NBC sitcoms, while also mocking that same history, throughout its run. They continue their run of doing corporate synergy that is simultaneously mocking corporate synergy with a guest appearance by Jerry Seinfeld in the **season premiere, "SeinfeldVision."** The episode has NBC digitally inserting Seinfeld into all of their current shows as part of a shockingly true-to-life "SeinfeldVision" stunt, à la classic network sitcom stunts like having all the shows on one night deal with the same situation across multiple shows—like a storm that affects both *Family Matters* and *Step by Step.*

But in the storyline, NBC didn't get Seinfeld's permission. Oops. So he threatens to sue. Getting Seinfeld to play himself was a big get for the show, even almost a decade after his hit sitcom had finished its run. He volunteered to be on the show, and *30 Rock* jumped at the chance—though he had only one day available to film. He'd made scarce appearances before *30 Rock* since his hit show wrapped up.

> **Tina Fey:** We could not be more excited to have Jerry Seinfeld on the show, because hopefully then regular America might actually find out that we have a show and watch it maybe at least that one time.

> **Andrew Guest:** There was this desperation to get Oprah, or get Seinfeld, because we needed ratings. Every week, everyone was looking at the numbers, expecting us to get canceled, and every week we were trying to have a promotable thing.

The stunt worked—the season premiere pulled in 7.3 million viewers. It wasn't as high as the series premiere, but it was a 2.6-million-viewer jump over the previous season's finale. It also helped set the show on a stronger ratings path, with this season's ratings remaining higher on average than Season 1's.

The show let Seinfeld promote his upcoming feature *Bee Movie* in the episode, showing the animated movie character, including a plug for the opening date, and characters mentioning the film. But according to the network, it wasn't actually a product placement deal—it was the show's writers going for another meta-joke. Seinfeld himself said he didn't ask for the plug.

> **Andrew Guest:** I didn't get to meet a lot of the guest stars, because I was mostly in the writers' room, but I remember it was such a coup. We thought, coming back for Season 2, that we had Seinfeld, which was amazing.
>
> There was such a level of amazing actors and actresses that were attracted to [*30 Rock*] because they watched the show and they loved the show. So you felt like you were part of something unique and cool.

> **Tina Fey:** We made him put on a wig that made it look like his hair from the nineties, this sort of mullet wig, and he was like "This looks weird." We were like "Nope!" His wife was like "No! That's what you looked like."

The season continues to follow Liz trying to get over her relationship with Floyd. She's made the decision to stay in New York rather than leaving for Cleveland, but there's a tinge of regret. And things get worse when Floyd comes back.

Liz goes through the agony of seeing Cerie move toward getting married—she invites Liz to be part of her wedding, with Cerie explaining in oblivious joy that Liz is her "something old." Liz ends up not coping particularly well and, when she goes wedding shopping with Cerie, ends up buying a wedding dress for herself as she continues to play at everything being totally cool.

Liz also realizes that she's doing a terrible job at taking care of herself, with her tooth even falling out as she sits in her office.

As much as *30 Rock* wears its cynicism on its sleeve, Liz ultimately ends up getting some much-needed advice from Seinfeld on getting closure in a relationship following her breakup with Floyd. He delivers a perfectly Seinfeldian line, with the observational comedy approach that he made famous, explaining to Liz that the relationship isn't over until you pick up the phone.

"You say, 'I don't love you anymore,' they say, 'I don't love you anymore either,' you go, 'Great, I'll pick you up in twenty. Let's grab a scone.'" Though Liz doesn't perfectly execute—when she calls Floyd, a woman picks up. Panicking, Liz pretends that she's giving a fake survey.

As Liz explains this to Jerry—while wearing that wedding dress—she discovers that, when she's upset, her voice sounds like a parody of Seinfeld's, culminating in her asking "What is the deal with my life?!" the same way anyone trying to impersonate Seinfeld would do a "What's the deal with" question over the years.

The show went even harder at its NBC overlords in Season 2, mocking the trends in reality television. Jack explains that all the summer replacement shows that he'd put on the air were big hits, including *America's Next Top Pirate, Are You Stronger Than a Dog?*, and the big one that they would continue to develop over the course of the season: *MILF Island*. It was somewhere between *Temptation Island* and *Survivor*, with a little *Are You Smarter Than a 5th Grader?* thrown in for good measure. Jack describes it as "twenty-five super-hot moms, fifty eighth-grade boys, no rules." While Liz points out that one of the women turned out to be a prostitute, Jack defends her, noting that this doesn't mean she's not "a wonderful, caring MILF."

Jenna had her own issues over the *TGS* hiatus. It would've been easy for her to become completely unrelatable given her diva persona, but *30 Rock* continued to show that she had the deep fear and insecurity to balance it out. From "Muffin Top" last season to the aftereffects of the Broadway show she starred in over the break: *Mystic Pizza: The Musical*. Krakowski had hired a private trainer for the first time before Season 2—but after putting in long hours to get into shape, she got a call from Tina Fey explaining they were putting her in a thirty-pound fat suit

It took the suit weeks to be made, and Krakowski had to spend an hour in purple latex for them to create it. Jenna would go on to capitalize on the weight after it makes roller-dancing more difficult—when the new center-of-balance from her added weight leads to her falling, she gives in and delivers the catchphrase that writer Frank had pitched her after seeing her post-hiatus: "Me want food!" NBC would capitalize on this by even selling "Me Want Food" shirts in real life.

Jenna also tries out the "Japanese porn star diet"—only eating paper, but eating as much paper as she wants—as well as using crystal meth for weight loss.

Season 2 included a refreshed version of Jack's office as well. Alec Baldwin felt that his character had changed over the course of the first season and that he belonged in something warmer and more inviting now, insisting on having it redesigned.

Original production designer Keith Raywood had left *30 Rock* after the show's early episodes to go back to *SNL*—according to ongoing production designer Teresa Mastropierro, it was impossible for him to do both shows at the same time. He'd passed the baton to her, and encouraged the show to use the staff they had now for the redesign.

Keith Raywood: [Producer Jerry Kupfer] says, "No no no. Alec said, you're designing the set—it's either you or nobody."

Raywood met with Baldwin at his office in Central Park West, where Baldwin described the gentler environment that he wanted. He wanted it to more closely match Lorne Michaels's offices at the actual 30 Rockefeller Plaza, with English furniture, an antique styling, and more photographs. Raywood made the walls silk, bringing in a marble fireplace, matching leather loveseats, built-in bookshelves, and a wet bar.

Other characters' spaces started to change as well, including Jenna's and Tracy's dressing rooms.

Teresa Mastropierro: As the actors developed who they were, we followed their lead. We did a redesign of [Jenna's] dressing room at one point—she started putting a lot of pictures of herself up. Tracy was in a movie in an earlier episode and he mentions it—we will make a poster of that, and it'll show up in his dressing room and stay there for the rest of the series. As they embodied their characters, it informed me.

Those posters were also a part of the show that helped with filming—the camera crew had holes in the wall behind posters for when they needed to shoot those angles. They included such Tracy Jordan classics as *Who Dat Ninja*, *Black Cop White Cop*, and *Sherlock Homie*.

The season premiere was directed by Scardino. He noted that one of the perks of being producing director is that he got to choose which episodes to do, so he'd always look to where he could have the most fun. That usually included season premieres, season finales, and Christmas episodes.

Don Scardino: We were looking at some episodes recently, and they all still held up. In fact, not only did they hold up, but some of them became even sharper because of the writers and how they satirized the political scene.

That prescience is what keeps *30 Rock* feeling rewatchable today. While it's filled with cultural references, there's enough character-based comedy that the show still plays without knowing exactly what they're referring to all the time. A lot of the references were also on the cutting edge enough—like their mockery of short-form programming, or Jack Donaghy having a photo with then–New York business tycoon/reality TV host Donald Trump—that they're still relevant fifteen years later.

In **episode 2, "Jack Gets in the Game,"** Jack continues fighting to become the chairman of GE, going toe-to-toe with Devon Banks. He tries hiding his heart attack from the end of Season 1; as Jack copes with the new demands on his health, he requests that Liz let him watch her eating a steak in front of him, since he can't. But Kenneth accidentally lets the heart attack news slip to Banks. Banks literally tries to kill Jack, forcing him to play football, eat red meat, and drink red wine as he promises Jack that he's going to make his heart explode. Both Will Arnett and Rip Torn received Emmy nominations for their appearances here.

The episode features the first appearance of Kathy Geiss (Marceline Hugot), GE Chairman Don Geiss's apparently autistic daughter—and Banks's date, despite Banks being gay and the fact that he would much, much rather be kissing Kenneth, as he repeatedly makes clear. But Banks claims to have been turned straight by the Church of Practicology, a fake religion with some deep Scientology vibes. The show cites Marvel Comics legend/human mascot Stan Lee as one of its practitioners.

Marceline Hugot (Kathy Geiss): I had seen the raw, rough first season that had already taken place. I had not become an avid fan right from the beginning, but I saw the rest of them before I auditioned. The actual role was just a one-page, not much of a description.

John Riggi: What we were trying to do was just get a total dichotomy. The idea of it was the total opposite of what her father would be like.

Marceline Hugot: I thought to myself, *I don't know what to make of it, but let's see what I can do to make myself laugh.* It was clear from the dialogue that she was not attractive. I thought, *Well, what can I do that will be funny?* Not just show up with a gap between my teeth, but *actually* something funny.

So I flattened my hair, the way Kathy [has hers]—and that made me laugh. What's interesting as an actor going in is, everybody thinks, *Oh, I'm auditioning for a network TV show*. No matter how the description is, people put makeup on and look nice. Well, I didn't do any of that. Tina thought that was very funny.

When I first came on set, the hair guy said, "Ah, finally an actor who's an actor who doesn't care—they're not asking me to make them look pretty. They want the character to look right." The makeup people, they said, "I don't think she wears any makeup." I said, "Bring it on."

The part starts small, but Hugot's performance caught the attention of the writers and helped inspire them to continue building on the idea of Kathy Geiss.

Marceline Hugot: Let's be honest, it started as the Alec and Will Arnett Show when it came to that storyline. And I was the sight gag of the obvious gay guy who is going after this crazy woman, and that's never going to be real anyway.

Michael Engler was the director of that episode, and after working on that one little scene a bit with Alec, it was his idea that Tina supported: Why don't we not have her speak at all? So they just let me improvise, and an interesting thing started to happen. I was new to television, but Tina—she moved to another room next door and, I suddenly realized, had been just watching me move around and play with the character.

I've always loved broad comedy. If you can pull off a triple take, why not try a quadruple take? I'm one of those rare women that actually likes *The Three Stooges*. As a kid, I wasn't allowed to watch TV, but I was allowed to watch cartoons on Saturday, and there's a part of me that thinks that learning from those great cartoonists was some of the best pratfall comedy training you could ask for.

This episode also sees a potential actual origin for Liz's favorite exclamation: a cutaway to Ikea furniture in boxes labeled "Blërg."

But what most of the audience remembered most distinctly was something entirely different. We're long past the golden age of novelty songs, but in 2007, humanity was gifted with a "Monster Mash" for a new generation.

"Werewolf Bar Mitzvah, spooky, scary." Those immortal words got lodged in the minds of *30 Rock* fans, likely the show's most famous quick cutaway. Tracy's going through some of his stuff when he finds the novelty song he recorded—an obvious get-rich-quick scheme combining Halloween with Jewish coming-of-age parties.

Robert Carlock wrote the episode, while writer Tami Sagher wrote most of the lyrics. The line was in his writer's draft, inspired by a pop hit from the time.

Robert Carlock: This was around the time of the Black Eyed Peas song where they have "mazel tov" in there, "I Gotta Feeling." It felt like they were clearly just trying to get played at bar mitzvahs. I thought Tracy would have his own take, but not really understand the event, and try to double down on the Halloween novelty song—combine the two.

That was the thinking: *What are things that people do to try to make sure those BMI and ASCAP [royalty] checks keep coming?* We always talked about Jenna trying to do a Christmas album just because Christmas albums sell, and she's going to write new Christmas songs. We never quite got there.

But it was also all those terrible novelty Halloween songs that get radio time every Halloween—like "Zombie Jamboree." So part of the fun was can we mash up—almost werewolf-like—these different kinds of music, in an effort to exploit all of them.

Tami Sagher: It was Robert's script, and I think he had "Werewolf Bar Mitzvah, spooky, scary." I pitched "Boys becoming men, men becoming wolves."

Robert Carlock: On some level, it makes sense. If boys become men on this special night, then, perhaps, what's to keep men from becoming wolves? It's such a good joke. And I wish it were mine.

There's also Jeff Richmond's music to begin with, which is pretty earwormy. But also, you get "Oh OK, Tracy was being cynical, and I've seen people do that kind of novelty song thing," and you understand what it is on some level—it can't just be completely random.

My oldest kid had his bar mitzvah season, and said he heard it got played at one of the bar mitzvah or bat mitzvah parties he went to. So I guess the irony is, *I'm* getting the ASCAP checks.

The song played at Sagher's nephew's bar mitzvah, too. The song has even started to become a thing that people revisit and check out at Halloween time. But beyond those two little lines, the show took it to another level.

John Riggi: We wrote that, then somebody was like "We need to do a video." It was always like: How can we now take that joke, which is such a silly joke, and make it even more? How can we personalize it and put it out in the world, and even what's the next step beyond someone just saying it?

Well, the next step is somebody makes a video about it. And the next step is we get to see the video. We just kept layering it. Also, that was because, pick any two words and put them together, and Tracy at some point has probably said that. There's a randomness to the way he thinks. "Werewolf Bar Mitzvah" was a good example of that.

Tina Fey: He talks a lot of good nonsense—it's very helpful to us.

Tracy Morgan: A lot of times, I'll come to the set and just start talking. I start doing bits just to get a rise out of people, and the writers are there, and they hear it. Next thing you know, it's in the [show].

Robert Carlock: We were just learning, "Oh, this is time consuming and expensive to do these little jokes that are just these cutaways!" You walk down there and realize, *Oh, we've built a cemetery set for these eight seconds of time, and we're taking three hours out of our day to get these eight seconds.* But it didn't stop us from continuing to do that forever.

As Tina Fey put it, on *The Simpsons*, they could just draw these moments. Here, not so much.

Tami Sagher: Even though it was just an eight-second, swish, cut-to, it was so perfect—Tracy's werewolf costume, and they managed to do live-action cartoon in the best way.

Sagher credits the art and props departments for making that video really work, with them being fully engaged in the process. Often, she'd go down to the Silvercup Studios stages to see something being shot, and she'd spot a hilarious joke the crew had come up with on their own as part of the scene.

Tami Sagher: Then, that was a big hit, unexpectedly. It was one of those things where, after the episode aired, people really loved it. And NBC did that thing [online] where they showed a thirty-second commercial just to see that eight-second clip.

Born of frustration with that, but also because Halloween was coming up, musical director Jeff Richmond suggested writing a full song.

Tami Sagher: I think I'm the only Jewish person in the writing credits for it. So I wrote the lyrics and sent them to Robert. His note was to have it go off the rails a little bit more, having the Tracy character just lose his way more. I mean, honestly, it was me doing some Wikipediaing.

Donald Glover also worked on the lyrics, though the whole writing team pitched in. They recorded it in Richmond's office. Tracy Morgan himself wasn't around, so Glover stepped in and did a spot-on Tracy impression to help fill in the song, along with some other ad-libbed talking.

Robert Carlock: Donald's all over that track. If only I knew that I would be producing Childish Gambino.

Tami Sagher: Having written those lyrics, it was surprising how easy it was for a bar mitzvah to turn into a werewolf party.

"Werewolf Bar Mitzvah" was just one of numerous stops along Tracy Jordan's career on the show, one of the antics and get-rich-quick schemes he would often participate in. But the song makes its appearance as part of a storyline with some real emotional resonance—Tracy's strained relationship with his wife, Angie (Sherri Shepherd), which continues to be an issue going forward.

Robert Carlock: There were a couple things that we always tried to keep in mind with [Tracy]. One was that he'd been everywhere in his career—from doing stand-up as a way out of a certain kind of life, and doing it in some messed-up places, to being the biggest movie star in the world for a little while, then falling back into TV sketch.

Whether it was a Japanese commercial for some weird soda, or it was "Werewolf Bar Mitzvah," you could place where he was in the wild swings of his career. And I think people get how stars can go through those kinds of vacillations.

The other thing, the thing that I loved about the character, is from day one, we said, "He talks a big game about the stuff he's done, and about women, but he's really a family guy." Everything he does is out of fear and love, for and of his wife. We thought, *OK, you can get pretty desperate, especially if you're trying to hold onto something, if you're trying to hold on to it for these other people.* So it allowed us to go to some weird places.

We didn't want him to be the cartoon stereotype. We wanted him to be someone who knew that what the wider audience wanted from him, to hear from him, was "Oh, I'm wild and crazy!" But the reality was, he's just a guy trying to make his way in the world and do it for his family. So you could see him selling out, *a lot.*

As Tracy grapples with his emotions over Angie, he says that she's in the past, "like Dracula and broadcast television." But Tracy and Angie would ultimately reunite, with Angie playing a much larger role in later seasons.

Halloween was also a time used to bring the cast and crew together on the *30 Rock* staff, with Tina Fey hosting Halloween parties where parents were invited to bring their kids. The crew would be free to leave the set and check out the party, providing a respite from the intense work that went into producing the show.

Episode 3, "The Collection," marked the first of ultimately six appearances by Steve Buscemi on the show as private eye Lenny "Len" Wosniak. Buscemi would eventually go on to direct two episodes of *30 Rock*, as well as an episode of *Unbreakable Kimmy Schmidt,* and received an Emmy nomination for this episode. With Angie and Tracy back together, Tracy worries that he's whipped. She's making him get up at seven thirty in the morning, where he discovers that in the morning, they have "food, TV, almost everything."

We also received another *Studio 60* reference here with Liz asking Kenneth to walk and talk with her, which Kenneth explains he can usually do, but now she's got him in his head about it. He goes on to walk awkwardly, with his words largely incoherent: "Jenna with problem I have." The show claimed the walk-and-talk for itself here following *Studio 60*'s cancellation and *30 Rock*'s ultimate victory. The episode also features an early reference to Kenneth's mom's friend Ron, who Kenneth always despairingly refers to—until it ultimately pays off with an appearance of Bryan Cranston as Ron several seasons later.

Episode 4, "Rosemary's Baby," features one of the show's most widely beloved guest appearances. Riggi described it as the turning point of the show, with Carrie Fisher guest starring as old-school comedy writer Rosemary Howard. It was a blending of truth and fiction, with the real Fisher being known in Hollywood as a behind-the-scenes script doctor who helped to fix numerous screenplays, from *Sister Act* to *The Wedding Singer*. The episode lets Liz connect with Fisher as Rosemary Howard, a famed comedy writer whose rebellious streak, combined with a lack of keeping up with the culture, makes her a less-than-helpful guest writer on *TGS*. The character was rumored to be based on a real-life *SNL* writer from the show's early years.

Star Wars references were frequently woven through *30 Rock*, with Liz being a huge fan herself, so it was another blending of worlds. Both Fey and Morgan were big real-life fans of the films, as were many of the writers. Fey said that it started organically, as they realized they had *Star Wars* references in almost every episode at one point, then tried to keep it going. She credits Carlock with many of the deep references.

Andrew Guest: All the writers felt like [that episode] clicked in a way. The difficulty for the show was never the comedy. But having an emotional story for Liz was always hard. One of the reasons that "Rosemary's Baby" was such a good episode is that it felt like "*Yes.* This is something Liz would actually care about." Her mentor, and the person that she looked up to and inspired her to be writing comedy, is something that she's very invested in.

John Riggi: Liz quit because Jack said, "Get rid of her." That was actually based on something that I had said once in the room: that I was working on a show with the creator of the show, who was also the actor in the show. We had a writers' assistant in the room, and he was not particularly great at his job—and the creator was laughing, and having a great time with him. As soon as the writers' assistant left the room, the creator of the show looked at me and said, "Fire him."

Showing the depth of the connection between Liz and Rosemary, her apartment was actually Liz's apartment, just re-dressed.

Teresa Mastropierro: Every production designer, you ask yourself and you ask the writers, "How do you think that person came to be in that environment? How long have they lived there?" Let's say it's an apartment—did someone pass it on to them, or is this the apartment they aspired to their whole lives and they've finally gotten it?

You want to know their history, and if you don't have access to it or no one's really written their history yet, you make one up. Tell a little story about it to my crew to explain how we're going to get it there. "This person lived in this apartment for thirty years and never threw anything out." That's a big obvious thing to say, but we tried to give people a little bit of a history behind the only moment that we're going to encounter them in.

Vanja Černjul (cinematographer): Because there were all these amazing people, I always thought it would be unprofessional for somebody in my position to ask for a photo. But I completely forgot about that professional standard with Carrie Fisher. We were a little embarrassed. She hugged us like little kids who she knew were in love with Princess Leia. She just knew what it was.

The episode also strangely foreshadowed what would become a near obsession by the *30 Rock* writers with blackface. When Rosemary comes to pitch ideas with the *TGS* writers, she says that race is the last great taboo, so they should put Josh in blackface and have Tracy call him the N word. Liz objects, telling Rosemary that they can't do race stuff on TV because it's too sensitive. They'd go on to do blackface on the show in three more episodes, starting in Season 3 and doing it multiple times in Season 5.

Fisher was nominated for an Emmy for this episode. The other reason this episode became pivotal for the series is that it had a moment that crystallized the Liz and Jack relationship, and helped the show fully define the dynamic that let Liz/Jack storylines take center stage week after week.

John Riggi: We kept struggling with, how are we going to get Tina and Alex in the same space? Because Jack worked on the fifty-second floor, and the writers were on the fourteenth. But we knew that they were good gasoline for the show together. So, in that episode, Tina quits, goes and sees Carrie Fisher's apartment—which is pretty much a big bummer—and comes running back for her job, saying, "Oh my god, her life. Jack, you couldn't believe it." First of all, he said one of the greatest things we ever wrote, which was "Never go with a hippie to a second location."

He said, "I'll mentor you, Lemon. I'll show you how to run your life so that you won't ever have to be like her." We were shooting it—Jack Burditt wrote that episode. We're looking at the balcony of Jack's office, and they were both having red wine. I looked at Jack [Burditt] and said, "I'm so mad at you right now, because I think you just cracked it." And I wish I would've cracked it. I was looking at the two of them, and I was like, that's the show right there. We had just put it in the center square of the show, and it locked everything in.

Jack Burditt had lived a wild life—one he would go on to mine for material on multiple hit shows over the years. It included him working at a theme park amid riots, working for Lockheed during the Cold War on top-secret weapons systems that he still can't talk about, and outrunning the police while riding his motorcycle in a high-speed chase.

Daisy Gardner: Burditt just looks like this dark, handsome drifter, wearing a denim jacket that says *Mad About You* on it. And you're like "Who is this dude?" Then all of a sudden he comes out with the craziest, darkest, funniest shit you've ever heard.

Jon Haller: Jack Burditt is often described as the nicest man in show business, and he is. He has a wealth of stories. Tina and Robert adored him. He was just a calming presence. I don't want to call him the Yoda, but he never said a bad word about anybody. He would go off and write these amazing scripts, listening to music while he wrote.

So, of course, they honored him by making him play a homeless guy on the show, which he absolutely adored doing. He would go off and do [another show], then they would pull him back. He's somebody who would sit in a room and be silent for two hours, then he would pitch this amazing, well-thought-out thing, and it would be like "Holy shit, this is why you are a legend among comedy writers."

He was a master of the kind of idea that could completely unlock a show, like he did here in bringing Liz and Jack together. Burditt also worked as a 1980s rock critic, developed substance issues, and worked as a business journalist. All those different life experiences made him a TV writing muse, always ready with a story that helped spark more ideas.

It's never been simple to break into TV writing—Burditt got into comedy writing through a gig as a script reader for Disney, working on the crew of Disney's Sunday-night movie. Burditt broke the rules and took home a script from Disney, did a rewrite on his own, and ended up getting hired to do the official rewrite for the company. He comes from a TV writing heritage—his dad, George Burditt, wrote for *Three's Company*, while his mom wrote on mystery shows and created *Diagnosis: Murder*.

"Rosemary's Baby" was also famed for a scene with Jack trying to help Tracy through a therapy session, role-playing as different members of Tracy's family—his father from "Funky North Philly" with a "droopy lip," his mother, Tracy himself, the white man his mom left his dad for, even a Latina neighbor. The accents Baldwin uses might not make it to air in 2021, though the therapist working for the network in the episode points out what a bad idea this is at the time. The scene was widely praised as a hilarious moment that showed off Baldwin's great skills as an impressionist. It was inspired by late Black comedian Redd Foxx, with stories being warmly shared about what they loved about his work—according to Baldwin, it wasn't meant to be any sort of put-down.

Alan Sepinwall: When we're talking about great moments, you can't not talk about the Tracy and Jack therapy scene. That right there is an absolute classic TV time capsule kind of moment. It walks just on the knife-edge of being wildly inappropriate.

Alec Baldwin: The purpose of the show was to walk along that edge, and we think it would be disingenuous of us to pull our punches. Some of the most offensive things come out of Tracy's mouth. Our attitude is that we don't really worry about that.

Don Scardino: I didn't direct it, but I produced it. It was Alec's improvisation that took that to even the farthest place, of doing all of those characters. I asked some friends of mine, and nobody found it offensive, nobody found it racist. And fortunately (*knocks on wood*) that one has not been taken off [of streaming].

Meanwhile, Tracy is busy doing the one thing he's not supposed to do

Tami Sagher: [Tracy] was in this rebellious phase, and Jack says, "You can do whatever you want, just no dogfighting." So he's like "Dogfighting!" Grizz and Dot Com went and got two tiny little puppies, and they say "Awww!" Then in the script, Tracy's supposed to say, "'Awww?' No 'awww'!" But for some reason, he just went "*AAAAH!* No *AAAAH!*" Tracy's one of those guys who just does that. But whatever choice he makes—any other person, it would be a mistake, and with him, it would just be funnier.

It was also the first appearance of Kenneth's nemesis, evil page Donny Lawson (Paul Scheer), who mocks Kenneth in a series of extremely low-stakes power battles.

The high-stakes power battle of the strike continued to play out in real life. "Rosemary's Baby" was the last episode aired before the writers' strike kicked off. Due to the delay from producing an episode to it airing, though, several more episodes were still to be written before the interruption caused by the strike.

Episode 5, "Greenzo," was inspired by NBC's very real Green Week initiative, which featured multiple shows writing in environmentally minded storylines. On *30 Rock*, they personified the initiative with David Schwimmer as corporate mascot Greenzo—"America's first nonjudgmental, business-friendly environmental advocate."

But when Jared, the actor playing Greenzo, starts taking the environment *too* seriously for NBC's liking and turns against his corporate overlords, Jack tries replacing him with . . . Al Gore. At the same time as speculation around him potentially running for president again was rising, with *An Inconvenient Truth* having won the documentary Academy Award earlier that year.

Bellamy Forrest: Al Gore, there was an air of awe. Everyone was really smitten by him.

Vanja Černjul: I still have a picture of the camera crew with Al Gore—it seems like everybody who was relevant in the culture would be a guest that week on the show.

Gore ended up appearing in multiple episodes, which Forrest credits to the respect he had for Tina Fey and her work.

Kenneth throws a party in this episode that, while not attended by a former vice president, spawned one of the show's great recurring jokes: the relationship history between Liz and Grizz. Given the rhyming names, you'd think they would have played with that more.

Grizz Chapman: The moments with Tina Fey were always nerve-racking for me, because she's my boss. You want to do your best. She never put that type of pressure on me, but it was just me putting that pressure on myself. In Hollywood, in the acting world, you do one thing wrong and it's over. So any time I was in a scene with her, or being around her, I would want to bring as much funny as possible, to let her know that I belong there—and that she didn't make a bad decision by adding me to the cast.

The episode also features Pete's much-spoken-about wife, Paula, finally appearing on-screen, played by *SNL* and *30 Rock* writer/actress Paula Pell. And while she'd largely been a source of complaints in the past, this episode actually had sweet moments with the two reconnecting with some bedroom roleplay—in Liz's apartment.

Scott Adsit: When I first met [Paula Pell], I just thought she was an actress. And she was a really, really funny actress. By the end of the day, I found out she was this amazing writer. She brings this odd, left-field observation to everything, and can encapsulate it in the briefest of sentences, which then makes everybody crack up.

She's really game and wants to make everything better and funnier, and will do anything to make it work. I mean, the first episode she's in, maybe the first time we met, she was sitting on top of me with her top off, and my hands were covering her breasts. She didn't blink an eye. She was not shy about it, she thought the idea was funny, and that's the salt of the earth comedian that she is.

Jack finds a new romantic spark of his own in **episode 6, "Somebody to Love."** We'd seen the tease of Jack dating Condoleezza Rice before, but he meets a new political love interest this season: Celeste "C.C." Cunningham, played by Edie Falco just after finishing her run as Carmela on *The Sopranos*. But Jack quickly discovers that he's dating—*gasp*—a Democratic congresswoman from Vermont.

Baldwin had some dubious acting advice for Falco, new to the world of TV comedy.

Edie Falco (Celeste "C.C." Cunningham): I just felt, literally, like a fish out of water. But Alec came up to me—he said, "All right, you know all the years of acting, all the stuff that you've taught yourself over the years never to do? Do it here. All that bad acting stuff? This is where you do it. This is about being larger than life—it's not about creating real moments."

The episode also did a striking parody of continuing fear of foreigners following 9/11 and the ongoing Iraq War here. Liz's paranoia about her Middle Eastern neighbor Raheem (Fred Armisen) gets the best of her, leading to her causing her own neighbor's radicalization. After she calls the authorities, it turns out that all the training he was doing that she'd attributed to him being a terrorist turns out to have been part of his prep for going on *The Amazing Race*. And when he comes back from being detained, it seems like now he really might be planning some sort of revenge against the government.

The episode also included a blink-and-you'll-miss-it cameo by another former *SNL* cast member, Kristen Wiig, playing C.C. in the Lifetime movie about the congresswoman's life. It details the dramatic story of when she was shot in the face by her neighbor's dog, in *A Dog Took My Face and Gave Me a Better Face to Change the World: The Celeste Cunningham Story*.

Episode 7, "Cougars," provides one of the most blatant critiques of the Bush administration that the show did, mapping the Iraq War onto a Little League baseball team. It starts with Tracy having to do community service by coaching the team—at the same time as the real Tracy was dealing with his own run-ins with the law thanks to driving under the influence. The episode culminates in a troop surge—which translates here into Jack recruiting Grizz and Dot Com as ringers for the team. The script originally called for New York Met Mike Piazza to fill the ringer role.

You also get Jack standing beneath a "Fun Accomplished" banner, à la George W. Bush's infamous "Mission Accomplished" banner on an aircraft carrier.

The episode features Frank exploring his sexuality, developing a crush on the much younger coffee delivery guy Liz is dating, Jamie. It's a potentially dangerously offensive premise having Frank explore being gay in a somewhat stereotypical way for just one episode, though John Riggi's influence in the writing keeps it from ever coming across as saying something negative about being gay.

> **Judah Friedlander:** I played this role almost like a junior high or high school crush. It's their first, and they just go completely overboard and have no idea what they're doing, have no control over their emotions or their body, or anything they do, and they're completely obsessed. I had "Open Arms" by Journey playing in my head the entire time.

He also dresses like a gay stereotype, which Friedlander attributed to being due to the way Frank thinks—that he's the kind of guy who thinks in stereotypes, so when he develops a crush on another man, he starts dressing like what he thinks a gay man should dress like. Friedlander told wardrobe to put him in outfits like Cerie would wear.

Friedlander has a certain love for crafts, seen in the custom trucker hats that he created himself for every episode, as well as in a painting he presents to Liz here representing his love: an image of a part-unicorn mermaid being held by Bigfoot. According to Friedlander, the Bigfoot represented Frank, while the mermaid represented Jamie.

> **Judah Friedlander:** I actually had to do two, because I had one already done, but the mermaid was topless. Apparently you couldn't have a topless, crudely painted mermaid on TV.

This episode includes both Tracy's and Tina's stand-ins in small roles, including Tina's stand-in playing Frank's crush's mom in the end. When the show aired, it also featured one of the commercial tie-ins that kept the show profitable—American Express ads with *30 Rock* characters in them, with Kenneth giving out Christmas gifts. That was one of the ways that the show grappled with the ongoing rise of DVRs and declining network ratings, helping to convince viewers to stick around for the commercial breaks.

In **Episode 8, "Secrets and Lies,"** you get one of the most offensive things Tracy does in the run of the show—which is saying a lot. Tracy gets mad when Jenna wins an award for her *Mystic Pizza* musical performance, so Liz creates an entire fake awards ceremony for Tracy: the Pacific Rim Emmys. Tracy insists on accepting the award in order to not disappoint the Japanese audience, especially Godzilla. He clarifies that he's just kidding, as he knows Godzilla doesn't care what humans do.

While accepting his award, he puts into practice what he says is a popular Japanese practice called "sharking" and pulls down Jenna's dress. In the end, it turns out that *both* awards were fake, created by Liz as she did her best to keep both of her delicate, easily angered stars happy.

Jack and C.C. continue to face relationship struggles here, with C.C. suing GE parent corporation, the Sheinhardt Wig Company, after it poisoned a river and turned local children orange. *30 Rock* used Sheinhardt both to mock its corporate parent company and to give itself some cover.

Robert Carlock: If someone's poisoning a river, it's the Sheinhardt Wig Corporation and not General Electric.

The episode also features a guest appearance by James Carville, who continuously uses the catchphrase "Cajun style."

Episode 9, "Ludachristmas," set the standard for all the Christmas episodes to come. Those holiday shows often gave the show a chance to play around with the characters' family dynamics in new ways.

Don Scardino: You've already done the Halloween show in September, and sometime in October or early November, you get to decorate everything for the Christmas show. Some shows, you do a Christmas show, they're very sentimental—on *30 Rock*, they were very sardonic. [But] they assume a festive air that they don't normally have, and it's fun to play at creating your own Christmas movie.

While they were creating a jolly holiday episode, the writers' strike was looming behind the scenes. The episode remained untitled in NBC's press releases when it originally aired, before getting the "Ludachristmas" title on the second-season DVD.

This episode introduced Liz's parents, with Anita Gillette as her mom and legendary comedy writer Buck Henry as her father. Conan O'Brien sidekick Andy Richter plays Liz's brother, Mitch, who's suffered ever since a skiing accident with his memory stuck in 1985, perpetually a boy in a grown-up's body.

They play the happy Christmas family in their Christmas sweaters, much to the envy of Jack. But Jack's mom, Colleen (Elaine Stritch), doesn't buy it, promising to find out what's really going on in that family. She sets her plan in motion as they all go out to lunch together.

John Riggi: Elaine had this line that is basically a little grenade that she'd leave on the table, then she gets up and goes to the salad bar. She's rehearsing, and every time she reaches in to get salad, she bangs her head on the sneeze guard. She is cursing so much. The words coming out of her mouth, you would not believe—she's so angry, she's like "Why can't we get rid of this goddamn thing?"

So Griffin comes up to wire her [for sound] and says, "Elaine, just so you know, on my monitor, you can't see your hands, so you don't have to lean in to get salad if you don't want to, because nobody can see you." Elaine looked at Griffin, said, "Well, then if I'm not getting salad, what the fuck am I doing at the salad bar?" And that's exactly what she was like to work with. Everything had to make sense, because she was a stage actress.

Stritch was nominated for an Emmy for her role in this episode, following her win for "Hiatus" in the first season, though she didn't go on to win this time.

Beyond the more subtle allusion in "Cougars," Tracy's real-life ankle bracelet following his DUIs gets turned into a storyline here, as he wears a court-ordered alcohol-monitoring device. The real Tracy's sentences for his multiple DUIs included probation, fines, a mandatory alcohol education program, and a suspended driver's license—along with that alcohol-testing ankle bracelet.

> **Tracy Morgan:** When I got my second DUI, Alec was the main one counseling me. He's a passionate dude. I don't give a fuck what nobody says about him, dude been there. "You got an opportunity on *30 Rock*," he told me. I felt the love.

On the show, Tracy worries his ankle bracelet will keep him from attending *TGS*'s annual Ludachristmas party, which instead ends up being a victim to Kenneth explaining the true meaning of Christmas in his hillbilly way and inspiring everyone to tear down the giant 30 Rockefeller Plaza Christmas tree. You also get an appearance by Kenneth's much-referenced spiritual advisor, Reverend Gary (not to be confused with *Unbreakable Kimmy Schmidt*'s Reverend Richard Wayne Gary Wayne, played by Jon Hamm).

This season's tenth episode was the last episode produced before the writers' strike, which is the reason behind it getting the somewhat sterile title of **"Episode 210."** With the writers gone, the producers were so afraid of breaking strike rules that they didn't name the episode—it remains officially untitled.

"Episode 210" began shooting a couple days before the strike and was continuing to shoot after the strike started for another two and a half days. Some scenes in "Episode 210" didn't even have a director around to direct them, as the show's writer/producers weren't there to direct the scenes. The actors, along with the producers and directors guiding them, had to avoid ad-libbing due to fears of breaking the strike rules, sticking even more strictly to the script than usual. There were scenes where Tina Fey felt that some ad-libbing would have helped and normally would have happened, but the strike means there are some unusually bumpy moments here. As Tina said on the episode's commentary, "Here we are, not ad-libbing again. You're welcome, Writers Guild of America."

Tina Fey: We didn't break any rules, and anyone who thinks we did can bite me on the butt.

The episode was also a culmination of Jack's love affair with C.C. They try to make their love work, finding a place to literally meet in the middle: a town halfway between New York and Washington, D.C. But their respective commitments to their high-powered jobs keep them apart. In reality, Edie Falco was also sick while shooting her scenes, relying on cold medicine to power through it.

We see them meet in the fictionalized town of Hockassin, Pennsylvania, halfway between their cities—spelled slightly differently from the actual town of Hockessin, Delaware. They walk through the park together, enjoying the romance of small-town life and what it could mean for their love . . . just for a moment.

Tina Fey: Only on *30 Rock* would we double Central Park for rural Pennsylvania. What a colossal waste of money.

This was the end of Edie Falco's arc as C.C.—and despite this episode earning her an Emmy nomination, it marked the end of her interest in doing sitcoms.

Edie Falco: They were so patient, and so lovely to work with. But boy, I just never felt like I could get totally comfortable with it. I'm done [with] that kind of comedy.

The show finishes with a big song-and-dance number featuring the whole cast, with the actors actually singing themselves. They deliver a rousing "Midnight Train to Georgia," inspired by Kenneth deciding to return home after feeling his life go awry thanks to the sinful power of trying coffee for the first time—he's always avoided hot liquids, because that's the Devil's temperature. Alec Baldwin sings, though he was known to be shy about singing during the show.

Grizz Chapman: We did "Midnight Train to Georgia" with Gladys Knight, which was pretty cool, because we got an opportunity to go to the studio and actually sing. A lot of people don't know that that was really us singing. And doing those dance steps—they brought in a choreographer.

Grizz got mad at himself while filming, having trouble getting his moves just right. He was heard on set walking off and saying "mother f—ing two-step" to himself. But he came back and made it happen, putting in some deep concentration. The show also pays off the joke of this big Gladys Knight number by having the actual Gladys Knight show up on the *TGS* set—but she never sings.

Kevin Ladson: I was literally underneath the camera when they would do "He's leaving," and Gladys Knight was there. I went behind the set, and I started tearing up. I knew why: because I was having such a good time. It still makes me feel that melancholy way when I think about it.

This episode also lives on in online culture as a meme—Tina Fey giving herself a self-high-five from this episode proved to be a ubiquitous GIF.

After this episode, the season was broken in half due to the writers' strike. Airing midseason finales in order to introduce something fresh has become commonplace on network TV in recent years, but this was different. Network TV, before widespread streaming, often relied on reruns that served as the warm comfort food for viewers. You couldn't just watch episode after episode until Netflix asked, "Are you still watching . . .?"

Tina Fey and Robert Carlock expressed their support for the strike, signing on to a letter from numerous showrunners of other TV shows promising not to write, not to break stories, and not to ask their writing staff to do so either. While they may have privately been upset by the disturbances to their shows, with their own loyalties torn in their roles as both writers and management, they also expressed to the cast and crew their support for what the writers were fighting for. Tina Fey and Jack McBrayer even ended up joining picket lines, despite Fey being part of management and McBrayer being a nonwriting member of the cast.

Grizz Chapman: Tina Fey was so in tune with the show, and with everybody that was there. When we went on writers' strike, she had a meeting about it. She didn't have to have that meeting—she didn't have to tell us what was going on, but she explained her stance on the situation, on why we were striking, and why she's standing up for our rights. It was a touching moment, because she started crying, and it just showed me how special of a person she really is. Sometimes the celebrity, and the money, and the fame, and all this stuff goes to your head, but she's one of the good ones.

How much the strike hurt people varied—some, such as assistant director Bellamy Forrest, said that the timing worked out since she gave birth to her son during the January of the strike. But the strike was hardest on the lowest-paid members of the crew, those without savings and the same level of support as the producers, the writers, and the actors during this time.

Kevin Ladson: That was an emotional time, 'cause we didn't know how long we were going to be off. Tina came to the crew crying. She said, "I know you all have families and you all have homes. I'm just so sorry that we're going through this time." And that right there brought a camaraderie to the crew that I'm glad to have been a part of. We were *30 Rock* lifers at that point. Because it's rare when a producer/showrunner is expressing that kindness to the crew, and we really felt like a family.

While the show was shut down, the cast went and performed the "Secrets and Lies" episode as a staged reading at the Upright Citizens Brigade Theatre in New York before it aired on television. It was to show their support for the strike and to serve as a benefit for the show's laid-off production assistants, who didn't have the same support that those in writers, actors, or craft guilds might have, along with being far less likely to have savings.

The performances featured most of the cast, with Paula Pell filling in for Edie Falco as C.C. and Robert Carlock taking on the James Carville guest role, while Don Scardino served as the narrator. Jack McBrayer and John Lutz also put their improv skills to use, improvising fake commercials based off the audience's suggestions in between acts of the show. Several of the show's writers pitched in with small roles, including Donald Glover. Fey said that she was hopeful when doing the live show, as negotiations were set to start soon, and the hard-driving writer/performer wanted to be back at work.

> **Don Scardino:** Unlike a writers' strike when I was directing a soap opera in the eighties, where we kept making soap operas, this one, we had to shut down. And for me, it was just for want of being involved and having something to do, and something as great as that, and not knowing what the fate would be.

When the WGA finally settled its dispute, it ended up getting nowhere near what it asked for, though the payments for streaming were a significant step up from what the writers had been making for DVD sales. The WGA allowed showrunners to go back to work on February 11, so Robert Carlock officially went back to work, though there was speculation they were brainstorming ideas for new episodes during the strike. The rest of the writers returned to work two days later, after being on strike for three months. The strike lasted from November until February, keeping the show off the air from January until April.

30 Rock was one of more than sixty shows that had to shut down production due to the strike, without any new scripts to shoot, and it cost the economy billions of dollars. When shows began to return, ratings were down across the board, and traditional scripted programming had lost more ground to the reality TV that the networks had used to fill holes in the interim.

Due to the strike, *30 Rock*'s season was also cut from twenty-two to fifteen episodes. The strike may have hurt the show's momentum, coming off of major Emmy wins and increased critical praise. Only one of the post-hiatus shows hit its pre-hiatus average, and the show moved time slots the following week, dipping to between 5.4 and 5.6 million viewers for its last three episodes—below even its Season 1 average. That compares with 11.6 million viewers for the highest-rated scripted show at the time, ABC's *Desperate Housewives*—and 16.1 million viewers for the Tuesday airings of Fox reality series *American Idol*. Though it's not so bad compared with the biggest scripted show on NBC at the time: *Heroes*, which averaged 7.6 million viewers.

30 Rock also ended up behind schedule when it was back, forcing more packed shoots and multiple crews working at once.

Don Scardino: Tina being Tina, and Robert Carlock being Robert, they kept the ball in the air in terms of thinking up stories and talking with one another about when they came back. Out of the gate, when the strike ended, we came out with some really strong shows.

Marceline Hugot: When we got back on, they called and had written me in again for another episode—Don Scardino came down to the dressing room, and he said, "I've got interesting news for you, Marceline. What do you think . . . you want to be on for a while?" I said, "Well, let me think on it." (*laughs*) No, I said, "Oh my god, I'd love to."

She'd make her comeback just a few episodes after the show's return.

Before that, **episode 11, "MILF Island,"** let us finally see an extended segment of this horrific reality series that had been established as a bona fide NBC hit. The episode also had some more resonance given the way reality TV had rushed in to fill the void left by scripted programming during the writers' strike.

This show dug in deeper on an all-time memorable idea, presenting the season finale of *MILF Island*, which is essentially *Survivor* but with an island filled with twenty-five bikini-clad moms and fifty eighth-grade boys. NBC even sold real-life *MILF Island* T-shirts.

Tina Fey: We actually sat down and tried to figure out the rules of *MILF Island* and were not entirely successful. It involves something where the boys vote the moms off if they don't like them anymore. And then it involves physical challenges, and that's about all that we know.

The real kids surrounded by these bikini-clad women in the faux show's equivalent of *Survivor*'s Tribal Council were much more uncomfortable than what they were playing on camera—according to Scott Adsit, they seemed to get sadder and sadder as the day went on.

Pete, hyped to watch the *MILF Island* finale alone in his office (ew), ends up getting his comeuppance by getting his arm stuck in a vending machine as he tries to acquire a pre-show treat.

Scott Adsit: It ends in such a great way, where I finally dial a phone—but I dial my own office, [after] throwing all of my clothes at it. The props department built this fake vending machine to put on top of me, and I was under that all day. We worked out a lot of physical bits while we filmed it, because we had time and the interest to change it just a little, so it's not exactly what was on the page. We found new schtick within it, which is rare on [*30 Rock*].

Because the show is this really elaborate, beautiful Ferris wheel. It's ornate, this little toy wind-up merry-go-round, which is just perfect in all its elegance. There's a tendency for actors, when they get that beautiful creation on set, they want to change it *immediately*. We were all pretty aware of how pristine the scripts were when they arrived, so we didn't have to play with it much.

Coming out of the strike, "MILF Island" was a natural fit in the role of a pseudo-midseason premiere—it's focused around the main cast and features the uber-dramatic and topical *MILF Island* reality TV parody. With **episode 12, "Subway Hero,"** the show seems less interested in being easily accessible, bringing back Liz's ex Dennis and featuring a particularly New York City local news story.

The episode was built around the idea of Dennis becoming a subway hero, à la the real-life New York subway hero Wesley Autrey—a construction worker who saved a film student who had a seizure and fell onto the tracks. The even-more-NYC-than-usual episode had then-New York mayor Michael Bloomberg as a guest star, praising Dennis for his subway heroism. It was before the billionaire Bloomberg jerked around the Democratic Party with an ill-fated presidential run, back when he was busy jerking around New York City and those who love big sodas.

Jack's own conservative political machinations here include informing Kenneth that writing in the Lord's name when he votes counts as voting Republican, and recruiting Tracy to tell Black people not to vote because the amount of time it takes you to vote could instead be used on playing three games of pool. He also gets Tracy to tell his "fellow Blackmericans" that Dr. King had a dream: a 200-foot-high wall to keep Mexico out. Was Donald Trump a *30 Rock* fan?

The writers were particularly thrilled to have the legendary Tim Conway appear on the show in this episode—an appropriate choice for a program that draws inspiration from *The Carol Burnett Show*. Conway plays an old Hollywood star, Bucky Bright, star of *Wagons Ho*. Kenneth's the only one who really knows who he is, both a sign of Kenneth's country-bumpkinness and a nod to his potential much-older-than-we-know nature.

Conway makes a number of inappropriate jokes, and they also get in a nod to the real Conway's work on *McHale's Navy*. While Kenneth gives Bucky a tour of NBC Studios, what was actually happening was that Conway was giving McBrayer a tour.

Conway also paid a visit to the real *30 Rock* writers' room, for an extra level of meta. And while many of *30 Rock*'s guest stars were nominated, Tim Conway actually won an Emmy for his appearance here.

Episode 13, "Succession," marks one of the most pivotal turns in *30 Rock*—if this were a drama, it would be the one getting the dramatic teases and sinister deep-voiced commercials promoting it.

> **Andrew Guest:** [Getting to co-write an episode of the show] was something I had to fight for. There are certain bosses on sitcoms who are happy to hire from within and move people up the ranks, and that was my experience on *Hope & Faith* the year before. *30 Rock* was not that vibe.
>
> They had picked us up for only thirteen initially in Season 2. I had a drink with Robert Carlock and told him that I would love to come back as writers' assistant—but he had to guarantee me an episode. He said he had been talking to Tina about it, and it was something they were considering. He said, "I can only give you a co-writing credit, because some of our staff writers haven't even gotten a co-writing credit," so I said, "OK. I want to be guaranteed an episode in the first thirteen." And he agreed—I had him in a tight spot.
>
> I was very lucky in the end that I did that, because the writers' strike happened that year. My episode almost didn't get produced.

Guest was given a co-writing credit on one of the series' key episodes alongside veteran writer John Riggi, a huge turning point in Jack's battle with Banks.

> **Andrew Guest:** I have to give Robert a lot of credit—when it was time to actually do my episode, he was really sweet and wonderful about it, he wanted me at the writers' table during the story-breaking. He sat at the computer and put the jokes in while we were working on the rewrite, and let me sit with the writers—it was a great experience.

A sidenote: While they were working on this episode, Donald Glover was auditioning for *SNL*. He ended up having to settle for being a popular actor, writer, and performer in many other places instead.

This episode features the return of Kathy Geiss, initially in a background gag, before a much larger reveal by the end. She's first seen in a cutaway with Banks looking for flowers for their wedding—as Banks flirts with the flower guy, Kathy eats the flowers.

> **Marceline Hugot:** When someone you're making fun of or you're not even paying much attention to 'cause you're flirting with the flower guy, and she is just genuinely happy eating flowers, she's like Ferdinand the Bull, there's a part of you that goes, "Oh my goodness, look at this."

John Riggi: She really ate the flowers. We made sure that everything was not poisonous, because you hate to see that happen.

Despite Devon's willingness to jump into a sham marriage with Don Geiss's daughter, Geiss decides to give the GE chairman role to Jack. When Geiss tells Jack that he is finally going to get what he's always wanted—getting to be Geiss's successor—Jack gets overwhelmed by his emotions in this sheer moment of joy.

Just as he's about to announce Jack's future, though, Geiss asks Liz for a snack while everyone's attending Banks's bachelor party—and when Liz neglects to bring Geiss that snack, he slips into a diabetic coma. As Dr. Spaceman completely fails at reviving him. Oops.

The show was also finding a different approach to ending an episode than most classic sitcoms, where everyone tells each other they're loved, they hug, and the audience gets the feels. They combine the main "A" story, as well as the lower tier "B" and "C" stories, into something that gives the audience a sense of closure.

Andrew Guest: We did a lot of what we called "dovetailing" on *30 Rock*, where we would have an A story and a B story meet, and sometimes the B story would inform the characters' main decision on the A story, or thematically they would cross. This was something *Seinfeld* was doing before *30 Rock*—when you remove characters learning things emotionally and having a hug at the end of a typical sitcom episode, you don't have an emotional epiphany.

This was a pretty cynical staff, who was in it for jokes, and really didn't want characters to be learning and hugging. The writers discovered that sometimes those structural epiphanies justified why we had this crazy A, B, or C story, and none of the characters were necessarily going to learn anything from it. But, as an audience member, it felt like that's why these stories happened.

While Jack fervently claims to everyone who will listen that he was about to be named the new chairman—and that Banks knew about it—Banks plays dumb. And when Jack gets invited to a special board meeting, it turns out that Banks lied to Jack about when it was, already meeting with the board beforehand . . . and getting his fiancée, Kathy Geiss, installed as his puppet chairwoman for the sake of family continuity.

Kathy Geiss appears in a dramatic reveal at the end. As Banks details his plan like a Bond supervillain explaining everything in the movie's climax, we see Kathy sitting at a board of directors surrounded by the kind of weirdos that Kathy Geiss would install on a board.

Marceline Hugot: When you turn around in your chair, and you're the big scary owner now that your father is in a coma, and half your trustees are big dogs . . .

You can't take her seriously, and yet she's so genuinely pleased with herself and believes in herself that you don't hate her.

It was originally supposed to feature one of the oddly inbred royal line of the Hapsburgs, introduced in the classic Season 1 "Black Tie" episode with Paul Reubens. But flu struck the set, including the actress who was set to play that part.

One of the jokes in this episode was inspired by an awkward moment between Tami Sagher and Robert Carlock, when she laughed so hard at a choice Tracy had made during a table read that she grabbed Carlock's knee.

Tami Sagher: As Jew-y as I am, Carlock is WASP-y. I've never felt so completely aware that that was an inappropriate thing to do. We never even discussed it. But then a few months later, we had gotten through the writers' strike, and coming back, Yvonne Mojica, who was in the art department and did design, we saw each other in the hallway and we hugged. Because it had been a few months where everybody had been out of work.

Carlock witnessed it, and I could see that he was very confused. Even then, it took him until three in the morning that night to bring it up: "Did you and Yvonne know each other from before? Because I saw you guys hugged." And I was like "No, we're both just ethnic." She was Puerto Rican, and I'm Jewish.

Then I managed to bring up "A few months earlier, I know I gripped your knee, and that was weird for you." He was like "Yes, it was." Then we put in the script—it might have even been that night—where Liz tries to hug Jack, and Jack doesn't like hugging because it's too ethnic.

Riggi and Guest would end up winning a Writers Guild Award for this key episode.

John Riggi: I do hug a lot. I do hug a great deal, especially relative to [Carlock].

Andrew Guest: I felt very lucky that the way the abbreviated season worked, it meant that the episode I ended up writing was toward the end of what our season ended up being, and there were a lot of big stories happening.

The award-winning episode featured another off-the-wall storyline, one of the most memorable of the season, with a masterpiece created by Tracy. It starts with Tracy dealing with his son choosing not to tell him about his school's Bring Your Father to School Day, so he decides to make his children proud by doing something great—and it goes in a much grosser direction than its wholesome beginnings may imply.

Robert Carlock: When I watched this moment with my wife, she was very touched, and I had to tell her this was going to turn into a porn video game/*Amadeus* conceit. On a story about Tracy and his kids.

John Riggi: That's what we do on *30 Rock*. We make you think something touching's going to happen, and then we make you feel foolish for thinking that.

Tracy's efforts to achieve greatness lead to him combining two of his greatest loves: video games and pornography. The storyline culminates in a riff on the 1984 film classic *Amadeus*, with Tracy as the Mozart of the storyline and office gross guy Frank as his inferior Salieri. But, you know, if they were into porn instead of classical music . . .

Tracy writes feverishly, proving to be a genius auteur—at least when it comes to making porn video games. Guest went and watched *Amadeus* to make sure they got all the beats just right.

Andrew Guest: There was a big moment in breaking that episode, where we came up with the *Amadeus* conceit. After Geiss goes in a coma, we were pitching carrying his body through the snow like when Amadeus's father died, and somebody started doing the music from *Amadeus*, and it all felt very exciting and like it was working. Somebody pitched Spaceman coming in in a cape, and there you go—that was it.

The episode brings in Mozart early, weaving in his music as Liz tries to kiss Banks as part of a blackmail scheme, working to protect Jack. *Amadeus* pays off as the link between each storyline, with Tracy's porn video game savant status turning Frank into his Salieri, jealous of Tracy's ability to do something he'd always longed for.

John Riggi: To us, the essence of the joke is that people would take it that far. That someone would take something that sort of obscure—and yeah, it was a great movie and everything, but the idea that these two grown men would get that involved in it was just funny to us. So the more we could dig into it, the more we could get into the minutiae of it.

Again: *30 Rock* doesn't care if you get its references. If you do, great! Fun for everyone! If you don't, there's another joke coming—just hold on five seconds.

This episode helps to crystallize the Frank character and just the kind of creep he is. According to Judah Friedlander, Frank was based on at least two writers that Fey had worked with at *SNL*. But the character also seemed like a genuinely funny comedy writer at times, particularly with his use of his hats to comment on the episodes. Friedlander would come up with the ideas for the hats and make them himself—something he'd already been doing for more than a decade before *30 Rock*. He would take his ideas to Tina for approval, but she would usually sign off. Then Friedlander would have to spend his time off camera actually constructing all those hats in his dressing room.

Friedlander noted that the Writers Who Never Talk were the ones he actually would talk with the most, in between takes, thanks to the writers always sitting around the table waiting for their next scene when they weren't necessarily the focus.

Another of the small delights in this episode: Tracy yelling "calm down" at a bunch of people who are, in fact, actually calm. It was inspired by Morgan yelling in real life at a perfectly calm Donald Glover to calm down behind the scenes at *30 Rock*.

Episode 14, "Sandwich Day," marked another particularly memorable episode of the series, with a character-defining moment for Liz and her love of food.

While the rest of the *TGS* team tries to convince the Teamsters to tell them the location of where they get their fabled sandwiches each year, Liz is focused on the return of Floyd (Jason Sudeikis), who's in town looking for somewhere to stay while in New York City on business. Liz spent much of this season working on herself, not settling into any other significant relationships after Floyd left—then given the chance, she sets about making Floyd jealous with a flashy red dress. It was the same one that Cameron Diaz wore to a movie premiere, which Fey said she hoped would never be seen side by side.

Tina Fey: Because that would be rough days for old Liz Lemon.

She also used her powers as executive producer to cut a Floyd POV shot that she found unflattering. But she's fine being intentionally unflattering, going on to subvert that moment of manufactured stunningness by following up with Liz sleeping in socks, wearing Tina Fey's actual retainer, and without makeup as she answers her door to find Floyd.

Tina Fey: Liz Lemon sleeps with socks on, because nobody in TV land needs to see my feet—that's private. Feet are private. Let's all remember that when we wear flip-flops on planes, nonsense like that. I would rather see your genitals.

The big, romcom-style run to the airport as Liz chases Floyd in the end runs into a roadblock—thanks to the dipping sauce for Liz's sandwich, with the three-ounce limit still a somewhat fresh annoyance in post-9/11 flying. The power of a sandwich let the writers find a new way to do the run-to-the-airport storyline, all built around the moment of Liz eating a sandwich in one take before working backward from there. The writers felt that they were creating a genuine dilemma for Liz: choosing between a delicious sandwich or the love of her life. She chooses the sandwich, at least for a moment.

Kevin Ladson: I felt like, Tina's not gonna want to eat these big sandwiches. But then she came to me and she said, "Kevin,"—'cause she knew I lived in Philadelphia—"Can you pick up the really big Philadelphia hoagies?" So I went to Philly, and I got these hoagies. Tina always surprised me, because when we came with the food, she would eat the food. Like I said "Oh my god, she's eating more than me."

Don Scardino: Tina said to me, "I want you to just keep the camera rolling—I'm going to eat that whole sandwich." And I said, "OK, well, I can't, I mean—" and she said, "No! Give me the big fat sandwich!" So I told Kevin Ladson, who was our genius prop master and designed all of those props that were so crazy, to pull out some of the meat and make it look big, but be a little smaller. And we cut away for a reaction shot to the TSA guard there, but she did—she ate that whole sandwich.

Tina Fey: And I'll tell you something—it was a *delicious* sandwich.

But Liz and Floyd's conclusion ends up being that they should just be friends, so it's another swing and a miss for Liz Lemon's love life.

Beyond the Sandwich Day itself, this episode features Jack dealing with Don Geiss in a coma and relegated to a job on the twelfth floor rather than the fifty-second. Rip Torn tried pitching writer Jack Burditt a line for his character—to which Burditt had to tell him, no, we can't do that, because you're in a coma.

The episode also lets us see the aftermath of Kathy Geiss being installed at the top—Jack's office has been redecorated with unicorns and Mark Wahlberg posters from his 1990s Marky Mark and the Funky Bunch "Good Vibrations" days.

Marceline Hugot: Some people say, "Why would you want to do a character that doesn't speak?" and think that's a lesser character. I never suffered from that mentality. The truth is, the character was a writers' dream come true. They were very respectful—they would come to me and say, "What do you think of the idea that she can't open the door, so she throws herself against the door as opposed to trying to open—would your character do that?" And the answer was always "Of course." Or "What do you think of her eating flowers?" "Yes!"

It was great fun, the whole choreographing how to throw myself against the door. With [the show's] connection to *Saturday Night Live*, the person who taught John Belushi how to do it came down and taught me. [She] can't open the door and so takes it upon herself to throw herself against the door. It's ridiculous. On some level, it's a sight gag. But on another level it's like, well, you've got to give her an A-plus for trying.

This season's star-studded finale, **episode 15, "Cooter,"** features Matthew Broderick, Edie Falco, and Paul Scheer in guest appearances. The season ends with Jack ousted from GE/NBC by Banks's machinations, at work in Washington, D.C., in a new government job. But he finds government work no more satisfying, working alongside Matthew Broderick as the ineffectual Cooter Burger at a terrible, underfunded agency as part of the Bush administration. As with many of the ways the show's characters grew, it also mirrored Baldwin's own very public flirting with the idea of potentially running for office, along with his outspoken politics.

Matthew Broderick brings his part to life with the same sort of sweaty desperation that he brought to *The Producers*.

Matthew Broderick: I was a big, big fan. And I've known Alec forever. Alec's just a wonderful actor, and he's perfect at that kind of comedy. We had done a movie together [*The Last Shot*], which had almost the same relationship. I got there—you could tell he had been doing it a while. He was like "Where's the camera gonna be? Where's this?" Not in a bad way, but just like he was very comfortable.

The word "cooter" was a favorite of Fey's, which she used frequently while anchoring *SNL*'s *Weekend Update*.

Tina Fey: I *do* love "cooter." I suppose I like "cooter" because it's one of the least graphic ways to describe a lady's genitals. Not that I don't have an appreciation for other euphemisms.

It's revealed that George W. Bush gave Cooter Burger his name—two nicknames. "Cooter" because Bush thought he looked like a turtle, and "Burger" because he saw him eating a hamburger—once. His real name is the perfectly respectable "James Riley."

Matthew Broderick: No matter how much you're being disrespected, you put a positive spin on it if you're in politics. If you're working for the president, whatever he says, you try to just make it into some sort of compliment, or that it's an affectionate name, which I doubt it is. And the way politics are now, there's a different feel to that sort of a joke. It feels more serious now to me.

Jack quickly realizes that this endeavor isn't a good idea, but when he tries to quit, his letter of resignation is rejected. So he conspires with Cooter and his ex-girlfriend C.C. to approve research into an old, abandoned project: a "gay bomb." As Jack notes, it's an idea that's offensive to "both the red states and the gayer blue states," and will surely get them fired.

Alan Sepinwall: That they were able to get away with that stuff on a broadcast network show back then was really something.

Matthew Broderick: It's really vitally important that satire happens, from the court jester. Since the beginning, powerful people need somebody to point out who they are and make fun of them.

The episode also features one of Kathy Geiss's most memorable moments: when she pulled a race car out of her mouth.

Marceline Hugot: As time developed and we got to know each other and had more fun with it, Will [Arnett] started to develop, and then Tina and the writers started writing in, this genuine fear of Kathy Geiss and never feeling comfortable with what he'd gotten himself into. The temper, the growling, all of those things that started to develop later, was all part of what we played with and what we came up with.

So one thing led to another, and out of it came Tina's brainchild—the Matchbox car in the mouth.

John Riggi: Because she spoke so infrequently, we were just like "Well, what if she pulled a little toy car out of her mouth?" Because the thought process would be like, what would be a funny reason why she doesn't talk? The more you embrace the insanity of what you're writing about, the more stuff would come out of it.

Marceline Hugot: That launched her and launched the character. And clearly Tina was intrigued with what she could do with Kathy Geiss. If it hadn't been for the right chemistry of myself, the timing of the writers' strike, then giving the character a bit more life here, it probably would have been a one- or two-episode sight-gag deal, and it would have been over. But somehow it just clicked.

This episode was also one of the first that really started to explore how deeply weird Pete's background is, and the heights that he had fallen from. We learn here that he was supposed to be an Olympic archer, but his dreams were dashed due to the United States boycotting the 1980 Summer Olympics.

Scott Adsit: I'd done archery as a kid at camp, so I thought I knew about archery. The first thing I did was stretch the bow without an arrow in it, which is a *big* no-no. Then I let it go, and it snapped so hard against my forearm—that very soft, doughy, lizard's underbelly of the inside of my arm—and it scraped me so bad that I had a mark there for a month.

The storyline also served as NBC's own tie-in promoting that summer's Olympics coverage. A joke to watch for eagle-eyed viewers: In Pete's office, after his archery history is revealed, a bow and arrow suddenly appear in the background on his wall that aren't there before the flashback.

Scott Adsit: I got in costume for the flashback, where I had the big John Oates [of 1980s blue-eyed soul act Hall and Oates] outfit on. The director had to ask me to go bigger, and bigger—the scene where they tell us that we're not going to be in the Olympics. And I had this enormous take, and they just said make it bigger, bigger, bigger, and eventually it was just this enormous, ridiculous face.

Kenneth was also working in this episode to get sent to work as a page at the Olympics, but his nemesis, evil page Donny (Paul Scheer), works to stop him—leading to a showdown in Chinese between Kenneth, Jenna, and Donny.

The other big season-ending storyline involves Liz mistakenly believing she's pregnant with Dennis's child—but while that ends up not being the case, it inspires her to look into adoption. The reason she thought she might be, aside from an ill-advised one-night stand with Dennis: the Sabor de Soledad cheese curls she's been eating have a tangy flavor that, she discovers, can lead to pregnancy-test false positives. Because that flavor comes from evaporated bull semen.

This also happened to air right around the release of *Baby Mama*, so Liz having a pregnancy scare may not have been a coincidence, but another moment of cross-promotional synergy.

The episode ends with quick teases of stereotypically classic cliffhangers, some of which get paid off and some of which don't, using a flash-forward. Porn video game, yes; Kenneth being an apparent ladies' man while in China for the Olympics, not-so-much.

There was originally another teaser shot for the end of the season, paying off the adoption storyline with Liz bringing back an adopted fourteen-year-old from Eastern Europe because she wasn't able to adopt a baby. But the network pushed back against the idea, and the writers agreed to drop it and go in a different direction.

The show had survived the strike and come back with an undiminished creative energy. And it would take that energy and more into Season 3—along with the added aid of a comical Alaskan governor who claimed she could see Russia from her house.

Of course, the ratings weren't there just yet. The last three episodes were the lowest rated of the entire season. Over the summer, Tina Fey joked at a critics awards ceremony that *30 Rock* was "the highest-rated cable show on broadcast TV" with its combination of critical praise and low ratings. She compared broadcast television at the time to being a vaudeville performer in the 1960s.

And later that summer, Alec Baldwin was feeling a lack of support for the show, and he wasn't afraid to let anyone who would listen hear it. Baldwin told the *New Yorker*, "If the show does succeed, it'll be something of a fucking miracle, because NBC hasn't done a fucking thing to help this show at all. This show is the red-headed stepchild in the lineup."

The show hadn't hit ratings gold. But it was about to.

SEASON 3

(2008–09)

Tina's Doppelgänger Celebrity

The praise for *30 Rock* continued, with the show being showered with Emmy nominations for Season 2—seventeen nominations, a comedy series all-time record. And it won seven of those Emmys, including best comedy series, as well as Alec Baldwin and Tina Fey winning for their leading roles. Tina picked up another for her writing on the Season 2 episode "Cooter," and Tim Conway was rewarded for his guest appearance in "Subway Hero." On the technical side, the show won for both its excellent casting and its sound mixing.

> **Paul Feig:** The one thing that I always held one slight grudge against the show was that Alec beat out Steve Carell for best actor on *The Office* [twice]. And having worked on *The Office* for so many episodes, I feel it was very unfair that Steve didn't get a couple of those. Because Alec had a very showy part, but Steve was working just as hard—and I would dare say, occasionally harder.

While Tina Fey had spent the last few years breaking out from her *SNL* past and had this huge awards momentum on her side, 2008 brought a siren's song so powerful that her old home reached out to pull her back. On August 29, Republican presidential candidate John McCain made a surprise vice presidential selection, picking Alaska governor Sarah Palin. Palin had been low-profile at this point, with few expecting to see her show up in national politics.

And there was something else—she bore a striking resemblance to one Ms. Tina Fey. From cultural commentators to social media, everyone was commenting on the likeness, practically begging for Fey to appear as Palin on *Saturday Night Live*. As *SNL*'s season premiere approached, with the show returning from hiatus just two weeks after McCain's announcement, Lorne Michaels acknowledged that they were in talks with Fey about her appearing and playing Palin. As he put it at the time, "The whole world cast her in that role." Reportedly, Fey's own daughter looked at a photo of Palin and said, "That's Mommy." But with all the pressures Fey was under as writer and star of *30 Rock*, she hesitated.

> **Jovan Vitagliano (Jane Krakowski's personal hairstylist):** We were all in the room when [Tina] told the story of how someone had said to [Lorne Michaels], "You know, Tina Fey looks a lot like Sarah Palin." And [Tina goes,] "They want me to do Sarah. I don't have the time. I'm on this show—I'm writing, I'm work-ing, and then I have to give up Saturdays and rehearsal . . . I can't." But then she said yes.

As the clock struck eleven thirty P.M. on Saturday, September 13, 2008, the show delivered, with Fey as Palin alongside Amy Poehler as Hillary Clinton in the cold open of the show. Fey and Poehler had co-written the sketch with then–*SNL* head writer Seth Meyers. They addressed sexism in politics, with Hillary getting increas-ingly agitated about Palin's selection after Clinton's own primary campaign against then-Senator Barack Obama. But while there was sharp comedy at the heart of the sketch, the biggest response came with Fey quoting Palin and her infamous line that she could see Russia from her house, leading to a sustained applause break.

Fey was praised for capturing Palin's Alaskan accent, along with her manner-isms. Given the resemblance, her transformation into the governor was largely made with a combo of a hairdo and her distinctive glasses. Even the real Palin responded, noting that she thought the visual resemblance was perfect.

> **Don Scardino:** So she became this other, hyper-phenomenon playing Sarah Palin. And, God bless her, damaging that candidacy.

It was a shift for Fey, who despite her assertions that she's never been good at charac-ters, had found an impression that was widely agreed on as one of the best in *SNL*'s history. With the popularity of the sketch, Fey came back several more times—two weeks after her debut, she did a parody of an interview with Katie Couric where Palin had come off as poorly informed. Palin's performance was seen as so absurd that Fey quoted large portions of it verbatim, with little heightening needed to make it play as comedy.

Tina's pop culture domination brought ratings gold for *30 Rock* when it returned on October 30, just days ahead of the 2008 presidential election. Scardino described the extra attention from Fey's Palin as a "booster rocket" for *30 Rock*, combined with the show's Emmys success.

Chris George: She all of a sudden became the most famous woman in the world. It felt that way, anyway. We had to increase our security presence on set, everywhere. We absolutely had security at Silvercup [Studios]. There were certainly some people out there who were upset with Tina for her impression—she probably got some threats.

The season premiere set show ratings records with 8.7 million viewers, and that was topped again with its Christmas episode pulling in 8.9 million viewers. Its previous record was 8.1 million viewers, all the way back in the pilot, and the premiere was a 3.1-million-viewer jump over its Season 2 finale. Airing after *The Office* as that show continued to grow in popularity also helped as NBC created a modern Thursday-night dynasty.

The show would go on to break its own Emmy record this season, nominated for twenty-two Emmys. It was the most of any show, comedy or drama, period. Several actresses would be nominated for Emmys for their guest-starring roles this season—but they ended up losing to Tina Fey for her *SNL* Sarah Palin.

All that critical acclaim also paid off in earning a more well-to-do demographic of viewers, becoming the most popular show in that much-coveted-by-advertisers demographic.

Nate Corddry: It was really smart on [NBC exec] Kevin Reilly's part. He knew, if we have shows that don't have high ratings, but they have this classy credibility wrapped around them, they will survive in the long run. They cost nothing to make. A handheld camera, no lighting basically. You're only paying for the actors.

In the **Season 3 premiere, "Do-Over,"** Jack quickly tires of Washington, D.C., and makes a return to GE, reentering battle with Devon Banks. He sets about working his way back up, starting at the bottom with a job in the mailroom—at least until Kathy Geiss shows a sexual interest in him and he realizes he could help his former coworkers by getting back into power faster.

Marceline Hugot: I loved working with [Alec] because he's an *actor*, so he's great with actors. Even the scene where I had to put my hand up his thigh, as we were gearing up for it, he was like "All right, Marceline, bring it on. We're gonna do it. Don't be shy."

But Jack and Liz figure out how to manipulate Kathy and win her over without Jack getting more intimate with her, playing up an imaginary romance between Jack and Liz—and teasing a kiss. Soap opera fan Kathy Geiss was rapt, calling out for them to kiss.

Marceline Hugot: There wasn't a clue that it was going in the direction [of that "Kiss! Kiss!" scene], except I think Tina wanted her to finally have at least some kind of love passion amid all of this. It played around with the tension between Alec's and Tina's characters. It wasn't as if we sat around and said, "Well, what are some of the things that Kathy Geiss does?" It came more of "Well, she does any- and everything we want her to do, so what would be funny, and what would bring it together?" There's not ultimately a mean bone in her body except toward Will [Arnett]—toward her husband. Boy, did he ever earn it. (*laughs*)

But just as her character was peaking, with the writers finding new ways to build her from week to week, Arnett decided to leave *30 Rock*.

Marceline Hugot: When Will Arnett decided to leave the show and was ready to move on to other things, they wrote him off. There was nothing left to do for my character.

But Banks would pop up again down the road—as would Kathy Geiss.

While the show never wanted a baby to be the main character's driving force, this season also follows Liz exploring adoption. Children are clearly meaningful to Tina Fey—her production company Little Stranger's title card featured her daughter throughout the series, and Fey herself has said she sees herself as a mom first, writer second.

Picking up from last season, Liz meets with Bev (Megan Mullally) from the adoption agency. Her storyline parallels Jack's, each of them looking for a do-over—Jack in a grander way, taking another shot at his life's ambition (albeit at an accelerated pace as he moves to be quickly promoted), while Liz gets a more literal do-over. That's because Bev gets a head injury while touring the *TGS* studios, resetting her memory to the beginning of a visit that wasn't going particularly well for Liz. But when her memory resets itself once again, they're forced to give up and actually help Bev to seek medical treatment.

Episode 2, "Believe in the Stars," brought the show's history of pitting women and minorities against each other to the forefront. It starts in the DNA of the show with Tracy coming into *TGS* and usurping the power position held by Liz and Jenna, but it gets taken to a whole other level in this infamous episode.

Tracy ends up getting rich—well, richer than his character already was—thanks to the huge success of his pornographic video game, *Goregasm: The Legend of Dong Slayer*. Jenna's not having it, as she feels that she deserves credit for her moans she recorded for the game contributing to its success, so she sues Tracy.

Before things escalate too far, an NBC human resources mediator tries to resolve the situation. It's the first appearance of Jeffrey Weinerslav (Todd Buonopane), a character who's a trans HR rep and who makes several appearances over the run of the show. Their fight includes Tracy declaring that "white people stole jazz, rock 'n' roll, Will Smith, and heart disease!"

The fight ultimately leads to Jenna trying to show that white women have it worse, while Tracy tries to show that Black men have it worse, and the way they do so is problematic. In June 2020, this was one of several episodes of the show that Fey requested be removed from streaming platforms, as well as from syndication, due to the use of blackface.

"As we strive to do the work and do better in regards to race in America, we believe that these episodes featuring actors in race-changing makeup are best taken out of circulation," Fey wrote in a letter to the platforms that were either streaming or selling the show. "I understand now that 'intent' is not a free pass for white people to use these images. I apologize for pain they have caused. Going forward, no comedy-loving kid needs to stumble on these tropes and be stung by their ugliness."

But she stays away from actually using the word "blackface," seeming to obfuscate what was actually in these episodes.

Alan Sepinwall: For someone who has gotten a whole lot of critical acclaim, I don't think that Tina Fey generally responds that well to more pointed criticism. She writes it into the show, and it often comes across as a bit tone-deaf or overly defensive.

Don Scardino: I understand, Tina's nothing if she's not current—she's very much plugged into what's happening now. She always has been, and she still is. And she just felt the last thing she wanted, in this climate, was to be offensive.

Tina Fey: From the beginning, as soon as we had [Tracy Morgan, Alec Baldwin, and me], I thought we could deal with race, gender, and power.

Jesse Thorn: It's obviously a show, and this comes from Robert Carlock and Tina Fey, that above all else values a perfect joke. So at the end of the day, that was always going to be the tiebreaker. And there's a part of me that wishes that sometimes they had just used a different one of the pile of perfect jokes they had on their desk.

The episode includes Jenna going into blackface to make her point, while Tracy dresses as a woman and puts on white makeup—it's not quite as involved a costume as a movie like *White Chicks*, but, well, he goes for it.

Don Scardino: The argument at the heart of that episode is whether it's harder to be a white woman or a Black man. Both those groups feel like they have not gotten their just due in the world of white men, and that's true. That's what the show was about, and that's what it was taking aim at. I didn't see anything offensive about it.

Emily VanDerWerff: I don't want to say [pulling the episodes is] a bad idea, but it is an easy way that Hollywood patted itself on the back for dealing with the structural racism that is inherent to Hollywood without actually dealing with the problem. Just being like "Oh, here's some things we're going to put down the memory hole, and now we can pretend there was never an issue."

Don Scardino: In fact, I thought of it as championing the fact that these groups have been pushed to the side by white men—and that liberal white men were some of the worst, because they don't believe they're racist. So I thought, *Why? Why take it off?* But someone might just look at the surface of that, particularly Jenna dressed as a Black man, in about a thirty-second scene. And it's not even like she's doing some sort of *Amos 'n' Andy* dialect, or anything offensive.

The show would come back to characters doing an *Amos 'n' Andy* dialect with Jon Hamm a few seasons later during their second live episode—along with more black-face, both there and elsewhere.

Don Scardino: Toofer steps up and says, "That's racist! That's offensive!" We let every point of view be known, and we also know the point of view of the filmmakers, and where we come down.

The writers knew they were on the edge of taste at times. Jokes like Tracy talking about opening a school in Africa like Oprah in Season 2 would lead to a discussion among the writers. But the room would usually trust that if the joke seemed funny, and they could get away with putting it on TV, they should go for it. There may have been some differences if the show had a more diverse room, or more diverse show-runners. Out of twenty-nine credited writers over the course of the series, just four weren't white.

Ira Madison III (critic/TV writer): I don't think Black comedians are that interested in writing about blackface. A lot of liberal comedians think that tackling the taboo is what makes things funny. When you're tackling blackface, you really just have to ask yourself the question, why are you tackling blackface? What about it is giving you this need to be like "This is an issue I really need to tackle as a white person," because my question would be, maybe a Black person on staff would really want to do this joke and find a nuanced way to make it funny in a way that we haven't seen before. But you don't really have any Black people on the staff to do that.

Emily VanDerWerff: That's an issue anytime you have a show featuring a lot of characters of backgrounds that aren't represented in the writers' room. You could level that charge against *30 Rock*, you could level it against *The Office.* You could level it against any number of other programs, especially from that era, and probably right now.

Alan Sepinwall: The stories, especially the ones where Jenna is doing black-face, are meant to be a commentary on the awfulness of it, the cluelessness of white people. But I don't know that white creators should necessarily be the ones doing that kind of story to begin with. It's a bummer that the totality of these episodes have now been scrubbed from the internet.

Jesse Thorn: I don't think that removes those episodes from the Library of Congress. If it was a question of removing them from the historical record—if they ceased to exist, like *Song of the South*—that's a problem, because you need to be able to access problematic things to understand why they're problematic.

Prop master Kevin Ladson, who is Black, said that he thought the use of makeup here worked.

Kevin Ladson: That didn't bother me, because I understood the comedy behind that.

But he would go on to be deeply troubled by other episodes of *30 Rock* that chose to use blackface later on, with another featuring Jenna during Season 5 being the most upsetting. The show didn't face stronger criticism at the time, both due to the way our society has changed in the past decade and because of how funny the show was. The writing was so strong that there was a willingness—particularly among white audiences—to look past these issues. You also had Tina Fey as the face of the show, a breakthrough for women in entertainment, along with Tracy Morgan in the cast, helping to protect the show from criticism. But that also means this was a show that thought it was acceptable, in the 2000s, to use blackface multiple times.

The reason this show ran into problems was that the writers were trying to comment on race in what they thought was a positive, more enlightened way. It's far from the first show to suffer from problems around a lack of diversity and the way it treats characters that aren't white males.

Todd Buonopane: Any white person that is creating right now has to be brave enough to get it wrong, and then accept responsibility for getting it wrong. Thank god we had someone like Tina taking chances. But there are a few things she got wrong, and she would admit that.

It's hard—you watch *Cheers* now, and *Cheers* is still brilliant, but the sexual politics of *Cheers* are *very* complicated. The way they treat the women on that show is, *whoo*, it's rough. And that show doesn't attempt to say anything about race, because they were just writing about white people.

Other shows tried grappling with their past at the same time as episodes of *30 Rock* were being removed from streaming. Three shows that shared Thursday nights with *30 Rock* at some point during their run also had blackface episodes of their own that streaming networks tried to deal with in the summer of 2020: *The Office*, *Scrubs*, and *Community*.

Community's "Advanced Dungeons & Dragons" was pulled due to Ken Jeong's character, Ben Chang, wearing makeup resembling blackface while cosplaying as a dark elf. Streamers pulled a scene from *The Office* at the request of creator Greg Daniels. The episode involves Dwight celebrating a real Dutch Christmas tradition—which has widely been acknowledged as racist—and has a white colleague dress up as "Black Peter."

Daniels explained the decision at the time in a statement, which ended with Daniels saying, "Blackface is unacceptable and making the point so graphically is hurtful and wrong. I am sorry for the pain that caused." And *Scrubs* pulled episodes featuring Zach Braff's and Sarah Chalke's characters in blackface. Beyond NBC's own lineup, Netflix pulled the entire British comedy series *Little Britain* due to its blackface, and late-night hosts/Jimmys Fallon and Kimmel both apologized for past uses of blackface.

Showing what a delicate line that *30 Rock* and all of these other shows were walking, an episode of *The Golden Girls* was pulled where characters wear mud masks—clearly not blackface, though the white characters in the episode worry it might be perceived as such. That show features numerous other racist and problematic moments, from Blanche doing a stereotypical Black voice to jokes made about Dorothy being drugged and raped. The fact that the mud masks episode was the one that got pulled makes removal seem more like performative wokeness than actual thought about the troubling way that Black people, women, and many others have been presented throughout TV history.

Other recent shows that used blackface include *It's Always Sunny in Philadelphia* (which also made use of brownface and yellowface), *Mad Men* (which added a title card giving context for the episode's blackface), *Saturday Night Live*, and more. And HBO Max temporarily pulled the film classic *Gone with The Wind*, before adding it back with an intro video addressing the troubling way it depicted slavery.

There have always been troubling depictions throughout entertainment history, many of which continue to resonate in our culture, as far back as the potential antisemitism of Shakespeare's *The Merchant of Venice* and beyond. And satire like *30 Rock* was trying to do in several of its episodes that included blackface makes it likely that more moments like these will happen in the future. Satire often includes reflecting back ugly moments in culture so that people can more clearly see what is wrong with this behavior, reminded that practices like racism still permeate our culture. Doing so perfectly is perhaps impossible, and even more so when the voices behind it are from the same group as the perpetrators of the injustices.

Buonopane's OK with episodes of his that included blackface being removed from streaming.

Todd Buonopane: If I have to lose, what is it, thirty seconds of me on television, it's not a big loss to me. I do hope that, years from now, we are able to look at this medium the way we look at Norman Lear stuff from the seventies, where he was writing about inappropriate people. But that is not up to me. We have a lot of racial stuff to solve way before that. And to be honest, getting the entertainment community to listen is a heck of a lot easier than getting a lot of other communities to listen.

While Jenna's blackface was the most obviously controversial moment of the episode, there was also the issue of having a non-trans actor playing a trans man—and him being trans played as a joke, with the surprise delivery of this HR officer interrupting a fight between Tracy and Jenna with his exclamation of "Do you have any idea how hard it is to be an overweight transgender in this country?" The use of "transgender" as a noun is also something that likely wouldn't be done today.

Todd Buonopane: We are a wiser people now. And Jeffrey Weinerslav is a [transgender] man. I am not a transgender man.

Jesse Thorn: It was insensitive. And if there had been a gender nonconforming person with power around, they would have said, "Come on." I don't think they did it because they're hateful, but I also don't think that should be the standard.

When actor Todd Buonopane heard about a potential part on *30 Rock* for a character just named Jeffrey, no last name at the time, he was hyped. It was just a five-line role, but he was already a big fan of the show. Buonopane asked his agent to submit him for it, but his agent was reluctant to push for his relatively no-name client. Still, he did it, and relayed back that the casting people would see Buonopane—if he could get down to 30 Rockefeller Plaza by five P.M.

He went to audition, working to memorize it on the train on the way over. When it came time for him to perform, he knew that he did well. He ended up getting a callback the next day with Don Scardino at Silvercup Studios.

The audition room was full of the same actors who played funny weirdo parts that he'd see over and over at other New York auditions. When Buonopane auditioned, Scardino asked him if he'd like to do another take.

Todd Buonopane: I said, "No, I don't," because I did what I wanted to do. And he said, "I totally agree with you."

Tina Fey wasn't there, but Buonopane was excited, because he knew she would watch the tape of his audition. The next day, he fired the reluctant agent and walked in to sign with a new agent. As he signed with a new agent, he also booked the gig on the same day. Buonopane said that getting those five lines made him feel like he hit the jackpot.

Buonopane has since grappled with what it meant for him to play a transgender character. The fact that Weinerslav is a transgender man is referenced only in the one episode of the show, though the character would make further appearances, and Buonopane says that he wasn't trying to make fun of anything himself. *30 Rock* had already made multiple jokes in its first season derisively using the slur "tranny," though trans TV critic Emily VanDerWerff notes that the problem with trans depictions on network television goes far beyond *30 Rock*.

> **Emily VanDerWerff:** You look at the sitcoms that aired in the mid to late 2000s, and they all just have a host of transphobic jokes. *The Office* has some, but it doesn't go all in on it like *How I Met Your Mother,* especially. *30 Rock* has quite a few. There is a conservative streak to Tina Fey's humor that serves her well in a lot of ways. She's one of the best pure joke writers to ever live, but it also gets her into weird areas where she's like "Well, everybody can take a joke." In theory, yes, but I am much more likely to take a joke when I know where it's coming from, a place of someone who either understands my experiences intimately or has done the work.
>
> I don't want to see things get pulled off the air forever that have transphobic jokes in them, because then you're pulling off basically every comedy from before now—but also, who is to say?

Tina Fey may not have been coming from the most enlightened point of view at the time—in both a 2006 *Howard Stern* appearance and a 2008 *Playboy* interview, Fey criticized the appearance of Paris Hilton and others by comparing them with trans women, referring to them with the same anti-trans slur used previously on the show. Fey did go on to express regrets about the language she used when discussing Hilton.

> **Emily VanDerWerff:** A lot of my trans friends who are really into comedy are deeply suspicious of Tina Fey. It's that white woman over forty-five thing. As a white trans woman, even when they are supportive, you'll hear certain code words and certain joke structures within *30 Rock*, and especially within *Kimmy Schmidt*, that make me feel like "Oh. They haven't really bothered to think about the lived reality of being a trans person." They don't have to. I'm not saying that they can't write good comedy without doing that, but it's a lot harder to write comedy that doesn't seem like it's picking on myself and my siblings.

I want to read stories about trans people that are as complicated and messy and real as my own life, but they probably have to be written by trans people. At the same time, if I'm like "Oh, cis person, you can only write noble good trans people who do the right thing," that's boring. I screw up all the time. Every trans woman is Liz Lemon. (*laughs*)

One positive that Buonopane saw coming out of his role was getting to offer trans representation at a time when there weren't a lot of trans characters on television, particularly not in positive roles.

Todd Buonopane: I was in San Francisco, and people kept coming up to me on the subway and thanking me. Because there was no transgender representation, and I wasn't making fun of anybody. I have trans friends that are like "'Do you know how hard it is to be an overweight transgender?' while a funny line, really rings true to me."

While I have transgender friends that think me playing this part is OK, and what I did was fun, I'm sure there are people that are offended that I played it. And I'm terribly sorry about that. I think we finally have welcomed transgender people into our business, so we actually have transgender people to cast. We weren't doing that at that time. And hopefully, there are transgender kids that see themselves represented in media, and think that they can actually do that.

While none of my friends are offended by me playing that [part], and I'm proud of my work, I wouldn't even audition for that now. But it was described as a soft-spoken human resources [person]—it said "a transgender"—and it said, "but has an anger boiling under the surface." And I'm really good at the kind of awkward sweet guy trying to hold it together. In the film world, that's where I live.

Emily VanDerWerff: You have to work to make sure the representation you do doesn't reduce your characters in either direction to the body they occupy. A joke about a trans person being trans is bad, but so is a trans person being trans just to be there.

Buonopane didn't get a lot of direction. But he caught the attention of the writers, and they started rewriting his scene as he was performing.

Todd Buonopane: Because they liked the way I said "O-kay"—this kind of high-pitched "Okay." And so they might add more "Okays" in the scene, and almost every scene I ever did had some kind of "Okay" in it, because they liked the way I did that.

Buonopane also credits his popularity with people at the show to there being something enjoyable about seeing this gentle actor/character get aggravated, or putting him in uncomfortable situations. As he noted, this uptight, sweet, nerdy corporate character likely isn't used to dealing with people like Tracy Jordan and Jenna Maroney often, so he doesn't always know how to deal with it.

> **Todd Buonopane:** Leaving that first day, I saw John Riggi, and he was like "Great job"—I was like "Have me back!" That's so cheesy, but then they had me back a few times.

Beyond the controversy, the no-longer-streaming episode also featured one of the show's biggest guest stars of its entire run. The episode also features one of its most memorable *Star Wars* references, which would be called back to several times as the show continued, including at Liz's wedding. While Liz is trying to get out of jury duty—in Chicago, because she never changed her voter registration—she dresses up as Princess Leia to try to come off as a kook.

As she's on a flight back to New York, she takes a sedative given to her by Jack. This leads to her getting emotional and spilling her guts to one of Season 3's biggest guest stars. The writers had a handful of dream guest stars in mind from near the beginning, and this season they landed one of them: Oprah (no last name needed, but, you know, Winfrey). Scardino expressed regret that that storyline isn't available to be streamed any longer.

Winfrey played a version of herself sitting next to Liz—before it turned out to be a drug-induced hallucination, when the twelve-year-old girl Liz *thought* was Oprah turns up later as Liz tries to have her settle the dispute between Tracy and Jenna. And Oprah Junior actually ends up successfully mending fences.

Tina had been planting Oprah references in the show for a long time, with Liz identifying as an Oprah acolyte herself and Tina talking in interviews about how she wanted to spend time with Oprah. It was also a step up from when the show previously had Tracy play Oprah in drag.

> **Ken Eluto:** There were so many great guest stars over the seasons. I mean, in addition to the wonderful regular cast, it takes forever to scroll the IMDb pages.

The show clearly knew it was using a plethora of guest stars, and it made fun of that fact in **episode 3, "The One with the Cast of *Night Court*."** Jennifer Aniston made an appearance, still just a few years removed from the finale of *Friends*, and *30 Rock* handled it in the most *30 Rock* way possible: by having the episode revolve around the fact that it *also* featured the cast of classic 1980s sitcom *Night Court*. Aniston played Liz's ex-roommate/party girl Claire Harper, another in the string of "would this person actually be friends with Liz Lemon?" personalities à la Jenna.

The title pays tribute to the *Friends* "The One With . . ." episode naming convention, while not really being about their big *Friends* guest star. Jack has a one-episode fling with Claire, before finding out how wild she actually is when she plants a gun on him just for kicks.

Meanwhile, Tracy wants to cheer up Kenneth, who's upset about new gray NBC page uniforms due to his love for the traditional NBC blue page attire. Kenneth notes he's been wearing his page jacket since "nineteen . . ." before trailing off. He explains that the old uniforms were "timeless, practical, sexy," but that the new ones are an outrage. Given Kenneth's love for NBC's history, Tracy recruits Harry Anderson, Markie Post, and Charlie Robinson from *Night Court* to stage the wedding that Harry's and Markie's characters/will-they-or-won't-they couple, Harry and Christine, never got.

This season also gave us Jon Hamm and Salma Hayek as love interests (more on them later), Steve Martin, Alan Alda, John Lithgow, Peter Dinklage, and the aforementioned Megan Mullally. And of course, with her appearances as Sarah Palin, Fey brought her own special-guest-star-esque star power with her every week.

Episode 4, "Gavin Volure," featured Steve Martin as a rich, reclusive weirdo. Martin had previously played Tina Fey's boss in *Baby Mama*. They were in a mutual appreciation society, with Fey honoring Martin when he was given a lifetime achievement award by the American Film Institute, while Martin honored Fey when she won the Mark Twain Prize. He even hosted a live conversation with her when her book *Bossypants* was released. Both widely acclaimed for their sharp writing skills, their minds felt like a match.

But it was harder to work in the connection between Volure and Liz. She attends a fancy dinner at his estate, and he starts to act like he's pursuing her romantically. But it turns out that he's a con man who's actually on house arrest, and the potential affair quickly fizzles.

John Riggi: That was a tough one to write, because we crafted Liz Lemon as being like "I don't have relationships with anybody." So even though that wasn't a real dating relationship, she got pulled into Gavin Volure's world. I had to get help from the other writers because I just didn't know how to get in there with that one, and it still was tricky for me to really make that work.

Alan Sepinwall: They did a bunch of guest-star-driven episodes in a row— that felt a little tired. I think they wasted Steve Martin. I'm not sure how that happened.

John Riggi: Working with Steve Martin was such an honor and a treat. He is a very private person, [but] he was always open to everything. If we gave him anything to do, he'd be like "Oh yeah, great." But it wasn't like between takes we were just going to sit down and shoot the shit with him—that was not going to happen. And not in a mean way. I would have liked it better if I had a bunch of selfies with him, and I don't, but that's OK.

Episode 5, "Reunion," is best remembered for six legendary words: "I want to go to there." The show uses the phrase twice in the episode, nailing it into your brain. Fey credits her daughter, Alice, with being the origin of the phrase, with that perfectly delightful little-kid grammar.

Don Geiss also wakes up from his coma in this episode. Jack is initially elated, but when Geiss declares that he's not going to give up being head of GE after all, it sends Jack into an existential spiral.

"Reunion" digs in deep on the Jack and Liz relationship. As Jack mopes, he looks to get away from it all, but ends up getting snowed in with Liz at her twenty-year high school reunion. Without being constantly interrupted by Tracy and Jenna, there's a certain sense of melancholy to the episode.

They each have their identities challenged, with Liz learning that while she felt like the lonely nerd, everyone else saw her as a poison-tongued bully using her wit to poke at their deepest insecurities. Meanwhile, Jack is mistaken for one of Liz's classmates, Larry Braverman, and uses the opportunity to escape his life for a night. When Liz questions how Jack's managing to pass as one of her classmates, he explains, "Rich 50 is middle-class 38."

The West Wing's Janel Moloney has a small role here, showing up as Larry Braverman's ex and revealing that the real Larry has a son. *Gossip Girl*'s Blake Lively and Leighton Meester were originally set to guest star as Liz's classmates in a flashback, but those appearances fell through. It would have been a natural fit and an easy cameo—both shows shot at Silvercup Studios. Blake Lively's half-sister Robyn *did* guest star in the episode, playing one of Liz's classmates.

> **Beth McCarthy-Miller:** We were in this high school gym for three days, and we're shooting Friday. [Tina] left me at nine or ten o'clock at night, went to *SNL*—because it was the first time she was playing Sarah Palin—rehearsed that Friday night, went home, Saturday morning was in the makeup chair at *30 Rock* again for a seven A.M. call time. So she was probably in the makeup chair at five thirty, maybe six A.M., because she was also shooting the Oprah Winfrey stuff from a previous episode, because that was the only day Oprah was available. Then she left, went to *SNL*, did the first Sarah Palin on *SNL*—run-through, dress, and air. And then Sunday, I think she threw a birthday party for her daughter at her house.

Just hearing Tina Fey's schedule is exhausting.

In **episode 6, "Christmas Special,"** we get what is perhaps the most iconic episode for the dynamic between Jack and his mother, Colleen. While in Florida, he accidentally backs into her with his car. He's instantly beset by that special combination of strict mother guilt with Catholic guilt. And to make it worse, he later reveals that he waited eight minutes before calling 9-1-1.

The episode was based on a real story from the writers' room, with one of their nieces hitting a writer's mother with her car. They weren't sure if they could do the storyline because they weren't sure if the mom would be OK, but when she was fine, they decided this would be perfect for a Jack/Colleen Christmas story.

Jack ultimately brings Colleen to *TGS* and celebrates Christmas with her on a special holiday episode of the show, finally realizing how much she cared for him growing up. They sing a duet of "The Christmas Song" together for the special.

In **episode 7, "Señor Macho Solo,"** Jack falls in love with his mother's nurse, Elisa (Salma Hayek).

> **Alan Sepinwall:** Salma Hayek, for the most part, is not cast in comedies. If she is cast in comedies, it says "The Beautiful Woman Who the Funny Character Is Lusting After." I feel like Fey would see a comic potential in people that had not necessarily been exploited to its fullest extent.

Her character falls into a bit of a broad stereotype, with Mexican actress Hayek playing the Puerto Rican part with a thick accent. But the show finds strong jokes for her when they get away from the racial stereotypes.

At the same time, this episode confronts biased perceptions as the series often does: by letting its own characters look like dummies. Liz, still thinking about having a child, sees a boy on the street and pats his head—before realizing that's no boy, it's a man. Peter Dinklage plays Stewart, and is about to tell Liz off before she claims that she was trying to get his attention, and agrees to go on a date. But Liz can't help herself from treating Stewart as a kid, even though he actually seems like a match for Liz. He's a successful man who can also match her *Star Wars* reference for *Star Wars* reference.

But when they end up on the Brooklyn Bridge in an ending that riffed on the finale of the *Sex and the City* movie, Liz mistakes an actual little boy for Stewart—and Stewart shakes his head, realizing it's never going to work between them. He also gets to continue a *30 Rock* catchphrase. Starting at the end of "Fireworks," Jack and a stage monitor yell "Shut it down" at the end when they realize what a bad idea fireworks in Manhattan are. The phrase became a running joke on the show, both on-screen and behind the scenes, with the show's own assistant directors saying to shut it down. Here, Dinklage delivers it when he realizes it's time to pull the plug on this relationship.

We also get Tracy reminiscing about another of his classic films, noting that he was in a remake of *An Affair to Remember*, *A Blaffair to Rememblack*.

In **episode 8, "Flu Shot,"** the flu is starting to make its way through the *TGS* cast and crew—and Liz secretly gets to jump ahead of the line to get a flu shot before anyone else (an idea that recently became relevant again with the clamor for COVID-19 vaccinations). As the show continues, people get sicker and sicker. Director Don Scardino tried to capture the emotion of that in the way the episode was filmed.

> **Don Scardino:** Liz is trying to pretend she didn't get this shot boost from Spaceman. But the show almost becomes Liz's horror movie. As it progresses, we're shooting in our usual style, but as people get sicker and sicker, the camera starts to Dutch angle, twist more, and go lower. By the time she runs into the last guy who's well, Hornberger, he says, "Oh!" and she's just relieved—"Pete, it's you!" He sneezes—and when he comes back up, the whole thing turns into a horror movie.

The network also made the show cut a joke about the US government running out of flu shots because government officials thought that recent hurricanes were going to kill more people.

Tracy and Jenna want to think of themselves as humanitarians, so they decide to do something nice for the crew and to get them all hot soup. But their idea of getting soup for the crew is to tell Kenneth to do it. He explains that he can't, because all the other pages have gone home sick, but Jenna and Tracy can't comprehend the manual labor he's describing to them.

Kenneth tries to go step-by-step, but Tracy objects at every point, incredulous at the idea that he could go pick up soup himself. "With what? My arms?"

This show also has a surprise treat for Michael Bublé fans. As Jack and Eliza drag the somewhat out-of-it older man she's caring for, Mr. Templeton, around the city for the sake of their love, we get a crooner theme for him sung by Bublé. In their montage around New York City, much of it was shot on green screen to allow them to get more locations in during their limited schedule, especially given that the scenes involved Baldwin and his more limited availability. But the green screen use ended up being more trouble than it was worth, so the show decided not to make extensive use of the technique in later episodes.

The song was a payoff for Jack and Elisa—she'd marveled in the previous episode at Jack's large collection of Michael Bublé albums. Both Hayek and Baldwin were reportedly real-life fans of Bublé. (Your author is, too, as he has deeply uncool musical taste.)

The episode holds the remnants of a lost storyline from Season 1. The show had planned an episode about the cast and crew visiting the Hamptons. Whether they thought it reflected too much privilege, it wasn't relatable enough for a broader audience, or they just couldn't make it funny enough, they never ended up doing that story. The one joke that survived from that idea to Season 3: the tankort, a bathing suit with culottes and sleeves.

Tina Fey drew a rendering of the tankini/skort Frankenstein and handed it to *30 Rock* costume designer Tom Broecker, who constructed this mad imagining from Tina's mind. According to Fey, the actual suit proved popular with women on the crew thanks to its combination of comfort and coverage—the suit ended up in script supervisor Claire Cowperthwaite's hands for the summer.

Episode 9, "Retreat to Move Forward," was the first episode directed by Steve Buscemi, after previously appearing several times as Jack's personal PI, Lenny Wosniak. Jack takes Liz to a management retreat, inspired by the real management process utilized by Jack Welch at GE: Six Sigma. The real one is not as delightfully strange as the version championed by Jack Donaghy—though there *are* actually Six Sigma Black Belts.

In **episode 10, "Generalissimo,"** we meet what may be the most foolish person in a series filled with fools. While Dennis always called Liz "dummy," this season featured Liz's romance with the most handsome, biggest dummy of them all: Jon Hamm's Dr. Drew Baird. The *30 Rock* writers were big *Mad Men* fans.

> **Tina Fey:** A lot of times when we're writing we'll have an actor in mind and we'll keep referring to them. Like for this we said, "Then Hamm comes in, blah blah blah." And I kept saying, "You know, you guys, we probably aren't going to get Jon Hamm."

But it turned out to be easier for the show to land Hamm than it might otherwise have been, thanks to *30 Rock* shooting while *Mad Men* was on hiatus.

> **Tina Fey:** So I called over [to *SNL*] and asked them (*whispering*), "Hey, is that guy funny? Tell me the truth."

> **Jon Hamm:** When I was hosting *SNL* the first time, I got a phone call in my dressing room. It was after readthrough, and Robert Carlock said, "Oh, we had an idea—do you want to be on *30 Rock*, do you want to do this thing?" And I said yeah, I would. He said, "Well, do you want to hear what it is?" I said, "Nope, whatever it is, I'll do it." Then he pitched it to me anyway, and I thought it was funny.

The relationship starts innocently enough, with Hamm as Liz's new handsome neighbor. But the episode ends with her accidentally roofieing him.

It also features a Spanish soap opera with an evil character—the Generalissimo—who happens to look just like Jack, causing Elisa's mother to hate him, until he pulls strings to change the show and have the General fall in love with an elderly lady.

One thing this episode has come under fire for is that, at the same time as it was depicting Elisa as a rather broad character, the actor behind the Generalissimo is also portrayed by Alec Baldwin. And he's wearing makeup designed to make Baldwin look more Latino—a role for which he'd win an Emmy.

> **Jesse Thorn:** Spanish-language soap operas are such a clichéd premise, that even though they do a pretty good job of it, it's insensitive to say the least. And I think that their attitude toward Latinx characters in general is not as nuanced as it is toward African American characters—and it's not that nuanced toward African American characters.

For **episode 11, "St. Valentine's Day,"** *Community*'s Gillian Jacobs was initially up for the role of a date for Kenneth. That role, playing a blind woman, ended up going to actress Maria Thayer.

> **Gillian Jacobs (*Community* actor, *30 Rock* superfan):** I auditioned for an episode of *30 Rock* once, which would have been the crowning achievement of my career.

While writing this episode on a Thursday in November, the day before table read, the writers were working late into the night to get a joke involving Jesus and a bowl of soup just right.

> **Tom Ceraulo (writers' assistant):** We were hopelessly stuck on a crucial second-act scene in which Jack Donaghy sees the face of Jesus in a bowl of soup. Carlock was out sick with pneumonia. Tina, who'd joined us after a fourteen-hour day of shooting, was literally slapping herself to stay awake. Jack Burditt insisted that she go home and sleep, but she refused. There had been and would be later nights, but few that seemed as dire as far as getting a script ready. The mood was grim.

> **Kevin Ladson:** So we're sitting in the production meeting, and Tina says, "Oh, don't worry. Kevin will figure it out." Friday night I'm like "Oh my god, how do I figure this out?" And we were going to shoot it on Monday.
>
> It came to me in a dream—and sure enough, it worked. What I did was I had a thick soup, then I made a stencil, where I used pepper to create the Jesus. I go in on Monday, and I'm just so proud of myself—"Look, I made Jesus appear in a bowl of soup."
>
> Then Tina says, "Oh yeah, that scene's been cut." I said, "Oh my goodness. Well, I can guarantee you, next Thanksgiving, Jesus is gonna be in all the soups I serve."

This episode is also the beginning of Dot Com's interest in Grizz's romantic partner, Feyoncé, though Grizz himself doesn't know about his friend's feelings. It would ultimately pay off with Grizz and Feyoncé's wedding in Season 4.

In **episode 12, "Larry King,"** Tracy Jordan incites absolute panic throughout New York City during a guest appearance on *Larry King Live* when Larry asks Tracy for his opinions on current events. Which he should have realized was a terrible idea. It leads to markets crashing as Tracy continues to spew misinformation.

Things get so dire that Jack pops in a video that's meant to be played in the event of a global catastrophe, recorded decades prior by Don Geiss. As he watches it, Geiss provides his advice for what to do if the unthinkable has happened and capitalism is coming to an end, which Geiss attributes to either the Soviets or "something ridiculous, like a woman president." Geiss adds that he's recording this message in 1987, "but the message is timeless: Avoid the Noid!" The reference to the 1980s Domino's Pizza mascot proves unhelpful, but Jack is still able to weather the storm. After surviving the harrowing experience, he decides to follow his heart and pop the question, proposing to Elisa.

Episode 13, "Goodbye, My Friend," sees Liz's desire for a baby continuing to be amped up, with Liz befriending a pregnant teen and trying to adopt her baby—before the teen and her boyfriend are reunited through the power of terrible, terrible song. The episode was written by Ron Weiner, who became known for his talent at creating funny songs for the show.

This season marked another catchphrase taking off, at the expense of one of their cast. Poor, poor Lutz. While Liz isn't a fan of Frank, she's even less of a fan of Lutz and his lonely manchild failures. He's often well intentioned, but "Shut up, Lutz" became a signature line for Liz, as well as other members of the *TGS* crew.

This episode, built around *Harry and the Hendersons* references with Frank taking on the metaphorical position of the Bigfoot Harry, allowed Friedlander to once again explore his Bigfoot obsession as Frank.

Frank had several evolutions over the course of the show, where he would take on a different persona and style for an episode. This episode features Corporate Frank, complete with suit and eighties business shark ponytail.

Judah Friedlander: There were some girls I could tell really liked me the way I looked. People were telling me I should keep my hair that way, and I'm like no, not at all.

Stage legend Patti LuPone made her first appearance on the show here as Frank's mom, Sylvia—her own take on the Italian mother.

Patti LuPone (Sylvia Rossitano): Judah was terrific, really terrific. And because I am Italian, I really didn't have to do much thinking about it.

Sylvia reveals to Jack that Frank can't become a corporate lawyer, because of his family's ties to the mob. She slaps Jack.

Patti LuPone: And that was a hard slap, because he didn't move. I actually hurt my wrist.

Judah gets to put his Bigfoot knowledge to use as Jack tells Frank that the corporate lawyer life isn't for him, sending a hunched-over Frank heading back to the writers' room, à la Bigfoot returning to the forest.

This episode also marked writer John Riggi's first time directing on the show—he would go on to become one of the show's most prolific directors with a total of fifteen episodes under his belt by the end, the third-highest number behind Don Scardino and Beth McCarthy-Miller. By Season 4, he was directing more than he wrote.

John Riggi: From the beginning of my career—even on *Larry Sanders*, Paul Sims was like "Come down to the floor with me, I think you're good on the floor." I had directed a couple things in the past, and I liked it and thought I was good at it. I was good with the actors. So, when we got to Season 3, I asked Tina if I could start to direct. And to be really honest, the writers' room of *30 Rock* was an intense place to be, and we worked really late hours. Directing is hard, too, but I got to come home at eight o'clock at night and have dinner. That's not the reason I did it, but I honestly wanted to be able to say I wrote it, and I directed it.

It made me a better writer. I wish other writers would direct, because it gives you a perspective on your writing that you don't understand until you actually get it on its feet and go, "Oh, this scene would actually work better if this happened here."

Peter Agliata: He gravitated to the camera department almost right away. He's like "I don't know how you guys do this." He was constantly seeking us out, just hanging around joking with us, but quite often picking our brains. When it came his time to direct, we'd had a long, easy running relationship.

He came to the cinematographer and to me, and he's like "I'm going to need you guys' help. I'm going to rely on you so much." He's so smart, we already knew he was beyond needing help, but you're terrified doing a new thing for the first time.

Other directors have come to me in the past, where they're scared that they don't have a plan: "How do I come up with a plan? Shouldn't I know the shots or see it in my head?" Everyone's got this vision of the maverick, who visualizes it then executes it with brilliance. I always tell them, "Look, it's story." I told this to John: "Stage it truthfully."

Don't think about cameras and shots and coverage. Just move the people through the room the way you want, when you want, how you want to make your dramatic or your comic point. Then it's going to reveal itself to you.

In **episode 14, "The Funcooker,"** Liz once again tries using her Princess Leia costume to get out of jury duty. But this time around, she fails.

This was also the episode where one of the Writers Who Never Talk, Sue, gets her first actual lines after years as an extra—and when she does speak, we discover she has an absurd Franco-Dutch accent.

The real Sue is from outside of Philadelphia. Sue Galloway joined John Lutz using part of her real name for her character: Sue LaRoche-Van der Hout. Lutz and Galloway had also been dating before appearing on the show, and ended up getting married. See, *30 Rock* really does love a happy ending.

Also in this episode, Jenna finally finds her star vehicle. Well, a significantly discounted one, at least. While she was cast in a Janis Joplin biopic earlier this season, it's one without Joplin's life rights, or songs. She starts shooting the film, using pills from Dr. Spaceman to stay awake as she shoots the biopic at night and *TGS* by day.

But these pills are from the world's quackiest doctor, and it turns out they might kill her if she doesn't go to sleep. Spaceman tries knocking her out during a *TGS* taping, at which point Tracy drops trou and shows off his "funcooker"—which Kenneth had pitched as a name for a pocket microwave being marketed by GE, not remembering that he heard that term before from Tracy.

The short-lived run of Dr. Drew Baird as Liz's boyfriend comes to an end in **episode 15, "The Bubble,"** as Liz is confronted by his complete idiocy and the fact that all his success comes from his immense handsomeness. Jack explains the phenomenon to Liz, showing a photo to her of himself when he was younger and even more incredibly handsome. He describes it as a bubble, changing the way that you experience life and protecting you from reality, and he encourages Liz to enjoy living that life with Drew.

Years before Hannibal Buress's stand-up put Bill Cosby on the public hotseat, and even longer before he eventually faced charges and was convicted, this episode features a joke taking on Bill Cosby's alleged sexual assaults. When Jack tries to get Tracy to come back on the show after quitting, he has one of his employees do a Bill Cosby impression, with Cosby meant to entice Tracy to come back. Tracy's enraged response: "You've got a lot of nerve getting on the phone with me after what you did to my Aunt Paulette!" Buress was a writer for *30 Rock* as well, and it was an issue Fey went after Cosby for all the way back on *Weekend Update*.

The episode features a cameo from Calvin Klein (the father of *30 Rock* executive producer Marci Klein) offering Drew a job as an underwear model. And sharp viewers may catch Tracy dropping a couple of *M*A*S*H* references, calling Kenneth his "Radar O'Reilly" and telling him to rub his feet "until you hear a chopper coming"— just a few episodes before *M*A*S*H* star Alan Alda would show up on the program.

In another blending of reality and fiction, Jenna makes a plan to cut her hair and references "the Rachel," Jennifer Aniston's famous *Friends* haircut, after just having the actress as a guest star earlier in the season.

While Dr. Drew drives off on a motorcycle—badly—to end the episode, Hamm himself wasn't allowed to drive the thing due to safety and liability concerns. He's a star, after all. But his character would prove such a hit that, while his arc was over, he'd make a number of appearances on future episodes. And he would just get dumber from here.

Alan Sepinwall: Tina Fey writes for Jon Hamm better than anybody, other than maybe [*Mad Men* creator] Matt Weiner, ever has. I would love to see her make a comedy for him at some point. Hamm really blossomed when he was doing it.

Episode 16, "Apollo, Apollo," is centered around Jack's fiftieth birthday and his desire to find what made him happy when he was young. The double Apollo references come from Jack purchasing a model Apollo Lunar Module that he discovers made him happy in a video from his tenth birthday, along with Tracy's efforts to travel to outer space. While his colleagues doubt him, Tracy is determined to go to space—and in an attempt to keep the star happy, the show fakes a space launch for him. Along the way, Tracy asks, "What is this, Horseville? Because I'm surrounded by *nay*sayers. Wordplay!"

Jack wishes that he could see the world through Kenneth's eyes, and we discover that Kenneth sees everyone as Muppets. It's one of a number of Muppets-related bits on the show, including Kenneth showing up as a Muppet when seen on an HD camera in Season 4, culminating in Kermit the Frog appearing at the funeral of Jack's mother in the final season.

The episode also gave birth to the terms "jack" and "lizzing"—when Jack gets too excited, he vomits, as he did when receiving that gift as a child. And when Liz laughs too hard, she urinates, leading to "lizzing" being used as a term meaning a combination of laughing and whizzing.

The next week, Tina Fey's former *SNL Weekend Update* co-anchor would take up residence alongside her on Thursday nights in *Parks and Recreation*. The show had an even rougher first season than *30 Rock*, with the advice *Parks* fans generally give being "You can start with Season 2." The show would start out as an underdog, but ultimately contributed to a fondly remembered era of NBC Thursday-night TV and found its footing—with its ratings beating *30 Rock* in that show's later seasons.

In *30 Rock* **episode 17, "Cutbacks,"** Liz is confronted with having to cut the show's budget. Consultant Brad Halster (Roger Bart) is her nemesis, forcing the changes, and leads Liz to make a choice: using her sexuality to get him to change his mind. After sleeping with him and finding out the cutbacks are still happening, she gets mad—but Brad had thought there was an actual emotional connection, and feels used.

This all leads to the return of Jeffrey Weinerslav in HR, thanks to Liz's unprofessional behavior. She also faces a sexual harassment lawsuit. Weinerslav became a regular part of the NBC/Sheinhardt Wig corporate family, with Jeffrey always just a few floors away from the main characters if they wanted to write him in.

Todd Buonopane: When you have a group of people like they had on that show, you're going to need human resources a bunch.

While HR is generally designed to protect the corporation more than the employee, Buonopane said, he believes that Jeffrey is there because he wants to help people. But that he's ultimately controlled by his corporate overlords at the Sheinhardt Wig Company.

He also had the chance to work with both Tina Fey and Alec Baldwin several times in his *30 Rock* appearances, often being the one delivering a monologue at them due to the way someone at *TGS* has screwed up. Buonopane was thankful that he got to work with them directly, rather than having stand-ins while his scenes were shot—though he did always have to be filmed first.

Todd Buonopane: When they're choosing sides to shoot, they always shoot the least famous person first, so everyone else can be sure to know their lines—it's really scary.

When he was brought in for "Cutbacks," he didn't know that they already had his next appearance in mind.

Todd Buonopane: A PA came up to me after I finished—I only had one scene in "Cutbacks." And they said, "They wanted to invite you to the table read for the next one." I said, "Oh sure, that sounds so fun." Don Scardino came down to get me, and we're walking there, and I was like, "Oh, I'm just happy to get a free lunch." He goes, "Did they not tell you you're in the next episode?" And I said, "No!" He's like "You're only in this episode because you have a much bigger part in the next episode." I was like "Ohhhh! Great!"

Buonopane got to go to his first-ever table read for **episode 18, "Jackie Jormp-Jomp."** He sat down next to writer Kay Cannon.

Todd Buonopane: I'm like "Hi, I'm Todd," and she's like "I know, I wrote the episode." (*laughs*) The sweetness of Jeffrey is kind of like the sweetness of me when I walk onto a TV/film set, because I don't want to even . . . I mean, I *want* to eat the food, but I always want to be like, do I have permission to eat the food? I'm such a good kid.

Buonopane described his table read experience as one where everyone was both sincere and completely insincere. They laughed at the jokes because they were funny—but also because the network execs were watching over a video feed.

Todd Buonopane: I was terrified, because I was like, if I don't get a laugh on this, I will be cut from the episode. You just end up thinking the worst, but none of it is actually true.

In the episode itself, Liz is suspended from work thanks to her sexual harassment in "Cutbacks." She goes on to learn more about the lives of the idle women of means who don't need work in order to find fulfillment. Liz becomes enamored with their lifestyle of day-drinking, thinking she's found a new, perfectly valid way to live her life.

She initially tries to get back to work, due to her love of her job, which includes her going through group counseling sessions with Jeffrey Weinerslav. Liz is finally being allowed back, with Weinerslav awarding her a certificate for completing her harassment training. But she starts freaking out as he describes the stress that she'll be facing once she starts working again.

Todd Buonopane: When we shot Tina's side, I had to sit on a box, start the monologue, then lean over ninety degrees and keep talking so the camera could go past me. I was like "This is *hard!*" That's when Tina taught me that, if it's not my coverage, it doesn't even matter if I say the right words. She said, "I'm still trying to teach Tracy that, and it's his third year of the show."

Buonopane enjoyed getting to bring more of the character's gentle humor to the show in this, his third appearance.

Todd Buonopane: He's actually incredibly straitlaced. The fact that he thinks, someone that wants to return to work—now *that's* a good joke. His jokes are just like Ziggy calendars.

People at *30 Rock* loved Buonopane so much that one of the show's editors came down to set to tell him how much she loved editing him—and when he gave his sexual harassment seminar, she insisted on being one of the sexual harassers.

Todd Buonopane: Guest starring on TV is stressful and awful, but everyone on *30 Rock* was always very kind. No one ever made you upset or nervous. If anything, it was Tina sitting across from you while we were rehearsing, and she had to approve a bunch of props, and just say, "I'm not going to be fun for you today, I'm sorry," because she had so many other things to do.

Liz ultimately returns to work after finding out that the women she's been spending time with are in a secret fight club—that's where they actually get their joy from.

The episode marks the end of Jenna's efforts to play Janis Joplin—the movie ends up being a hard sell because Sheinhardt-Universal never acquired the rights to Joplin's music, or her life rights, and instead name the character "Jackie Jormp-Jomp." Jenna is set to appear on Nickelodeon's Kids' Choice Awards, to which she agrees to set aside her feud with *That's So Raven*'s Raven-Symoné for one day, "but she knows what she did." But when the awards show accidentally includes Jenna in its "In Memoriam" montage, Jack plots to use the publicity to sell the film. It almost works, but as *TGS* hangs a tribute poster to the deceased Jenna that includes her *actual* birth year, Jenna refuses to play dead and reveals that she's still around, keeping her true age a secret and ruining the publicity stunt.

Instead, the Jackie Jormp-Jomp movie must live only in our hearts.

This episode was also Tracey Wigfield's first episode with a written by credit, co-writing it with Kay Cannon. Wigfield had started as a writers' assistant in the second season, but quickly rose at the show. She'd become a regular part of the writing staff in the fourth season.

Jon Haller: She had this meteoric rise on the show from assistant to co-writing the finale with Tina. And Tracey is her own force of nature

Bellamy Forrest: It's the real American Dream, right? You put the work in, you work your tail off, you commit one hundred percent, and look how far you can go.

She would ultimately write Liz Lemon's wedding episode, as well as create the NBC show *Great News* with Fey and Carlock as executive producers, before later delivering a critically acclaimed reboot of *Saved by the Bell*.

In **episode 19, "The Ones,"** Tracy reveals a softer side of himself, telling Jack that he's never actually cheated on his wife, despite his big talk—but that he *is* a high-functioning alcoholic. When he meets women at the club, he just hands out Brian Williams's phone number—we get to see Williams picking up a call from one of the women who wants to get together with Tracy, and Williams actually seems pretty into it.

As Jack purchases an engagement ring with help from Liz, she drops a ring and goes to hunt on the floor for it, her butt sticking up in the air. The jewelry salesman uncomfortably describes her as "spirited. Like a show horse." He adds that Jack's a lucky man, before Jack clarifies that she's not the bride and gets out a photo of Elisa. The salesman apologizes and takes Jack to the *real* showroom.

When he goes to be with Elisa, she ends up revealing a dark past as her anger fuels her to be jealous of Jack's relationship with Liz. This marks the end of her arc, the last appearance of Elisa until the series finale. On commentary for the episode, Jane Krakowski and Jack McBrayer both acknowledged the somewhat blunt racial lines written here—including a shocked Liz yelling "Puerto Rican!" when she walks in to find Elisa in her office. The point of the joke is that Liz is showing her white privilege—Elisa calls her out for that reaction—but with how our culture has progressed since then, there would likely be a bigger reaction to these words. Another line from Liz to Elisa: "How are you so quiet when your parades are so loud?"

Jack delivers a cocky callback to a line he delivered in "Reunion" about how old someone seems if they're rich versus if they're poor, telling Liz, "I'm fifty. To put it in perspective, that's like thirty-two for ladies."

Elisa ultimately explains that she murdered her first husband in a crime of passion after finding out that he had cheated on her, with the reveal including a folk song providing a grandiose version of the murder in another quick-cut musical number.

The episode also features another of the show's popular catchphrases: Liz singing that she's "working on my night cheeeese" to the tune of Bob Seger's "Night Moves" as she lies on her couch in a Slanket, eating from a block of cheese. The ultimate in comfort.

But getting the rights to "Night Moves" for that fleeting joke cost NBC a pretty penny. The line cost NBC around $50,000, according to composer Jeff Richmond, and the network wasn't particularly happy.

The episode made fun of how fans would constantly accuse the show of using product placement when it wasn't, after initially building product placement into a storyline. When Jack barges into Liz's office, she's wearing a Slanket and cries, "It's not product placement—I just like it!"

One of the weirder ongoing jokes of the show starts to become more explicit this season: that Kenneth is, somehow, immortal and/or of an age much more ancient than his youthful looks may portray. He reveals here that his real name—just like that of Don Draper with Jon Hamm's secret past on *Mad Men*—is "Dick Whitman."

John Riggi: Robert [Carlock] was obsessed with this Kenneth character who seemed to be immortal. The way we were building this was always like, OK, here's this kind of goof-ish, oafish, backwater character who doesn't really seem to be on the ball. And you've seen that bumbling kind of character before. So, what could we say about that guy that would be surprising?

Jesse Thorn: He becomes more and more important as the years go by, simply because [the writers] realize that with someone who is that sweet, you can make them do anything on screen and have it feel relatable and credible. So they take the idea of "cornpone hick," and they take it to the most insane, obscene edges of madness.

That's what's also so great about Tracy Morgan. You can have him do anything, say anything, and it will make sense, because he is saying it, because he is so grounded in insanity, and so obviously a sweet guy. You would love Jack

McBrayer if he was talking about how he had dismembered your mother, so they're like, what are the most bizarre things we can have him say and do, with the simple premise this guy loves NBC and is a hick?

There's something to the fact that he has the uniform as well. He has these magical golf caddy qualities, and you realize, oh, we can *Bagger Vance* the heck out of this guy.

John Riggi: There was always a little bit of horror in the things we were trying to do. Like, oh my god, is he like *The Walking Dead*? A typical *30 Rock* joke would be if Kenneth would tell a funny joke and he'd start laughing, but all of the sudden he had these razor teeth. Then you'd look again and they'd be gone. Because we'd like to give the audience a sense that Kenneth isn't who you think he is.

In **episode 20, "The Natural Order,"** Tracy and Liz fight over which of them is getting preferential treatment—Tracy for being a star, or Liz for being the boss. They wrote a gibbon into this episode as Tracy's replacement for himself at rehearsal, which ended up becoming an accidental ripped-from-the-headlines storyline with Jenna getting attacked by a monkey.

Tami Sagher: That was another all-nighter, and then we got out, and literally that morning, the monkey attack where the woman's face was torn off happened. It was such a bizarre confluence—I remember being like "We have our fingers on a very fucked-up pulse of America." And also, the panic of "Can we still do this?" Because we worked very hard on it. Our messed-up writer brains were completely in line with a rabid monkey.

The episode ends with an event that inspires Jack to search for his biological father: His mother, Colleen, mentions that her husband left her from the spring of 1957 until returning and asking her to go see *Some Like It Hot* with her. But since that movie didn't come out until 1959, and Jack was born in 1958, Jimmy Donaghy couldn't be his real dad.

Episode 21, "Mamma Mia," features the beginnings of another of the show's catchphrases: "That's a dealbreaker." It was an obvious breakout joke for the program. In the world of the show, it would ultimately go from a hit sketch starring Jenna to a hit book and talk show for Liz.

Alan Alda (Milton Greene): I wondered when I saw this if they were getting two birds for the price of one, because they're getting the great joke about the dealbreaker on the show-within-a-show, but they got their own catchphrase.

While Jack begins a search for his real father, Tracy introduces his allegedly illegitimate son—who seems to be far too old to actually be Tracy's kid. Though it leads Liz and Pete to speculate about how old Tracy actually is, guessing that maybe he's secretly sixty. As Liz puts it, "He can't rap, he has diabetes, a lot of his friends are dead . . ." Pete notes that he falls asleep in chairs, doesn't know how to use computers, and is always mad at the TV. Toofer adds that his favorite show is CBS's *NCIS*, to which Liz responds that Tracy might just be seventy.

Jack finds three candidates who could potentially be his father, but all signs point to Milton Greene in what Liz labels a "Mamma Mia," with Jack arranging meetings with all three possibilities. Of the other candidates, one had his genitals blown off in World War II, and the other is Korean. Liz tries to relate to Jack and, pushing the importance of reconnecting with his real dad, awkwardly offers a lesson from her family in the *Sims* computer game: "When a child doesn't see his father enough, he starts to jump up and down, then his mood level will drop until he pees himself."

When Jack reveals to Greene that he's likely Jack's father, Greene embraces him—and explains that it's great news, because he needs a kidney transplant. Alda had worked with Baldwin before on *The Aviator*.

> **Alan Alda:** Almost the whole impact of that character I played was in one line. "I need your kidney!" When I read the script for the first time, I thought it was irresistible. Monumental egotism. You know where Alec's character gets his.

> **Kevin Ladson:** [Alan] would spend his lunch hours telling stories, and he'd have five of us sitting at his heel, just listening to his time in the industry and people he worked with.

His storyline crescendos into the season finale featuring a telethon for one man, **episode 22, "Kidney Now!"** It includes a joke referencing a classic scene from Alda's *M*A*S*H* involving a chicken and a baby. What was a deeply emotional moment on that program gets played for inside joke laughs here, and Alda wasn't a fan of making fun of that original scene.

> **Alan Alda:** That *M*A*S*H* scene, which I wrote, meant a lot to me. Something like it had happened in two wars that I know of. So I wasn't crazy about the joke. But I decided to be a good soldier and say it anyway. Actually, when I think about it, comedy has a license to poke its nose into pretty much anything, even things that are held dear. We need funny.

As he's trying to figure out what to do, Jack explains that he has "the entire liberal media establishment at my disposal. The same manipulation machine that got people to vote for Barack Obama and donate all that money after Rainstorm Katrina." Jack abuses his power to hold an epic telethon to save the man he believes may be his biological father.

> **Alan Alda:** I always enjoy working with Alec. I think we'd have fun working together on the stage sometime. He's really there when you talk to him. When

[Alec and I] run into each other now, he calls me Dad. If he does it again, I'm cutting off his allowance.

They share father–son moments in the episode, including accidentally playing catch, tossing a ball back and forth.

The episode leads to an elaborate "We Are the World" spoof featuring a cavalcade of musical stars calling for the gift of a "Kidney Now!" (Complete with exclamation mark.) The musical luminaries include Elvis Costello, Sheryl Crow, Adam Levine, the Beastie Boys, Clay Aiken (we still cared about *American Idol* and its Season 2 runner-up at this point), and many more. And it was all to record a song about Greene, "He Needs a Kidney."

Due to how far behind schedule they often are by the end of the season, the script was completed about a week before being shot—and Tina Fey's assistant, Eric Gurian, managed to book all of this talent in that time. As the episode got closer, members of the crew felt an energy and excitement about the big performance

Don Scardino: When they wrote this "We Are the World" idea out, and we started getting people—one after another, all these huge music stars came, because they were all fans of the show. And we pulled it off in a day. In the morning, Jeff Richmond was pre-recording, first the orchestra, then the singers. Then, the end of that day, I got them all for two hours—I think it was the last day of the season, shooting-wise.

We had scenes with Mary J. Blige, Michael McDonald, Clay Aiken, and Elvis Costello in Jack's office. They were all so happy to be there. I said to Michael McDonald, "You know, I've been a fan of the Doobie Brothers forever, I've been a fan of your voice forever, so to get to work with you is such a thrill." And he said, "Are you kidding me? I'm finally cool in my house. I have kids who don't care that I'm in the Doobie Brothers, who don't care that I had million-selling records. But when they heard that I was going to be on *30 Rock*, finally Dad was cool."

It was another callback, the show living its dreams in success—they were making Michael McDonald jokes back in Season 1. Tina couldn't believe they got him to show up, due to how many jokes they'd made mocking him over the years. Norah Jones was among the collection of stars that brought this ridiculous song to life, as well as getting to pretend to be drunk while doing so.

Norah Jones (guest star, musician): They just had us all come pre-record our part there in the studio right before we shot it. I was really nervous but also really excited. It was my dream come true, doing a joke. My dream of my whole life was to be on *Saturday Night Live*, since I was a kid. Maybe I was taking my part too seriously. I think I did have a bottle of vodka in my dressing room.

Bellamy Forrest: There's no other show, besides *Saturday Night Live*, that's getting that kind of talent in there. We had campers, and we had to organize dressing rooms all over the building—just random rooms that we had to rent for that.

Norah Jones: I don't think [Tina] knew who I was. Because I had just for some reason cut my hair short and dyed it blonde for the first time in my life. So I was a little incognito.

Tina Fey: This whole day, I kept thinking that I wanted Norah Jones's haircut, and then I realized what I wanted was Norah Jones's face, and that was never going to happen.

Sheryl Crow joked that this many huge music stars wouldn't turn up for an *actual* charity.

Tina Fey: If it had been something really for good, they would have been like "*Aah*, I'm not doing it." But because it was actually a complete waste of time, they showed up.

Norah Jones: Yeah, it's kind of true.

The show did something good for those suffering kidney problems with this episode, beyond raising awareness—the "He Needs a Kidney" music video was released on iTunes, with proceeds going to the National Kidney Foundation.

Wyclef Jean pranked the cast and crew by taking the issue behind the fundraiser quite seriously. Jeff Richmond was teaching the song to the show's cavalcade of guest stars, with groups of three coming in to record their parts. Wyclef was recording alongside Michael McDonald and Steve Earle.

Tina Fey: In the middle of it, so deadpan, [Wyclef] just goes, "You know what? I can't do this. I have a friend who needs a kidney, and this is F'd up." And started to walk out, and about a hundred people in the room were like (*gasp*). Jeff was like "Well, it's gonna be for charity," and then [Wyclef] walked ten feet, and was like "Aaah, I'm just messing with you." And you felt everyone's butt just relax.

The kidney issue was one that affected the show's actual cast—both Tracy Morgan and Grizz Chapman received kidney transplants in real life. That wouldn't come until later, but the issue apparently influenced the show's storylines even here.

Grizz Chapman: I can't say that it was all about me, but I won't deny it. Because it was so close together, and then me and Tracy Morgan were going through our issues at the time.

John Riggi: Nothing happened in the real world that didn't affect us in some way when we wrote the show. So the "Kidney Now!" thing, I'm sure, came out of how we were all feeling about Tracy.

They'd also been making jokes about diabetes running in Tracy's family since Season 1.

Grizz Chapman: I thought it was amazing that [the writers] would bring that type of attention to a situation that needed that. Because, in today's society, people don't take things seriously until it's knocking on their door. A lot of Americans don't even know that they're going through those issues. So that really hit for me, hit home for Tracy, and hit home for a lot of other celebrities.

The episode saw Tracy Jordan getting an honorary diploma after dropping out of high school, based on Tracy Morgan also getting an honorary diploma from the high school he dropped out of. But the emotional heart of the show was the giant musical number.

The idea was likely meant to serve as a ratings stunt for the actual *30 Rock*, but it didn't end up drawing big numbers—the episode was the second lowest-rated of the season, with 5.7 million viewers. The show had peaked when it came to the size of its audience, with ratings declining in each subsequent season.

But things were looking up for Liz and Jenna, with both becoming bigger stars—Liz's work on *Dealbreakers* would give her a star opportunity, while Jenna would follow up *Jackie Jormp-Jomp* with an international release. Meanwhile, Jack's power would decline as an old enemy returned to exert his own power. And both the real and fictional shows would get some new blood, while saying goodbye to the corporate power of GE that had kept the lights on all these years.

SEASON 4

(2009–10)

Selling NBC, a New Cast Member, and the Quest for the EGOT

As the show returned for its fourth season, the series had just won the Emmy for Best Comedy for the third time, along with three other Emmys, and set a record with twenty-two nominations. This year also saw Tracy Morgan, Jane Krakowski, and Jack McBrayer nominated as supporting actors. Tina Fey wouldn't get a repeat win as an actress, but Alec Baldwin picked up another Emmy for his work in "Generalissimo." And the writing was so outstanding that the show not only won, with writer Matt Hubbard taking home an Emmy for "Reunion," but his competition in the category included three other episodes of *30 Rock*.

While the Tracy Jordan character might have started working toward an EGOT awards quadfecta this year, the show itself dropped this season both in the ratings and in critics' estimation following an outstanding Season 3. The season premiere would draw 6.4 million viewers—up from the 5.7 million that the Season 3 finale drew, but significantly down from the 8.7 million viewers it'd had for its season premiere a year earlier amid the hype for Tina Fey as Sarah Palin on *SNL*. Reviews remained largely positive, but it's the season with the lowest Rotten Tomatoes score, with just 72 percent of critics rating it favorably—that compares with 92 percent in Season 3 and 94 percent in Season 2.

> **Jesse Thorn:** The funny thing about *30 Rock* is that it came just late enough that intensity of audience, plus Tina Fey's celebrity and Alec Baldwin's celebrity, were enough to make it through all of those years. If it had gone on TV five years earlier, when the definition of a hit sitcom wasn't dropping by 5 million viewers per year, it could never have outlasted *Studio 60*.

It was known heading into Season 4 that GE was considering selling off NBC to Comcast—everyone was wondering what would happen if the deal went through. But critics didn't seem to take strongly to the increasingly inside baseball jokes of the show, and episodes this season were seen as being more uneven than the extremely high levels that Seasons 2 and 3 had reached.

Scott Adsit: The reason it stayed *on* the bubble is that you could always rely on it. There are no really bad episodes of *30 Rock*. And thankfully, the characters were intelligent enough that you want to spend more time with them. What I find is, if characters on the show are trying to seem smarter than me, rather than talking down to me like I'm a dummy, then I want to spend more time with them. The smarter people on the show—Liz and Jack—that's who I want to spend time with, because they will have a great point of view that is thinking on a level I wish I could think on.

The episode "Lee Marvin vs. Derek Jeter," which came in the latter half of the season, hit an all-time series low of 4 million viewers, breaking low ratings records set in the show's first season. The season would end up averaging 5.9 million viewers, good enough to make it eighty-sixth in the Nielsen rankings for the year. It also received fewer award nominations than the record-setting Season 3. There were still plenty to go around, but *30 Rock* didn't win in any of the categories it was nominated for in Season 4.

And while there were still plenty of guest stars this season, the show aimed to reduce them and move away from what was seen by some fans and critics as stunt casting. They wanted to take the chance to grow their own cast—among the beneficiaries was John Lutz, who started out as an extra before getting promoted to the main cast this year.

The season brought on an influential crop of new writers. Vali Chandrasekaran, who would go on to be an executive producer on ABC's *Modern Family*, was coming on in just his second TV job ever. He was following a stint writing for NBC's *My Name Is Earl*, interviewing alongside his friend Steve Hely. They'd been classmates at Harvard, writing for famed school comedy magazine *The Harvard Lampoon*, and had written a book together—*The Ridiculous Race*, about the comedy writers racing one another across the globe. It was an *Around the World in 80 Days* for our time. Their dash through TV writing continued with both being hired.

Vali Chandrasekaran (writer): It was a really intimidating group of people, because everyone was really funny, really skilled. To enter that, there's definitely a feeling of "Don't mess this up. Don't screw up the show." I was fortunate that I started with a bunch of people that were new at the same time, so we had each other, and I got along with everybody. It went as well as it could have gone, but definitely, you leave work on the first day, and there was kind of a "Welcome to the NFL, kid" moment in the elevator.

He was also able to bring experience from the corporate world, working as a business strategy consultant before becoming a TV writer. It was something he spoke with Fey and Carlock about a lot before being hired to write about the fake corporate world of *30 Rock*.

Vali Chandrasekaran: I spent two years in that world, and I just hated it. I thought it was so stupid. One time we were talking about products that we had helped clients make that were really successful, and one of them was these DVDs that you could buy when you were at CVS and checking out. It was your favorite moments from movies, a huge supercut—this was before YouTube. Not all of *Jerry Maguire*. I was thinking, *Well, those moments are great because you build to them.* It seemed to be just missing the whole purpose.

Meanwhile, Steve Hely brought a literary eye to crafting jokes.

Jon Haller: He would have these very dense jokes. Now I work on a multi-camera show, and writing jokes for that, you have to write a joke that can hit an audience in the back row, so it has to have this succinct nature. Whereas *30 Rock*, you could have all different kinds of joke. You could have these literary jokes, these completely dense wordplay jokes, cultural references, cutaway humor. What Robert and Tina did was they had a variety of writers who could provide all those things.

Jon Haller, who came on as a writers' assistant, would write two episodes of the show and go on to be a writer for *Last Man Standing*.

Jon Haller: I ended up reading all of the scripts for the first three seasons before I started. And that was actually ideal, because I could digest the show at my own speed. I was allowed to enjoy the seven jokes that were on a page in my own time, versus you hear the third one, you're laughing, you miss the fourth and fifth one, and then you maybe hear a little bit of the sixth one, and you're on to the next page. When you read a script, it's a different experience, and you have a much higher appreciation for it.

Vali Chandrasekaran: The first year is always terrifying on a new show. You're really trying to just learn what [the other writers have] done.

Haller even got to fly out with the rest of the team for the Emmys, right after being hired on the show.

Jon Haller: I came in out of nowhere, and I was like "Really? I'm getting to go to LA? They're flying us out?" What was so funny is I had to sit next to Grizz and

Dot Com during the Emmys ceremony, and they are large men, so it was a very small seat I had sitting next to those guys.

This fall was also the beginning of one of the network's most critically praised Thursday-night comedy lineups, with the addition of freshman show *Community*. Its tone was somewhere in between the biting joke-heavy ride of *30 Rock* and the hey, can't we all ultimately get along vibe of *Parks and Rec*.

> **Alan Sepinwall:** Of the four shows that were in that classic NBC lineup of *Community*, *Parks*, *The Office*, and *30 Rock*, I probably had more of an emotional investment in the others—but more often than not, *30 Rock* was the one that I would wind up laughing the most and the hardest at.

In *30 Rock*'s **season premiere, "Season 4,"** Jack tries to figure out how to crack getting the Middle American audience to watch *TGS*. One part of his plan includes encouraging Jenna to get back in touch with her country roots. This leads to one of the show's great musical contributions: her NBC promo advertising "Tennis Night in America," trying to convince people that tennis is hella country. As Jack sets about trying to broaden the show's appeal, Josh, frustrated by the new competition, quits the show.

> Jane Krakowski told *USA Today* at the time, "Even though the (premiere) episode starts with us trying to appeal to the heartland of America, in my heart of hearts I don't think *30 Rock* will ever be that show. I think we've gotten used to not getting good ratings."

The episode also features Kenneth discovering the giant corporate bonus that Jack gets while the pages have their overtime frozen. The incident followed a controversy earlier that year over AIG execs getting huge bonuses at the same time as the country was going through 2008's Great Recession, with AIG itself getting large taxpayer bailouts. And it's a storyline with echoes in how some large companies took COVID-19 pandemic relief money while average Americans continued to suffer.

Kenneth leads a page strike that seems to incorporate elements from the real-life Writers Guild strike—the writers had enough distance at this point to make it a storyline. Just like with the writers, the pages don't get much in the end beyond a moral victory, with Kenneth accepting Jack admitting he's a "big ol' liar" to end the strike.

And as part of the show's endless obsession with food, this episode also includes Liz describing the commercial for one of her favorite snacks, Cheesy Blasters. She sings the theme: "You take a hot dog, stuff it with some jack cheese, fold it in a pizza—You got Cheesy Blasters!" She adds that all the kids in the commercial say "Thanks, Meat Cat," and then a wave of embarrassment falls over Liz as she explains that Meat Cat then flies away on his skateboard. We'd go on to see Meat Cat appear later this season in a dream sequence and, somehow, riding in a non–dream sequence elevator with Jack.

In **episode 2, "Into the Crevasse,"** Liz faces haters while on the way to *Dealbreakers* success. Her book, based on the hit "Dealbreakers" sketch, gets a negative response from the different types of guys that she warned women to stay away from. As he looks Liz in the eyes, a bookstore employee (played by comedian Jon Glaser) tears apart a cardboard stand-up of Liz after pointing out where it says, "If your man is over thirty and still wears a nametag to work, that's a dealbreaker."

Her warnings have also managed to ruin relationships for many of her coworkers, from Pete and Tracy to Subhas, the janitor. It's in the tradition of dating books like *The Rules*, though it may have been a play on the hot dating book of 2009: *He's Just Not That Into You*. Tracy complains that a book hasn't given him this much trouble "since *Where's Waldo* went to that barber pole factory."

> **Beth McCarthy-Miller:** Subhas was the Silvercup [Studios] janitor. Originally, he had one line in an episode I did. You know where he came in and he's like "*You* are the dealbreaker," and he threw her trash on the ground? Well, we had a bunch of actors come in and do it. And they were totally overdoing it. So, Tina and Robert are like "Maybe we should just see if Subhas can do it." He was really just natural and funny.

> **Vali Chandrasekaran:** We had people audition, and we asked him to also audition. He gave the best audition, and was really great in it.

> **Beth McCarthy-Miller:** At *SNL*, all the writers would be there all night. They knew all the night janitors, all those people that have the thankless job of cleaning up after everybody overnight. There was one who was a real character, her name was Janie—she was so funny and so sweet. Everyone had such a soft spot in their heart for Janie and the other people that worked overnight at *SNL* that Tina started writing that stuff into the show, and Robert, too.

Will Arnett makes his return as Devon Banks here, now working in the Obama administration after befriending Obama daughters Sasha and Malia and becoming their gossipy pal. He brings in government oversight, pushing for the conservative Donaghy to accept government bailout money. Their verbal sparring in this episode includes a debate over whether cold pizza or hot pizza is better, with Banks explaining that revenge is a dish best served cold, like sashimi, or pizza. Jack declares the idea that cold pizza is better than hot pizza as "insane," while Banks extols the virtues of a cold pizza the morning after ordering. To be fair, they both make strong cases.

Jack relates a story to Liz about going "into the crevasse," where you actually escape by going *deeper* into the problem, as Jack did in 1994 after he fell into a crevasse and hurt his leg while ice climbing. He went back to camp and told the person who cut his climbing line, TV news anchor Connie Chung, that she did the right thing. In the present, Jack metaphorically goes into the crevasse by accepting the bailout money and the subservient position to Banks that this puts him in. Robert Carlock compared the storyline to the "car czar" in the Obama administration at the time, who helped lead the auto industry through the Great Recession. Banks was that, but for network television.

In order to make up for causing Tracy's marital problems, Liz tries going into the crevasse, too, selling her life rights to Tracy and allowing him to make a pornographic film about her. This followed an actual *30 Rock* porn parody being released that previous summer—yes, apparently *30 Rock* was popular enough to warrant a porn version, featuring "Liz Limon," "Jake," "Trey," and "Jenny."

As concern grows among the *TGS* stars about competition with the show potentially bringing in a new actor to freshen things up and help Jack appeal to that Middle American audience, Jenna protests by heading to shoot a movie in Iceland rather than being available for her job on *TGS*.

Episode 3, "Stone Mountain," follows Jack and Liz going down south in their quest to find the perfect new "regular person"–type cast member that will appeal to Middle America. Donald Glover wrote on the early seasons of the show, and while he had moved on by Season 4 and was devoting more of his time to his role on *Community* (before becoming a rap superstar), one of his lasting legacies was Kenneth's hometown: Stone Mountain. It's a real place, the town where Glover grew up.

> **Donald Glover:** The first day, we were talking about Georgia, and I said I was from Stone Mountain. They were like, that really sounds like a hick town. I was like, well, it has this big stone mountain in the middle of nowhere that has the Confederate leaders scrawled on the side. Everybody doesn't believe me! And there's a laser light show. The writers were just like, that's insane, that's going in the show.

Jack McBrayer himself is from Kennesaw, Georgia, just a little west of Stone Mountain itself. Liz and Jack bunk together on the trip, which leads to Jack experiencing Liz's morning breath, which he describes as smelling like she'd eaten a diaper she just found on the beach.

> **Gillian Jacobs:** I love how Tina Fey lets Liz Lemon look like crap on this show. I really admire that a lot about her. How she will wear a nightgown, a sweatshirt, and pants at the same time.

Liz and Jack find themselves watching a fictional Southern puppet comedian, played by famed actual Southern puppet comedian Jeff Dunham. While they initially think this might just be the guy for *TGS*, they change their minds when he uses his puppet to call Liz ugly and basically act like a jerk, screwing up his own chances of joining the cast. Jack, in a weirdly sweet moment, storms the stage and destroys the puppet in Liz's defense.

This episode also features Tracy being worried that celebrities die in groups of threes following the deaths of "world-famous clog dancer Jugbert Cody" and "Fred Dawkins, the incredibly overweight guy that Pac-Man was based on." Tracy's response is to say he'll eat a bowl of cherries and some "ghost meat" in Dawkins's honor, before going on to try taking out other celebrities to save his own life. You can catch a callback to Alan Alda's role as Jack's father in Season 3—when Tracy calls Betty White to try to startle her and kill her, she's reading Milton Greene's Jimmy Carter biography, *From Peanut to President*.

The episode includes one of several references on the show mocking news site the *Huffington Post*. When Kenneth mentions the celebrity clogger's death, he notes that he died "doing what he loved most: blogging on the *Huffington Post*." Alec Baldwin himself was known at the time as a popular *Huffington Post* blogger, regularly sharing his liberal political opinions.

We finally see an all-out audition for the new *TGS* cast member spot in **episode 4, "Audition Day."** The cast of *TGS* isn't a major factor in the show beyond Tracy and Jenna most of the time. Josh peaked early, before fading into the background to the point that the fact that he was still working there until recently was a joke—back in Season 2, Liz quipped that his job was safe because Jack had forgotten that Josh was a person. The character never really broke out.

Andrew Guest: You go back to the pilot—we thought Josh was going to have a bigger role, obviously. And then it didn't end up happening.

Lonny Ross: The ensemble was a comedy all-star team. I was happy to come off the bench and take a few shots.

Liz and Pete have a plan to make sure Jack picks their choice of a new cast member, Jayden, despite Tracy and Jenna's jealousy—but it all falls apart. Liz realizes that Jayden's references were all actually celebrity impressions that he does, and that he is completely insane. *30 Rock* landed Martin Scorsese, Christopher Walken, and Gilbert Gottfried as actual guest stars to do the voices.

But Jack ends up going a different way. He contracted bedbugs earlier in the episode, and when the one person who doesn't shun him is a silver robot street performer, Jack casts that spray-painted robot man on the show. Episode writer Matt Hubbard had a deep understanding of what Jack was going through—he'd had his own bedbug experience in the show's early days, ending up with the worst case anyone in the writers' room had ever seen.

The actor playing the street-performer version of Danny is different than the man who plays him in the next episode—Cheyenne Jackson apparently doesn't have mad robot movement skills.

The auditions provide a great chance for a ton of character bits, including NBC anchor Brian Williams making his second of numerous appearances on the show with an overly cocky impression of a Jersey wiseguy. We even get to see Josh return after quitting a few episodes earlier, auditioning to get his old job back after his attempt to launch a movie career doesn't go so well. It seems like a cruel bit when the actor is *actually* leaving the show—this was his last regular appearance—but his lines are painfully funny and give the audition episode a real anything-could-happen feel, weaving in this real-life element.

And they're not the only familiar faces we saw return for this episode, thanks to Susan Boyle going viral performing *Les Misérables'* "I Dreamed a Dream" on *Britain's Got Talent.*

Marceline Hugot: Tina called me and she said, "Marceline, I think we figured a way to bring you back."

Behind the scenes, some new blood was getting featured this season in a different way. With such a stellar lineup of talent, *30 Rock* started to produce more original content for digital. Grizz and Dot Com starred in a web series together during Season 4, *Livin' XL with Grizz & Dotcom* [*sic*].

Grizz Chapman: I wish that they continued it. I also wish that I took more advantage of that situation. I didn't take full advantage when it was on and crackin'—at that time, a lot of people loved the *Livin' XL* skits.

It was part of multiple efforts by the show to expand into the nascent world of digital programming, including *Kenneth the Webpage*, Q&A's with Tina Fey, and more. One of those other online features was a series, *Frank vs. Lutz*, with the writers set against one another.

Jon Haller: They were giving the opportunity to up-and-coming writers to try these things. Eric Gurian, who was Tina's assistant, he always had his hand in a lot of pies, and it was a way for him to showrun the webisodes. That was the first year the Writers Guild started acknowledging web content as well, paying for it and giving out awards for it.

It was the kind of content that writers had fought to be compensated for during the 2007–08 writers' strike. These features also allowed them to produce something more akin to sketch comedy, a natural fit for the improv and sketch backgrounds of many of the show's performers—and the world of *TGS*. But higher quality.

In **episode 5, "The Problem Solvers,"** Danny (Cheyenne Jackson) makes his debut as the new cast member. Well, "Jack" makes his debut . . . before Jack Donaghy makes the hapless performer change his name to Danny.

Jane Krakowski was working with Jackson on Broadway in *Damn Yankees*. Tina Fey came to see the show, and Jane told Cheyenne that Tina wanted to say hi afterward.

> **Cheyenne Jackson (Jack "Danny" Baker):** Of course, I said, "That would be incredible." And I met Tina afterward. She said, "I like your big Midwestern face. And your timing." I said, "Thank you, Tina Fey. Thank you, thank you for coming." She said, "I have a part on *30 Rock* that I want to gauge your interest in." And I said, "Well, my interest is high."

Although he's since appeared on shows including *American Horror Story*, *Watchmen*, and the *Saved by the Bell* reboot from *30 Rock* writer Tracey Wigfield, *30 Rock* was Jackson's first real television show, and it was a learning-on-the-job experience.

> **Cheyenne Jackson:** My very first scene on the show was where I meet every-one, and that's real fear—that's real confusion on my face. My first take, I come around the corner, and the whole cast was standing there meeting Danny for the first time, the silver robot. To come around the corner and to see everybody standing there was so daunting. I was super prepared, and I was just pumping myself up—then I overshot my mark. Alec puts his hand on my arm, and he goes, "You're *in* my *light*." Gruff, scary—but with a twinkle in his eye.

When Danny makes his first appearance, he also joins in one of the show's ongoing predictions that pays off in the finale: mentioning that Kenneth might one day run the network, which is why he refuses to join in with Tracy and Jenna in treating Kenneth badly.

> **Cheyenne Jackson:** Tina thinks Canadians are funny, so he's Canadian, and there was a whole episode about me not being able to say "about." I could pull on my own feeling of being the new boy, the outsider, not really knowing my place.

Jack offers Liz her own show here, based on the success of the "Dealbreakers" sketch. Tracy and Jenna convince Liz to hire an agent for negotiations over the new show. There's only a thin veil of reality between our world and *30 Rock*'s, and the creation of Liz's agent Simon Barrons—based on writer Simon Rich—is one of the best examples of that, beyond the main cast.

> **Simon Rich (comedy writer):** It would have been either Steve Hely or Vali Chandrasekaran [who created the character]. I was a freshman on the [*Harvard*]

Lampoon when Vali was a senior. He was one of my all-time favorite *Lampoon* writers, a hero of mine, and one of the funniest writers on the magazine when I was starting.

Vali Chandrasekaran: In my mind it was Matt Hubbard [who came up with the character]! But all of us could be wrong. I had a lot of fun writing in Simon's voice for that character. He was definitely the inspiration.

Simon Rich: The thing about comedy writing is, if you're physically weird-looking, your fellow comedy writers will typically notice. I was an extra in a lot of *SNL* sketches, usually used as a sight gag. I never had any lines, because of my total lack of acting experience or ability.

Whichever former *Lampoon* writer came up with it, Vali called Rich at his *SNL* office.

Simon Rich: He was like "Hey, will you audition for this part that's based on you?" I thought, *If I'm ever going to audition for a role, this is the time. You have to—if you don't go out for this part, then you're never gonna go out for a part your entire life.*

I went downstairs. It was my first time ever auditioning for anything, and I read the lines on camera. As it was happening, I realized very quickly that not only was it my first audition, but it would certainly be my last, because I was so uncomfortable and terrified throughout the experience. I don't know if the footage still exists somewhere. Hopefully it does not.

Josh Fadem (Simon Barrons): I was visiting New York—I lived in LA—and I had a meeting with the casting directors. They said, "There's a part on *30 Rock* that you happen to be right for, this week. Do you want to put yourself on tape?" I went home, and I obsessively made my friend read it with me *so* many times. It drove him crazy.

Simon Rich: I was so bad at acting that I couldn't even get a callback for a part based on me. It was the beginning and the end of my acting career, but I still was excited that I could, to this day, tell people that I auditioned for *30 Rock*.

Josh Fadem: The first time I did it, I was twenty-eight or twenty-nine. I looked like a really young twenty-eight, twenty-nine. I mean, I was just kind of a spaz—I'm sure I still am. Many people were like, it seems like this part was written for your sense of humor. I'm a big dog person. There was a joke where we're sitting down, and Liz pulled the chair out for herself to sit in, and I sit in it. There's lots of things like that where it's embarrassing to admit there's a time I could imagine myself doing that.

Simon Rich: The detail that I think was most based on me was the fit of the sportscoat, which definitely resembled how I would have looked going to a party with Vali when he was a senior and I was a freshman, and that might have stuck in his mind.

Josh Fadem: That was all scripted—that he had an oversize suit, as if it was his dad's. The only thing in the script that seemed that physical was the hiccups, but I did a lot of that stuff on stage already.

Simon Rich: It was hilarious, and I really like Josh Fadem. I didn't know him at the time, but our paths have crossed since, and I'm a big fan of his work in general.

Josh Fadem: Liz Lemon is the relatable character for everyone—she's trying to pull it together, but she's surrounded by people that make it difficult to pull it together. If she's trying to look like she's got the big brass to take on Jack, who's the worst person she can bring in the room? That was how I interpreted it—how can I make it more difficult for Liz, even though it doesn't seem like I'm trying to?

It was surreal, because it was the first time I'd done anything on a set of a show that I'd watched. I watched it over and over beforehand—to the point where, you ever binge-watch something and you just have it so in your brain that you almost dream it? When I walked on, it was the first time I was like "I'm in it! I'm inside of it! I'm in the show!"

Fadem also managed to get in trouble while shooting due to his inexperience, and it temporarily left him half-blind.

Josh Fadem: The glasses I wore on the show were my real glasses, and they put a nonreflective thing on the lenses for the next time, and they're like "We'll have them on there the next time you come back!" But I forgot that I need my glasses to see, so I left, and I'm like, I can't really see. It was nighttime in Queens.

He didn't know the subway and was feeling scared, but managed to catch a cab back to where he was staying.

As Danny is getting his feet wet and Liz is negotiating, Jenna and Tracy take it upon themselves to team up in order to solve everyone at *TGS*'s problems, naming themselves the Problem Solvers. They even got matching T-shirts.

Josh Fadem: The Problem Solvers, they switch T-shirts, and they were trying to decide whether to do a take where the shirts are too small. [Tracy Morgan's] like "You've *got* to go smaller."

So that's how Jenna ends up in a shirt that looks like a night shirt and Tracy in a tight belly shirt.

Josh Fadem: Tracy Morgan, I was in a scene with him and he was just the funniest guy I've ever seen in my life. Cracking everyone up, constant jokes—he seemed to give a dissertation on all the variations of big-belly jokes. He'd hit his stomach and be like "That's a mating call!" He would change his physical performance between takes, just goofing, and he'd be like "Look! Now I'm doing a Will Ferrell." He'd change his body and he'd be like "Now I'm in a van by the river," doing Chris Farley.

After that scene, they broke for lunch. He was walking with a group and talking about big bellies. I was walking alongside him, so I chimed in—I said, I have a belly issue, when I go too far on the cookies and ice cream. And he turns and goes, "Cookies and creeeeeam! What show you on?" I didn't know what he was asking, so I said, "Just this one, today." And he was like "You funny. You're old-time funny—old-timers do anything for a laugh." He kept talking about "old-time funny," telling me this is what old-time funny is.

Morgan recognized Fadem when they ran into each other two years later. Well, mostly—Morgan asking him if he'd opened for him once.

When it turns out that Simon isn't much of a power agent, Liz arranges her own meeting with slick *Sports Shouting* producer Scottie Shofar (played by Shawn Levy, director of Tina Fey movie *Date Night*). But when she realizes how little he's invested in her and her success, including not noticing as she holds her sleeve over a candle so long that it catches on fire, she sticks with Jack—and Simon.

This was one of the first episodes that John Riggi directed. Fadem noted that everyone was supportive of Riggi, and that they made sure to take the time to get the jokes just right.

John Riggi: We never really wrote much stage direction. But in "The Problem Solvers," when Jack finds Liz on the plaza and they run toward each other, and he goes, "It's you, Lemon, it's always been you"—it said, "They run together like in a romcom." Just that one sentence. And I was like, I want it to be like a romcom.

That final moment is prompted by Jack offering Padma Lakshmi (playing herself) the *Dealbreakers* talk show as part of hardball negotiations with Liz—but when Padma says it would change her life, Jack realizes he wants to change Lemon's life instead.

John Riggi: I said, "OK, here's what we're gonna do. I guess what we need to build is kind of like a Lazy Susan. We'll put them on it, and it'll be like a merry-go-round. We'll mount the camera in the middle, we'll shoot Alec on one side, then we'll shoot Tina on the other. And what'll happen is, the world will spin around them, but they'll stay stationary."

There was a guy in the art department—I had drawn a little picture of it. And he said, "I know what you're thinking, but that's not going to work that way. He will still spin." And I was like "Buddy, listen, I was a science major. It's physics. The camera's stationary, and the object is stationary. So, if I point my stationary camera at my stationary object, I can spin the world. I understand what you're saying, and you're wrong."

Then we built it. It was really cold on the plaza that day, and we shot it, and it was just so beautiful, and I loved it so much. It was a really, really fun thing to shoot—and it was also fun to be right.

The episode also featured one of the all-time most-cutting lines in *30 Rock* history. When Liz asks Cerie, "Do I look OK?," Cerie cheerfully responds, "That's *exactly* how you look!"

While making the classic episode, the real world was intruding on the fictional one. Tracy Morgan was having kidney issues that would grow worse, ultimately leading to him missing several episodes in Season 5.

John Riggi: When we did "The Problem Solvers," [Tracy] was sick then, too. And I was really, really worried about him.

In **episode 6, "Sun Tea,"** Liz tries purchasing the apartment above hers in a deeply upper-crust New York storyline, emblematic of her character growing more successful at work while her love life remains a mess. Her neighbor, a gay hipster cop, is played by Nate Corddry, cast member from early *30 Rock* rival *Studio 60 on the Sunset Strip*.

Nate Corddry: I wasn't able to watch [*30 Rock*] in the second season after we were canceled, because my ego was hurt too much, and I blamed them. Then I got over that and started watching the show from the beginning. I got the DVDs, and I love *30 Rock*.

Corddry got the gig on the show and remembers Fey as warm and welcoming. During his first day shooting an episode, a reporter from *USA Today* was following her for a profile.

Nate Corddry: As soon as the reporter left at six, she said, "Now that he's gone, let's get down to it." I was like "I can't wait." She was like "So did you guys hate us as much as we hated you?" I was like "Absolutely." It was a real competitiveness, because we were the Yankees and they were the Toledo Mud Hens. They didn't have a chance. Then they dominated, they exploded, and we fell by the wayside.

Corddry was also blown away by Fey as a writer/performer, impressed with her ability to be present and find a new way to deliver a line after several takes.

The title references Frank keeping jars of urine in his office. It was inspired by an actual practice at *SNL* where writers would urinate in their offices rather than going to the bathroom as they worked through the night. It's a technique that Liz uses to get Corddry's character to move out of his apartment so that she can take it over and expand her own place.

This episode also somehow lured in Al Gore, which means that former vice president Al Gore made *multiple appearances* on the long-running sitcom. The show was another in NBC's series of Green Week programming, with a storyline focused around Kenneth being tasked with reducing *TGS*'s carbon footprint. Gore advises him to recycle everything, including jokes—then exits with the same joke from his first appearance: "Quiet . . . a whale is in trouble. I have to go!"

Episode 7, *"Dealbreakers* **Talk Show #0001,"** features the beginning of Liz's new talk show, but it's also the beginning of the idea of the EGOT—the effort to win an Emmy, a Grammy, an Oscar, and a Tony. Tracy stumbles on the idea while shopping for his wife at Yakov's Nubian Bling Explosion, trying to butter her up for the idea of having a daughter to join their two sons. But his eyes instead land on an EGOT necklace that belonged to *Miami Vice* star Philip Michael Thomas, aka Tubbs.

That necklace is a real thing, and it belonging to Mr. Thomas was a *true story*. Thomas apparently had big aspirations, with a necklace of the awards he planned on winning—though his was far more tasteful, as opposed to the blinged-out version created for *30 Rock*. Thomas coined the term himself, telling reporters what it stood for and that he planned to win those awards in the next five years. (Though he'd later change what it meant, claiming it was for "Energy, Growth, Opportunity, and Talent"—as well as the name of an alien angel character that he'd created.) The idea came up in the writers' room in an episode ultimately written by Kay Cannon.

On *30 Rock*, Tracy decides to execute on Thomas's dream for himself. And as he uses Grizz and Dot Com to conduct his research, he finds that most EGOT winners have been composers, so he decides to start making music to get closer to his goal.

> **Kay Cannon (writer):** In the first three seasons, we didn't really do as many arcs for characters. Then you get to Season 4, and this EGOT arc was really important for Tracy. It was the first time we were ever doing something like that with him, where we were giving him a real want and a real goal.

He also puts up a one-man show so that he can win the Tony—and his somewhat haphazard approach to doing so was inspired by Morgan's own plans ahead of a big solo show.

> **Don Scardino:** We said to him, "So are you rehearsing?" And he said, "No, I'm just going to wing it, go out and talk about whatever I'm thinking." We were like "Oh, Tray, do you really think you should?"

The concept was so grabby that "EGOT" became a term used by the public more broadly, with news stories coming out whenever someone seemed to have a shot at landing all four. Lin-Manuel Miranda seems tantalizingly close to the honor at press time, currently holding an EGT but only being an Oscar nominee, not winner—Billy Porter is in a similar position, among the dozens hanging in the realm of three of the four awards won.

Morgan still has his EGOT necklace in storage.

While shooting the episode, Morgan continued to deal with his ongoing health issues—he was recovering from foot surgery. Scardino had to avoid showing his feet on camera, as Morgan was in a large surgical boot.

30 Rock had continued to shoot on film throughout its run, but they used the opportunity of Liz's TV gig to play with the idea that high-def digital cameras show who someone *really* is.

> **Don Scardino:** What was fun about that episode, and really tough to pull off, was when they realize that the camera is revealing the true personalities of the characters. So that Kenneth walks on, he's a Muppet. Or Jack, this younger version of himself from the Jack Ryan movie.

Alec Baldwin had already shot his scenes, but editors managed to track down footage from *The Hunt for Red October* that closely matched Jack Donaghy's movements here. The bit almost didn't happen, with the show working to avoid Alec having to be compared to his younger self. Other ideas for what Baldwin would actually look like in high-def that weren't used: an eagle, Ronald Reagan, and other American symbols.

Liz, thrust into the performer role, also starts to have her own personal breakdown thanks to Jack's critiques of her appearance.

> **Robert Carlock:** Liz starts the whole series having a lot of the things she wants. She has a show on TV, she has a nice apartment on the Upper West Side. And the things she doesn't have, it's the perfect mate and the family and the whole picture: happiness, having it all. So a lot of her stories end up being other people causing problems for her. And "Dealbreakers" was an attempt on our part just to take a break from relationship stuff.

Liz's insecurity makes the talk show an unusable mess, with the treatments she's taken to become TV-friendly leading to her crying out of her mouth and her personality split in two, going Jekyll and Hyde with another version of herself in the mirror. Jenna explains to Jack that he's put too much performer pressure on Liz—she even starts overenunciating "cam-er-a" like Jenna does—and ultimately, they have to shut the talk show down.

In **episode 8, "Secret Santa,"** we're introduced to one of Jack's old flames, his high school girlfriend Nancy Donovan. She's played by Julianne Moore, with a completely over-the-top Boston accent. The character was part of an effort to start getting Jack into more adult relationships, with something deeper between them.

Alec Baldwin: Fifty-year-old Jack running around still using women like a drug is not where I'd like him to end up.

Beth McCarthy-Miller: Julianne Moore comes on the first time—it was one of those moments where you're shooting outside at 30 Rock, it was October, and we were making it look like Christmas. And Alec and Julie were having these scenes together. I would get lost in the scenes; I would forget to yell cut.

Nancy's marriage falling apart leads Jack to the temptation of sweeping in himself. Baldwin and Moore's acting jumped off the screen. Writer Vali Chandrasekaran said this was one of the few times working on the show that he wished they could slow down those scenes, despite the breakneck pace of *30 Rock*.

Vali Chandrasekaran: Maybe it was just the magic of being around Julianne Moore and Alec Baldwin at the same time—I loved those scenes so much in person. On screen, as much as I loved them, I thought they were even better when I was watching them on stage.

As the show continued to develop Danny's character, the storylines started setting him against Jackson's real-life friend and creating a rivalry with Jenna. Jackson's favorite moment was when he sings for Jenna for the first time, and the fact that he's actually great gives Jenna a "rage stroke," with blood dripping out her nose.

We also get Kenneth having the chance to be even more of the embodiment of kindness than he already is, coming in for a Secret Santa—and forcing his coworkers to participate, each of them terrified at their inability to escape. Director Beth McCarthy-Miller decided to shoot it like a Japanese horror movie, communicating the horror these characters are feeling.

In **episode 9, "Klaus and Greta,"** we get to see a little more of Jenna's love life. It hasn't always been a major focus of the show, but she's involved in several major storylines this season. One of the most memorable is when she agrees to a fake celebrity relationship with James Franco, who plays himself. She helps him to cover up something he doesn't want to become public—his deep, passionate love for Japanese body pillows. He's named his "Kimiko-tan."

Robert Carlock: Jenna discovers it isn't fulfilling for her, and she has an emotional realization that she wants more, which is a cool turn for that character after three years of thinking that all she wants is to have her picture in the paper and have her hair look good.

Tina Fey: We realized we never put her in a genuine relationship of any kind.

Franco's storyline was inspired by a *New York Times Magazine* article about a man who carried a body pillow featuring an animated Japanese woman on it, treating it as his girlfriend.

The episode also continued the show's love of making its characters speak German, not infrequently.

> **Jon Haller:** Tina and I were maybe the only people that knew how to speak German—I just took German in high school, so I knew it. When we would write a joke for Tina [in German], or any of the characters, I would call my German family member, and be like "Hey, is this the right way to say this?" But one day, Tina wasn't on set. So they're like "Oh, Alec is having problems with this German phrase. He needs somebody to walk him through it."
>
> He does not know German, and I walked up to him. He's like "Who are you?" I'm like "I'm Jon, I'm the writers' assistant, I've phonetically written this thing out." He's like "OK, show it to me." And he's literally about to walk onto the set to do the line. I was like "Here it is, and you say this line like this." He's like "Great, got it," and then he's gone, and then he does it! I don't know how people do that. It was a curse and a blessing to be the one knowing German.

Episode 10, "Black Light Attack!" gives Danny a major spotlight. He bonds with Jack, who is thankful to finally have a guy around who he sees as someone cut from the same cloth. Jack explains how he's had to spend years making do with "what passes for men around here, with their untucked shirts, boneless faces, their Stars, both Wars and Trek." But as Jack pieces together that Danny is in a secret relationship with Liz, it ruins his male bonding. Jack finds Danny's overly descriptive stories of his romantic life with Lemon distressing.

> **Cheyenne Jackson:** When I saw that that episode, and that I was going to be dressed as a guy from *CHiPS*, and Grizzly Adams, I [was given] a lot of references from Tina.

Liz turns Danny into her studly boy toy. The show also makes another reference to *30 Rock*'s real-life Silvercup Studios neighbors with Jenna auditioning for *Gossip Girl*—and preparing to read for the part of the daughter, instead of the mom they're actually trying to cast her as, forcing her to once again confront the fact that she's aging out of youthful roles.

This episode also features a classic Lutz moment: when black lights at a dance party reveal that he wears a bra. Lutz tries to clarify to the stunned onlookers, "It's not what you think—it's something I need to wear to support my breasts!" The episode ends with a tag featuring Lutz enthusiastically dancing, his chest continuing to glow.

John Lutz: Sue and I are actually married in real life, so it's always fun for her to see me doing embarrassing things on the show.

Sue Galloway (Sue LaRoche-Van der Hout): It's very similar to what he does at home, so I just want the world to see all of it. All of it, so they see what I suffer through.

John Lutz: They really like to make fun of the writers for not being in shape.

After setting up in the previous episode that Tracy wants to add a woman to the entourage, as he develops a deeper appreciation for women, Sue gets that spot here. This episode later features Sue referencing being roofied, while Tracy dismisses her concerns—showing that Tracy hasn't really learned to take women more seriously.

Episode 11, **"Winter Madness,"** follows Liz taking the *TGS* team on vacation to help them deal with the New York winter—but due to his interest in Nancy Donovan, Jack determines that they're actually going to take a trip to Boston. Given all of the *30 Rock* writers with connections to Harvard, there was plenty of Boston knowledge that went into this episode.

Vali Chandrasekaran: There were a lot of Boston people on the show—Robert, Hubbard, Ron Weiner, Steve Hely had grown up there, I had spent a lot of time there, my wife was from there—we all had a lot of strong opinions about Boston.

It came more out of New York City, than the winter of it. As much as everyone loved New York, I would go insane every six or nine months and have to just leave it for a little bit. I would go to my parents' place in Pennsylvania for the weekend. It would usually come in the winter, when you were particularly cloistered.

Beth McCarthy-Miller, who directed the episode, described the grind of working on *30 Rock* as "blood, sweat, and tears, seriously." The episode played to the midwinter desperation that those long hours inspired.

Beth McCarthy-Miller: I would do some episodes in the beginning of the season, and I would come back around Christmastime, and everyone would be gray. No one had flesh-tone color anymore. Robert would look like he had been I-don't-know-where and back. It was just nuts what they did to themselves.

The storyline let the show bring back Julianne Moore as Nancy Donovan, following the success of her first appearance.

Jon Haller: Once Julianne Moore comes on the set, you're just like, whoa, Jesus, she's fucking amazing, and I haven't seen her do comedy before like this that I can remember. So let's write more to her.

Liz turns the *TGS* team, unhappy with their vacation destination, against an imaginary (or so she thought) enemy: Dale Snitterman. The reveal ends up being that the name was one she saw on an actual office door—and the staff takes the rage Liz has inspired in them out on the real Snitterman.

This episode also continues Tracy's apparent love for American history. After previously trying to create a movie where he played Thomas Jefferson, this one sees him taking on the historical veracity of the actors on Boston's Freedom Trail.

Episode 12, "Verna," had one of the most abrupt cold opens the show did, featuring a dream sequence with Liz giving birth to . . . Cheesy Blasters mascot Meat Cat, with Jack as the father.

> **Don Scardino:** I was the voice of Meat Cat. "Hey-hey!" (*evil laugh*)

> **Tina Fey:** That dream sequence took care of a lot of things. It hopefully gave the internet people who so badly want Liz and Jack to get together someday some kind of weird satisfaction, to see she had a stress dream in which she is married.

We also get to see a little more of how Jenna ended up so broken. Just as Jack found his biological father last season, Jenna meets her mom, Verna (*SNL* and *3rd Rock from the Sun* alum Jan Hooks).

> **Tina Fey:** [Jane]'s so good, and Jenna so rarely gets to have any human feelings. We had to coax Jan out of retirement, sort of. Or not even out of retirement, but I guess out of Woodstock, New York—which I guess is like retirement.

Her 2010 appearance on *30 Rock* was her first on-screen role since 2004's *Jiminy Glick in Lalawood*. The show paid homage to Hooks's famed Sweeney Sisters character with a completely inappropriate duet between Verna and Jenna, singing Captain and Tenille's "Do That to Me One More Time" to each other as a mother–daughter team. It also ended up working metaphorically, according to Fey, with the idea that Jenna knew her mother was just going to screw her over again—but that she'd rather that than have no mother at all.

You can spot Alec Baldwin having a hard time not laughing as Verna flirts with him. She describes her tattoo as being of Captain Morgan having sex with a mermaid—Alec Baldwin loved the idea so much that his season wrap gift for his colleagues was a picture of that very tattoo, his favorite thing the entire season.

As Liz continues to leave the extra apartment upstairs under construction, it serves as a metaphor, according to Tina—it's the unfinished personal work that Liz still has to do on herself.

We find that Pete has finally found a little me time to himself in the mornings. It's almost immediately ruined by Kenneth seizing on it as a chance to share his own weird and/or boring stories.

Scott Adsit: Pete felt sorry for Kenneth in the beginning, because I imagine maybe Pete had been a low-level at NBC at some point—I don't think he was a page, but he knows the animal that is the page. Kenneth is an odd one, but he knows what the deal is. But then Kenneth slowly reveals himself to be something other than just a page, whatever he is. And so like most everything in life, he grows afraid of Kenneth, and his power.

This episode also lets Tina act opposite Judah Friedlander thanks to a rare Liz/Frank scene.

The food delivery service in this episode—Noofüd, somewhat ahead of food delivery services becoming as big of a trend as they did in the later 2010s, and even more so during the COVID-19 pandemic—was inspired by a real meal delivery service diet that Tina Fey was on. It worked for her, but eventually, she just couldn't take it anymore.

The episode ends with an extended improv run from Jack McBrayer about the way TV used to be.

Episode 13, "Anna Howard Shaw Day," features the debut of Jack's other big Season 4 love interest: Avery Jessup (Elizabeth Banks), who he meets while making a CNBC appearance on her business show *Hot Box*. They match when it comes to their conservative politics and their immense career ambition.

Elizabeth Banks (Avery Jessup): She's basically Sean Hannity in a skirt. What's great about her relationship with Jack is they're equals. She's not some [pretty] young thing that he has a fling with.

Banks was already a fan of *30 Rock* and started putting feelers out, letting them know how much she'd love to be on the show. She wanted to nail the fast-talking vibe befitting both *30 Rock* and cable news shows.

Elizabeth Banks: I begged them to put it on a prompter for me. They said, "No problem." But I got there that night and there was a problem. They couldn't figure the prompter out. It came down to me throwing fastballs at Alec and him batting them back as fast as possible and hoping they could cut it together faster than we were doing it.

Banks was able to deliver as an actress on the show, but the show didn't seem to find a strong comedic voice for her. She wasn't able to be unique, essentially playing a female Jack in many ways.

Alan Sepinwall: If one of them was in a relationship that was not necessarily working, that could be a bit of a drag. Elizabeth Banks, I understood what they were trying to do with that character, but she was not necessarily as funny as a number of the other women he'd been paired with.

The *New York Post*'s Page Six claimed at the time that Avery was based on CNBC anchor Melissa Francis, citing a source close to the show. But Banks tweeted that the story was "completely false." Francis knew Carlock from college and had been sending him ideas about how she could be written into the show, but Tina Fey credited the inspiration for the part to Carlock's wife, Jen Rogers—Rogers also happens to be a business reporter.

> **Melissa Francis (CNBC anchor):** There's a lot of debate about that. At some point, I pitched something about Jack, who is such a straitlaced kind of guy, falling in love with a business anchor from CNBC. I thought, *Hey that could be me!* I hounded [Carlock] for a long time, and lo and behold Avery Jessup shows up.

The other big guest star appearance here is Jon Bon Jovi, playing up the fact that he was legitimately participating in NBC's "artist in residence" program to help promote his band's new album. He appeared on a variety of shows as part of the initiative, though *30 Rock* took it to another level with Bon Jovi as a contestant on *Top Chef* and playing the *NBC Nightly News* theme on his guitar.

With Jack working to impress Avery at a network party, he uses Grizz and Dot Com as fake security. Donaghy thanks them for pretending to be bouncers, to which Dot Com replies, "Maybe someday we'll live in a world where you ask us to pretend to be scientists." Neither of them looks particularly happy putting on a show for Jack's romantic interest.

As Season 4's Valentine's Day episode, Liz's most notable past boyfriends pay a visit—via a dentist's office medication-inspired hallucination sequence that lets her reunite with Floyd, Drew, and Dennis.

> **Jon Hamm:** That was given to me literally the day before we shot it. They were like "We wrote some more stuff, so we'll see you tomorrow." I was like "OK, how much more can it be? Oh great, it's a completely different take, awesome."

They all take on the role of Jamaican nurses in the episode's tag due to that Liz hallucination, so you can judge for yourself how you feel about these three white male actors doing Jamaican accents.

Episode 14, "Future Husband," delivers what would be a meet-cute in any other show. Liz discovers an entry on her phone that she doesn't remember putting there, labeled "Future Husband." She realizes it must have happened at the dentist's office while she was all doped up. She heads back to the dentist to investigate, discovering that it was an initially charming Englishman—Wesley (Michael Sheen). He pulls up his phone and we see the entry for Future Wife—and then they go on a first date that is as painfully awkward as so, so many first dates in one of the most relatable moments the show ever finds.

They quickly realize this just isn't right, but fate continues to insist on them being together, eventually breaking them both down.

The turning point for the series that we see here is how the show begins to turn NBCUniversal's real-life acquisition by Comcast into drama for *30 Rock* in the seasons to come. The move gave the show a new life, with a whole new world of corporate parody open before it. Rather than the real-world Comcast, *30 Rock* gave us Kabletown buying out NBC with Jack cut out of the deal. The purchase also gave the show an excuse for a run of Philadelphia jokes, since Kabletown and Comcast both just happen to be based there—the city is also Tina Fey's hometown.

To add insult to injury, it was revealed that Don Geiss (Rip Torn) had died, and that the higher-ups had kept it quiet. Jack doesn't even find out until discovering it's been covered up as the deal with Kabletown closes. Torn hadn't appeared on the show in more than a year—there'd been speculation that he was written out due to an alcohol-related arrest in January of that year, with an inebriated Rip Torn found asleep after breaking into a bank that he said he thought was his home, while carrying a loaded gun. But Fey said that the episode was shot before that incident and that it had more to do with a symbolic changing of the guard. The death of Don Geiss was used as symbolism for the end of an era for GE, with the transition to Kabletown as their new corporate parents.

John Riggi: We let our opinions be known. The idea that Comcast was going to buy the company, to us, was so . . . honestly, I don't think "repugnant" is too strong of a word. Especially for Tina, because Tina had her home at NBC, and now this cable company was going to buy this pedigree that we all grew up with. We were poking it in the eye a bit—that's why we called it Kabletown. We wanted to point out that this was absurd and weird, and where things were going.

We were always looking and trying to honestly reflect what was going on in the culture at the time. Sometimes that worked great in the sense of, we were really saying something, but it also dates us a bit—you're just going, "Oh, that's when that merger happened." So it's not like watching an episode of *Friends*, and other than their clothes, that could happen anytime. We were really commenting on our own world, even though our own world was made up on a certain level.

We worked on this fictitious show, but you knew we worked at NBC, and so this big thing happened at NBC and it felt like there wasn't any way *not* to do it. We didn't want to not take an opportunity to take on all these mergers and this company swallowing this other company, and then a bigger company than that coming and swallowing those two companies.

The show had initially planned on spelling the fake company's name as "Cabletown," but NBC's legal team informed them that there was an actual company with a similar name. So Kabletown gets spelled with a K, somehow making the slightly fictitious company that much more absurd.

Tracy also continues his quest for an EGOT here with a one-man show to make himself eligible for a Tony, but has to face the struggle of putting on a show that he can do more than just once and isn't completely spontaneous.

The opening of **episode 15, "Don Geiss, America and Hope,"** originally featured six pages of Jack and Liz with dueling Boston and Philadelphia references, written by Jack Burditt. It ended with Jack singing rock group Boston's "More Than a Feeling" for three-fourths of a page, while Liz delivered the far more obscure "TSOP (The Sound of Philadelphia)" by MFSB—the song was a disco soul instrumental. The show trimmed this, deciding that as funny as it was, they could keep this Boston/Philly battle to the highlights.

This episode continues to pay off the discovery of Wesley as "Future Husband" in Liz's phone. While many viewers assumed that Liz and Wesley's date in this episode—going to see *Hot Tub Time Machine*—was product placement, episode writer Tracey Wigfield said it was not. But the *Hot Tub Time Machine* team *did* send Wigfield two men's XL *Hot Tub Time Machine* T-shirts as their way of saying thanks. The episode also features Liz going back to her dentist's office to find out more about how she and Wesley matched up in the first place.

> **Tracey Wigfield (writer):** Poor James Rebhorn (who plays Liz's dentist), in one of the takes, opened the door and hit himself right square in the middle of the forehead, and had a pretty serious gash. But we were almost done filming. They just put makeup on it and said chill out for a moment, let's keep going, instead of addressing it or getting him stitches.

Liz and Wesley realize the impact the dental anesthetic had, helping them to put less importance on running into each other again and again. They try to separate themselves, but fate throws them together once more. It leads to Wesley making the pitch to Liz that he is her "settling soulmate." Liz rejects the idea, while also discovering that her beau's last name is "Snipes," as in famed tax-evading actor/*Blade* star Wesley Snipes. Wesley makes a good point: If you look at the other Wesley Snipes, then look at him, his upper-crust Britishness *does* seem like a better embodiment of the names "Wesley" and "Snipes."

Liz tracks Wesley down one last time in this episode, knowing he couldn't resist a tasting of the white wines of Scotland. A background joke to watch out for: the text of the sign advertising the tasting, written by Robert Carlock and including jokes about "ossified Viking bones" and other jokes explaining why Scottish white wine is an absolutely rotten idea.

Tracy grapples with a tell-all book from his former nanny that reveals how remarkably normal and faithful to his wife he is. It puts his endorsement deals at risk due to his wild larger-than-life image, and those paychecks being threatened ironically puts Tracy at risk of raising Angie's ire. It's a callback to Season 3 episode "The Ones," where Tracy confided in Jack that he'd never actually cheated on his wife. The storyline also offers a mirror image parallel to golfer Tiger Woods's affairs, which had made headlines the previous fall. He worries that Angie will be madder than a bat in a suitcase, which reminds him to check that bat he left in a nearby suitcase.

While Jack wasn't included in the merger negotiations, he tries to strategize how he can play a key role in the new Kabletown monolith. But he realizes that the new company has little interest in making things, leaving him and his desire to always be creating and doing something new unfulfilled. It's a twist for a character who started in a role that seemed designed to squelch our hero Liz's creativity, but it lets us see what his corporate version of creativity is all about.

Don Geiss's funeral inspires Jack to create a new product for Kabletown: porn for women, where nudity is replaced by handsome men listening patiently. Don's daughter, Kathy (Marceline Hugot), also makes another appearance at her father's funeral.

Marceline Hugot: I was going to sing "Ave Maria" to go along with this whole thing that I was a great singer [from the season's earlier "Audition Day" episode]. But then at the last minute, good old Jeff [Richmond] said, "Marceline, if you can learn to play the trumpet in, I don't know, forty-eight hours, let's do that. What do you think?" And, of course, I said, "What do I think? I say, yes, of course she plays the trumpet."

The frozen-in-carbonite Don Geiss (à la Han Solo in *Return of the Jedi*) seen at the funeral would go on to live in the *30 Rock* writers' room, though it began to seriously crack rather quickly. One joke cut from the funeral: the introduction of Don Geiss's mistress, and his manstress.

While he appeared via hallucination a couple episodes prior, Jason Sudeikis returns in **episode 16, "Floyd."** Liz hopes that Floyd visiting New York and asking her to dinner means they can get back together, but it turns out that he wants to let her know that he's engaged to another woman. Liz tries giving Floyd food poisoning as revenge, but accidentally pushes the recovering alcoholic off the wagon via the restaurant's whiskey-based fish sauce. Her penance: being invited to be part of the wedding.

As she pines for Floyd, Liz sings a bit from the imaginary song she thought Christopher Cross would sing about their love when they eventually got together. While his version didn't end up on the show, Cross extended the song himself, and the fully produced epic ballad appeared on the *30 Rock* soundtrack album. And it's perhaps the first hint of Liz's ultimate one true love: Criss Chros (James Marsden). The two-disc (two disc!) album features the show's score, along with the numerous absurd songs featured throughout the series' run to that point.

The episode features another musical moment: Danny gets nominated for Canada's version of the Grammys, a Juno Award, thanks to recording a psych-up song for hockey team the Ottawa Senators. His competition in the category: "Sir Dave Coulier."

> **Cheyenne Jackson:** [The song] was actually longer. We shot a whole music video, but for time they always cut stuff. There was a whole call-and-answer to the people of Nova Scotia.

In **Episode 17, "Lee Marvin vs. Derek Jeter,"** Jack feels he has to choose between his two great loves of the season, once and for all: Nancy or Avery. Nancy is his high school girlfriend, the hometown girl-next-door, while Avery is the fellow conservative, high-powered, take-no-prisoners powerhouse. The choice is prompted by Nancy getting a divorce, forcing Jack to deal with his old flame finally being available.

We also see Toofer grappling with the fact that he may have been hired due to affirmative action. He quits, but ultimately gets hired back after Liz realizes she's also been the beneficiary of affirmative action due to a Title IX college scholarship and *The Girlie Show* itself being picked up due to complaints about NBC's completely misogynistic action drama *Bitch Hunter*, with Shane Hunter (Will Ferrell) as a bounty hunter.

> **Scott Adsit:** My favorite Pete line was to Liz. We were in this kitchenette in the writers' room, and she's having some self-doubt. She says, "I'm not supposed to be here"—meaning in this life, or this job. And I put my hand on her shoulder and said, "Liz, this is America. None of us are supposed to be here." I love that line. White privilege, and the fact that we have this assumption that America is the greatest place in the world, because we are the people running it. We came here and conquered *several* Indigenous peoples, and decided we were the good guys, after doing all of those horrible things.

It's a line that Fey wouldn't necessarily take to heart, with a later storyline on *Unbreakable Kimmy Schmidt* causing controversy when it's revealed that Jane Krakowski's character on that show is actually Native American, leaving critics unhappy with some of the stereotypical Native American aspects of the story and a white woman playing a Native American.

When Toofer returns to the show, he tries to get people to stop calling him by the inherently insulting name—"two-fer" referencing that he's great for the show because he's both Black and a Harvard grad. But the effort to change his identity fails, with everyone coming up with even more insulting nicknames.

> **Keith Powell (James "Toofer" Spurlock):** They kind of warned me about that one—I thought it was a really fun thing because affirmative action has permeated corporate culture.

Liz and Jenna also attend singles events together in this episode, where they run into writer Steve Hely as Jerem, a snooty attendee who consistently shuts down Jenna.

> **Jon Haller:** Steve Hely had this way of pitching this one character, that they ended up casting him as Jerem. He just did it so well in the room, and you're like, well, if you're doing it so well here . . .

Episode 18, "Khonani," was perhaps the most in-depth mapping of a real-life situation onto the show—or really, the most elaborate mapping of a real-life situation onto any show, even those *Law & Order* ripped-from-the-headlines episodes. Friend of the show Conan O'Brien being pushed out of *The Tonight Show* in a feud between O'Brien and Jay Leno turns into a storyline centered around *30 Rock*'s janitors jockeying for a certain late-night janitorial time slot.

> **Vali Chandrasekaran:** No one gave us any flack. Leno was then doing the show right after us—we were at nine thirty, and Leno was at ten. There was a joke at the end, Jack Donaghy says something about "stay tuned for Leno," and then Leno opened his show, which it opened right into, with a bit that referenced "Khonani." So I think they took care of it on some sort of corporate level.
>
> I was a little bit scared about how close it was hewing to [the real events], but Tina had a good instinct on how to do it and how to make it work.

The episode featured Subhas in an expanded role.

> **Beth McCarthy-Miller:** When they got to "Khonani," we hired an actor to play the other role, and the first scene that we were shooting with them, Alec was brokering the deal in the janitor closet. And Alec was like "Who hired Subhas?" 'Cause it was his first time doing a lot of dialogue, and he was having a hard time. I'm like "No no no, Alec, he's the janitor." He's like "I know he's the janitor, but who hired him?" I'm like "No Alec, he's *the janitor*." And Alec immediately took him under his wing and was giving him helpful hints during the scenes.

Vali Chandrasekaran: It's him and Alec negotiating with each other, and Alec was really great with him—Subhas went toe-to-toe. It was really funny, where you sometimes were watching and thought, *Man, this show sometimes is just blessed. This guy is not trained as an actor.* I'm not exactly sure how you would direct another actor to make his choices, but something about what he's doing is really funny and viscerally interesting.

But some assumptions were made about Vali on this episode that left him calling in an emergency helper.

Vali Chandrasekaran: My wife came to set that day, because I looked at the call sheet, and they had me down as the Hindi translator. Carlock asked me if I knew Hindi, and I said no. So I had to frantically call Nithya and ask her to come up to Silvercup to make sure we were pronouncing everything correctly.

Nithya went on to be elected to the LA City Council in 2020—no word yet on whether she'll introduce an annual 30 Rock Day in Los Angeles.

Episode 19, "Argus," was Tina's husband, Jeff Richmond's, first time directing. He got the script around a week before shooting and found an unexpected surprise: He was directing a whole bunch of scenes featuring a live peacock and Alec Baldwin.

The peacock, Argus, was a final gift from mentor Don Geiss to Jack, given to him at Geiss's will reading and serving as the living embodiment of the NBC symbol.

Jeff Richmond: What you really want to do when you first-time direct is you just want those days with Alec to be nice and easy and professional. And I find out, oh great, every scene he's going to have to sit with a live, dirty, fevered, diseased fowl of some sort.

In a walkthrough with the peacock, it took a dump backstage. But somehow, Richmond pulled it off, though there are a handful of shots with a puppet. A frightened Liz yells "living dinosaur" when she sees the peacock—a metaphor for the state of broadcast television, according to Fey.

Richmond also had to grapple with a huge snowstorm that shut the city down, with the show ending shooting early that day. Line producer Jerry Kupfer was afraid the crew would be stranded at the studio.

Jack becomes convinced that Don Geiss's soul is inside Argus, helping him as he processes his grief over Geiss's death. But Jack accidentally hastens the animal's death, as while it's already acting peculiar, a drunk Jack offers the peacock a drink of its own.

Kathy Geiss makes an appearance at the will reading, receiving her father's pocket watch with strict instructions not to get it wet. Uh-oh, it's already in her mouth.

Meanwhile, Grizz is getting married to his fiancée, Feyoncé, setting up the season finale. But he's forced into the awkward position of choosing either Tracy or Dot Com as his best man. It also gave Grizz the opportunity to reference his largely nonexistent romantic past with Liz, inspired by the one-off kiss we saw at Kenneth's party several seasons back, with Grizz describing their relationship as the Sam and Diane of the *TGS* offices.

This season also introduced the love interest that finally stuck for Jenna: herself. Or, more specifically, straight Jenna Maroney drag impersonator Paul, played by Will Forte. Whose last name is as unimportant to the show as it is to Jenna, with the last name "L'Astname."

Alan Sepinwall: I'm such a sucker for funny names and I'm not sure there's ever been a show that has more, better funny names, both for characters and for fake movies.

You couldn't put her with a normal person, because even more than Tracy or Kenneth, she was maybe the biggest caricature among the regular characters. You had to put her with someone who was ridiculous and weird, and the fact that they had this whole kinky gender queer bond between one another going on was basically the most likable I tended to find Jenna.

The show plays with your expectations, as Paul initially comes across as a relatively square guy—before the truth is revealed and he's used both to amp up Jenna's self-obsession and to kick her public displays of sexuality up to another level.

Vali Chandrasekaran: My biggest memory for Paul was when we had Paul dressed up as the Jenna Maroney impersonator, making out with Jenna, and I was watching it on the monitors thinking, *This is hilarious. But we have just given up on entertaining people who are not like us, and that's what makes me love this show and working on this show so much.*

The role was designed for Will Forte from the beginning. Forte committed completely, shaving all his body hair—and giving all that hair to *Saturday Night Live/MacGruber* writer John Solomon as a prank. The show continued to walk a tightrope in its depiction of people outside the cis, white world.

Episode 20, "The Moms," paid tribute to the *SNL* tradition of doing a Mother's Day episode featuring the writers and the cast's mothers, bringing back both the characters' mothers who we'd seen before along with a couple new additions. That includes stage greats Elaine Stritch and Patti LuPone coming back as Jack's and Frank's moms, as well as John Lutz playing his own mother.

Patti LuPone: Elaine is a character, and there's only one Elaine Stritch. She was very welcoming to me. Not that she wasn't welcoming to everybody, but I felt especially chuffed that she would extend herself that day when we worked on the set together.

The art department worked episode director John Riggi's mother's name, Madeleina, into the episode, using it as the name of a restaurant. He still has one of the menus.

The writers had a surprising moment at the table read involving another of the episode's special guests.

> **Jon Haller:** The one moment I try to tell people about to show the surreal nature of the show: Table reads are given a kind of theatrical importance, so that means you are a very polite audience member. You laugh, but you don't make any extra noise, you turn off your cell phones, you treat it like a live show.
>
> At one point, in the middle of the table read, somebody's cell phone went off extremely loudly. The ringtone was the sound of a spaceship's bay doors closing—that EHHN, EHHN, EHHN. It went on and on. You could see Carlock looking around, like who the fuck's phone is going off?
>
> And it was Buzz Aldrin. Buzz Aldrin was sitting in the audience of the table read, because he was doing his cameo. We were shooting that week with Buzz Aldrin, and somebody invited him to the table read. As soon as we all knew it was Buzz Aldrin, we were like "Oh, it's just Buzz Aldrin's phone," and we go back to the table read.

Yes, the episode featured astronaut/legend Buzz Aldrin, second man on the moon. Liz discovers that he was her mom's true love, a play on Liz's own imaginary dream man, Astronaut Mike Dexter—the Mike Dexter actor, John Anderson, portrays the young Buzz Aldrin. And Buzz and Liz end up yelling at the moon together, with Buzz continuing to have strong feelings about the object he once stood on.

> **Buzz Aldrin (guest star, astronaut):** I had to think about it a little bit. The first thing I thought of was *3rd Rock from the Sun*. Then somebody said *30 Rock*, and I was like "What does that mean?" "That's 30 Rockefeller Plaza."
>
> **John Riggi:** He could not remember his lines if his life depended on it. When we shot that scene, we tried everything. I had little mini–cue cards made that we put right next to Tina's head. But his eyeline was so far off that he just looked like he was looking off at a closet or something. So when we shot that scene, I was sitting on the floor between the two of them. When he would have to answer, I would say, "Your line here, sir, is this." And then he'd say it.

Aldrin reveals to Liz that he spent many of the years after being with her mother as an alcoholic, so it was a good decision on her part not to be with him. Buzz and Liz yell at the moon together, Buzz yelling, "I own you! I walked on your face!" while Liz tells it, "You dumb moon! Don't you know it's day? Idiot!"

John Riggi: But what was really cool about [Buzz] was, he still had this aura about him as this guy who had been on the moon. We got done shooting, and our AD Steve Davis said, "Ladies and gentlemen, that is a wrap on Mr. Buzz Aldrin." The crew applauded, and Buzz Aldrin looked at the crew and said, "And now, onward to Mars!" and threw his hand up in the air. The entire crew went, "*Yeah!*"

The episode features another appearance by Will Ferrell as Shane Hunter in *Bitch Hunter*—with the episode of the fictional show credited to *30 Rock*'s Jack Burditt, along with the creator of prestige television hit *Mad Men*, Matthew Weiner. It's one of multiple *Mad Men* references in this episode, including Liz's mom graduating from secretary school and getting a job working at that show's ad agency, Sterling Cooper.

Episode 21, "Emanuelle Goes to Dinosaur Land," featured one of the best runs of jokes by Tracy in the show's history. And that's saying a lot considering how absurd basically every line he says is. As he visits the old neighborhood from his past that he's spent so many years trying to repress, the emotions overwhelm him, remembering such events as sleeping on an old dog bed stuffed with wigs, watching a prostitute stab a clown, and using a rib cage as a basketball hoop.

Jack McBrayer: Oh my god, this was the hardest. It was terrible. There were several takes that they could not use because me and Dot Com are just sitting here laughing [in the stairwell with Tracy].

The pain overwhelms Tracy as he films *Garfield 3: Feline Groovy*, making the family comedy he's shooting while wearing a motion capture suit to play Garfield not so joyous.

Tina Fey: This guy played this director Shawn one time, and he was so funny we just brought him back anytime we needed a director of anything. He's really funny. I like how he screams "action."

Jack McBrayer: Tracy kept mispronouncing "Nermal."

Tracy uses the torment in his efforts to become a serious actor. He stars in an emotionally painful movie titled, appropriately enough, *Hard to Watch*, helping move him another step closer to that EGOT. His other painful memories in this episode also continue his well-documented love for American history, as he cries, "The projects I lived in were named after Zachary Taylor—generally considered to be one of the worst presidents of all time!"

Meanwhile, Liz visits past boyfriends to find someone to go to Floyd's wedding with, but Drew and Dennis are, in fact, still morons. And she discovers that Drew is so dumb that he lost both hands and had to have them replaced by hooks, thanks to waving to a friend while near a helicopter—then celebrating his return from Africa with a bunch of fireworks. So, even though she hates his guts, she decides to attend the wedding with Wesley. At the wedding, she meets a guy who just happens to look just like her dream man, Astronaut Mike Dexter—but after discovering that the guy is a plushie, she agrees to marry Wesley.

This episode marked Dean Winters's return to television after suffering a bacterial infection—his heart stopped in an ambulance on the way to the hospital, where he would end up spending three weeks in the ICU. He went septic due to an illness he'd had when he was a kid. Winters went on to develop gangrene, and over the next year, doctors were forced to amputate two toes and half a thumb at the time. His surgeries included skin grafts and an operation where a forearm muscle was used in rebuilding his right hand. He ultimately underwent seventeen surgeries and a total of nine amputations. "Emanuelle Goes to Dinosaur Land" was a return to acting for him.

Dean Winters (Dennis Duffy): While I was having my tenth surgery, Tina Fey called and said, "I'll put you back on 30 Rock," and after I got out I was on the set the next day. They put me in a cast because they'd cut off my baby toe and work gloves because my hands were still healing. I'm indebted to Tina for life.

Jack has also continued his relationship with Avery, and while he tries not to also pursue Nancy, he ends up sleeping with her. They go to Floyd's wedding together, and Jack decides to tell Nancy about his relationship with Avery in the middle of the wedding's Catholic mass. Nancy vows to leave him as soon as the mass is over, so Jack texts Liz to stall and give him more time to make her stay, since the deeply Catholic Bostonian would never leave in the middle of mass. Which leads to Liz reading completely inappropriate scripture passages in the ceremony, largely from the Old Testament.

The wedding continues in the **season finale, "I Do Do."** Season 4 built to the most intricate dovetailing of storylines the show ever did, with three weddings in one episode: between Liz's ex Floyd and his fiancée, Kaitlin; Cerie and her Greek shipping heir fiancé, Aris; and Grizz and his fiancée, Feyoncé. Cerie's storyline was a reference to celebutante Paris Hilton—Hilton was engaged to a Greek shipping heir at the time.

The featured spot makes Season 4 one of Grizz Chapman's favorites, though he said that he loved Season 3 as well. Grizz's wedding was originally supposed to be at a Marriott, with the three weddings in different places, but the writers instead set up his wedding at the TGS studio so that the standard 30 Rock sets would be used at least once in this episode, keeping the episode's budget under control. The cake in Grizz's wedding was created by the bakers from the Food Network reality show *Ace of Cakes*—in an unusual crossover, an entire episode was dedicated to the creation of both that cake and the cake for *30 Rock*'s Season 4 wrap party.

Susan Schectar (hairstylist): There was a wrap party, and there was this [Meat Cat] cartoon cake that was amazing looking.

Cerie's relationship with the unseen billionaire shipping heir Aris had been referenced as far back as the first season. More absurd details were layered on that relationship, including her fiancé being kidnapped by pirates, until paying off with Cerie *finally* getting married. And, because either he's a gentleman or he's suffering Stockholm syndrome or both, the pirates are part of the wedding party.

Jack chooses Nancy—but after Nancy discovers in the women's restroom that Avery is pregnant, she shares the news with Jack and says goodbye. Jack goes to Avery and proposes, a new engagement to end the season.

Don Scardino: Julianne Moore, she would come—she knew it cold, knew what she wanted to do. Then one day, that big wedding where they had the bust-up scene, we were rehearsing it, and she was just kind of marking it. And I said, "Oh don't forget, this hurts a lot." She said, "Oh Don, is this about the acting part?" I said, "Yeah." She said, "Oh don't worry, honey, I got it." And she did.

Michael Trim (cinematographer): If you're going to give working pros a note, you better be really sure that it's a note that they haven't thought of five moves before you.

While Liz and Wesley Snipes decide that they must settle for each other and just get married, a non-plushie version of Liz's dream man comes in at the end to save her: a pilot, Carol, played by Matt Damon. Liz breaks up with Wesley, refusing to settle as this opportunity for a dream guy flies into her life. Damon had come up to Tina Fey at the Golden Globes and said that he wanted to be part of the show.

Jon Haller: Matt Damon shows up, and you're like, he is so funny—let's do whatever we can to get him back. This happens on TV shows all the time—you have a master plan, but then you have this actor that shows up and is so captivating that that's the new muse you end up following.

Peter Agliata: You're going to get punched in the eye as an actor if you come in. They're not going to be kind to you. That's precisely why people want to show up. Matt Damon—he's in the height of his *Bourne Identity*, super macho, killer guy. He's delivering movie after movie. He's more fierce every time—and he shows up, he's going to play a guy named Carol. He's going to be a crier—the littlest thing, he starts getting frazzled and starts crying. They did this with everybody.

This also marks the end of Kenneth's run as a page. When he finds out that a promotion is going to send him to Los Angeles, he does an intentionally terrible job—forcing Pete to fire him. It was a sign of things to come, with Season 5 throwing major wrenches in many of the show's key dynamics, from Kenneth's new role and Jack's longest-lasting relationship, to experiments with the format of the show itself.

SEASON 5
(2010–11)

Breaking the Format

This season featured some of the show's biggest swings, with a live episode, their hourlong 100th episode, and turning one episode into a fake reality show, *Queen of Jordan*. That restlessness for something new comes as *30 Rock* was coming off of its worst reviewed season to date, with no Emmy Award wins for the first time, despite a number of nominations.

Ratings were down in Season 4, and they continued to trend down this year. They'd remain on that track until their final season, coming at a time that the entire television business was transforming. Netflix had introduced streaming in 2007, just after *30 Rock* first launched, and the toll of streaming competition was starting to be felt in network TV ratings, which took a hit beyond just *30 Rock*. The show also moved to eight thirty from its nine thirty P.M. slot the year before, and, instead of having the continued strength of *The Office* as its lead-in, it had the weaker *Community*.

Still, you can see a renewed creative enthusiasm here. The dedication of the writers continued—Vali Chandrasekaran got engaged and married during this time, but dealt with a long-distance relationship with his wife in a job in India. He said it took a toll on his personal life, but at the same time, these writers had the chance to contribute to one of the best-written shows in TV history.

Season premiere "The Fabian Strategy" features Tracy missing his boy Kenneth, who follows up his firing by going to the opposition, working as a CBS page for the *Late Show with David Letterman*.

Jenna Maroney gets a producer credit on *TGS* this season, one of the biggest inside-Hollywood moves that *30 Rock* has portrayed. But she ends up showing a preternatural talent for budgets and realizes her own producer credit is an unnecessary expense, so she asks Pete to fire her.

And yes, Liz's love interest's full name is shared by a famous comedienne who happens to be one of Tina Fey's heroes—his name is Carol Burnett. Liz continues pursuing the relationship this season, despite Carol's frequent absences due to his work as a pilot (and Matt Damon busy being Matt Damon).

The biggest threat to the relationship is initially Liz's own intimacy issues, which are set up here when we catch her in her sleep crying out, "No, Tom Jones, no!" We eventually learn the root of her problems (and don't worry, they aren't as potentially upsetting as her words could make it seem). But in the meantime, she's not having Carol sleep over, and Carol gets emotional not knowing where their relationship is headed. When they part, they tease the date they're planning to be back together—which happens to be the date of the show's first-ever live episode. Delving into Liz's psychological depths was also a shift in the type of quick comedy the show had become known for, with the writers weaving in more character work that at times came at the expense of the laughs.

Showing that the *30 Rock* writers might just hold a grudge, there's also a subtle *Studio 60* joke here, where the credits for *TGS*—established by this point as a somewhat terrible sketch comedy show—include Ricky Tahoe and Ronnie Oswald. They're the infamous former head writers of the fictional show-within-a-show of *Studio 60*, who were also known as complete hacks.

In **episode 2, "When It Rains, It Pours,"** Paul Giamatti had a cameo, once again showing that he's an actor's actor by playing a character with few redeemable traits. He portrays bullying *TGS* video editor Ritchie. When Liz flirts with him to get him to do his job faster, he starts spreading a rumor that they were sleeping together. But while he approaches it in a completely creepy fashion, Liz finds out that he's actually trying to make his assistant editor, Donna, jealous. Liz agrees to a fake breakup with Ritchie to help him attract the woman he's actually interested in.

Jack also worries in the episode about being an old dad, recording advice for his unborn child in the event that he's not around to share those moments. Baldwin himself only had one child at this time, who was then a teen, but he would go on to be an older father himself—he's had five children with his second wife, Hilaria Baldwin, between 2013 and 2020.

Tracy also laments that he missed the birth of both of his children for "very legitimate reasons," which Dot Com clarifies were "cooking a French bread pizza" and "forgot."

In **episode 3, "Let's Stay Together,"** the Kabletown takeover continues, with Jack appearing before Congress to testify about the acquisition of NBC in front of

Rep. Regina Bookman (Queen Latifah). Bookman demands more diversity from the network. As Jack testifies, he goes searching through his memory for a response and struggles to remember the name of "the black kid on *Community*," aka former *30 Rock* writer Donald Glover. He tells Bookman that he doesn't see color or gender, calling her "Mr. Chang."

The storyline was inspired by NBC exec Jeff Zucker attending a House Judiciary Committee meeting and being asked by Rep. Maxine Waters why NBC hadn't created shows appealing to the Black community.

"Is there some assumption that Black programming is not profitable?" Waters asked Zucker at the time. Zucker said that this wasn't the case, but Waters wasn't convinced when he started listing shows from NBC's past. "That was then and now is now. Black viewers deserve the kind of content they feel good about. . . . I don't understand why you don't pursue it and why you don't do it."

Jack recruits Tracy and Dot Com to develop a new show for the Black community. It starts out as a show created by Dot Com about a Black family in the 1970s, with grit and depth behind it, but Grizz suggests adding a talking dog—which Tracy agrees to. *TGS* also promotes Toofer to the position of co–head writer to diversify their show, but Liz grows frustrated at Toofer getting credit for her work. "Let's Stay Together" has similarities to classic sitcom *Good Times*, with the father from that show—actor John Amos—cameoing as the lead in Dot Com's new program. The watering down of the show's themes reflects real complaints about the writing on *Good Times*, with Amos complaining about the writers pushing the J.J. character and his "DY-NO-MITE" catchphrase over meaningful dialogue. Amos said that he was ultimately fired from *Good Times* for being too outspoken.

Grizz Chapman: What the writers would do, is they would just walk around and watch [me and Dot Com]. When we would have lunch, the writers would sit, and they would watch us, and see how we would interact with each other, and then they came up with this dynamic of putting me and Dot Com against each other. We were supposed to be such good friends, and then we turn out to be rivals because he wanted to push his plays and his scripts, and I wanted my own TV show.

When Bookman comes to visit the *TGS* set, the recycling bins have been moved, so she finds labels reading "white" and "colored"—whose placement makes it look like they're instead referring to the restrooms.

Todd Buonopane: I still think we need to be able to joke about bias. We need to joke about how corporate culture pretends to work, but it's just doing it for show. The recycling, and separating the whites and the colored—which is,

I mean, actually a very funny joke. But you could also understand someone would be like "That's not something I want to laugh at." And as a white man, I don't know if that's my decision to make, whether that's offensive or not.

Kenneth was always the much-picked-on, lovable underdog, but this season ratcheted that up with Kenneth having to work his way back from being fired. Jenna works with Kenneth to try to get him back into the NBC Page Program, explaining that she'll need to break Kenneth down and build him back up, "just like Mickey Rourke did to me sexually"—one of the long-running jokes of Jenna's sexual relationship with Mickey Rourke, which ended with a fourth-wall breaking nod that it wasn't a thing. But the pressure to rehire Kenneth leads to HR rep Weinerslav having to replace the initial Native American pick for the page position with white male Kenneth.

> **Todd Buonopane:** I have what I thought was a really funny line at the time, that I said I want to hire a Native American fellow named "Runs for Sandwiches." Which, that's a joke about white people's perceptions of Native Americans, and Kevin Costner in *Dances with Wolves*. But I could also very well understand if a Native American person doesn't want to laugh at that, and doesn't appreciate that.

Buonopane said he wasn't sure if Fey's justification for using blackface and making a larger cultural point would apply to the jokes based on race in this episode. They aren't as in-your-face offensive as the show actually using blackface, but it seems to indicate a blind spot in the writing when it comes to Native Americans that would go on to be a bigger issue on *Unbreakable Kimmy Schmidt*.

Jack ultimately praises the importance of diversity, describing it as the engine that drives this country—with the first generation working hard to make things, the second generation going to college, and the third snowboarding and taking improv classes.

Episode 4, "Live Show," did a network favorite to grab viewers' attention by using a live episode. The inspiration came from a combination of the live-performance backgrounds of much of the cast, including on *SNL*, as well as the success of the live performances of an episode they did at UCB during the Season 2 writers' strike. There had been a plan to do a live episode during Season 4, but they were unable to schedule it.

This could easily have been nothing more than a gimmick, but the comedy is still high quality enough to keep it from feeling rote. The cast and crew did the show live for both coasts, with some jokes specific to each version of the episode.

> **Chris George:** I was standing in the corridor at *SNL* and Alec came walking down. He's like "Mr. George, great find again." Just making fun of me. Clearly, I had no role in finding Studio 8H.

Vali Chandrasekaran: It was crazy. Because first of all, our show is a version of *Saturday Night Live*, so our sets look like the *SNL* writers' room, and *SNL* stage, and all of that. Then we shot the live show in 8H, on the *SNL* stage. You're in the rafters, you look down on the stage, and it is a slightly smaller version of the *Saturday Night Live* stage, built inside *Saturday Night Live*.

The set designers re-created the *30 Rock* sets from Silvercup Studios in *SNL*'s Studio 8H.

Vali Chandrasekaran: It's like when you're in a museum, and they have a scale model of the museum you're inside of that you're looking at.

Some of the sets had to be rethought, designed to allow for a live audience to watch what's going on. They also had to be a bit smaller due to the relative lack of space in 8H.

Paul Feig: The set on *30 Rock* looked like you think the set looks like when you go to see *SNL*. And when you get to *SNL* you go, "This looks nothing like I thought."

The *30 Rock* writers would go back to the *SNL* offices to write while that show was on hiatus, including for the live episode.

Vali Chandrasekaran: It was nerve-racking to be a part of, because I had never worked in live TV before. The pacing of a regular *30 Rock* episode is really fast, and you can't do that with a live audience. We would do the table read and the run-through, and it would feel totally different.

Tina and Robert, having spent all that time at *SNL*, they knew. They just said, this part is going to work—it can't be the same way we do it normally, because there's just not time for the camera to swing and for the audience to look around the room. They're not going to enjoy it in that way live—the live audience doesn't like it. I had never even worked on a multicam with an audience, and they were so even-keeled and great.

A massive rainstorm that night had cast and crew worried whether the audience would show. But even a torrential downpour couldn't keep fans away, so there was a show to put on. To open things up, along with introducing the cast, they tasked their resident Broadway stars with delivering songs to warm up the crowd. Jane Krakowski got to sing the *actual* "Piece of My Heart" by Janis Joplin rather than the Jackie Jormp-Jomp version, and Cheyenne Jackson delivered Stevie Wonder's "Superstition." During the actual live broadcasts, the actors also sang versions of the show's theme song, with slightly altered lyrics for each coast.

30 Rock director Beth McCarthy-Miller had directed *SNL* episodes for eleven years. She took the lead in bringing the live version of the show to life, with Tina Fey saying there was no one else that could have called this show.

Beth McCarthy-Miller: It was insane. I had 120 camera cuts in the first act. After the cold open, I'm like "Oh well, at least I can roll the opening credits." They're like "No, we're gonna sing the opening credits."

Jon Haller: The week of the live taping, she got some sort of virus. So she had this insane head cold, and then she was in the director's booth directing two hundred-some shots in that episode, all while we were honoring *SNL*.

The *30 Rock* crew collaborated with the *SNL* crew on this cultural exchange between one kind of faux reality and another.

Beth McCarthy-Miller: We used a bunch of the *SNL* camera guys, too. Honestly, that's the greatest crew in television, and the other greatest crew in television was *30 Rock*. I had the *SNL* stage managers working with the *30 Rock* first ADs, and it was the perfect synergy of two of the greatest crews I've ever worked with in my life.

Original *30 Rock* Jenna and Tina Fey confidante Rachel Dratch made her return to the show—appropriate for an episode that borrows deeply from *30 Rock*'s *SNL* roots, as well as Tina's longtime collaborations with Dratch in live shows.

Beth McCarthy-Miller: It was so fun to see Dratch and Fey together again.

Tina Fey: We rewrote it that morning, *SNL* style.

Will Ferrell was asked to bring back his *Bitch Hunter* character as a cameo in this episode, but was unable to appear due to a scheduling conflict.

Speaking of *SNL*, the show found a way to do the quick cutaways that the show was known for even in the live format by using different actors to play the characters during those cutaways. That includes Julia Louis-Dreyfus doubling for Liz in the version of her we see in Liz's mind. The crew had to do those whip-pan camera moves that go into flashbacks on the show live.

Peter Agliata: Oh my god. The communication and timing to get them—I had to do one of the whips, then a cameraman five sets away was marrying his whip to mine, and then he would have to whip back [to me]. It was a little bit of guesswork when the whip was happening. We tried it in rehearsals, and it was a disaster.

Beth was laughing and said, "I don't know if this is going to work." It was very hard to call it live, but it actually worked out when we did it.

Tina's brainstorm to lure Julia Louis-Dreyfus into playing the younger version of Liz in the live show's flashbacks: She figured Louis-Dreyfus would want to come out to the East Coast to visit her son Henry at Wesleyan in nearby Connecticut. The show tried to get Billy Baldwin to play young Alec, but he was in Hawaii at the time.

Due to the show being live, they also had very specific timing they had to hit. When they got behind during a commercial break, Tina and Alec had to come back talking *verysuperquickly* because they didn't have quite as much time spread between jokes as they needed with the audience response.

Beth McCarthy-Miller: The scripts in *30 Rock* are so dense as it is. I was like "You're gonna have to write the shortest script ever," and they were like "Yeah, yeah, yeah." Then we go into the first commercial break and we're two minutes over, and you can't just cut stuff. It's storyline.

Tina Fey: We all messed up a little bit. That's how you know it's live.

Beth McCarthy-Miller: And Tina's like "OK, we'll just talk faster." In the second act, she and Alec spoke at a rate that I have never seen before in my life, and they made up over a minute.

The time they gained was also aided by some Capital One product placement they'd arranged before the show. The goal: a Capital One commercial in their dialogue giving them more time than they'd lose talking about Capital One—Pete and Jack deliver the plug in just two lines. Alec Baldwin went on to become a pitchman doing full, actual Capital One commercials.

30 Rock took advantage of the live format and being at the *SNL* stages to actually show you a *TGS* sketch for once, as well as including some fake commercials starring Dr. Spaceman.

They also lured back Matt Damon, even though his wife was about to have a baby. He does a short scene where he calls Liz while flying and going through turbulence. *SNL* alum and *Barry* star Bill Hader also appeared as his co-pilot. The pitch was made to Damon while he was shooting another *30 Rock* episode.

Tina Fey: I literally get emails from friends of mine from college—I got an email from my friend who was furious with me that I didn't write in something where I made out with Matt Damon. I'm like, I can't do it!

Though, she noted, she did kiss Jon Hamm, because Liz deserved *something*.

The fake plane was staged under the *SNL* bleachers, which is where Lorne Michaels normally stands to watch the show—and during the live show, Julia Louis-Dreyfus, Jon Hamm, Matt Damon, and Chris Parnell all stood there to watch the show, too.

Jane Krakowski was pregnant when this was shot, but it was before she'd made the news public. The show would work around her pregnancy as the season progressed, coming up with increasingly more elaborate ways to hide her midsection.

The show-within-a-show wraps up with the whole *TGS* cast on stage—the small, small *TGS* cast, since it usually seems like Tracy, Jenna, and Danny are their only performers. They even include the *TGS* robot (Sketchtron 6000) and bear, frequently seen in the background on the show, in the cast shot to help round out their numbers. As Tina Fey noted, the way *TGS* works doesn't fully make sense.

Part of the conceit to explain the live show was that Jack wasn't drinking while Avery was pregnant, and it made everything look more garish—the same way live TV video cameras do versus film that's been properly graded, as *30 Rock* usually had due to shooting on film. Liz is frustrated during the episode that everyone has forgotten her fortieth birthday, but she finishes by making a birthday wish: for Jack to have a drink with her. He concedes, and the show cuts to a piece taped weeks earlier on glorious film, his world—and *30 Rock*'s—finally back to normal.

> **Beth McCarthy-Miller:** There are so few watercooler moments anymore, because we're in a world of video cameras at every single thing that happens in the universe now. When I was growing up and there was a really great episode of TV, the next day you talked about it. Now, you can talk about it online while it's happening. Some of those live things are real watercooler moments, where people the next day do talk about them.

The live-show stunt worked. This episode drew the highest ratings of the season, with 6.7 million viewers, compared with 4.9 million the week before and 5.85 million in its season premiere. It was good enough for *30 Rock* to beat a rerun of *Grey's Anatomy*, which had just 4.08 million viewers, though it was still far behind first-run episodes of *$#*! My Dad Says* on CBS (10.16 million viewers) and *Bones* on Fox (9.58 million viewers).

The original East Coast episode is a bit lost to time—while the West Coast episode is a DVD extra, the main version used is edited together from portions of both versions of the show, designed to provide a smoother experience.

This episode was also among the shows pulled from streaming when Tina Fey asked for episodes to be pulled following the 2020 growth of the Black Lives Matter movement and the murder of George Floyd. While this episode didn't feature blackface, the East Coast version included Jon Hamm's Dr. Drew Baird in a controversial fake commercial, revealing that he's had one of his hooks replaced with a hand transplant from an executed prison inmate—which happens to be a Black man's hand, meaning that Hamm is both wearing a Black man's skin and the show is using the stereotype of Black men being criminals. And then the hand, apparently possessed by the spirit of the executed man, tries to strangle him.

The West Coast version initially remained available, but was later pulled. In that version, a woman's hand was used, which seems somewhat less offensive. But both versions featured Fox News parodies with anti-Obama chyrons that could have been part of what drew more attention in 2020, with the East Coast version advertising "exclusive interview with Kenyan liar," while the somewhat more subtle West Coast version reads, "impartial interview with Barack Obammunist." It's clearly a parody of Fox News's hyperbolic, less-than-fact-based coverage of the former president, but it might not be something that *30 Rock* wants to be putting out there even in parody form given the way politics had evolved since then under President Donald Trump.

In **episode 5, "Reaganing,"** Jack introduces "Reaganing" as a concept. It's when you're on a roll, making one perfect decision after another for 24 hours—"a magic zone of error-free living," à la the way conservatives believe President Ronald Reagan lived. The only men who've ever accomplished it, according to Jack, are "Lee Iacocca, Jack Welch, and—no judgment—Saddam Hussein." Jack makes use of a Reagan favorite, jelly beans, to help Tracy say a line in a commercial that he is repeatedly failing at. The solution: have him chew on jelly beans, with Jack doing his (somewhat offensive) Tracy impression on voice-over to deliver the line.

Jack also helps Liz find the roots of her intimacy problems, tracing them back to when she was a kid and had a Tom Jones poster fall on her just before her mom walked in. Believing that young Liz had been masturbating, her mom took away all of her posters.

Kelsey Grammer makes one of several *30 Rock* appearances here as himself, conspiring with *TGS* cast members to scam ice cream franchise Carvel out of money using a card Jenna received that entitles her to free ice-cream cakes for life. Their big score: eight hundred bucks. It was based on Lindsay Lohan's mom, Dina Lohan, *actually* abusing a real Carvel black card that the company had given out to celebrities. The show's in-depth plot also includes nods to classic con-artist film *The Sting*.

In **episode 6, "Gentleman's Intermission,"** Avery grows concerned about Jack and Liz's close friendship. But she grows to understand it in an episode that once again reminds viewers that Liz and Jack were never, ever getting together.

We also get just a touch of old-people racism from Liz's dad, Dick Lemon. She explains that he doesn't have to say his name every time he calls her, but he explains that telephone etiquette is important because "it lets people know your race even when they can't see you."

With **episode 7, "Brooklyn Without Limits,"** Tracy's Oscar-bait film *Hard to Watch* makes its way around the awards circuit. Tracy realizes he has a shot at that EGOT he's been dreaming of. He tells Jenna—with ample use of air quotes—"The 'pundits' think I have a 'chance' at an 'Oscar,' and I just learned about 'air quotes.'"

Tracy Morgan: They took that from my real life, because I love quoting.

Jenna attempts to sabotage his potential Golden Globes win due to jealousy of his acclaim. She tells him that he should try to bribe the Hollywood Foreign Press

Association, despite Jenna getting banned from awards contention for doing the very same thing in the past—but when she sees his film, she ends up so moved that she comes clean and stops Tracy from offering a bribe.

In another *Mad Men* universe connection, John Slattery makes a memorable guest appearance as conservative/insane Tea Party politician Steven Austin, who goes by "Steve" so that people think they're voting for WWE pro wrestler "Stone Cold" Steve Austin. Some of his political ideas include declaring that, if we have to have government, it should be as small as possible. A traditional conservative idea, until he adds examples: "Dwarves, tiny buildings, pizza bagels for lunch."

Jack attempts to use him to take out the congresswoman who's been breathing down his neck, Rep. Bookman (Queen Latifah). He sees vulnerability: Her citing the youth vote means that she's desperate—Jack's assistant Jonathan adds a shot at young people with his follow-up, "My generation never votes. It interferes with talking about ourselves all the time." *30 Rock* often showed its writers biases, including a disgust with young people that runs throughout the series, all the way back to Liz's approach to Cerie in the pilot.

But Jack decides he can't unleash this pizza-bagel-loving madman on America. The 2010 episode ridiculed the real-life Tea Party movement that had just happened to get started shortly after America's first Black president took office in 2009, and laid the groundwork for the conservative movement to come. The things Steve Austin says don't sound that outside the realm of political discourse a decade later.

In both the political storyline and in Liz's, the show makes one of its sharpest critiques of consumerism. After Liz buys jeans that magically make her butt look great, Jack reveals to her that the store she bought them at is owned by weapons manufacturer Halliburton. She tells Jack that he doesn't know what he's talking about, showing off a label that looks like it says they're handmade in the USA—but Jack explains that she's mispronouncing that and that "they're Hānd made in Usa. The Hānd are a Vietnamese slave race and Usa is their island prison. Want to know how they get the stitching so small? Orphans."

In **episode 8, "College,"** Jack's voice is used by an online dictionary site, leading the *TGS* writers to use it to prank Pete into thinking Jack wants to be his friend. Jack mentions that his voice has been used for *Thomas the Tank Engine*, a reference to Alec Baldwin actually being a storyteller on the *Thomas and Friends* show and playing Mr. Conductor in *Thomas and the Magic Railroad*.

As they filmed **episode 9, "Chain Reaction of Mental Anguish,"** Jane Krakowski's pregnancy was starting to show. But the writers opted not to have Jenna get pregnant on the show. Both Jack and Tracy were having children on the show this season, so the writers were looking to avoid every character having a kid at once. They also knew that Jenna wouldn't be a particularly fit mother.

This episode featured more bad business ideas from Tracy's adult faux son, opening a fine dining establishment that held regular battles between knockoff versions of Godzilla and Mechagodzilla fighting through the seated diners. Despite how awesome that sounds, it mostly leads to upset customers who just want to eat.

Liz uses Kenneth as her relationship therapist, but her complex problems break Kenneth's brain. When Jack tries to help him, Kenneth breaks Jack's brain. It's essentially horror movie *It Follows* in comedy form, with each of them passing on their brokenness to a new carrier.

When Paul asks Jenna to meet his parents, she panics and decides to break up with him. She wants a wild sex partner, not a commitment—a struggle that she would continue to face as the relationship developed for the next several seasons.

In **episode 10, "Christmas Attack Zone,"** Jack finally tells his mother about Avery's pregnancy—and Colleen (Elaine Stritch) is less than excited, due to the couple not being married. Jack invites his liberal father Milton (Alan Alda) to try setting Colleen straight, but Colleen responds by faking a heart attack and winning both Milton's and Avery's sympathy. Jack and Avery announce that they're getting married over New Year's and that they'd been planning to elope.

While Alan Alda knew Elaine Stritch beforehand, this was their first time working together. This episode also serves as a reveal that Milton got the kidney transplant he needed—and that it was sent to him by "He Needs a Kidney" benefit singer Elvis Costello.

In order to keep his quest for an EGOT on track, Tracy buys the rights to the *Nutty Professor*–style comedy he just shot, *The Chunks 2: A Very Chunky Christmas*. The goal is to maintain his image as a serious actor, shelving the film to avoid perpetuating his foolish image. But when he goes to do a charity event for a women's shelter, where the audience includes a lot of kids, he decides that laughter is a far better Christmas gift than showing them all a bummer awards contender and he decides to screen *The Chunks 2*.

This was among the episodes pulled from streaming and syndication over its use of blackface. Jenna and Paul dress up for the New Queer's Eve party, an event where you have to dress like a pop culture phenom from the previous year. The idea, which brings the couple back together: *Black Swan*. So, Will Forte dresses as the ballerina from the Natalie Portman film, while Jenna dresses up as . . . former Pittsburgh Steelers player Lynn Swann. In blackface.

Kevin Ladson: I remember when we did the Lynn Swann episode. And I read it in the script. I was there for the meetings and everything. And I said, "How are they going to pull this off?" My office was on the main stage—where we had the *TGS* stage—right up in the corner. And when Jenna came out, they were going to talk about how she was going to come to do the reveal. She was on the way to set. I came down and I saw Jenna, and that . . . that really hurt. And I said, "I really want to know how this gets a pass."

When she came out and did the reveal, everybody was laughing. And I really stood outside myself to see what my reaction was going to be. I said, "I'm not feeling that comedy."

Ladson retreated to his workshop office above the stage.

Kevin Ladson: I went back to my cage upstairs, my office. And I said, "This kind of stings a little bit."

John Riggi: As far as the blackface, I think we made the right decision to pull it. The insensitivity of the time was not as apparent as it is now. And I'm honestly sorry—I mean, I think if we had literally thought about it a little bit more, we probably wouldn't have done it in the first place.

Jesse Thorn: I mean, I'm completely unconvinced that Carlock and Fey have a sophisticated understanding of the problematics of the show. They didn't have a good answer when I asked them about that [in an interview for public radio show *Bullseye*]. And I didn't ask them gotcha questions. *Kimmy Schmidt* is full of problematic stuff, and I love *Kimmy Schmidt*, too. I think they just are from a different generation, and they have not had the full reckoning. But that also doesn't mean that I think that they are malicious, or jerks, or what people think of when you say "racist."

Emily VanDerWerff: Hollywood should be more open to people from any level of production challenging certain things within the show. If you are a guest star who's coming in for one episode and you say, "This line feels wrong to me," that should be a challenge to the writers to either make the line better or make the context surrounding it better.

This was different than when Jenna wore blackface in Season 3. This time, it wasn't being used to make a dramatic point about racism and sexism—it was about the absurdity of these two white characters thinking this was a good idea. The storyline didn't feature any actual Black characters this time, so there isn't Tracy Morgan's involvement to hide behind. The episode is credited to white writer Tracey Wigfield. She went on to develop the 2020 *Saved by the Bell* reboot for NBC streaming service Peacock, which deals with race throughout its first season and features one of the most diverse casts in television. She also acknowledged that on the show she created in between *30 Rock* and this reboot, *Great News*, her writers' room wasn't diverse enough. She set about intentionally changing that with *Saved by the Bell*.

In *30 Rock* Season 5 **episode 11, "Mrs. Donaghy,"** we open with Jack and Avery married. Kind of. Jack discovers that, due to a mix-up in their French Caribbean wedding ceremony thanks to not knowing the language, their officiant married him to Liz. While this could be an excuse to go into that Jack/Liz relationship that was much speculated about early on, the idea continues to be played as completely absurd—Jack is overwhelmed with disgust, while Liz needles him about what it would be like if they were a genuine married couple.

She tries to leverage their marital status to get Jack to give *TGS* back its budget, with their feud escalating and Liz announcing a public donation to create the Jack and Elizabeth Donaghy High School for Teen Drama, the Arts, and Feelings. HR mediator Jeffrey Weinerslav comes in to save the day, pointing out the romantic-like qualities of their relationship and making Liz and Jack realize how meaningful their mentor–mentee relationship is. Each of them gives the other what they want.

> **Todd Buonopane:** Tina said that that episode was kind of their answer to NBC, because the NBC execs kept saying, "So, when are Liz and Jack going to get together?" And Tina kept saying, "That's not what the show's about. They're friends." This is a show about a friendship, ultimately, and NBC is always looking for the next Sam and Diane.
>
> People have been programmed to think, there's a handsome man and a handsome woman that are the stars of the show—they will eventually get married.

Buonopane said that he always loved working with Alec Baldwin, because Baldwin has an almost needy energy.

> **Todd Buonopane:** He immediately is like "Tell me about your life, what's been happening?" I know he has this reputation of being a bully in real life, but I never, ever saw that.
>
> When you walk into being a guest star on a show, you are walking into a world that operates every day without you. And then suddenly, you have to be a big focus of it—and you don't even know where the bathroom is.

This would end up being Buonopane's final appearance on the show, which he said was always a good experience.

> **Todd Buonopane:** It was fun to do the rehearsals, because the crew would just sit there and laugh at you. It was a rather joyous place to be—and I have been on other sets that were not joyous at all.

Danny returns for another episode here, with Jenna's dressing room rented out to save on the show's budget and forcing her to room with her rival. Their dynamic shifts to that of an old married couple, with Kenneth as the lonely child caught in the middle, and Jenna ultimately forces Danny out of his own dressing room.

> **Cheyenne Jackson:** I'm so grateful to Tina, because Season 5, I was doing *Finian's Rainbow* on Broadway. And they let me do both. So I was only on maybe four or five episodes a year, but they let me do it in the morning. Then at night, I would be done in time to get to my call and do the Broadway show. I was so exhausted. And it was hard on my leading lady on Broadway—but really, what a wonderful problem to have.

The episode features Tracy's wife, Angie, getting her own reality show, with the end-of-episode tag showing the opening sequence of *Queen of Jordan.*

> **Paula Leggett Chase (Randi):** Tina Fey was a big fan of *The Real Housewives of Beverly Hills.* And the whole thing was just an audition to come in and do, "I'm Randi, with an 'I'"—one of those things, like on *Real Housewives,* where they show the person and a fan is blowing on them.

30 Rock went on to do a full episode of the faux show later this season.

In **episode 12, "Operation Righteous Cowboy Lightning,"** Jack comes up with a plan to take care of celebrity benefits for natural disasters by pre-recording a benefit before the disaster ever happens. It even includes Robert DeNiro coming in to tape potential disaster options, such as "When the birds first started attacking us, we all thought it was pretty funny and made Hitchcock jokes, but we're not laughing now, because our laughter excites the birds sexually."

This was one of the first episodes with a full-length storyline featuring Lutz, as well as his real-life partner Sue Galloway, in a big storyline.

> **John Lutz:** We had already met two months before [*30 Rock*], but then we were extras and sat in extra holding together, and that's where our love bloomed. *(laughs)*

> **Sue Galloway:** It sounds gross when you say it like that.

As the *TGS* writers consider what they would do in the event of an emergency, Lutz brags that he owns a car and would be able to help them escape the city. The other writers all try to convince Lutz why they're worthy of joining him in his car, with Sue taking her top off as her way of making her case.

In Lutz's ever-evolving gender expression, he's also in some subtle makeup here.

Sue Galloway: I'd like to point out that John had eyeliner on for like the next four days. I don't think men are good at removing eye makeup.

John Lutz: But for those three days, my eyes really popped.

Jack sees Lutz and is . . . not pleased.

John Lutz: The best thing—that was something that Alec just did naturally when they saw me, so they just put it into the script. He looked at me, disgusted by what I was wearing.

Sue Galloway: No one knew if he was ever acting or not.

John Lutz: We don't know if he really hates the character Lutz, or if he hates Lutz.

It turns out that the disaster the network deploys its pre-made benefit for is on a sex island owned by Mel Gibson—but the special still ends up being a success.

Before there was a full *Queen of Jordan* episode, the fake reality show's crew was shooting at *TGS* and following Tracy around. It forces Tracy to be on his best behavior so that he won't show up on the reality show, which Liz tries to take advantage of by turning him into a better-behaved cast member. But he realizes he can say terrible things, he just has to do it to the tune of songs that would be expensive for the show to license—he sings his insults to the melody of Billy Joel's "Uptown Girl." He also insists on only doing serious movies, explaining that the only movies he's going to make from now on "are about the Holocaust, Georgia O'Keeffe, or both."

Starting in **episode 13, "¡Qué Sorpresa!,"** Kabletown gets a new personification this season, with the cable giant run by the affable, grandfatherly Hank Hooper (the late Ken Howard). It's a great contrast with Jack, a shift from Devon Banks and their mano a mano battles, two equals going up against one another, or Rip Torn and his gruff older businessman. Here you find Hooper's friendliness completely confounding Jack's cunning business instincts.

They gave Howard a fake mustache—Don Scardino said they felt it gave him more of a country bumpkin air. He meets Jack and gives him a big ol' hug.

Alan Sepinwall: I don't know that Don Geiss was ever quite as funny as the show thought he was, but then Ken Howard comes in as Hank Hooper, this nice and gentle family man running this company utterly incompetently.

Vali Chandrasekaran: It was never a question of if we would do it, it was a question of how we would do it. To Comcast and GE's credit, they never harassed Tina and Robert about it. They were really good about giving them their independence. I wonder if [the execs] maybe even liked it a bit.

Hank turns NBC's executive dining room into an "Everyone Dining Room," leaving Jack appalled. They filmed it in the actual 30 Rock building's Rainbow Room, a private events space—which proved technically difficult for director John Riggi, working to get all their equipment to the top floor of this 1933 building.

In **episode 14, "Double-Edged Sword,"** Liz and Jack both realize their partners have similar traits to their own, a "double-edged sword" with the situation both helping and hurting their relationships. Jack and Avery visit Toronto, where Avery goes into labor. The conservative couple tries to get back to the US so that their child is born on American soil, but despite the help of a meth smuggler who happens to be named Lorne (played by John Cho), they don't make it.

Meanwhile, Liz travels with Carol serving as the pilot. But as the plane gets stuck on the tarmac, with Carol constantly telling the passengers that they'll leave "in about half an hour," Liz joins the passengers in revolt. It was Damon's last *30 Rock* episode. Liz's moral indignation on behalf of everyone onboard comes into conflict with Carol's moral indignation for how terrible passengers are on planes, and the battle leads to them breaking up.

After Tracy finally completes his EGOT, it's a monkey's paw, with his wish to be an award-winning actor leading to the actually kind of boring life of a serious actor. Which isn't at all what Tracy wanted. So he flees, allegedly going to live in Africa (à la when Dave Chappelle left for Africa at the height of his own *Chappelle's Show* fame).

Tracy Morgan: Being in Africa, that was a great, great thing for them to write for me. I was able to heal and come back to the show.

The storyline was designed to give Tracy Morgan time for a kidney transplant, writing him out of the show for several episodes and pulling him out of storylines he was set to be a part of. He missed the next two episodes entirely, and was used in smaller roles on other episodes this season. It was hard for the entire cast and crew, both due to their personal connection with Tracy and the difficulty in writing around his absence.

John Riggi: What I really remember was how concerned I was about him—we all were. I loved them all, but I loved Tracy and still do so much. He's one of the nicest people I have ever met in my life. He's one of the craziest people I've ever met in my life.

Vali Chandrasekaran: First of all, you immediately want Tracy, who's one of the world's best men, to just get better and be healthy. Because he's a delightful person, and no one should be unhealthy.

John Riggi: When we would put stories up on the board, the way we would break stories in the room is we'd have a column that was usually the Liz and

Jack story, or the Liz and somebody story. If there was a separate story, then there was a Jack story, and quite often, the third story was Tracy, or Tracy and Jenna. He was such a big part of the series, that to lose him for those episodes . . . I mean, we worked around it. But it was hard, and we were honestly concerned about him, because for a long time he was really struggling. Trying to get his health issues under control was a challenge.

Working with Tracy could be a challenge, with colleagues citing his lack of discipline as a performer, coming in unprepared and at times struggling to deliver a scene. But they felt he was magic onscreen.

One of the ways that they started to fill the Tracy-sized gap was doing more storylines centered around Pete. He'd started the show as Liz's conscience, an advisor and a listening ear, before she just started telling Jack all of her problems.

Alan Sepinwall: Pete in theory is the most normal person, and the longer the show went on, the less Scott Adsit had to do. It quickly became a show without a need for a Pete Hornberger type.

Vali Chandrasekaran: Tracy often got to play, even in the world of *30 Rock*, some of the more absurd storylines, and it freed up more of the absurdity tank that we could sprinkle around to other people.

John Riggi: Scott's an amazing actor, and we tried to give him some oxygen—let's do a Pete story. But because of the way Tracy was as a character—like, Tracy's hanging on to the ceiling of the elevator. Tracy's bigger than life. So it was a lot to try to fill that spot, and everybody helped out with that, but it was a hard time.

Jon Haller: Adsit is just so fucking good. He was such a team player. He was just happy to do whatever material you came up with. They did a Pete story and Adsit, like he does, knocks it out of the park.

Vali Chandrasekaran: I'm glad we were able to pull it off for a little bit, but I'm also glad that we didn't have to do it for too long, because it really would have hit the show.

We see Pete get that spotlight in **episode 15, "It's Never Too Late for Now."** With Liz still fresh off breaking up with Carol, she's largely given up on life. So, in a storyline that plays on *Murder on the Orient Express*, it's ultimately revealed that her coworkers conspired to give her a perfect one-night stand as she gets back on her feet, in an intricately layered plan.

Judah Friedlander: This is one of those episodes where I actually had to ask what was going on, because I really wasn't sure.

It's a long setup that gets Liz back to her old self. Even while she figures out what happened and gives a long monologue with all of her colleagues assembled, detailing what they did, she chooses to believe that the romantic one-night stand they arranged for her was actually just a lovely moment. Unlike Liz's usual fight for the truth, she chooses, at least one time, to live in a bliss that actively ignores what actually happened.

Meanwhile, Pete and Frank reminisce about Pete's time in 1980s band Loverboy, and they come up with their own retro-rock song, "It's Never Too Late for Now."

> **Vali Chandrasekaran:** Ron Weiner came up with that line, while we were breaking the story. Just the *dumbest* song. And it made us laugh. Ron writes songs himself, and I feel like that show ended up happening because Ron came up with that idea.

In actuality, Friedlander was a much worse singer than Adsit—he praised Adsit for carrying the vocals. Friedlander had been told in sixth grade that he was tone deaf, and felt that music never became a strong point for him. But for the one shining moment of this episode, he got to be a rock star. *30 Rock* hired a Broadway singer to hit some of the particularly epic notes for the song's recording.

> **Scott Adsit:** The costume was very, very tight for the flashback—the music video. I got self-conscious, because I've got an inch or two I can pinch in my middle. I was thinking, *OK, well I don't want to look bad. And I want to look like a rock and roll guy back then, not from now.*

> **John Riggi:** I'm a weirdo in that there are certain things that I would shoot, and they would be really funny, but they would almost make me cry. I was so happy for Pete in that moment, watching him live a dream that he had. It bled over into me dealing with Adsit and Judah. I was like, I one hundred percent want to believe that this is happening. So I am going to shoot the shit out of this video, because I want them to have a great time with this.

> **Scott Adsit:** I had them put some Spanx on me, underneath. It took forever because they had to cut it, and change it, and alter the Spanx. It took a day for them to get just right, and finally it was there, my belly was flat, and I looked younger. We get on set, and they strap this guitar to me, and the guitar just blocked my entire middle. The wardrobe people and I just looked at each other and shook our heads, and thought, *Well, this was a great waste of ego and time.*

Jack also finds his negotiating put to the test, with his daughter, Liddy's, night nurse playing hardball. Her negotiating tactic is simply eating a tangerine and remaining stoic throughout—a technique Jack puts into play for himself while negotiating with Kabletown.

Episode 16, "*TGS* Hates Women," took on cultural critics with an episode satirizing women's blog *Jezebel*. Tina Fey made headlines while making *Unbreakable Kimmy Schmidt* for the way she responded to complaints about how race was depicted on that show, particularly with its depictions of Asians and Native Americans. But the subtler approach to criticism here proved more successful—though it was easier for the writers to have some distance in this case, since it wasn't about a specific critique of *30 Rock* itself.

The show substitutes in fictional blog *Joan of Snark* for *Jezebel*. It was a play on an article that criticized hiring Olivia Munn, then a model and former host on geek/gamer TV network G4, as a *Daily Show* correspondent. *Jezebel* had criticized *The Daily Show* for hiring Munn, seeing the move as one meant to appeal to a male audience. Munn had previously been best known for sexually provocative moments as a host, as well as appearances in *Playboy* and *Maxim* magazines, rather than for her humor. But this *30 Rock* episode also plays as a critique of how women are treated throughout comedy, the entertainment industry, and, you know, the world.

TGS hires Abby Flynn (Cristin Milioti), a comedy writer who seriously plays up her sexuality. Liz tries to act like her feminist friend, but ends up coming off as a hypocrite.

> **Beth McCarthy-Miller:** I love that idea of perception and the idea of the way women sometimes feel they need to carry themselves to get ahead in life.

> **Tina Fey:** It's a complicated issue, and we didn't go much further on saying anything other than to say, "Yeah, it's a complicated issue and we're all kind of figuring it out as we go." I don't have the answer. But I find it interesting that Olivia gets people who go after her on some of these sites because she's beautiful. I think if she were kind of an aggressive, heavier girl with a Le Tigre mustache posing in her underpants, people would be like "That's amazing. Good for you."

> **Jon Haller:** When Cristin Milioti came and played the bimbo girl writer, Tina was just aghast—Tina was like, she's really good. So then we would watch the dailies. I just thought, *Please let this person become a star*.

> **Beth McCarthy-Miller:** One of the great things about a well-written comedy is that you can take a little look at yourself, and without being heavy-handed, you can send a message. Tina and I were in all the auditions for that, because we wanted someone specifically that could handle it. She played that role perfect.

Milioti went on to have a bigger breakthrough as the mother on *How I Met Your Mother*. *Salon* writer Rebecca Traister noted how closely the Abby character mirrored the comedy and even the voice of Sarah Silverman, and writers' notes from the show indicate that this was at least partly inspired by Silverman. It was a part of discussions among the writers as far back as Season 1, before landing in the show here. There were also similarities with the way comedian Janeane Garofalo was treated in her short-lived run at *Saturday Night Live*—she would go on to describe working on *SNL* as one of the worst experiences of her life.

Jack faces another seemingly opposite adversary this season: Hank Hooper's teenage granddaughter, Kaylie Hooper (Chloë Grace Moretz). But while she appears innocent to begin with, we quickly learn that she's just as much of a conniving business snake as Banks ever was.

> **Vali Chandrasekaran:** She was such a good foil for Jack. It was something that made us laugh a lot when we were pitching it, then when Chloë showed up and would really just scream at Alec Baldwin, and he would scream right back at her, it was really funny to look at on screen. Especially just size-wise.

The show shot scenes with her character outside the Museum of the City of New York doubling as her school, a location also used on *Gossip Girl*.

Beyond the live episodes, this season also included **episode 17, "Queen of Jordan,"** the in-universe reality show about Tracy's wife, Angie. Like the live episode, it was filmed on video to give the episode a different, reality show feeling.

Doing the fake show allowed them to play with the tropes of reality TV, particularly the *Real Housewives* franchise, just as reality shows were having a real moment. Tina Fey and episode writer Tracey Wigfield were both big reality TV fans—Fey described the episode at the time as her thrusting her own TV viewing habits onto *30 Rock*'s audience.

> **Tracey Wigfield:** So much of writing the episode was figuring out how exactly do we do this, why would the cameras be following our characters? This was Tina's idea—one thing that they do a lot on these *Real Housewives* kind of shows is they're always following people through a doorway, or girls are having an argument about something in a bathroom and they're filming from under the door. I know this because I watched over four thousand hours of reality television.

> **Tom Ceraulo:** My biggest memory of the writing of this episode in the room was us watching episodes of *The Real Housewives of Beverly Hills*.

> **Tracey Wigfield:** You watch something like that, and you're like, why would you ever be a writer of television, when this and *America's Funniest Home Videos* is a thousand times better than anything you could ever write?

The episode featured wine throwing galore, in true reality show fashion.

> **Paula Leggett Chase:** First, it's like, I'm going to throw wine at this dog. So here's this dog, this really sweet German shepherd with a little birthday hat on,

sitting next to me. I'm sitting there, and the dog's trainer crouched down right in front of me. It was grape juice—it wasn't actually wine.

And [the trainer] said, "Throw it kind of toward, but not exactly in his face." So I did that. Then they're like "OK, no, we're gonna do it again." I'm like "OK," and then I did the same thing. Then [director Ken Whittingham's] like, "Paula, you gotta throw it. Are you having trouble? Are you not close?" I was like "Oh no, they think I'm a dullard." But I wasn't gonna rat her out either. So I threw it in his face. He didn't care one bit.

Tracey Wigfield: The problem was the dog kept licking the wine.

Chase found years later that her throwing wine at the dog had become a popular GIF.

The special episode also helped fill the gaps while Tracy Morgan was getting his kidney transplant. He'd been gone for four episodes, so "Queen of Jordan" let them do an episode largely without him, although he's in some flashback scenes that Morgan filmed when he came back.

The opening sequence was used as an end-of-episode tag earlier in the season, a satire of the promos for this kind of reality show, with this episode being another example of *30 Rock* taking a small joke and heightening it to a level far beyond your standard sitcom. These episodes also helped lead to the discovery of actor Tituss Burgess as Angie's gay friend D'Fwan, with Burgess being brought back by Fey and Carlock as a star on *Unbreakable Kimmy Schmidt*.

Tracey Wigfield: These were actors who were cast not to say dialogue or anything, just to look like weirdos, so we really lucked out. Because before the table read of this episode, it was like, uh-oh, I hope everybody knows how to act!

Jesse Thorn: I had no idea who [Tituss] was—he was on screen, the first time he did that, for ninety seconds or something—and I thought, *Oh my god, this guy's fantastic! Who is this person?* I was totally stunned, and totally unsurprised when I learned that basically that was the reaction Tina Fey and Robert Carlock had.

Paula Leggett Chase: At the table [read] for the second episode, D'Fwan—Tituss—and I are sitting together. Both of us were just like "This is wild." Because neither of us had had this large of a TV thing.

Burgess had come in to get some extra work while working by day on Broadway. But he was such an inspiration that the show used him multiple times, with Fey then writing a whole part around him on *Unbreakable Kimmy Schmidt*.

They had to re-cast Angie's friend Portia from her previous appearance, as the previous actress was filming a Queen Latifah movie in Atlanta.

You could see the season progress in how it filmed Jane Krakowski, who was around seven to eight months pregnant at this point. At this point in her pregnancy,

Jane would shoot with tape across her chest to help mark where she had to be shot above—that tape was slowly moving up her body.

Tracey Wigfield: All her shots are framed lower boob up.

She still had a chance to be glamorous. With the reality show conceit, Jane Krakowski requested that she wear five different cocktail dresses.

Tracey Wigfield: Even though there's no reason for costume changes [here]— like if you do the day to night, you should only change one time.

The episode features a brief flashback to Tracy and Angie getting married. The original idea was for them to get married in a Chuck E. Cheese, with ShowBiz Pizza keyboardist/monster Mr. Munch as his best man, but that sadly never happened anywhere but in our hearts.

The episode still had plots featuring the show's regular cast, including a storyline that the writers' room had long discussed: Frank having had an affair with his elementary school teacher, Lynn Onkman (Susan Sarandon). The *New York Post* published a story at the time citing sources that said Friedlander and Sarandon had "hooked up." But Friedlander clarified that they're actually friends from the New York City ping-pong world thanks to Sarandon owning a ping-pong social club. (Yes, this is a thing.) According to Wigfield, she got the impression that Sarandon actually enjoyed the Page Six speculation.

Randi does a scene where she has to show off strip aerobics skills—which the real actress had never done.

Paula Leggett Chase: We sat there at that table read, and I'm reading through it, and then it has in the script that Randi's hanging upside down on this pole. I was like "Oh, OK." They knew that I was a Broadway performer. Jerry Kupfer came up to me afterward, and he's like "So yeah, do you think you can do that?"

Tracey Wigfield: Paula is a dancer, definitely, but had never been a stripper—a pole dancer—so she took an intensive class to learn how to do that. It was really impressive.

Paula Leggett Chase: I did have to do it at some place in Manhattan at eight o'clock in the morning, over and over and over again. Until I was hanging anchoring the weight of both legs upside down. So I go into this place, and we go into this darkened room. I'm looking around and I'm like "OK, where are the mirrors?" And they were like "Oh, no mirrors because—" I said, "No, no, no. I need mirrors, because I want to know what my bits and pieces are going to be looking like hanging out on this."

The show brought her strip aerobics instructor on set to help out.

Paula Leggett Chase: My son was in high school and was watching all of *30 Rock*. He brought his friends over and I remember first meeting all these kids, and realizing they're looking at me kind of like, "Hello, Mrs. Chase. You were on *30 Rock*." And I say, "OK, now listen, boys. I was. And yes, that was me. But I am not a pole dancer in real life."

The show's climax features Liz getting her reality TV moment, repeatedly saying "let me talk" when no one's trying to interrupt her and while she doesn't have anything of substance to say. She closes with a trope from the *New Jersey* edition of *Real Housewives*, saying that her family is "thick as thieves."

Episode director Ken Whittingham had directed a lot of episodes of *The Office*, so he brought his experience shooting a documentary-style sitcom here.

The episode originally ended even more off-the-wall, with Angie's meth-addict nephew Michael dying, along with accidentally killing the dancers in Angie's music video. But they decided to pull back, just a touch.

Similarly to when Wigfield put a *Hot Tub Time Machine* reference in an earlier episode and was rewarded with T-shirts far too big for her, she got a free *Queen of Jordan* shirt—size large. She gave it to a male friend.

The episode was such a creative success, including critical praise, that it led to another *Queen of Jordan* episode in Season 6. As **episode 18, "Plan B,"** was being filmed, there was another pregnancy in the cast other than Krakowski's—this one still under wraps. Fey described herself as being tired and secretly pregnant while working on the episode.

At the same time, Tracy Morgan was starting to be eased back into the show. In the storyline, *TGS* was put onto a forced hiatus by NBC until its star, Tracy Jordan, returns to the program.

Jeff Richmond: He had a kidney transplant, and part of his foot is gone at this point.

Tina Fey: He's trying and doing his best, but I've had so many conversations with him where I'm like "Buddy. You can't have a twenty-piece McNugget meal." And he's genuinely like "Really?" And, of course, I don't know what he's supposed to eat.

She noted at the time that he still didn't miss the Super Bowl, or any Knicks games, while he was recovering.

The episode includes Jack discussing a recent acquisition of a TV network for gay men called "TWINKS," inspired by the growth of the LOGO TV network. Fey defended the show's approach to edgy comedy on this episode's DVD commentary.

Tina Fey: It's the intention behind the joke, and also it actually being formed into an actual joke, that makes it OK.

When Jack is advised by Kabletown boss Hank Hooper to either drop TWINKS or find a gay version of himself to run it, he realizes there is a gay Jack Donaghy: Devon Banks (Will Arnett). Banks is recruited to save that network, but ends up turning down the job to spend more time with his children, leading Jack to realize he hasn't been spending enough time with his own daughter.

As Liz looks into alternate career options as *TGS* runs into trouble, she contacts her terrible, terrible agent, Simon (Josh Fadem), in a return appearance.

Tina Fey: From the moment we brought him in, we thought, we gotta have this guy back again—he's such a good weirdo.

Josh Fadem: It gave my résumé credibility. I have a respectable character actor résumé, and that was the first recurring thing that I did. Even back at comedy shows, it was nice to be able to, when they say "What should I say when you come on stage?" to just say, "You saw him on *30 Rock*."

I drop Liz as a client, and then I say, "This is what I tell my dogs," and I start doing a Cesar Millan [*Dog Whisperer*] kind of thing. There was no script for that sound, and I remember just going off and doing different versions, and Tina going along with it. It was that feeling of "Hey, we're acting with each other! I do a thing, you do a thing, I'd respond to the thing, she'd respond to the thing." You have those little fan moments, where you're like "Hey! I'm a little guy here getting to come in and play with the big people, and the big people are playing with me. Good job, Me."

Tina Fey: Even his hair's too big for his head.

Jack gets Liz an interview for a writing job on a cappella singing show *The Sing-Off*, where she meets her competition: Aaron Sorkin. It's a punctuation mark on the *30 Rock/Studio 60* rivalry, another reminder that *30 Rock* was the ultimate victor—and that the *Studio 60* side didn't seem to hold the same animosity for its comedy competition. It's a chance for one more walk-and-talk, featuring the man who popularized the technique.

Jeff Richmond: [We used] the hallway that takes you around to the writers' room set, but we re-dressed it that morning. If you'd have gone another six feet, you would have been in the writers' room. We didn't have enough hallway for a Sorkin-style walk-and-talk. It was fun to see him do a walk-and-talk, because he was very good at it, and he barely ever messed up any takes. But he was putting so much pressure on himself to do it right. I said, "Yeah, you've asked a lot of actors to do this in your life, you've got to do this."

Sorkin flew in from picking up a BAFTA award for *The Social Network*. On the show, Sorkin tells Liz that writing is a dying art. Liz starts to mention *Studio 60*, at which point Sorkin tells her to shut up.

When Kenneth mentions that the pizza place Tracy orders from on the video calls they have with each other is the same one Liz likes, she realizes he isn't really in Africa and must be hiding out in New York somewhere.

The episode also includes a reference to Liz finding mouse poop in her slippers at *TGS*, drawn from Tina Fey's own experience.

> **Tina Fey:** True story. That happened at Silvercup Studios. Which is mouse-ridden—the old bread factory where we shoot our show. I had some slippers, I left them out. It looked like someone poured chocolate sprinkles over them when I came back.

> **Daisy Gardner:** If you were still there when the mice came out, you knew it was gonna be a long night. And we pretended it was only one mouse, named Mousington. But as soon as Mousington appeared, you'd be like "Aw crap, we're here."

While Liz and Kenneth search for Tracy in **episode 19, "I Heart Connecticut,"** Jenna stars in torture porn *Take My Hand*. But as Jack tries to make everything the company is involved with profitable, kissing up to his Kabletown overlords, that includes completely selling out the production of this film. He adds product placement for Walmart, promotion for Connecticut tourism, and a celeb cameo paid for by *Everybody Loves Raymond* producer Phil Rosenthal. That's all topped with a rewrite making it a family film.

> **Vali Chandrasekaran:** We talked about the nature of entertainment existing within a really buttoned-down organization, like General Electric, a lot. A lot of people on the show had read [GE chairman/CEO] Jack Welch's autobiography.

Tracy is finally found in the end, living in Liz's spare, unfinished upstairs apartment. Liz tells him that he is off the leash and can be a complete dirtbag in order to destroy his fancy filmmaker reputation. Tracy excitedly rips off the African top he's been wearing and gently knocks over Liz's lamp as he sets off to demolish his image.

Pete has an extended storyline where he gets to be an office arm wrestling champion after defeating Frank in a battle to determine where they're going to order lunch. It leads to an intense competition with a member of the crew played by Rob Riggle, a battle for arm wrestling supremacy. Pete even gets to take down Jack.

> **Scott Adsit:** We had to shoot that scene, and Alec is quite an alpha. So we rehearsed it, and he let me know—not in a jerky way, but "just so you know"—that there's no way I could ever beat him in an arm wrestling contest. He does have a *thick* arm, and we played it, he fought it, I beat him.

Jack tells Pete congratulations and that, by the transitive property, he's just beaten dictator Muammar Qaddafi in arm wrestling.

Scott Adsit: Then between takes, we would do a little actual arm wrestling. I would put my whole back into it, and he would just look at me, blink, and not move at all. It was like walking up to the Chrysler Building, putting your hand on the cement, and trying to wrestle the Chrysler Building to the ground. He's a very strong man, and I would never, ever want to take his parking space.

But in the end, the arm wrestling victories are all in Pete's head—he snaps out of it to find himself still arm wrestling Frank, and losing.

Vali Chandrasekaran: Making it a fantasy was something Carlock came up with. He discovered it the day before the table read, and wondered if that was the funnier way to go—having it be totally fake. I remember his eyes lighting up, him pitching it to us—what if we made *that* the version. That none of it happened. And the rest of us couldn't stop laughing.

Don't try to work out the timeline of this episode's events running concurrently, with the rest of the show moving on before cutting back to the arm wrestling contest—it's impossible.

The show did a special hourlong episode for the **20th episode this season,** **"100,"** celebrating both *TGS* and *30 Rock*'s 100th episodes. Thanks to *TGS*'s terrible ratings with Tracy Jordan gone, Kabletown's Hank Hooper threatens to cancel *TGS*—but agrees to hold off for them to prove themselves with their one hundredth episode, with Tracy's return.

Pointing out how terrible *TGS* is supposed to be, the show pulls out "Pam, the Overly Confident Morbidly Obese Woman," character seen in the pilot—which Pete notes they've done 107 times in one hundred episodes. Meaning there are episodes where it's done more than once. Or possibly just one episode in the middle somewhere where they did it 105 times.

The episode featured several homages and flashbacks to the early days of the show, including Tracy running through the street in his underwear in the pilot yelling, "I am a Jedi!" You also get a retcon for Liz and Jack's first meeting, with the reveal that Jack had originally been planning to fire Liz when he came in to NBC, rather than Pete—but that Pete stepped up and sacrificed himself for her.

Michael Keaton made his return to television here, and a return to comedy. Producing director Don Scardino said that Keaton came in with a million ideas but was worried about being too broad in his choices. After it aired, Keaton left a voicemail for Scardino. His question: "Too big?"

Scardino credited the ability to do something like pulling Keaton back to TV to the show having a cool reputation, shooting in New York, and the smart writing. Actors knew they'd be well served.

Keaton plays one of the show's many janitor characters, finding a gas leak making everyone in the building dumb and/or hallucinate. Jack meets with three other Jacks produced by his hallucinatory visions in this episode, meaning Alec Baldwin had to play whole scenes against himself. They used stand-ins that were similar to Alec from behind, but he didn't want them to speak and influence his reactions—he asked the script supervisor to read the lines, and sometimes he would read them himself while also playing the part they were shooting. The other versions include a less warm, even more business-focused version that's more similar to how Jack was portrayed in the series' early episodes.

Alec didn't want to change clothes more than once for the different characters, so Scardino had to figure out how to shoot the scene with that limitation, as well as under TV time pressures.

The gas main gets repaired—but Liz's ex Dennis breaks it open again to get her to rekindle their relationship, making her temporarily dumb enough to ignore his flaws.

Danny makes another appearance here, though Jenna's convinced that he's the same person as previous *TGS* cast member Josh. Danny tries to explain that there used to be another guy, but Jenna isn't having it. Ultimately, even Danny is gaslit into believing he's the same guy—in a flashback sequence, Danny's flashbacks are all scenes featuring Josh.

Cheyenne Jackson had hoped to do more episodes of the show, but enjoyed when they found a spot for him.

Cheyenne Jackson: There were so many characters to write for. I always waited for the call, because that show really changed everything for me. People saw me in a different light. It showed people that I could hang and be fun. It did a lot for my confidence.

This was the one time when Jane Krakowski's pregnancy was actually written into a storyline and allowed them not to hide Jenna's midsection, through the device of her character having a hysterical pregnancy.

There's a big climax with Tracy holding a gun on the roof, trying to ruin his award-winning actor reputation so that he could go back to being himself. But the real 30 Rock building wouldn't let the show shoot there, particularly with a gun-toting Tracy. Instead, they shot on a terrace outside the building's old Rainbow Room dining area, which was closed.

This leads to a chase through the stairwell that features cameos by *30 Rock* regulars including news anchor Brian Williams; a group they refer to as "recurring hobos," which include *30 Rock* writers Hannibal Buress and Jack Burditt, as well as real New York homeless personality Radioman (aka "Moonvest" on the show); and GE lawyer Alan Garkel (Eric Dysart) in his wheelchair.

Jack advises Tracy to ruin his movie star image by returning to *TGS*, as appearing on television is a quick way to get kicked out of the A-list. The advice mirrors some of Baldwin's own feelings about appearing on TV, telling Tracy that coming back to the show will make sure that no one ever takes him seriously again. "It doesn't matter how big a movie star you are, even if you had the kind of career where you walked away from a blockbuster franchise or worked with Meryl Streep or Anthony Hopkins, made important movies about things like civil rights or Pearl Harbor, stole films with supporting roles and then turned around and blew them away on Broadway."

It's even more surprisingly true to life when you realize that Baldwin had been wanting to quit the show at the time, despite it apparently being a cushy gig for him. As Lorne Michaels put it, Baldwin "guards against enjoyment."

Lorne Michaels: I'll say, "Alec, you have one of the best writers in television writing this part for you. It's shot in New York, where you chose to live. You work three days a week, you get paid a lot of money, you're getting awards. It's a great time in your life. And, if you were capable of enjoying it, it would be even better."

Alec Baldwin: On a television show, precise acting isn't the order of the day. It's a sitcom. The idea is to hit certain beats, and we do it cleverly. But you do a television show, you become a pastry chef.

Nathan Lane: It's a twenty-two-minute story. Alec used to say, "I make little delicious pastries. That's what I'm serving up."

The gas main is once more repaired, but Liz breaks it open yet again to save *TGS*. That's because she discovers that the writers had written the show while high on gas, with the episode's writing being bonkers/unusable, so the only solution is for Hank and the audience to *watch* it while on gas too. They do, and they think it's *hilarious*.

The episode closes with a special appearance by Tom Hanks, calling other members of the actor A-list to get Tracy kicked out of the group when he sees the *TGS* episode.

Jon Haller: Nobody knew what that cameo was going to be. At one point they were thinking about trying to get George Bush to do it. I remember us realizing, really? Are we going to try to get Bush on the show? Is this a thing? And they're like, oh, maybe it'll go to Clinton. That's a crazy show, when you're like "Who's going to do it?" and then Tom Hanks is the one.

It was really hard to get ahold of Tom Hanks. At one point, *30 Rock* was shooting in Central Park. They were going to have to shoot this cameo in two weeks. Tom Hanks's movie *Extremely Loud and Incredibly Close* was also shooting in Central Park. And there is a character on the show named Moonvest, who was based on a real homeless man named Radioman. He is this eccentric homeless guy in New York, who knows all of the film crews. Everybody knows him and loves him, and he walks back and forth.

Eric Gurian, Tina Fey's assistant, saw him on the set in Central Park and was like "Hey Radioman, we're trying to get Tom Hanks to be on our show— will you go ask him?" And Radioman went over to the *Extremely Loud and Incredibly Close* set and asked Tom Hanks if he would do *30 Rock*, and Tom Hanks said, "Sure!"

Hanks improvised by singing the theme to his pre-stardom 1980s sitcom *Bosom Buddies* while he watched *TGS* on TV—and even though the show had to pay for the song, they thought the reference was so funny that they had to go for it.

The end of the episode cuts forward to a future where the characters are all dead in five years. The semi-exception: Kenneth, whose arm shoots up from under the dirt, as a true immortal character's arm should.

In the second-to-last episode of the season, **"Everything Sunny All the Time Always,"** the show gets mixed up in international politics, with Jack's wife, Avery, being detained in North Korea. Years before Seth Rogen and James Franco caused an international incident with *The Interview* and made a bunch of Sony execs embarrassed about their emails, *30 Rock* started taking shots at North Korea's dictator—at the time, Kim Jong-il, father of Kim Jong-un.

Margaret Cho (Kim Jong-il/Kim Jong-un): They had reached out a couple of different times, but the timing didn't work out. It's always exciting to go down to work in that building, [30 Rock]. It's an iconic and special place.

The storyline was inspired by North Korea's history of kidnappings and detentions, which had recently included Lisa Ling's sister (and fellow journalist), Laura Ling, in 2009. Kim Jong-il claims in the episode that Laura Ling left the country because "she can't party as hard as we can." He was known in real life as such a big movie fan that he famously kidnapped filmmakers to appear in and create his films.

It plays into the episode's tag, with Kim Jong-il filming his own tribute to Alec Baldwin's body of work, which Tracy Jordan also appears in. In an instance of life imitating art, this was before Dennis Rodman visited North Korea and befriended Kim

Jong-un—and Rodman's larger-than-life personality might be the closest our world has come to Tracy Jordan. (Well, except for Kanye.)

> **Margaret Cho:** That was fun, 'cause it was just so meta, many things referenced—both Alec Baldwin and *Glengarry Glen Ross*, and then Tracy Morgan, and "coffee for closers," and North Korea. I love a meta-joke.

Cho connected with episode director John Riggi—they had both worked in the 1990s as stand-up comics. She made her name in the nineties playing herself, and members of her family on her sitcom *All-American Girl*, but this was a chance for her to dive into another personality. She has family from both North and South Korea.

> **Margaret Cho:** It's exciting to play a different person. I mean, it's different to play a man, and it's certainly something I could play, somebody as notorious and crazy and scary, and also somebody that has that crazy kind of a legend around him. And then my own family history around North Korea, too. It's a big deal. It was really easy actually—it's harder for me to turn into myself as a woman, to play myself. I easily slide into male drag.

But she didn't get much chance to interact with her co-stars, coming in from another show shooting in Atlanta.

> **Margaret Cho:** A lot of it was shot separately with different units because of my schedule. I shot a lot with Tina, and she was on set for most of my coverage, because she wrote everything and wanted to be there.

Cho said that everybody was such a big star on *30 Rock* at the time, they were all doing other projects. While on set, she did see Elizabeth Banks as they were each getting their makeup done.

> **Margaret Cho:** There's so many big stars on that show, that there's the most levels of different kinds of stand-ins that I've ever seen. You would think that you were in the presence of the star, but actually you were in their stand-in's presence. But not just their stand-in, but their body double, or their hair double, their hand double, or their back double. All of the different parts of them were represented.

The role was such a hit that Cho was nominated for an Emmy for the role.

> **Margaret Cho:** I didn't know what to expect. I'd never been nominated for an Emmy before, but I was really excited to have that happen.

While Fey would come under fire while shooting *Unbreakable Kimmy Schmidt* for some of the ways that the show depicted Asian characters, Cho loved that Tina provided an all-too-rare opportunity for an Asian actress. But she also attributed her love for playing this role to the simple fact that there weren't a lot of roles for Asian actors.

Margaret Cho: I love Tina. My generation of Asian American actors, we just want to work. I just want to be out there. I always wanted to be working in any capacity. There's so little that we could choose from in terms of opportunity and access. So, I always appreciated Tina for the opportunities that she provided us. It's one of those things where you're just like "I'm just trying to get seen. I wanna be visible." And there's no other way.

Jack tries getting an ex-girlfriend that was referenced way back in Season 1 to help— Bush administration official Condoleezza Rice, who appears and plays herself for the first time (while using her real-life skills as a concert-level pianist). But she's unable to save Avery.

Avery's absence was also necessitated by Elizabeth Banks's own packed schedule, including working on *The Hunger Games*.

Robert Carlock: We finally got burned by our insistence on bringing in the splashiest people to play love interests. Liz [Banks] was perfect for that role, but she's a busy lady. We went down that road with our eyes open in terms of her marrying [Jack] and everything, but our mutual hope that it would work out perfectly didn't happen. We were telling some stories that we had intended to tell with her there, then she couldn't make it. And that was frustrating, combining with the Tracy situation.

Liz uses the occasion of kicking Tracy out of her home to finally clean it up and take control. But she's foiled by a plastic bag.

John Riggi: We did an episode where there was a bag in a tree outside of Liz Lemon's apartment, and she got obsessed with it. And that was an absolutely one hundred percent true story. Tina and Jeff had gotten a new apartment. It's beautiful, and it was on the corner. They moved in and they had it all decorated. But outside their bedroom window, there was a tree. Tina was showing me around and there was a Gristedes [Supermarkets] bag in that window—in the tree. She goes, "See that bag? That is driving Jeff out of his mind." I was like "Really?" [She's] like "He's called the city. He's tried to get rid of it. He's like, we've got this beautiful apartment and I've got to look at that bag every day when I get up."

Riggi thought that was such a funny idea that they should do a whole episode about it.

In the **season finale, "Respawn,"** Liz leaves for the Hamptons on her summer vacation—but her relaxation is thwarted by Tracy Jordan happening to be staying next door. She takes inspiration from the *TGS* writers playing *Halo* endlessly and decides to "respawn" by blowing up her own vacation. She refuses to pay a fine and gets sentenced to community service, which lets her live the outdoor gardening life she'd dreamed of. She's just doing it as legally required community service.

Jack struggles dealing with Avery's kidnapping, uncomfortably trying to use Kenneth to fill the missing affection in his life. That includes him making Kenneth put on her robe—and asking him to put on some of Avery's perfume.

Jane Krakowski gave birth just weeks after this episode was shot. In the culmination of creative ways to cover up her pregnancy, she wore a full dog costume in this episode while walking Paul by a leash, a kink which leads to the end of her role as spokesperson for the Wool Council (led by a very proper Victor Garber).

This was also the season when Tina Fey's autobiography *Bossypants* came out, somehow written between acting/writing/producing/parenting/life-ing. The book was a bestseller and received widespread critical acclaim, as well as giving more insight into her life and work on *30 Rock*.

Dennie Gordon: She was busy as hell. I don't think anybody since Lucille Ball has worn that many hats, plus been a mother of two.

Jon Haller: [Tina] came in, trying to figure out what she wanted to be on the cover. She's like "I think I just want to have some man hands, holding my face up like this."

Paula Leggett Chase: *Bossypants* was dropping at the same time [as "Queen of Jordan"]. I mean, oh my god—the drive to do that. I've always thought myself to be a very driven person—stayed in the business as long as I have and to still be going. But that was like "Oh, OK. All right. I can do anything if she can do that."

Jon Haller: A conversation with Tina, it was like talking to somebody who's juggling ten balls at once. She's married, has a kid—one kid at that time—and then starring in and writing the show. And in Season 5, she was writing her book. So, if you got a little snippet of time with Tina, it was amazing. My experiences with her were like, she'd be on set, she'd be in hair and makeup, and they would need to run joke-alts by her. You would take down three alts for what they were about to shoot, and say, which one of these do you like? She would read three, and love them, and then pitch you a fourth one that was amazingly brilliant while she was getting her hair made up.

But the success of the show meant that it would lose a longtime, key member of the show's crew. Director/producer Don Scardino left at the end of Season 5 to shoot his first major feature film, *The Incredible Burt Wonderstone*.

Don Scardino: That was tough. I mean, I've had some wonderful jobs in television, and been a part of some really incredible shows, but without a doubt, on a day-to-day, everyday basis, *30 Rock* was the greatest job I've ever had. From the writing, the playing, the guest stars, all that—and the freedom that we were given with the camera style, and the directors are really allowed to direct. It was very hard to leave.

30 Rock, and the Emmys, put me in a different league, like the actors who became stars after. In fact, Steve Carell, who was producing and starring in the movie, was friends with Tina, and I'm sure that helped. So it was bittersweet. It was like leaving home, leaving family. And Tina was very gracious about it. If it weren't for the fact that it was a movie, and it was a break into a much higher level of making features, I would have never gone away—I would have stayed until the bitter end.

Writer Jack Burditt also left at this time, along with writers' assistant Jon Haller. Burditt had been absent earlier in the series' run, spending time in LA writing on Julia Louis-Dreyfus's *The New Adventures of Old Christine*. But now he was leaving for good.

Jon Haller: Jack Burditt said, "I just got approached to write a pilot for Tim Allen—he wants to come back to TV. I guess I'm going to do it." Jack wrote this pilot, and then that was the one that Tim Allen chose. So Jack's like "I guess I've got to go to LA now." And I was like "Hey, do you need an assistant?"

Longtime cameraman Peter Agliata, who helped define the show's visual look, also left at the end of Season 5. He chose to step away from doing handheld camera work due to the physical toll it would take.

That changing of the guard would give Season 6 a different feel. Season 5 was full of big swings that didn't always work, but showed a spark that many fans and critics felt was missing from Season 4. Maintaining that in Season 6 would prove a challenge. Finding viewers would also prove a challenge, with Season 5's finale pulling in just 4.2 million—down more than 1.5 million people from the season premiere, and down 2.5 million from the live episode.

SEASON 6
(2012)

Jack vs. North Korea

30 Rock was bumped to midseason this year rather than its normal September or October debut, thanks to Tina Fey having her second child. Similar to Jane Krakowski's pregnancy, Tina's wasn't written into the show. But the late start gave the season a different cadence, with the show's January debut meaning no Christmas episode this year, the entire season compacted into just a few months. It also included the show's lowest ratings of its whole run, with the season premiere drawing 4.47 million viewers—down from 5.85 million in Season 5. The viewership dipped as low as 2.8 million this year, both for episode "Nothing Left to Lose" and again for the season finale.

During the show's long break, Tracy Morgan came under fire after making violent homophobic comments during a stand-up comedy show in an extended riff about gay men. These included saying that if his son was gay, he "better talk to me like a man and not in a gay voice," or Morgan would stab and kill him. He even told the crowd that he didn't care "if I piss off some gays," adding that they can take a joke.

The comments led to calls for Morgan to be removed from *30 Rock*. Morgan may have been helped by the show's delayed start, as it allowed for more time to pass after his spring 2011 comments before the show came back. Jack McBrayer quipped shortly after the incident, "Half the stuff that Tracy says in real life, they'll put in the script. I mean, maybe not recently."

Morgan issued an apology at the time, saying, "I want to apologize to my fans and the gay & lesbian community for my choice of words at my recent stand-up act in Nashville. I'm not a hateful person and don't condone any kind of violence against others. While I am an equal opportunity jokester, and my friends know what is in my heart, even in a comedy club this clearly went too far and was not funny in any context."

A gay colleague on the show, Cheyenne Jackson, put out a statement at the time, saying that he was "disgusted and appalled" by what Morgan said. "The devastating repercussions of hate-filled language manifest in very real ways for today's LGBTQ youth. I've known Tracy for two years, spent many long hours with him on set, and I want to believe that this behavior is not at the core of who he is. I'm incredibly disappointed by his actions, and hope that his apology is sincere."

> **Cheyenne Jackson:** It was a tough time for everybody involved in the show. But I think he handled it well. I think the show handled it well. I had to say what I had to say. I spoke to Tina prior, and she understood my need to speak out.

Fey praised Morgan's apology and issued an apology on behalf of the show, which had previously been honored by GLAAD for its portrayals of gay themes and characters.

"Stand-up comics may have the right to 'work out' their material in its ugliest and rawest form in front of an audience, but the violent imagery of Tracy's rant was disturbing to me at a time when homophobic hate crimes continue to be a life-threatening issue for the GLBT Community," Fey said in her statement. "It also doesn't line up with the Tracy Morgan I know, who is not a hateful man and is generally much too sleepy and self-centered to ever hurt another person. I hope for his sake that Tracy's apology will be accepted as sincere by his gay and lesbian coworkers at *30 Rock*, without whom Tracy would not have lines to say, clothes to wear, sets to stand on, scene partners to act with, or a printed-out paycheck from accounting to put in his pocket."

> **Cheyenne Jackson:** It all worked out. I know Tracy's heart. He's a wonderful person. And, as we've seen with comedy and as we've seen with people, it isn't a linear thing. There's a growth.

The show would go on to satirize Morgan's homophobic idiocy with a two-part storyline about idiots in their second and third episodes this season, "Idiots Are People Two!" and "Idiots Are People Three!"

At the same time, while Alec Baldwin had played coy throughout *30 Rock*'s run about whether he would come back at various points, it looked more likely now than ever that Alec would leave. He announced that he was looking to expand his portfolio into other media, including launching public radio interview show *Here's the Thing* in fall 2011 and going on to develop a variety of TV shows with himself as a host. He even publicly claimed that the 2012 season would be the last season of the show, with everyone's contracts coming to an end. But his love of *30 Rock* would keep him through one more season.

Avery's ongoing North Korean misadventure proves to be this season's spine, with Jack coping with her absence and doing whatever he can to secure his wife's return—while also being tempted by a more age-appropriate match.

There was no Christmas episode with the midseason launch, but the **season premiere, "Dance Like Nobody's Watching,"** includes Liz doing a little tribute to regular Christmas episode guest star Elaine Stritch (Jack's mom, Colleen) with an Elaine-style musical bit early in the episode. It was the first *30 Rock* season premiere not written solely by Tina Fey—she co-wrote the episode with Tracey Wigfield, continuing Wigfield's rise through the show's ranks.

Tracy and Jack are puzzled in this episode over why Liz is actually happy for once. That is not a normal Liz trait, and it leads to Tracy acting like the rational one.

The episode ends with two joyful moments for Liz. The first is with Jack discovering that she has joined the Timeless Torches, a group of over-forty men and women who dance at WNBA New York Liberty games due to the love of dance. It started in the writers' room with a clip of the very real Timeless Torches being shared.

Tom Ceraulo: Within seconds of the clip beginning, she was on board.

Tracey Wigfield: We were trying to do a thing here with Liz where she's starting in a really happy, up place, because so often her life's falling apart, and she's stressed-out and upset. And it was nice to have her feel peaceful and calm and in a good place to start out the year.

The other ray of joy involves this season's love interest. Liz had bounced back and forth over the years between dreamy ideals like Matt Damon's Carol and Jon Hamm's Dr. Drew, and her sleazebag ex Dennis. But the man who Liz finds this season is one that's less about Liz searching for that ideal, while also not getting into a toxic relationship. It seems . . . almost healthy.

While she seemingly threw Jack off the trail, he spies her meeting a man and going to a movie. Her secret boyfriend is only seen from behind, yet to be shared with her coworkers. The show hadn't even cast him yet, with another actor used for his first appearance.

Kenneth exuberantly proclaims to the *TGS* staff that Reverend Gary did the math, and the world is ending the next day. It was a play on conspiracies about the world ending in 2012, as well as radio host Harold Camping. He was a conservative talk show host who predicted the "Day of Judgment" would begin on May 21, 2011, while October 20, 2011, would be the end of the world. (Note: The world did not end on this date. At least, we don't think so, even on days where it feels like it must have.)

The world doesn't end, but the writers take pity on Kenneth and take him to see the ocean. Which he says he has never seen, despite living in New York City. The episode includes a beautiful shot from the real Coney Island and its famed Wonder Wheel—for which the cameraman and John Riggi had to put on waders and get in the Atlantic to shoot.

In a riff on reality competition shows, Jenna becomes a celebrity reality show judge on *America's Kidz Got Singing*—a show somewhere between *American Idol* and *America's Got Talent*, but applying classic *Idol* judge Simon Cowell's meanness to children. D'Fwan returns as one of the show's judges, as does famed angry tennis player John McEnroe playing against type as the super positive judge (à la *American Idol's* Paula Abdul).

Teresa Mastropierro: We have limited stage space like everybody does in New York. The biggest space that we had to work in was the set which was the *TGS* studio. We would take that apart and put up something like a talk show or a game show, or a competition show like *America's Kidz [Got Singing]*.

The main thing was to make it feel more professional or high-end than the things that we would shoot within *The Girlie Show*. We relied a lot on lighting and tried not to over-research them—just get the gist and the spirit of this kind of show, and between the lighting, and the music, make a broad statement on those kinds of spaces. Not to make them too specific to copying anything in the real world, but to give that over-the-top feeling that those shows always have.

When *30 Rock* eventually ended, the show's stages were torn apart and given to other shows, including HBO's *Girls*. But before it all went away, Wigfield managed to get an ad that was hanging on Jenna's wall for *America's Kidz Got Singing*.

The episode ends with one of the kids singing an epic take on "Camptown Races," written by show composer Jeff Richmond.

Tracey Wigfield: This ballad version of "Camptown Races" is genuinely a beautiful song.

As it had done throughout its run, the show used **episode 2, "Idiots Are People Two!"** to comment on real life. Tracy Jordan makes homophobic comments, and Liz writes him an apology that includes calling Tracy an idiot. So Tracy leads an uprising of the world's idiots, including guest star Denise Richards as herself, gamely agreeing to be portrayed as an idiot who proudly tells everyone that she "played a nucular psychiatrist in a James Bonk movie."

Most of the plot unfolds in flashback, beginning with Pete being found uncon-scious in the supply closet. It turns out that Kenneth broke some lights in the closet that he was getting for Jenna's dressing room, leading Jenna and Kenneth to call in Kelsey Grammer—a callback to his team-up with with Jenna and Kenneth back in Season 5's "Reaganing" for their ice-cream cake scam—to frame Pete for the accident. They're a crack team of pranksters, treating their missions like *Ocean's 11* heists.

Liz has quietly started dating Criss Chros (played here by James Marsden), and despite Jack making fun of the spelling of his name and his lack of ambition, Criss genuinely seems to care for Liz. They move in together, living a life that's far more drama free than any of Liz's past relationships.

> **John Riggi:** The one thing about *30 Rock*, that T. Fey would be mad at me right now for saying—but I was always like, why are we pretending like Liz Lemon can't get a date? I don't buy this shit. I just don't buy it. So that's why when Jimmy [Marsden] came on as her boyfriend, I was thrilled, because I was like, I one hundred percent want her to have a boyfriend, this is great. But that was a lot of Tina writing the way she felt when she was in Second City, and she looked a lot different than she does now. What we all were feeling and what we had experienced, we were quite often putting into the show.

The idiot uprising continues in **episode 3, "Idiots Are People Three!"** In this per-fectly titled second part, Devon Banks offers to back off on attacking NBC for Tracy's offensive comments—but only if Jack gets his triplets into a fancy private school. Jack does it, but it turns out to be yet another element of one-upmanship by Banks. He's forced Jack to use up his favors so that Jack won't be able to get his own daughter into that school.

Liz ends up having to read an apology to the idiots, written by the idiots.

And Kelsey Grammer distracts everyone with a one-man, improvised show as Abraham Lincoln to allow Jenna and Kenneth to sneak Pete's unconscious body through the backstage area. In a stirring speech echoing a certain classic bar-set sit-com, he tells everyone that he knows that "future generations will forge a stronger country, and that, someday, America will be a place . . . where everybody knows your name." They set Pete up in his office to make it look like he was in the middle of auto-erotic asphyxiation. Like you do. Kelsey, Jenna, and Kenneth celebrate the success of their caper with champagne, declaring themselves the Best Friends Gang.

Kenneth makes some big moves up and some big moves down this year, all on his path to becoming the ultimate NBC employee. In **episode 4, "The Ballad of Kenneth Parcell,"** the plot swings into action with Jack eliminating the page pro-gram in a move to please Kabletown head Hank Hooper. Kenneth gets replaced by a computer named NotKenneth, voiced by old friend Rachel Dratch—though Jack sees the error of his ways before the end of the episode.

Vali Chandrasekaran: [Kenneth] was one of those situations where everyone loved that character—and also [Jack McBrayer], as a person, is so wonderful that you always wanted to be doing more stuff with him, and for him. A lot of that drive came from, there was a joke in the pilot that Tina wrote: Jack Donaghy saying, in five years, we'll all either be dead or working for him.

So Tina took that seriously, and was like "Let's figure out how everyone might possibly end up working for Kenneth the Page," and started to build that dynamic.

That decision would fuel Kenneth's character arc through both Seasons 6 and 7.

In a pitch-perfect parody of star-studded holiday films like *Valentine's Day*, *New Year's Eve*, and *Love Actually*, Jenna parlays her *America's Kidz Got Singing* success into appearing in Garry Marshall's *Martin Luther King Day*. Emma Stone, Andy Samberg, Nick Cannon, Kristen Bell, and John Krasinski all appear in the trailer for the faux film. It's a sign of Jenna moving into a new level of stardom, actually famous enough to be cast in a terrible, but highly commercial, movie. The cast list includes Liam Neeson, Amy Adams, Hugh Grant, and Vince Vaughn. And in quick shots at the end, the cast list *also* includes Matthew McConaughey, Ian McKellen, Abu Ghraib prison guard Lynndie England, the Plinko game from *The Price Is Right*, Inflatable Tube Man, the 1995 Quebec Nordiques, R2-D2, That Flight Attendant That Went Crazy, and Mankind (Mick Foley).

In **episode 5, "Today You Are a Man,"** Liz's horrendously bad agent Simon turns up once more—crawling out of a box that Simon has shipped himself in, playing to performer Josh Fadem's physical comedy skills in his third and final appearance.

Simon presents her with a new contract sent over by Jack, but he's such a terrible agent that Liz is finally fed up and decides to negotiate the new contract herself. We see the continuing evolution of the Jack/Liz dynamic, with Liz embracing what she can learn from Jack when it comes to contract negotiations. The situation echoed the fact that the *30 Rock* stars' contracts really were up with Season 6 of the show.

Vali Chandrasekaran: One thing that was fun to write was they really could go toe-to-toe with each other, and they were really different energies. Alec was this big, explosive, masculine character, and Liz was strong, but also Tina brought this silliness and self-doubt to that character, that Liz Lemon always wore on her sleeve. And those two characters—this headstrong character who's trying so hard to hide his vulnerability all the time, and Liz Lemon who was *all* vulnerability and trying to front this head strength—to watch them in scenes together playing like that was really, really fun.

The fact that we never went to romance with it kept us from having that out in a scene. So you could just keep turning it, and turning it, and the tension wouldn't have to break. The way the tension would break would be when Jack reveals himself to Liz in a way that he never revealed himself to anybody else. It was really loving and sweet, without being sexual—and I never had a chance to write that ever before.

Liz negotiates with Jack using his own techniques from a seminar he'd recorded, *Negotiating to Win*. What happens when two Jacks face off—Liz Jack and Jack Jack? She does pretty well, but doesn't perfectly execute . . . tempting Jack into negotiating on her behalf. He wins the negotiation, but in Liz's favor, as he played both sides with Alec Baldwin acting against himself. It's something Baldwin rejoiced in throughout the run of the show.

Although Kenneth gets his page job back, he realizes no one missed him while he was gone. So he introduces a new page, Hazel Wassername (Kristen Schaal), to take his place as he goes to work as a page on *The Suze Orman Show*. But the financial advice expert encourages Kenneth to seek a new position, explaining that the reason he isn't treated well is thanks to how much money he makes. He negotiates with Jack and lands a new role.

Hazel's character didn't end up being a hit—*Entertainment Weekly* ran a review headlined by the question of if anyone else was sick of her, and if you Google the character, one of the top results is fans discussing whether her appearance was where *30 Rock* jumped the shark. In a show filled with ridiculous characters, she was one who seemed not just crazed but actually mean-spirited. And she would go on to take that out on the characters we'd spent the past five years getting to know and love.

In another extended episode **"Hey, Baby, What's Wrong?,"** Liz battles through the crisis of choosing Ikea furniture with Criss. Their relationship survives the struggle in this Valentine's Day show. It also features Tracy putting some *The Game/* negging-style tricks into play as he teaches Lutz how to pick up women.

Kenneth works to train new page Hazel here, despite her own desires to be a star, not a page. Jenna sings live on *America's Kidz Got Singing*, and Pete's history as an Olympic archer comes into play—once he realizes she needs pain to succeed, he shoots her with an arrow.

As Jack continues to work toward his wife's safe return from North Korean imprisonment, he works with her extremely uptight mother, Diana Jessup (Mary Steenburgen). They have to deal with thick romantic tension while trying to keep the focus on Avery, working to avoid the completely forbidden match.

In **episode 8, "The Tuxedo Begins,"** Jack gets mugged on his way to work, leading him to consider a run for mayor. As he retreats from the world due to the fear this has inspired, he starts wearing a tuxedo all the time, while setting himself up as a defender of the city's wealthy. The episode was inspired by Baldwin's own flirtations with running for mayor of New York City in 2011, though his candidacy never materialized. It also satirizes the attitude behind conservative businessmen who jump into politics, coming after the infamous 2011 White House Correspondents' Dinner where President Barack Obama and comedian Seth Meyers's roasting of then–*Celebrity Apprentice* host Donald Trump may have helped inspire his later presidential run.

Meanwhile, Liz starts pretending to be a crazy old woman to scare people away on the subway, leading to her appearance becoming Joker-esque by the time of a climactic confrontation with the tuxedo-wearing Jack. It's the Batman/Joker showdown teased in the episode's title, a play on *Batman Begins*.

This episode also gave birth to one of the internet's biggest memes. When Jack calls in Steve Buscemi's PI character, Lenny Wosniak, following Jack's mugging, Wosniak reveals his past going undercover à la *21 Jump Street* in a high school. But as he walks up to students in a flashback with his T-shirt reading "Music Band" in the AC/DC style, wearing a backward baseball cap, and carrying *two* skateboards, he clearly isn't pulling it off. And he asks the teens this important question: "How do you do, fellow kids?"

Jenna and Paul realize that they're starting to settle down. They try to treat being normal as a cool new sexual fetish, but eventually have to admit that it's not. Their decision: to take a sexual walkabout for three months, independently pursuing their own sexual desires to see if they're actually ready to be together with one another permanently.

Episode 9, "Leap Day," became a signature episode from Season 6, a favorite both for the public and for the cast and crew. The idea: Leap Day is a jolly holiday that Liz somehow hasn't noticed before, a bizarre cross between Christmas and St. Patrick's Day. Kenneth dresses up as Leap Day William, a fabled mascot who lives under the sea and trades candy for children's tears. It filled the role the traditional Christmas holiday episode would have had, if not for the show's midseason debut.

Writer Luke Del Tredici was thrilled to be writing the Leap Day episode, as holidays were always an easier place to start as a writer, especially after more than a hundred episodes at this point. The writers got the idea after noticing that they had an episode scheduled to air on Leap Day itself that year.

Luke Del Tredici (writer): Someone in the writers' room was thinking out loud and said, "It's too bad that there are no traditions associated with Leap Day."

Robert Carlock: It was as if we had a completely untouched new Christmas.

The writers took the cue to make up all the traditions that might be associated with such a day. They wanted it to include weird traditions, like Santa coming down your chimney at night and watching you while you sleep. That inspired Leap Day William's home in the Mariana Trench, along with his gills and razor-sharp teeth. And Liz doesn't know what this holiday is because her White Haven hometown was founded by the Amish, and they only celebrated Amish holidays.

We even get Jim Carrey, as Jim Carrey, in a scene from the movie *Leap Dave Williams*, playing opposite Andie MacDowell in a role à la her role as the love interest in *Groundhog Day*. It's the type of role Carrey played during the peak of his movie stardom in films like *Liar Liar* and *Bruce Almighty*, with him crying out, "I saved Leap Day and connected with my son!" The writers created a full three-act structure for the film and wrote numerous scenes that didn't end up being used. They'd originally pictured it as starring Ray Romano and Rene Russo, but they ended up with what Del Tredici described as even better guest stars than they hoped for.

Of course, big stars also come with scheduling issues—Jim Carrey wasn't available until a month after they'd shot the rest of the episode, and was available for only one day. They had to get everything turned around in time for it to air, including special effects for his gills. Carrey came up with the idea for a scene where he's running down the street, tearing off his clothes—the writers worried about being able to do it at the last minute and make the costumes tearaways, but Carrey insisted, telling them, "We have to do it. Dave Williams needs to do it." Carrey had wilder ideas that they just didn't have the time to shoot.

Robert Carlock: Tina had to say, "We're shooting this tomorrow, Jim, I don't think we can go to the Empire State Building."

The *real* Leap Day William shows up at the end of the episode to inspire/potentially attack us all with those teeth. He tells the audience to "live every day as if it's Leap Day, and every Leap Day as if it's your last. Oh, and if you should ever see an old man in a blue suit busting out of the middle of the ocean, take the time to say howdy. It might just be worth your while."

The episode also included Tracy having to spend a giant Benihana gift card before its expiration date, inspired by the fact that Tracy Morgan genuinely loves Benihana.

Tracy Morgan: I love Benihana like I love my favorite strip club. When they put Benihana on the show—all the writers know that I love this place—that was the greatest compliment they could show me.

Morgan fell in love with Benihana when he visited one while on the road, and started doing stand-up comedy material with other customers around the table. Now he even has a hibachi table in his house. The show brought in actual Benihana chefs as extras when making the episode and to cook the food, and when they broke from shooting for lunch, Tracy Morgan got them to actually make lunch.

Luke Del Tredici: So, I sat with Tracy Morgan and Steve Buscemi, who directed the episode. It was just me, Tracy, and Steve having lunch at Benihana. Tracy got us all of these house specials that they never make for just regular people.

In **episode 10, "Alexis Goodlooking and the Case of the Missing Whisky,"** Frank continues dating his former teacher, Lynn Onkman (Susan Sarandon). Liz helps Frank hide the truth by pretending to be his girlfriend in front of Frank's mom, Sylvia Rossitano (Patti LuPone), making a return to the show.

Judah loved working with Patti LuPone as his mom. He noted that she was one of only two people in the business who read his book, satirical martial arts manual *How to Beat Up Anybody*.

Patti LuPone: I was really, really fond of Judah—because to be able to play opposite someone who was as welcoming as Judah was, is really lovely.

Kenneth has a new role in Standards and Practices. Jack encourages Kenneth to take down one of his new departmental coworkers, beginning to shape Kenneth in his own image. There's a bit with a couple of white characters in Standards yelling at their Asian colleague to shut up. According to Friedlander, it was a satire on show business and its lack of diversity. At the time, he said, "I think Hollywood is about fifty years behind the times, as far as race and representing all different types of people." You could argue that it's more than that, given America's complicated history when it comes to making opportunities possible for people who aren't white and don't come from money. It's also the show satirizing the lack of diversity, while in reality still giving speaking parts to more white actors.

Jenna revisits her role as Alexis Goodlooking, which she played in a police procedural TV pilot. Her powers: she's both good looking and good at looking for clues. Jenna pulls out those skills to find who stole Frank's whiskey. The episode plays with cop show tropes, including Lutz as the guy who's randomly moving boxes at the dock while being questioned—in this case, moving paperwork around his office for no reason.

In **episode 11, "Standards and Practices,"** the finale of the massively popular *America's Kidz Got Singing* gets ruined when the two child finalists show up drunk. The culprit: Kaylie Hooper (Chloë Grace Moretz) getting them drunk to sabotage Jack's big moment.

Kenneth gets promoted to head of late-night TV standards following the drunken children incident. Due to a fight with the standards department, Liz sends Tracy to go do his filthy stand-up act live on *TGS* in all the sketches, but Kenneth valiantly keeps the FCC at bay with a finger on the bleep button.

While Liz complains about all the words Kenneth bans, with the worst thing allowed being the word "dingbat," the actual show didn't have to deal with too much censorship. Robert Carlock would handle any calls from Standards.

John Riggi: No one ever came to us and said, "You guys can't do that." We'd get some censorship notes, but very seldom.

That isn't to say that Carlock wouldn't work with the network to make some tweaks. Way back in Season 1, "The C Word" featured one of the lewdest jokes that was in a writer's draft of a script but didn't make it to the episode's shooting script. It wasn't about the C word at all. It was one that location manager Chris George loved—the joke became something he and his wife would say to each other.

Chris George: Tracy is talking about when he was a young boy and his uncle would say to him, "Holes is holes, Tray, holes is holes." It was a very racy thing to have in the script. I laughed out loud when I saw it. Then when the next draft came out, that line was gone.

When he asked Carlock on set why they weren't shooting it, Carlock explained that the network thought that line was pushing the envelope a biiiit too much.

Chris George: I said, "Oh, that's kind of disappointing, because it's one of the lines my wife and I use on each other all the time." He looked at me and did a double take. He's like, "That sounds like you have a very good marriage."

The idea's one that stuck with Tina Fey, too—she used the line in a 2007 *Playboy* interview, while also criticizing the type of women that *Playboy* promoted in its magazine.

"Standards and Practices" includes Jenna meeting the children born thanks to the egg donations she made when she was starting out. The now-adult kids largely end up being Jenna-esque, status-obsessed monsters. When they get their own reality show, they kick Jenna out of the group due to her not being as young and beautiful as they are. But Jenna bonds with the one who isn't a blonde beauty, and vows to get to know her better, though the show wouldn't end up coming back to this storyline. Plus, Tracy has an important revelation, finally understanding the ending of *The Sixth Sense*: "Those names are the people who worked on the movie!"

In **episode 12, "St. Patrick's Day,"** Criss says "I love you" to Liz first, but Liz isn't ready for those three little words. When her ex Dennis shows up, Criss and Liz's relationship becomes strained, and she once again thinks they might break up.

Vali Chandrasekaran: [Liz's relationship with Criss] built to one of my favorite end bits, which is that St. Patrick's Day episode, where she thinks they were going to break up. And the only green thing that she can find was those Hulk hands, which was Colleen McGuinness's pitch, which made me laugh a lot. That was a great relationship for her, and it was nice to see Liz Lemon grow up in that way, and have Marsden say, we don't have to break up because we got into that fight. It was a time that we got to have a nice dynamic that wasn't just between Liz and Jack.

Liz finally proclaims her love for Criss on the streets of New York.

The episode was written by Colleen McGuinness, who joined *30 Rock* with Season 6 and would write on the show for its last two seasons.

Colleen McGuinness (writer): People online actually thought that I was a made-up name—because my name is so Irish and it was a St. Patrick's Day episode, they thought it was another trick that *30 Rock* is pulling out. But no, I'm real.

Hazel continues to be terrible at hiding the fact that she's insane, telling Kenneth, "I'm not about to screw this up, Kenneth. 'Cause I'd get kicked out of show business, and then how would I be famous? By starting a fire and then rescuing everyone from it, and then I'm a hero, and then I'm in *Playboy*?"

In **episode 13, "Grandmentor,"** Jack decides to produce a movie about Avery's kidnapping to keep attention on his missing wife. Jack recruits Liz to write it as Jenna lobbies to star in the film.

Hazel does a terrible job taking care of Tracy, relative to how Kenneth handled him. The situation leads to Hazel seeking out Liz as a mentor, with Jack becoming her grandmentor. Kenneth takes a fall down the corporate ladder, quitting his job in Standards as he feels his attachment to Tracy calling him back. He has to quit in order to be eligible to win a contest for a guest role on *TGS*, allowing him to give Tracy the medicine that Hazel has been neglecting to give him.

And in a great meta-joke about the nerdy obsessions of TV writers, Liz chastises the *TGS* writers, "Do not write another sketch with Krang from *Teenage Mutant Ninja Turtles*. No one knows who Krang is. It would be a waste of time to talk about Krang on television."

With **episode 14, "Kidnapped by Danger,"** Avery's mother, Diana, helps to oversee the production of the film about her daughter's kidnapping. Liz works to ease the romantic tension between Jack and Diana. She sets up Diana with the actor playing Jack in the movie, played by Alec's real-life brother, the now-available Billy Baldwin.

Jack fires Liz after she includes lurid details about Jack and Avery's relationship in her script, then sets about rewriting the script himself. But the writing makes him realize that their relationship wasn't exactly how he'd been thinking about it, and Liz comes back to do a new draft that isn't so personal.

Jenna gets into a feud with "Weird Al" Yankovic, who parodies the single Jenna releases to promote *Kidnapped by Danger*. She counters with a song that can't be parodied because it's too silly—then has to face "Weird Al" creating his own serious version of the same song.

The show would often keep following logical extensions from a one-off joke. What might have been a throwaway line elsewhere would come back in a big, fully imagined way—especially pieces set up in the pilot and in those first few episodes of the series. Kenneth returns to the show as a janitor, an idea that goes all the way back to Season 1, where Kenneth joked with a janitor that Kenneth might just take his job someday.

Vali Chandrasekaran: We took the stuff that was established in the pilot about the characters very seriously, and we would often come up with pitches—Josh Siegal was very good at this. Really smart about saying, that's who this character is, and so what if we did a storyline and arced a couple of episodes based on this characteristic that we established there? It was always very satisfying to see, because it would make us feel like they were real people.

The show was ahead of its time with a reference to a certain Hollywood producer's outrageous abuse of power that became widely known years later—Jenna says that she turned down having sex with Harvey Weinstein three times . . . out of five. It was another in a series of references to rumors within the industry, but that took until the #MeToo movement to break into the popular consciousness, and for the abusers in question to face actual consequences for their actions.

In **episode 15, "The Shower Principle,"** Jack tries coming up with the perfect business pitch to get Hank Hooper to reinvest profits into the company rather than giving them to shareholders. He applies the shower principle, using showers and golf to change his mindset and inspire the right idea. But he finds that the way the shower principle works in his own life is coming up with ideas while solving Liz's problems. As he helps Liz here, he develops a new plan: construct couches, allowing greater vertical business integration of the television-watching experience.

Jenna opts not to do a sketch for *TGS* based on *Macbeth*, but Cerie takes her place. Jenna starts to suffer a series of accidents, but it turns out that it's the crazed Hazel trying to manipulate her way into becoming friends with Liz.

In **episode 16, "Nothing Left to Lose,"** Pete has to do a self-evaluation for Kabletown. When it shows no ambition, Jack sees it as reflecting poorly upon himself. But when he tries to turn Pete's life around, it just ends up making things worse.

Scott Adsit: The funny thing about Pete is his strangeness—he's got a very weird life. But it's all hearsay, because it all takes place off camera. There are all these references to Pete's weird life, and occasionally you get a little peek into it. There was a great luxury for the writers to say anything they wanted about Pete that was funny, because as Tina has said many times, joke is king in that show. Anything that is about something that they don't have to prove is just gold. So he got weirder off camera, and then he would still be the straight man—or the desperate man—on camera.

When Jack laments the problem of NBC's writers being too white, Liz counters by throwing out a reference to *The Wire*. She plays into her whiteness, with her connection to Black culture consisting of critically acclaimed premium cable TV shows that make white people feel like they have some sort of insight now into the Black experience.

In **episode 17, "Meet the Woggels!"** Jack's mother, Colleen, gets sick and ends up in the hospital, which leads to him processing his feelings for her.

John Riggi: My mom was a big influence in my life, and so I really loved having Elaine on the show, even though she was a handful.

That attitude could show up on set with Stritch's interactions with Baldwin, the two legendary actors going back and forth with each other. There was a documentary crew on set during the filming of this episode, documenting Elaine for the film *Elaine Stritch: Shoot Me*. In the film, you can see them shooting a scene where Stritch improvs an extra line. Baldwin's reaction: "Don't you last-word me, you. It's my laugh-line, you bitch." She could take it as well as she gave, bursting into laughter— but Baldwin's patience was wearing thin.

Director Linda Mendoza tried to find ways to effectively work with Stritch.

Linda Mendoza: She was so difficult. One of the things I remember most is Beth McCarthy-Miller laughing at the fact that she'd been at *30 Rock* since the beginning and never had to shoot an Elaine Stritch episode. I go, and the two I get have Elaine in both of them.

I could see that Elaine was driving Alec Baldwin insane. I do a lot of work with children, in children's television. I'm used to shooting them out and figuring out ways to cover cleverly. I ended up using some very simple terms to make it seem to Elaine like I was doing this for production, but to really make it easier for me to shoot Alec without her. After my first day shooting with them in the hospital, he's like "Finally someone figured out a way to shoot Elaine." He was so grateful.

Stritch yells at Mendoza in the documentary, seeming to reject the director's guidance and asking, "What's my cue to talk? That's all I want to know. I need *no* justification!" After Mendoza gives her a friendly, enthusiastic goodbye, Stritch complains in the documentary, saying, "Everybody is just loving everybody too much for my money. I don't distrust them, I just . . . there's an awful lot of talk."

>   **Linda Mendoza:** I think that she was having her own personal issues. She was so mean to me. But what can you do?

Stritch gets a sweet moment in the documentary when she comes across Tracy Morgan backstage. She also suffered from diabetes, and greets him, "How's your blood sugar?" He tells her that it's good, and controlled—they exchange blood sugar readings.

>   **Tina Fey:** I feel like over those seven years that we've been working here, we know what to expect. But we still are always like "Whew! OK. Here comes Elaine." It's a bear. And it's always worth it. And there are very few people who are worth that. But I think Elaine is a great role model. She is confident, and brassy, and stylish, and gorgeous. She doesn't wear pants, and she lives the way she wants to live.

Mendoza had to shoot several scenes around the absences of different actors, including Will Forte shooting his appearance separately from Jenna, as well as Tina Fey at the hospital.

>   **Linda Mendoza:** Tina was not there because it was a Saturday, and Tina's a very responsible mother. Considering I didn't have Tina on the day when I was doing those big scenes, I thought it all tied in pretty well.

As part of Jenna's sexual walkabout, she dates a member of the children's music group the Woggels (a play on real-life Australian kids' act the Wiggles) and attempts to "Yoko" the band. She ends up somewhat more successful at it than Jack's ex Phoebe was at Yoko-ing Jack back in Season 1, with Jenna causing strife and division in the group. Jenna misses Paul, but when she sees him on his own sexual adventure with a woman and a couch, she continues on.

Mendoza tried to bring some of her real-life experience while shooting scenes that included sneaking the band out the back of a building as fans screamed.

>   **Linda Mendoza:** Especially after six or seven seasons, they want to come in, do their work, and get home. They don't want somebody coming in and reinventing the wheel. [But] I still think I was able to bring a lot to the table. I toured with Paul McCartney and I toured with Genesis.

In **episode 18, "Murphy Brown Lied to Us,"** Liz and Criss find some old papers from when she was considering adoption, and Criss encourages Liz to think about it again. Following an extra push from Jack, Liz decides to have a child. It's an abrupt shift back to the questions of adoption and Liz wanting a kid, after the concept was seemingly dropped for a long time.

After her discouragement at seeing Paul last episode, Jenna tries to win him back with a celebrity meltdown.

John Riggi: Production-wise, Jerry [Kupfer] would never say, "Guys, this is gonna cost a fortune." I had directed a few episodes, but I hadn't done stunts. I shot an episode where Jenna was pretending like she was having a mental breakdown so that she could get publicity. She was on *the Today Show*, and she ran across the set, jumped onto the *Today Show* desk, jumped through that pane of glass, and rolled out into 30 Rock Plaza. I figured out a way, but it was so exciting, because I was like "I hope this works." But it also felt like I could order anything I wanted and they would just give it to me.

Jenna ends up in the hospital, where she confesses her true feelings for Paul—who happens to be nearby, disguised as a nurse.

Jack's new couch manufacturing idea is a bust thanks to their American manufacturing making the couches deeply uncomfortable, despite ads promoting them with gruff *Mike Hammer* star Stacy Keach in a parody of Clint Eastwood's 2012 Super Bowl ad. Jack turns it around by selling the couches to the CIA as torture devices. And it all comes together, with the CIA using one of those couches to interrogate a North Korean spy, allowing them to recover Jack's wife, Avery.

In the show's second live episode, **"Live from Studio 6H,"** the writers tried to dive deeper into doing sketches to offer a storyline reason for it to be live. The initial live episode was a ratings success, with the network eager to do it again, and the show opted to give them what they wanted.

Beth McCarthy-Miller: The first one went off without a hitch and they were like "Oh, we can make it so much more complicated." With the second one, we had twice as many sets, all these costume changes—I was sneaking people out of Tracy's dressing room. It was relentless.

They had longer to rehearse than the first live episode—three days instead of just one. But Jack McBrayer was nervous, as they had a lot more complicated dialogue to deal with in this episode. Krakowski spoke with Jack McBrayer a month after the show aired, and he hadn't had the courage to watch it back yet.

Beth McCarthy-Miller: The second live episode, I was like, if you didn't give me a heart attack the first time, now we're doing costume changes in twenty seconds? It was nuts.

There was one costume change that Tina Fey never made in dress rehearsal, but managed to do once the show went live. The episode's opening featured Jenna, Tracy, and Pete during dress rehearsal.

Jeff Richmond: But under the bleachers, which is where you sit when you watch the shows, Lorne said, "You know what? I think we're introducing all our main characters too quickly, and we're not giving people entrances."

So the episode was redesigned to allow for some big entrances later in the show, letting the crowd give them some big welcoming applause when they first arrive. Danny made a surprise return, too, telling Jenna that the delivery she sent him to do landed him in a Singapore prison.

Cheyenne Jackson: My two favorite things were the live episodes. Tina asked me and Jane to sing, to do the warm-up. With the *SNL* band, I did some Stevie Wonder. Then I went and sat next to Lorne Michaels. Paul McCartney was sitting there, and he said, "You can really sing." And any feeling of me feeling sorry for myself that I didn't have more episodes completely dissipated. Because I was blissfully aware how grateful and how lucky this queer kid from Idaho was.

Jane Krakowski: The first year that we did this the adrenaline was so high, and I literally collapsed. To try to wake up again at midnight, to get back up to do the second live show was insanity. And we all made little bobble mistakes at the top of the West Coast feed. The one thing we learned this year was how to pace the adrenaline, because it's just so exciting when the audience comes in.

Flashbacks reveal that a 1986 telethon sparked the cast's love of live television. It features Donald Glover as a young Tracy, dancing and pulling up his shirt to do some of the belly-related humor Morgan was known for. Young Liz, played by the blonde Amy Poehler with no explanation (and surely for *30 Rock*, no explanation needed), learns to love rebelling through a prank call to the telethon. And a young Jack, played by Jimmy Fallon, answers the prank call and impresses Don Geiss, leading to a promotion.

Guest stars also include Fred Armisen popping up in the background throughout in a *Where's Waldo?*–style role, as well as Kim Kardashian and Paul McCartney in an effort to show that anything can happen on live TV. Kardashian appeared during the live West Coast airing, while Paul McCartney appeared for East Coast viewers.

Showing the level of sketches on *TGS*, this episode includes one focused on Prince William and Prince, the musician, as "Time-Traveling Fart Detectives." Paying homage to their *SNL* roots, Hazel seizes her moment by ripping up a photo of Sinéad O'Connor, as O'Connor did with a photo of Pope John Paul II on *SNL* in 1992.

And Jon Hamm appears in what could be seen as blackface in a parody of *Amos 'n' Andy*, leading to this episode also being pulled from streaming services and syndication.

Jeff Richmond: There was discussion about whether or not he should be in blackface or not. He's not. There was a lot of discussion, and Tina thought it might shock Emmys. Oh my gosh, how'd we get away with this?

Richmond credited the presence of Tracy in these scenes with making Hamm's not-quite-blackface makeup, and the jokes around it, acceptable at the time. Hamm, while speaking with a stereotypically Black voice, has a darkened face that looks somewhere in between full blackface and a chimney sweep. The sequence ends with Hamm going even more racially offensive, leading to Tracy's character choking him.

Jeff Richmond: Tina fought to keep this last beat in, because some of the writers thought we don't need that third beat.

Alan Sepinwall: I will admit when Jon Hamm dances in the blackface in the live episode, I laughed an awful lot, but I understand that it was probably not appropriate, and certainly in the modern lens is not appropriate.

Beth McCarthy-Miller was saddened that both of *30 Rock*'s live episodes were pulled from streaming.

Beth McCarthy-Miller: I don't think there was any ill will in it. I understand the sensitivity to it. And I'm just sad about all the events that took us to that place.

Kevin Ladson: The sting [from when Jenna dressed up in blackface as Lynn Swann] didn't *hurt* until I went to [the *SNL* stage] when we did *The Honeymooners* spot with Jon Hamm. And I had to leave the stage at that point.

When it was brought up recently, I wanted to email Tina and tell her my thoughts of the time, but I can honestly say that at the time, I didn't feel like I could express that feeling. And I was in such a great place, and working with great people, and it seemed like that was one of the skits that slipped. I'm looking at Jon Hamm—he's only doing his job—but, you know, it seemed like he one-upped his performance in the blackface role.

I went to the prop room, and I just watched it on the monitor. I couldn't stand it on the stage.

And then for it to rehash during this period in our history, Black Lives Matter and the atrocities of what happened with the abuse of police, I really had to go back to that time to remember that period. I kept a journal while I was on *30 Rock*, and I wrote in my journal how it stung.

So that's why when it was mentioned recently, I felt so like I needed to talk to Tina about it, and we've since talked after that, via email. And I'm still grateful for my time there. It was just one of those skits that slipped.

In **episode 20, "Queen of Jordan 2: Mystery of the Phantom Pooper,"** Jack gets a call revealing that the State Department has recovered his wife, Avery, via a North

Korean prisoner exchange. Jack endeavors to hide his relationship with Avery's mother, Diana, from the *Queen of Jordan* reality TV cameras, but he has to create increasingly bizarre excuses to hide the truth. Reality star Angie fights with husband Tracy, but he reveals his true gift to her in the show's climax: a drawn-out divorce storyline that can boost her show's ratings.

> **Paula Leggett Chase (Randi):** When you're a guest star and you come in, you probably haven't slept very well. I was always operating on four hours of sleep. I sat there [in hair and makeup], they're doing me up, and Tina's sitting there. They're blow-drying her hair 'cause she'd just washed it and came in with her wet hair. On lunch, they would be having a table read for the next episode. So she was working, writing on the next thing; she's acting in this one.
>
> Plus, her daughter was there—she had a five-year-old. And I thought, *Oh my gosh, I can totally do this*. You know, if she can do this—'cause at the time, my children were older than that, but I so know what being in the trenches is like—even if you have nannies and everything else that she has, and a car that's bringing her there, and I took the train in the dark to Queens every day.

The hours behind the scenes were still long, even in the later seasons of the show, with the cast and crew giving it their all. John Riggi faced some early call times when he was directing.

> **John Riggi:** I go up to my office, and I don't even turn the light on because I'm half-awake. I walk over to my desk and I'm like "Oh my god, I found my Chapstick. Here it is." I go down the hall and I get on the elevator, I put this Chapstick on, and I'm like "Oh my god, my lips feel worse. They're really chapped." So I put more on, and my lips are burning.
>
> So I go in to Tina, because I was directing, and I wanted to talk to her about a scene. She's in the [hair and makeup] chair. I start to put more of this Chapstick on, and I go, "Jesus Christ." She's like "What's the matter?" I go, "My lips are burning." And she literally, like a mother, reaches over and pulls it out of my hand and goes, "Riggi, this is a glue stick." I literally was putting glue sticks on my lips. Because I was that tired.

In **episode 21, "The Return of Avery Jessup,"** Jack helps Avery settle back into her life, explaining that not much has changed while she was gone. "There's an iPod 3 and a Mitt Romney 4," Jack explains. "They worked all the bugs out. He's not killing hobos at night anymore."

Avery offers a blanket forgiveness to Jack for any infidelity while she was away, which makes him suspicious. Jack believes that Avery may have cheated on him with another hostage who's being returned, broadcaster Scott Scotsman. Jack's guilt leads to him finally revealing his affair with Avery's mom, while Avery reveals that she was manipulating him to get him to reveal everything. Jack loves their competitive relationship, and they plan to renew their vows.

Avery's kidnapper, North Korean dictator Kim Jong-il (Margaret Cho), also makes an appearance—despite his death the year before. In *30 Rock*'s world, he faked his death, but keeps an eye on Avery as a waiter at Jack and Avery's vow renewal, with an apparent plan to interrupt during the "speak now or forever hold your peace" part of the ceremony.

> **Margaret Cho:** [Playing Kim Jong-il] worked out so well that it felt like a thing we had to do again. Also, it was such a fast thing [the first time]—it was great to come back and have more preparation. The first time I had gotten one of Amy Poehler's old wigs. When I came back the second time, they actually got a special ordered wig for me.

The appearances of North Korean dictators Kim Jong-il and Kim Jong-un showed how the *30 Rock* world could interface with reality. President Bill Clinton, while he never appeared on the show, came to visit the set.

> **Vali Chandrasekaran:** A stand-in was playing Margaret Cho for over-the-shoulder shots. When President Clinton was leaving, people were coming over and saying hello, and Margaret Cho's stand-in said, "President Clinton, I'm Kim Jong-un. Thank you for your service."

While Avery initially refuses to admit anything happened with Scott Scotsman, in the **season finale, "What Will Happen to the Gang Next Year?"** Jack deduces that they used a finger-tap code—as real prisoners of war have been known to do—in order to communicate. Avery confesses her feelings for Scott. They still go ahead with renewing their vows in a ceremony officiated by Liz. But when no one objects, they each turn to the crowd and call for someone to step up, as they only got married for the sake of their daughter, Liddy. The realization prompts them to agree to a divorce.

Hazel needs a place to stay, so Kenneth offers her to stay with him. He discovers that she sabotaged his efforts to get back into the NBC page program, but when he confronts Hazel, she tells him she has feelings for him—they kiss, and begin a dark, messed-up, manipulative relationship. On Hazel's part, because Kenneth is sweet and perfect.

Tracy faces accusations that his behavior has proven an embarrassment to the Black community, as well as encouraging racists. Cornel West makes an appearance in a meeting arranged by Grizz. Tracy visits a civil rights museum and decides to go full Tyler Perry, creating a film studio that will only employ Black people.

The episode's title also plays on the episode naming format of fellow joke-heavy show *It's Always Sunny in Philadelphia* and that show's reference to the main cast as "the gang." The show also nodded to *It's Always Sunny* in the second-to-last episode of Season 5, "Everything Sunny All the Time Always."

The Margaret Cho role was so popular that Cho returned as Kim Jong-un when Tina Fey and Amy Poehler were hosting the Golden Globes in 2015, satirizing North Korea's hack of movie studio Sony due to its film *The Interview* mocking North Korea's leader. Cho's character became a bit that Fey and Poehler returned to throughout the show. But the return of this character was not nearly as well received—many observers called the polarizing appearance racist and uncomfortable, with *Time* even describing it as "minstrely" given the character being one of the few Asians to appear on the show, in a broad character, for a largely white audience. Cho defended the appearance at the time, tweeting about her own Korean heritage and adding, "You imprison, starve, and brainwash my people, you get made fun of by me."

> **Margaret Cho:** I thought it was completely appropriate, and really funny, and really perfect. It's something that I will always treasure. And I think that they got a laugh too in North Korea. They've got to have a sense of humor to it, because it's really a great depiction, I think.

This season marked the last of *30 Rock*'s full-length seasons. There was also a larger exodus from the crew, with a number of writers and others moving on to new projects. Writer/director John Riggi came back to direct one episode in the final season, but left at the end of Season 6 ahead of its abbreviated farewell.

> **John Riggi:** When I left the show, I cried—I literally cried when I left New York. 'Cause my husband came out to New York and we packed up my shit, and we drove back across country. I drove out of New York for the last time and I was crying, because I was going to miss those people so much.

Writer Vali Chandrasekaran left to be with his wife—on another continent.

> **Vali Chandrasekaran:** I ended up moving to India and not working on Season 7. It was just thirteen episodes. My wife and I had met in college, we dated for a while, broke up for five years, and got back together and got married. But after getting back together, we had never lived in the same place—she was living in India. And getting older, it just got to a point where you think, *Ohhh . . . I have to live my life.* Working on *30 Rock* is so great, and wonderful, but I remember going to tell Robert and Tina that I didn't want to come back for a Season 7, and it being so rough. It was so hard to say.

But there was still creative steam left in the show. And with the knowledge that Season 7 would be their last, the cast and crew came back with one of the most critically acclaimed final seasons of all time, with ratings going back up for the first time in years.

SEASON 7
(2012–13)
Happy-ish Endings

Alec Baldwin tried to keep the show going. He told NBC he'd take a 20-percent pay-cut in return for renewing the show for full seventh and eighth seasons. But between the show's declining ratings and Tina wanting to go out on top and focus more on her children, that didn't happen. So Baldwin came back for the abbreviated final season, with just thirteen episodes.

Alec Baldwin: Over the years, I had bitched and moaned, as only actors can, about being tied to a contract for a show that would never be my own. After Season 5, I wanted to quit. I came back for Season 6, had a great time, and was ready to sign for five more years.

Don Scardino: It's like any sort of classic show that really takes hold. It did go six and a half seasons. And the only reason it didn't go a full seven seasons, which the network happily would have asked them to do, was that Tina had said, "Eh, let's go out high. Let's not go beat it to death."

Despite the short run, the show continued to be critically acclaimed, receiving thirteen Emmy nominations—the most of any comedy series that year. The show ended up winning two Emmys, both for the writing of the series finale and for the show's casting. It was a testament to the continued power of the writing on this show, and the long hours that still went into it, rather than anyone resting on their laurels.

Andrew Guest: Even Season 7, in pre-production, they were working on the first day until eleven o'clock or twelve o'clock at night. In Season 7 of a show.

In the end, the show received a total of 103 Emmy nominations over the course of its run. But it lost the best comedy series Emmy for the fourth year in a row to ABC's

Modern Family. That show would hold on to the top spot for one more Emmys season before the three-year reign of another acclaimed series with a female lead: HBO's *Veep*, starring Julia Louis-Dreyfus.

The final season gives viewers fan service, with the known ending of the show meaning that they had the chance to wrap up storylines and find satisfying conclusions for many characters.

> **Emily VanDerWerff:** The last season is like "Oh, right, we care about these characters and we love these characters. Even if we find them ridiculous, we want them to have something like happiness."

The final season was tightly plotted as the writers tried to fit in the final storylines and bring closure to the characters. This was helped by the shorter run, with few episodes feeling like filler—it's a storytelling trend that has continued in the streaming era, with often-shorter seasons for shows on Netflix or Disney+ keeping storylines from straying too far.

> **Andrew Guest:** The truth is, I love Seasons 1 and 2 particularly because I was there, and then Season 7. The last season, I thought the show, on a whole, went back to the standard of the first two seasons.

> **Vali Chandrasekaran:** I was able to just, in Season 7, watch the show as a fan again, which I wasn't able to do on 4, 5, and 6. Because you were working on it, it was hard to enjoy it. I spent so much time working on it, I was there all the time, and you kept thinking about choices that were made all along the way. Whereas Season 7, I just watched them when they aired. I would, of course, talk to people, but you're not as in it, and it was great. I *loved* Season 7.

The season opens with **"The Beginning of the End."** Jack finds himself unhappy as NBC's leader under Kabletown. He intentionally tries tanking the network, working to convince Hank Hooper to sell so that Jack can be out from under the bland leadership of Kabletown.

Liz catches on to Jack's plan, thanks to his terrible ideas for shows. These include *Homonym*, where contestants have to guess which version of a homonym the host is saying and where you're always wrong and there's no way to prove the host isn't lying to you about which one he said, and *God Cop*, with Jack as God. Liz agrees to help Jack, setting about making the already bad *TGS* even worse.

Despite Hazel largely being a psychopath whose values are completely antithetical to Kenneth's, their relationship has somehow continued to develop. And she quietly becomes responsible for the events that lead directly to the series finale. Hazel and Kenneth invite Tracy over, but Hazel starts to make a move on Tracy. She tells him she was just using Kenneth to get close to Tracy so that he would cast her in a film. But Tracy rebuffs her advances.

In **episode 2, "Governor Dunston,"** Criss and Liz continue their efforts to get Liz pregnant. While the show never wanted Liz's main goal in life to be having a baby, the writers finally pursue that storyline fully this year, as opposed to the halfhearted, start-and-stop approaches to the idea in previous seasons.

> **Vali Chandrasekaran:** We talked about it a lot. The show at its bottom is about, can Liz Lemon have it all? Can she have a professional life and a personal life? And what, for a person like Liz Lemon, is personal life success? It's not necessarily living in New Jersey with a house, a husband, and kids.
>
> But there was always this funny traditionalist streak within Liz Lemon, that she did like a lot of those things. There were lots of discussions, and Tina obviously, her instincts were what we followed on everything. She was really skilled at figuring out what would make Liz feel real and relatable. What is having it all?
>
> She gets better and better at life, and helping Jack figure out how to have it all himself—because he is a guy who is also obsessed with his career. They were so different, and they both were obsessed with the same thing, and had to help the other one get the same thing.
>
> When Jack started to have kids, what does that version look like in Liz Lemon's life, was something that we thought and talked about a lot. But at the end of the day, Tina knew Liz Lemon in her bones. If you woke her up in the middle of the night now and ask how Liz Lemon would deal with anything, she would have the answer that you would not bother even wasting time pitching on.

The show had fun with its take on Tina's cultural moment as Sarah Palin here, creating a storyline around a foolish politician who just happens to look exactly like Tracy Jordan. As Jack's plan to tank NBC continues, he insists that *TGS* avoid doing any political sketches, due to their popularity. But despite going along with the plan, the comedy writer in Liz can't resist when Tracy doppelgänger Governor Dunston takes Paul Ryan's place as VP candidate to Mitt Romney in his 2012 presidential run—Ryan gets disqualified after it turns out he was actually born in Kenya.

In order to keep her promise to Jack, they don't even write original dialogue for Tracy. He just says what Dunston actually said on the campaign trail, the same way Tina Fey used real Sarah Palin lines on *SNL*.

The episode brought Matthew Broderick back to the show as ineffectual Republican operative "Cooter Burger."

Matthew Broderick: I was delighted. I wish I could come back more. When I did come back, [Robert Carlock] said, "Yeah, there were some people, there's characters we just wanted to say hello to one last time, and you were definitely on the list."

Cooter pushes Jack to let Tracy make fun of this Republican vice-presidential candidate even more, because it turns out that the real Dunston is privately a monster. Making fun of his public foolishness is making him more relatable. You could argue that Baldwin would go on to do the same thing for President Trump on *SNL*—though Baldwin himself seemed to think otherwise, holding up a "You're welcome" sign on *SNL* after Trump's 2020 loss to Joe Biden.

The *TGS* ratings boost from the political sketches prompts Hank Hooper to order the show to start airing five nights a week. It makes Liz's life more complex—but she finds that having to intricately schedule everything makes her sexually excited, leaving her eager to get intimate with Criss. It helps to spice things up after they'd been focusing on having sex mainly for procreation purposes.

Kenneth's mom (Catherine O'Hara) visits with her "friend" Ron (Bryan Cranston), paying off previous references by Kenneth to their relationship. Ron accidentally reveals that he's been secretly married to Kenneth's mother for the past seven years, meaning they've secretly been a thing the entire run of *30 Rock*.

Episode 3, "Stride of Pride," takes on both sexism and ageism. Liz has to handle a magazine article proclaiming that Jenna is fifty-six years old—while Tracy says that women aren't funny.

The episode was partially inspired by a 2007 article in *Vanity Fair* by conservative thinker Christopher Hitchens, titled "Why Women Aren't Funny," which prompted responses from Tina Fey, Amy Poehler, and other female comedians.

Daisy Gardner: I mean, there were legit debates when I was a stand-up comic, and doing improv and writing sketches and writing my specs. People would seriously go, "Can women be funny?" What Tina settled once and for all is: Yes. And she can be better than you. And she can get it done in a way that doesn't compromise anything about her or her vision. And she can just be a badass.

Episode 4, "Unwindulax," aired just weeks before the 2012 election. Jack brings Liz to a Republican Party fundraiser, baiting her into a rant about her liberal political beliefs, which he uses to get those at the party to donate more to Romney.

The episode sees the expansion of the Lutz-o-verse, with *Twilight* actor Kellan Lutz (no relation to the real actor) appearing as Lutz's grandnephew. Liz uses him on *TGS* to promote the Democratic Party. Meanwhile, Jack bribes Don Cheadle with $10 million to promote the Republican Party and draw Black voters, to no avail.

Jenna turns herself into a Jimmy Buffett–esque figure with her song "Catching Crabs in Paradise," earning followers who call themselves "Crabcatchers." It's a payoff to a setup from "Governor Dunston," when Jenna asks Kenneth's stepdad Ron for song ideas—he described the kind of beach music she creates here. Her fans start camping outside the 30 Rock building, much to the annoyance of the *TGS* staff. But Pete comes around, and Jenna's fans help him to chill out and de-stress.

The episode ends with a cliffhanger—it turns out that Jenna's fans are a key voting bloc and that her endorsement could decide the election. In **episode 5, "There's No I in America,"** Liz and Jack hold a debate to win over Jenna, despite her complete lack of interest in politics. Jack wins, forcing Liz to work on convincing him not to have Jenna endorse anyone.

Liz tries to ruin Jenna's reputation, giving Tracy access to Jenna's Twitter account and getting her banned before she can endorse Republican nominee Mitt Romney against Barack Obama. Meanwhile, Pete tries to re-create the excitement of the 2008 election, thanks to the fact that office security guard Maria kissed him in excitement when Obama won. But no one else cares about the election this time around, and Maria leaves work before the winner is announced—with her boyfriend "Peter Horn," who happens to look like a fancier Pete. With hair. Kenneth votes for the first time, via absentee ballot from Stone Mountain. He's frustrated to discover how difficult making an informed decision is, but he ultimately finishes his ballot and sends it off. When he goes to cheer up Pete, Pete gives Kenneth that kiss he'd been saving for Maria.

> **Don Scardino:** I came back in Season 7 to do just two episodes, and also to play the meth freak in the clocktower of Kenneth Parcell's hometown for a John Riggi episode that he directed. Because Tina said to me, at that point, "We're in our last season, and you've never been on camera."
>
> I pushed back. I said, "Yeah, and that's the way it's going to stay." And she said, "No no, you've got to do something." So I was there prepping to direct an episode, and Riggi was shooting that episode, and she said, "You're going to play the meth freak in the clocktower." I said "ehhhh." She said, "No, you've got to, you've got to be on camera. I'm not taking no for an answer." You can never say no to Tina Fey. So I said OK, and went into hair and makeup. I said, "You've got to give me a lot of hair and a big beard. I just can't look like me."

So the meth freak that doesn't look like Don Scardino is Don Scardino.

Director John Riggi also had to figure out how to shoot some complicated stuntwork in this episode.

> **John Riggi:** Tina had to run through an obstacle course. She had to run down the hallway, slide under a pane of glass, get up, and Lutz was walking through

with a bowl of marbles. She has to get into the *TGS* set in time, and Lutz drops these marbles. And as opposed to just walking, she parkours off the wall and goes over the marbles. It had five different parts to it, and it was just like, this shit is complicated and we gotta figure out how to do it.

How are you going to let Tina Fey, on her face, slide underneath a big pane of glass like in a cartoon? While those two guys hold suction cup panes of glass, and you're on her face as she does it. All that stuff took time, but it was like a little puzzle, and it was using a whole different set of muscles that I wasn't using when I was writing. But there's also timing involved—you're visually telling a joke, as opposed to writing a joke.

In **episode 6, "Aunt Phatso vs. Jack Donaghy,"** Tracy makes a Jack-like figure the bad guy in his new *Aunt Phatso* movie—a riff on Tyler Perry's Madea films—*Tracy Jordan's Aunt Phatso Goes to the Hospital Goes to Jail*. And he's got another one on the way with *Tracy Jordan's Aunt Phatso's Jack Donaghy's We At It Again*. Jack and Tracy feud, including Jack attending the New York Philharmonic and finding that Tracy has paid them to play the *Sanford and Son* theme for four hours straight, ruining Jack's evening. In real life, Alec Baldwin is on the New York Philharmonic's board and has hosted its radio series, *The New York Philharmonic This Week*.

Hazel finally manipulates her way into an appearance on *TGS*, but when Liz discovers Hazel's machinations, Liz immediately fires her. Kenneth is angered by Liz firing his girlfriend, along with his treatment by other members of the cast. He declares that he is no longer their friend—a bold declaration for the man who's been an eternal friend throughout the run of the show.

In **episode 7, "Mazel Tov, Dummies!"** Liz learns that Dennis, thanks to being married, was allowed to adopt. Now he has a son who he calls "Black Dennis." While she has mixed feelings about the institution of marriage, Liz decides to have a low-key city hall wedding with Criss to increase their chances of being allowed to adopt. The key episode was written by Tracey Wigfield.

> **Tracey Wigfield:** Getting married in a sweatshirt, no bra, I feel like is something that I took from my life, because I do a lot of things in a sweatshirt, no bra. I wouldn't get married in it, but I would do more formal things than you'd think in it. Like go out to a store, or go out to a moderately priced restaurant.

An earlier version of the script included Criss and Dennis becoming bros behind Liz's back, but the storyline was cut for time. That version had them seeing the critically acclaimed *Beasts of the Southern Wild* together, but Dennis thought the movie was a porno.

While she thought the city hall wedding would be great, Liz has to admit that she actually does want a special day—and her friends, and even Dennis, work to deliver a Very Liz Lemon Wedding, featuring Liz as a space princess.

> **Alan Sepinwall:** [Criss] wasn't necessarily the funniest of the guys she dated, or the guy she had the best chemistry with, but you could understand why he was the one who lasted. You understood the bond between them. They brought that character to a nice landing place, where the romance wasn't necessarily the end-all-be-all for her, but she did wind up with a good guy and she got to get married in the Princess Leia costume.

> **Tom Ceraulo:** In [Tracey's] original writer's draft of this scene, [Liz had] a line I really enjoyed where they talk about how they feel about each other: "You do my laundry, and I bring you home soda from work, and that's love."

> **Tracey Wigfield:** It's so true. I feel so strongly about it.

The show tried making Criss look like a nerd at one point in the episode, but James Marsden was too handsome.

> **Tracey Wigfield:** We tried on three different turtlenecks, because everything he put on, it would just be like "Oh, you're like a J.Crew model, that *is* a nice turtleneck." We couldn't find one lame enough, and this was the best we had, because it has puffy sleeves.

Even though he was a dirtbag, Dennis gets to be a little sweet, in his completely criminal way—he steals flowers from a hospital for Liz's wedding and has his adopted son start the car.

> **Beth McCarthy-Miller:** Oh my god, Dennis running out of the hospital and going, "Black Dennis, start the car," and we were in this very sketchy neighborhood in Queens, and he was having to yell that.

McCarthy-Miller felt bad about everything she was having Winters do in this episode, given his physical limitations after his battle with gangrene.

> **Beth McCarthy-Miller:** But I had him running out, doing all this stuff. He had gotten better by then, but he had lost a toe. He had some definite issues.

Filming Liz and Criss finally getting married left Wigfield crying on McCarthy-Miller's shoulder.

> **Beth McCarthy-Miller:** I felt like that episode was a little bit of the beginning of the end. But it was so beautiful.

Criss also *finally* wins Jack's approval. Wigfield noted that she's been asked what Jack hands Criss near the end of the episode. When they'd met before, Jack handed him a card with wavy lines on it, indicating his disapproval—the new card has a star on it.

Jack even gets Tony Bennett to perform at Liz's wedding. Bennett showed up with his own longtime piano player, singing live for every take. He sang "I've Got the World on a String" and "Just in Time," which almost became the name of the episode.

Tracy is horrified when Dr. Spaceman reveals that Tracy is actually completely healthy now, and likely to live to a ripe old age. Tracy sadly realizes he can no longer behave as recklessly as he would like to.

> **Tom Ceraulo:** I was reading versions of this scene—there were so many things that we lost that were wonderful. Like, he lists things that he will now have to do because he will live a long time, like take trips with Angie. There's one line, he goes, "I don't want to see the splendor of Istanbul's Blue Mosque." And there's one where he says, "I promised Terrence Howard to go to lunch with him, and I'll have to do that."

But when Tracy gets hit by a taxi, he realizes he could die at any moment and that he should just live the way he wants to. With Tracy also putting his megastar power to use this season—running a movie studio—this episode includes a fantasy sequence after Tracy gets hit, where he's visited by Jack as Harriet Tubman. It inspires his next project. The plan had been to eventually get to Tracy sinking all his money into a Harriet Tubman biopic.

> **Tracey Wigfield:** With the thought that maybe Tracy would lose all his money at the end of the series—but we never did that. It almost happened—a lot of things almost happened.

> **Tom Ceraulo:** In the table read, Alec tried to do a voice for this.

But, following all the racial controversy over the years, the show opted not to let Alec do Harriet Tubman's voice. And he doesn't wear blackface. So you get Jack, in his Jack voice, as Harriet Tubman, which is still very, very funny, without nearly as many problematic issues as some of the show's previous choices.

Jenna discovers that a Surge Cola contest she agreed to participate in back in the nineties has given fan Terry (John Hodgman) ownership of Jenna. But Jack negotiates with the fan to give Terry her value in cash, which Jack calculates as $2,000. The valuation and his rationale for it depresses Jenna, but Jack explains that he's past his prime, too.

While the show got a hard time for product placement on occasion, one rejected product placement in this episode was from McDonald's. The production team sent the script to the fast-food company, but it passed thanks to a bit about Dennis's wife, Megan, finding a wire in the hash browns.

Tracey Wigfield: Which I don't understand, because I have done nothing but love McDonald's for many years, and pitch jokes with it in them for the six years I've been on *30 Rock*.

This episode also features a cameo from Tina Fey's daughter—she played Young Liz in a photo.

Episode 8, "My Whole Life Is Thunder," became an accidental Christmas episode when NBC changed the show's schedule, according to writer Colleen McGuinness.

Colleen McGuinness: So we threw up some Christmas decorations, and we mention Christmas. But I hope that it still felt like a Christmas episode, because Elaine Stritch was in it, and she was often in the *30 Rock* Christmas episodes.

Liz's surprise wedding in the previous episode ruins Jenna's plans for her own deeply kinky surprise wedding to Paul, which had been teased briefly earlier in the season. Liz tries making up for it by inviting Jenna as her guest to a Women in Media awards banquet with Gayle King, Andrea Martin, Pat Battle, Wendy Williams, Judy Gold, and other luminaries.

Colleen McGuinness: Tina wanted it to be a real thing for Liz, eighty women under eighty, New York ladies.

Linda Mendoza: One of the funniest things from that night—this is how real Tina Fey is. We're setting up and we're ready for her; she's finishing up a phone call. And she's like "OK, just for the record, I had to order dinner for my kids. I wasn't being Hollywood."

Jenna plans to hold her own surprise wedding at the women's event, but Liz thwarts her by throwing up unflattering lighting.

Tina's longtime friend, journalist Damian Holbrook, said that the version of Tina seen in flashbacks—working a college theater light board—was exactly what she looked like in her college years.

Colleen McGuinness: This is the last Liz/Jenna story we were going to tell. And Tina made a really good point: She said, let's make sure this story is about two friends, and not about a monster and a victim.

This marked the final appearance of Jack's mother, Colleen Donaghy (Elaine Stritch), on the show. She visits Jack and tells him she doesn't have long to live, and she ultimately dies during her visit.

Colleen McGuinness: For *30 Rock* to kill off a major character felt different, and I credit Robert and Tina for wanting to do that in their final season and not coasting.

Linda Mendoza: That was actually really an emotional thing, and she was very emotional throughout. She was very fragile.

The episode had a lot of heart, despite the often-terrible statements from Jack's mom about people who weren't like her.

Colleen McGuinness: She's older and from another generation. They were just racist.

A scene between Elaine Stritch and Alec Baldwin caused speculation online that they weren't actually filmed together—and there were times in the show's production where they were shot without the other. But according to writer Colleen McGuinness, they were shot together in this episode. The same was true for a ride with them in a carriage, where they share a genuinely emotional exchange. McGuinness said that the confusion was due to the way it was staged.

John Riggi: I won't say [Elaine] was a mother figure to me, but she was very much one of those big Broadway broads that they don't make anymore. We would have moments where we were like "Oh my god, what were we thinking?" But I used to say all the time, "Guys, when she goes, there ain't another one coming down the pike. There just isn't. They don't exist anymore. This is like having this crazy person from another time who's in our universe with us, for as long as she's gonna last, and I know it's difficult, but look what we get."

Stritch called Riggi after his mom passed away during the time he was working on the show. She told him, "Now you listen to me, John. I'm gonna tell you one thing about your mother. I didn't know her that well, but I'm gonna tell you right now: I don't think she would've been the kind of woman who would have liked to have had a lot of blubbering because she just left the building." It was the perfect Stritch moment, a hardass even in the face of death.

McGuinness noted they wanted to be able to bring back the Donaghy family for the funeral, but that it would be difficult arranging for all those stars—including Nathan Lane and Molly Shannon—to make a return appearance.

Jack vows to deliver the greatest eulogy of all time as he deals with his grief. We see brief glimpses of his eulogy, including deeply emotional stories, jokes, playing "Danny Boy" on the flute, Kermit the Frog explaining the afterlife, and more. Jack's eulogy is widely appreciated by those in attendance and does, in fact, seem like the best eulogy ever. During the eulogy, an emotional Tracy proclaims, "Today, we are all Irish!"

Jenna and Paul insist on staging their long-awaited surprise wedding at the end of the funeral. Jack gives it the OK, because he knows his mom would have hated it. Paul spent the whole funeral disguised as a statue, and their gimp comes in as the priest. Not everybody was shot together for this—Will Forte was shooting the movie *Nebraska* at the time and had to fly in separately to film his scenes.

Linda Mendoza: From that moment when Tina walks into the studio and he's up in the rafters to all the scenes in the church, Will and Tina were never in the same frame together. It was all doubles and very clever editing.

This episode featured a guest star appearance by Florence Henderson (*The Brady Bunch*)—filmed just before Hurricane Sandy, with the weather keeping her from being able to come back for the funeral scene at the end. Tracy invites her to *TGS* to cheer up Kenneth, due to him being a fan of hers, after he gets dumped by Hazel.

There's also a nod to the classic trope of *Roseanne*'s two Beckys, switching actresses and not looking much alike, with Tracy re-casting Hazel and setting up Kenneth with the Asian Hazel at the funeral.

In **episode 9, "Game Over,"** we get into the real endgame of the series. Hank Hooper announces plans to retire as CEO on his seventieth birthday, with his grand-daughter Kaylie set to take over after graduating college. Jack discovers that Kaylie has also been working with Banks. Jack meets with Banks and proposes a team-up, with Banks getting a role in the company.

But Banks turns on Jack. Kaylie reveals that they were still working together the whole time. Hold on, wait! Jack unveils one last twist. His plan was to spend a week distracting Kaylie, so she never sent Hank Hooper something that means more to him than anything: a birthday card. Jack has finally defeated Kaylie Hooper, topping her in Hank's esteem.

The episode includes Jack using his PI, Len Wosniak, against Kaylie, going undercover in her high school as drama teacher Jan Foster—before realizing that she prefers being Jan, and chooses to stay Jan from here forward. It's played for laughs in a time when trans characters were less prevalent, and it's one of *30 Rock*'s instances of what is considered acceptable to mock changing with time.

As Liz continues her adoption journey, she discovers that the waiting list for a newborn is four years long—but that she has the option of adopting a six-year-old immediately. At the same time, Tracy starts filming his Harriet Tubman movie, with Octavia Spencer as Tubman. But Octavia plays a comically hard-to-work-with version of herself, proving to be just as irresponsible as Tracy. Tracy praises Liz for being able to deal with someone like that all these years—which gives Liz the confidence to adopt an older child.

In **episode 10, "Florida,"** Jack and Liz visit the Sunshine State to settle his mother's estate, discovering that Colleen was . . . actually really nice, according to her live-in nurse Martha. Liz discovers that the "live-in nurse" was actually Colleen's romantic partner, but Jack refuses to believe it, arguing that two people can platoni-cally share a bed together.

When Martha assumes that Liz and Jack are a couple and makes up a bed for them, Liz challenges Jack to share that bed with her to prove his point. So, the audience finally got to see the pair in bed together. But there's still no romance. While Liz worries that it's because she's not interesting, or not spontaneous enough, Jack explains that their mentorship/friendship is more interesting than them getting together would have been—a pretty explicit statement from the writers, the subtext finally becoming text after all these years.

Jack initially believes that his mother's last words to him—that she just wanted him to be happy—were sarcastic. But he realizes that they weren't and, continuing the ennui he's been feeling this season, wonders whether becoming CEO actually made him happy.

Liz gets a call from the adoption agency, telling her that she can adopt right now—but only if she takes a brother-and-sister pair. She decides to be spontaneous and goes for it.

Tim Meadows guests as lawyer "Martin Lutherking," representing Hazel in a multimillion-dollar lawsuit against the show for inappropriate behavior. This was originally planned to be another appearance by HR rep Jeffrey Weinerslav, but due to Hurricane Sandy bearing down on New York City and actor Todd Buonopane living in LA at the time, they weren't able to fly him in.

> **Todd Buonopane:** Tim Meadows ended up doing most of my scene. And I'm like, I'm cheaper than Tim Meadows!

Lutherking explains that Hazel does lawsuits like this all the time and that the suit can be avoided if they all sign an affidavit denying any inappropriate behavior—but Kenneth tells the truth about all the inappropriate behavior he's witnessed at the show. Years and years of it. Due to the controversy, Hank Hooper's last act as CEO is canceling *TGS*.

In **episode 11, "A Goon's Deed in a Weary World,"** Liz works to save *TGS*, while also awaiting her children arriving at the airport in a few days.

> **Jane Krakowski:** When we did the readthrough of this episode, it was very emo-tional, because it was the first time we acknowledged the end of the series. And when she adopts the kids at the end, we really felt like "Oh, it's all wrapping up."

Krakowski left the room after the readthrough not looking anyone in the eye. Everyone at the show was trying to avoid the journalist who was there for the final table read, hoping he wouldn't catch them getting choked up and crying.

The episode finally brings the dream of Kenneth running NBC to a climax, with a storyline modeled after *Willy Wonka & the Chocolate Factory*. Jack allows Kenneth to be a page once more, giving a tour to the final five candidates for the role of NBC CEO—who all happen to look like adult versions of the kids from *Willy Wonka*, including an aptly named "Charlie McGuffin."

Kenneth thinks Charlie is the right choice, but discovers that Charlie plans to shut the network down and turn the building into a Forever 21 clothing store. Kenneth rails against Charlie, passionately arguing in favor of the power of television rather than concern about money. He even says that Jack wasn't the right person to be president of NBC either.

Jack gets to say the episode's title here, an elegiac ode to Kenneth finally getting what he deserves—and a play on the *Willy Wonka* phrase "So shines a good deed in a weary world." Jack admits that Kenneth is right, telling him, "Every show I was sure would succeed, failed." In an apparent reference to short-lived NBC sitcom *Animal Practice*, he adds, "I mean the monkey was funny, damn it." Jack names Kenneth as NBC's new president.

> **Jane Krakowski:** I remember Jack [McBrayer] really having a hard time not crying through a lot of the filming of this. Tina kept coming up to us and whispering in our ear, "If you cry too much, it can't be used."

With *TGS* barely hanging on by a string, Liz meets with a potential sponsor. They're the only ones who will consider sponsoring the show following the controversy from Hazel's lawsuit—leading to its short-lived transition to being known as *Bro Body Douche Presents the Man Cave*. And the sponsor has another request: rather than Liz being credited for her work, he wants Liz to credit the show to creator "Todd Debeikis." It's the name of the douchey sponsor's old frat bro, another indignity heaped on Liz, but she agrees in order to keep the show alive.

While Liz is willing to make that sacrifice, Tracy and Jenna step up and refuse to tolerate Liz continuing to kill herself for the show—she's staying focused on *TGS* as Criss goes to pick up their new adopted children from the airport. Tracy and Jenna quit the new, compromised version of the show. They announce that they will proudly do what they know how to do best: nothing. The rest of the *TGS* crew all joins them in quitting, from the Writers That Never Talk to Subhas, the janitor. Cerie, who played a smaller role in storylines following her wedding, shows up and explains that she actually quit two years ago. Everyone coming together like this lets Liz rush to the airport to meet her new adopted children, another example of the show twisting the classic run-to-the-airport scene.

When Liz meets her new kids, she finds that they are a mini Jenna and a mini Tracy. The young Terry, Liz's adopted Tracy-esque son, greets her with, "What up, Liz Lemon? I will not be able to attend school tomorrow because of an issue with my lizard."

Jane Krakowski: This young girl studied me a bit too much. She did a better me than me.

There was just one more show to do—an emotional, hourlong special bidding a final farewell to this special piece of TV history.

Don Scardino: Everybody says this a lot—we did so many years together, and it was like family—and it's true. People who work in our business—writing, acting—it is a family. *30 Rock* was another family. And the truth of that is, I'm still friends with so many of the people on the crew, and so many of the people who worked on it. I would work with any of them, whenever I could. And I always say to Tina, whenever you need me.

Grizz Chapman: You get an opportunity to be around these people, and you learn from them, what makes them tick. I've watched Tina Fey have kids, and the kids grow up. I've watched Alec Baldwin get married, I've watched his daughter grow up. It was just an all-around beautiful thing, a beautiful experience, all the way down to conversating with the craft services.

The plan for the series finale, which consisted of **episodes 12 and 13, "Hogcock!" and "Last Lunch,"** was to do one extra-long readthrough. But the storylines weren't settled on until just before Thanksgiving. They were going to read the script the next Thursday, with Robert Carlock and Jack Burditt writing a draft of the first half while Tina Fey and Tracey Wigfield wrote the other half. In their first draft, Tracey wrote the Liz/Jack storyline, while Tina handled writing Tracy and Liz.

The writers' room started working Sunday of the Thanksgiving holiday weekend to punch up the script. The episode paid homage to the show's beginnings while telling the story of *TGS*'s end. When Fey finished shooting on Wednesday night, she asked writer Tom Ceraulo to print out the current version of the last scene between Liz and Tracy.

Tom Ceraulo: A short time later, she came back with handwritten changes, some really beautiful dialogue—touching, honest, and perhaps reflective of Tina and Tracy's actual relationship, yet still *30 Rock*–funny. She then stayed in the room for the end of the rewrite and for the "ceremony" of checking the final scene number on the whiteboard. It was the first real instance of "this is the last time we'll do this," and though we weren't done until one thirty A.M., I was a little sad when the night was over.

People cried throughout the final table read. When Ceraulo posted a photo of the final page of the last episode online, Fey wrote back saying that she was honored by the gesture, telling Ceraulo, "You were meant to be trapped in that room with us."

Along with feelings running high, the show was frantic near the end, with multiple episodes being filmed at once. While normally the show had the luxury of coming back the next week, or after a Christmas hiatus, the cast and crew had no choice but to get everything done on time.

Beth McCarthy-Miller: With everyone being so emotional, it was really hard to get through all the scenes and get the performances we needed, but also be aware of the fact that everyone was very emotional.

Jane Krakowski: It was madness, especially the last two episodes, waiting for Beth McCarthy-Miller to direct both episodes—we'd be waiting on one set, waiting for her to come back to the other set.

Beth McCarthy-Miller: We were always behind schedule. We used to tandem sometimes, where we'd bring in a separate crew. Say I was working with Alec and Tina in the morning, and Don had to pick up scenes from another episode— he would shoot with Tracy and Jack in another location with a second crew. Well, by the end of it, I was tandeming with myself. So I would set up a scene, rehearse it. They'd light it, I'd go to the other crew, shoot one side of that scene, then come back, shoot one side of the other scene.

Longtime *SNL* and *30 Rock* director McCarthy-Miller had been selected to direct the finale.

Beth McCarthy-Miller: I don't know [why they chose me]. I hope it's because they trusted me with it. I was thrilled and honored. Maybe I was the one that was available. I certainly made myself available when they called me.

I'd started living in California by then. I was doing the reverse commute—I was having to leave my family that I'd moved to LA to fly back to New York to do *30 Rock*. So, I could only do a few a year by the end of the last couple seasons. I said, "I would love to do the finale." Jerry Kupfer emailed me back, and he said, "Tina and Robert are thrilled about that idea."

The episode itself opened with Liz adapting to her new life without *TGS* and with two children, living as a stay-at-home mom. Liz goes to 30 Rock to deliver a pitch to Kenneth, now head of NBC. Her idea: a *30 Rock*–esque show about her life. But Kenneth rejects it thanks to the "television no-no words" the pitch includes. He shares the list with Lemon, including such words as "woman," "writer," "shows about shows," "New York," and "quality"—words that don't appeal to a broad audience, at least according to Kenneth. Near the bottom of the list: "immortal characters."

Tina Fey: We wanted Jack Donaghy to have a fancy new office, but we were broke. But we changed the view out the window. Jack's office [was] re-dressed to be Kenneth's office, with homier touches. And I have to say, we all felt it was much homier in there, immediately. A less intimidating space with that afghan.

Jack is now working as CEO of Kabletown, but continues to feel unfulfilled. He creates the Six Sigma Wheel of Happiness Domination to find happiness in the different areas of his life, checking off goal after goal, including arranging a threesome with love interests Nancy and Elisa. But he's still not happy, and decides to quit.

Robert Carlock: Don't try to track the days on this particular episode. I'm assuming that Jack did his whole montage in an afternoon.

Liz discovers that Criss would rather be the stay-at-home parent, while Liz needs to be back at work. It ends up being one of the reasons that Criss is perfect for Liz, as it's the thing that lets Liz actually have it all, working in her dream career and still having her children taken care of at home. It's a relationship dynamic that many couples aren't lucky enough to have, as well as putting Criss in the role women were traditionally forced into that kept them from seeking their own career satisfaction outside the home. Maybe this is what genuinely makes Criss happy, but without his choice, Liz might not have been able to become the fulfilled character she ends up as.

Robert Carlock: That was nice we were able to trick him into hanging around and being the guy. Because we kept casting these wonderful dudes who would have to go be famous at other stuff, but we somehow managed to get him at the right time. Didn't have to put hook hands on him.

Tina Fey: Robert had been pitching James Marsden for a couple years as a possible Liz Lemon love interest, and I just kept refusing it because he was just too implausibly handsome. And I think we can now agree that I was right.

Liz tries pitching Jack a dumbed-down show, but he reveals that, due to their contracts, they need to produce one more episode of *TGS* to avoid having to pay a penalty to Tracy.

Jenna pursues her next gig, but only finds work as a corpse in an episode of *Law & Order: SVU*. When she decides to head west and work to become a movie star in LA, she gets off the plane and discovers it's all young, impossibly hot women there. She immediately turns around to get back on the plane and head east.

The first part of the two-parter—which aired as one seamless episode, and is presented that way on streaming and home video—ends with Jack complaining that Liz made him care too much about things other than work, while she complains his mentorship made her care too much about work. They decide to end both their friendship and their mentorship.

Robert Carlock: We were maybe accidentally smart to do things like get Liz married, and kill Colleen, and the big things early so, even though we had a fight between Jack and Liz, we still could make room for stuff that felt like *30 Rock* stories, and not get weighed down in the goodbye.

The writers studied other series finales to see what worked and what didn't, ultimately looking to give viewers a mix of characters being able to say goodbye to one another, while also staying true to those characters and letting them continue being who they've always been.

Tracy tries to keep the last episode of *TGS* from happening, apparently so he can get his payout, while Lutz torments his colleagues with one last lunch order since it's his turn to choose. Lutz chooses Blimpies, which isn't that bad a sandwich place, and we're not quite sure why everyone hates it other than that it's coming from Lutz.

It was the culmination of numerous lunch-based storylines over the years, likely inspired by the limited lunch choices available to the *30 Rock* writers at the somewhat out of the way Silvercup Studios.

Vali Chandrasekaran: Our hours were very, very long on *30 Rock*, and over the course of the season, we would stop having real experiences of the outside world, so we really devolved into picking lunch being a very big part of our day.

With the final *TGS* episode on the way, Tracy goes missing. Liz finds him at Dark Sensations, the same strip club he dragged Liz to in the pilot.

Beth McCarthy-Miller: I'll never forget the first time I've ever overslept in my life. I had flown in. In the middle of the night, there was a power surge, and it turned off my phone, and turned off the alarm clock—and the alarms. I woke up almost at my call time. I was in New Jersey, and I needed to be in Queens. We were shooting the scene where Tina and Tracy say goodbye to each other in the strip club, and I was panicked. I left my house in three minutes. I brushed my teeth, wore what I was wearing to bed to set and literally just got in the car. And I got there in time for the first shot.

Tracy reveals that he wasn't trying to stop the last *TGS* for the money—he was stopping it because he didn't want to say goodbye to everyone. Saying goodbye is something he's been doing his whole life, ever since his dad went out for cigarettes and never came back. Liz tells him that they might drift apart, but that she still loves him—he agrees to return to the show.

Beth McCarthy-Miller: A little bit of Tracy Jordan is a little autobiographical of Tracy Morgan. And especially that scene where they say goodbye to each other was very poignant for both Tina and Tracy. They had spent a lot of time together. I mean, he was on the cast of *Saturday Night Live*, and then they went to *30 Rock*—that's a long time.

We went through a lot with Tracy. He had a lot of health issues. He split up from his wife. There wasn't a dry eye in the house for the first take that they said goodbye to each other. I thought the words were so well chosen by Tina, for Liz Lemon. A lot of those scenes where people said goodbye, the words were so carefully chosen and really beautiful. But it made it a very tough scene, because you couldn't go, "OK, let's do that again."

Jenna and Tracy get their own final farewell moment, embracing as Jenna tells Tracy that she'll miss him. Jenna also enjoys a final montage with shots of her looking in her dressing room mirror, before it's removed. It's the moment that actually makes her emotional about the show coming to an end, as the mirror is relocated to Brian Williams's bathroom.

Tina Fey: I found this actually weirdly so moving, and it's just funny, she really cried when they took her mirror out. This actually makes me cry every time I watch it—the montage and her reaction.

It all leads to Jack having some dark moments, with the tease that maybe he's even going to commit suicide. While thinking about Jack potentially killing himself, Pete starts to fantasize about what a joy faking your own death to escape your problems would be. It's a storyline Carlock had insisted on doing, despite the finale having a lot of other storylines going on—and it was one of those bits that preserved the *30 Rock* weirdness that could have been pushed aside in favor of big finale moments if he hadn't championed it.

The Big Moment of the finale is one last Jack and Liz moment. Liz finds a video suicide note Jack left behind following his earlier sadness. But in that romcom way, Liz runs to save the day—with Jack, at least—in their completely platonic, mentor–mentee relationship, tracking his phone to the waterfront.

Beth McCarthy-Miller: That was the hardest episode of *30 Rock* I ever directed, because there were a lot of locations. It was the middle of the winter. Trying to find locations to do things like the boat is really, really hard to find in New York that time of year.

When she shows up and finds him on a small yacht, with the tease that he's going to sail off and start a new life, what actually ends up happening is more of a real human interaction that reflects everything that this friendship/mentorship was all about.

The Newtown school shooting had just taken place the morning of filming that scene. This genuine farewell provided a welcome respite at that dark time. Much of

the writing staff came out to watch the filming, sharing dinner with Tina, Alec, and McCarthy-Miller. Even Lorne Michaels was there in the wee hours of that shoot.

Jack's actual plan: to sail off and find what will finally make him happy. He tries to tell Liz that he loves her, beginning by saying, "Lemon, there is a word, a once-special word that's been tragically co-opted by the romance industrial complex, and I would hate to use it here and have you think that I am suggesting any type of romantic sentiment, let alone an invitation to scale Bone Mountain." Yes, *30 Rock* still found room for a sex joke inside of a truly sweet moment. He goes on to describe the word's origins, still distanced from expressing any emotion—but Liz, seeing through him, interrupts with "I love you too, Jack."

Alec Baldwin: Freezing my ass off on a boat floating in a marina in Battery Park City, Jack groped his way toward telling Liz he loved her. That night was tough. The best job I ever had, that I will ever have, was over.

Vali Chandrasekaran: What helped that finale moment really land so well, when she tells him she loves him—it felt really true, and real, but also you know it was never about lust.

It marked the climax of perhaps the longest-lasting, deepest male–female friendship in TV history. From Jack's initial antagonism when he arrived in the pilot, mocking the way Liz dressed and approaching her from a cold business perspective, to seeing potential and ultimately offering advice on every aspect of her world, he's finally come around to seeing Liz as a valued member of his life. She's everything she was ever meant to be, and Jack knows deep down that she would have gotten there even without him—but he's thankful to have been part of her journey.

Jack starts to sail away. But he quickly turns around, struck by a brand-new idea: dishwashers you can see inside. The idea gets Liz hyped, because that would in fact be pretty cool.

Tina Fey's own last scene shot as Liz Lemon was less momentous—merely a shot of her on her infrequently used treadmill, one last time. But Tina stood on Liz's living room steps (yes, Liz is fancy, her living room has steps) to deliver a speech to the cast and crew:

"A lot of times in interviews people will say to me, 'How are you different from Liz Lemon? I can't believe I didn't think of this answer until tonight, but the way that I'm different from Liz Lemon is the *TGS* crew are a bunch of jerks who don't help her . . . They don't care. And in real life, nothing could be further from the truth."

30 Rock was a show that played with power dynamics at work and in society, and it seems appropriate that Fey would wrap up praising the breadth of the show's staff that made it all possible—while also holding space for Fey at the center, the one who gave birth to the ideas that started it all.

While Jenna was unsuccessful in finding another role on TV or in film, she decides to go back to Broadway and closes the last *TGS* with a song from the musical version of *The Rural Juror*.

> **Tina Fey:** We wanted Jane to sing at the end, and we were trying to think of, what is that kind of "One for My Baby" song, and somehow came upon this idea of going back to *The Rural Juror*, which was so much cheaper.

> **Beth McCarthy-Miller:** That was amazing, except for it was a very emotional night for Jane, so it was tough. It was literally the last thing we shot—we shot everyone on stage saying goodbye, and then Jane singing. Jane was a trooper. She could barely get through it, and she just rocked it.

> **Tina Fey:** I felt like this was a completion of our thesis that music can be moving and meaningless at the same time. Manipulatively moving. And the music turns back into the original Liz Lemon theme from the pilot.

> **Todd Buonopane:** Somehow, at the end, Jane sings the *Rural Juror* song, and it's preposterous, and you find yourself bawling your eyes out listening to the *Rural Juror* song. They had held off for so long, that when you give us some big emotional payoff, it *really* works.

The show features a Marvel Cinematic Universe–esque post-credits sequence, showing what everyone is up to one year later. Things were so busy that Robert Carlock directed part of the flash-forward sequence himself.

> **Robert Carlock:** I directed part of this because Beth had to do so much stuff to get these two episodes before the whole thing shut down. Beth was literally running around the city.

Pete *did* fake his own death, but eventually gets discovered by wife, Paula.

> **Scott Adsit:** Everybody ended up in the right place, I think. [Pete] had his lost weekend where he got lost, very purposely so, and found himself and found his true happiness. Given who he is and his lot in life, he has to go back. But he had that moment. He's like a mannequin in the Twilight Zone—he gets to go walk around the store for a day, and then he has to go back to being a mannequin. But he had that year off where he got to grow a mustache and be somebody else. And I don't know if he would be happy being happy. He is a miserable beast.

> **Vali Chandrasekaran:** That character is not even necessarily beaten down by life—he never had a good life, at all. At no point did he think anything would be better for him. His life sucks now, and he's so enraged by it, it always made me laugh.

Liz produces a new sitcom starring Grizz, *Grizz & Herz*. Tracy's dad actually comes back after decades out getting cigarettes, reuniting with his son. Jenna pulls a Kanye and tries stealing a Tony from another actress. Jack's dishwasher idea lets him finally become CEO of GE. And Kathy Geiss creates a hugging machine that kills old people, inspired by real-life Kathy Geiss model Temple Grandin's hugging machine (that is significantly safer).

> **Tina Fey:** For years we wanted to do a whole arc of Kathy Geiss inventing a machine that hugs old people, then she becomes kind of a Temple Grandin, and then Jenna was going to play her in a movie. Then she was going to have to go around the whole awards circuit with Kathy Geiss, the way Claire Danes had to spend the whole awards circuit with Temple Grandin. You know what, maybe let's just make it a movie. It's a movie.

> **Marceline Hugot:** Even 'til the very end, Tina had always wanted me to make a spoof on [Temple Grandin]. I had heard from early on that this was an image, an idea that she had wanted. Tina lived out all of her possible ideas that she wanted with that character throughout the years. To me, that's the best compliment you can give another actor—she kept bringing Kathy Geiss back every once in a while. I'm not trying to suggest that she's the only great writer, but she was master puppeteer, certainly for Kathy Geiss. She had a soft spot for Kathy Geiss, and I was the beneficiary of that.

We also get to see Kenneth, continuing to be ageless as he runs NBC into the distant future. He has a snow globe containing Rockefeller Center in a tribute to the finale of famed soap opera *St. Elsewhere*, with Liz's great-granddaughter pitching a show based on Liz's life.

> **Jon Haller:** We were talking about where the show would ultimately end up, even in Season 5. There was just pitching—they weren't really trying to figure out what the finale would be. But [there was a pitch] that in the finale, Kenneth would leap out, and we would realize that Kenneth was actually Dr. Sam Beckett from *Quantum Leap*, and after saving his last person, would leap home.
>
> And I, as a lifelong *Quantum Leap* fan, thought that was the funniest thing I'd ever heard. I remember bolding it in the notes. And then sitting at home, waiting when I saw the finale, hoping that Jack McBrayer would get to leap home. But they obviously chose a funnier and more interesting thing.

Jane Krakowski and Jack McBrayer joked on the Season 2 DVD commentary that Kenneth would end up running NBC in five years—when Alec's contract ran out. They were dead on with the time frame, but Tina was the one to pull the plug.

Among the nods to the beginnings of the show, Tina wore several of her Season 1 outfits in this episode. It featured a cameo from the namesake of Jack Donaghy, Tina's high-school friend Michael Donaghy. There was also a cameo in the episode from someone who'd created a Facebook campaign to get a line on the show. But while the person got to come to set and film that line, the campaign an apparent success, the line got cut in editing—just like so many other *30 Rock* lines over the years—and didn't make it into the actual episode.

30 Rock was one of only two shows still shooting on film by its final season, with the other being *Two and a Half Men*.

The finale also included the characters guessing what the end of *Mad Men* would be.

Tina Fey: This was our legitimate attempt to ruin the ending of *Mad Men*.

Vali Chandrasekaran: The end of Season 7—the finale was so, so good. I was bummed I didn't work on that. I was bummed in the professional sense because it was so good, but getting to live with your wife is really nice. So that was also good.

Kevin Ladson: I stayed with the show to the very end. The last shot, the last scene, I sat by a little backdrop, and everybody was huddled together, watching the scene. I just had to reminisce from day one when we started, that it was coming to an end.

And that was really emotional for me, because it was almost like watching a child grow up and them leaving to either move out the house or go to college. And I said, "Well, that show was a really good run."

As the show wrapped up, NBC asked for all of the props back.

Tina Fey: We got a fifteen-page list of everything NBC wanted back, and things were on it, like literally on the list was the saltwater taffy that Nancy Donovan gave Jack Donaghy in Season 4. Things that were long gone.

NBC later auctioned off many of those props, so someone has Tracy Jordan's lizard in their home to this day.

Many of the cast and crew would continue to work on other projects over the years. But this marked an end to the most fondly remembered one. It's a series that led television's march toward shows that were more specific and finely crafted. TV comedy writing has rarely hit the heights of *30 Rock* in the years since.

30 *Rock*'s Legacy: From *Unbreakable Kimmy Schmidt* to *Mr. Mayor*

With *30 Rock* over, what now? NBC initially seemed eager to remain in the Tina Fey and Robert Carlock business, asking Fey and Carlock to develop a show for actress Ellie Kemper. NBC ordered *Unbreakable Kimmy Schmidt*—originally titled *Tooken*—straight to series in October 2013, not long after *30 Rock* ended. It seemed like a show built for the network, tying these two dynamite creators with rising *The Office* star Kemper as its lead, along with *30 Rock*'s Jane Krakowski returning as a new character.

But as network ratings declined, NBC took a second look at this quirky comedy from creators who'd created a show that was a critical hit but not, you know, a *hit* hit. They were already shooting their twelfth episode when the creators were told by NBC Entertainment president Jennifer Salke, "We're not feeling confident about watching comedies," according to Fey, with the network cutting back at the time on airing sitcoms.

After looking at running it as a summer series, or possibly midseason, NBC opted to sell the show—about a girl who gets kidnapped and spends years being held underground by a crazed reverend, before emerging and applying her childlike wonder to life in New York City—to Netflix in November 2014, which gave the show a two-season commitment. Fey described it as being "like when your spouse says you can sleep with other people."

Jesse Thorn: *30 Rock* is basically "What if Mary Tyler Moore was at *SNL*?" And that's a great idea for a sitcom that stars Tina Fey. In a lot of ways, *Kimmy Schmidt* is the same themes, in that it is still about a young woman trying to figure out how to be an adult in the big city. But it is built around two things:

one is Ellie Kemper, who is a really special performer, in a way that maybe Tina Fey isn't. Without casting any aspersions on Tina Fey, who's a wonderful genius. But Tina Fey is a perfectly good performer, and a brilliant genius comedy writer.

It's a show with almost no straight white dudes, which in comedy is a big deal still. It is also fundamentally a show about feminism in the context of trauma, and what that means. *30 Rock* is about feminism in the *Mary Tyler Moore Show* sense. Tina Fey was also a victim of trauma as a young woman, and wanted to make a show about that with elements of what's special about Ellie Kemper, which is that she can make anything seem magical.

Jeff Richmond: [Tina] is somebody who has gone through something. And I think it really informs the way she thinks about her life. When you have that kind of thing happen to you, that makes you scared of certain things, that makes you frightened of different things, your comedy comes out in a different kind of way, and it also makes you feel for people.

When Fey was just five years old, a stranger attacked her and cut her face, right in her front yard. Fey said that she dealt with the trauma well, not having to fully confront it until she started appearing on camera and had people take greater notice of her scar. *Kimmy Schmidt* was an opportunity for her to more fully deal with that trauma, but she may have made missteps when addressing issues that weren't as close to home for her—like having Tituss dress up as a Japanese geisha to make a point about political correctness.

Longtime *30 Rock* director Don Scardino was among those who would come back to direct episodes of *Kimmy Schmidt*, but his schedule only allowed him to do a few. Along with other connections with *30 Rock*, *Kimmy Schmidt* cast *30 Rock* actors like Mike Carlsen and Todd Buonopane in new parts. Buonopane had a beard at the time, and Robert Carlock told him they didn't even realize it was him when he was cast. And many of the crew members were holdovers from *30 Rock*.

The *Kimmy Schmidt* writers' room included several of the *30 Rock* writers, with episodes written by alumni Jack Burditt, Lauren Gurganous, Dylan Morgan, and Josh Siegal. The show also continued to develop talent, with writers from the show going on to work with Fey and Carlock on other projects.

Bellamy Forrest: I know that [Tina] really likes the same people around her. That's very important to her, and you can see that from what happened with *Kimmy Schmidt*. I mean, people are very, very loyal.

The same held true on other projects Fey and Carlock have gone on to do since. She'd made clear to crew during the final season of *30 Rock* that she wanted to keep a lot of them on board.

Fey and Carlock were also executive producers on *Great News*, a show written and created by *30 Rock* writer Tracey Wigfield about a TV newsroom and including multiple *30 Rock* alum as both writers and directors. In a way, it's not far off from Fey's original pre–*30 Rock* pitch, focusing on a producer at a TV news show, though Wigfield has her own fresh dynamic with the centerpiece being the main character's mother becoming an intern at her daughter's office. Fey and Carlock each co-wrote a handful of episodes, with Fey herself appearing as a character in the second season after the first season's so-so ratings.

She portrayed Diana St. Tropez, a network exec who plays like a gender-swapped Jack Donaghy, with a more feminine energy. The show took a beat to find its voice, but so did *30 Rock*. *Great News* developed a kinder, gentler approach to the workplace comedy, remaining just slightly more grounded than *30 Rock* as it centered itself around a mother–daughter relationship, but still hitting you with rapid-fire jokes. NBC would opt to end its run after two seasons from spring 2017 through spring 2018.

While there's still more to come from Fey and Carlock, not everything they touch turns to gold, or even makes it to air. *Studio 60*'s Bradley Whitford was cast in a pilot that Fey and Carlock were producers on: *The Sackett Sisters*, written by *30 Rock* writer Luke Del Tredici. The show was set to be about two estranged sisters played by Busy Philipps and Casey Wilson, with Whitford as their dad.

Bradley Whitford: Tina Fey is a joyous hero. An unpretentious, productive, show-business, delightful hero of mine. Nothing made me happier than the prospect of working on a show with Tina's company and Robert. *The Sackett Sisters*, I was like, I know I want to live with these people who know how to make a show like *30 Rock*, forever.

But the show wasn't picked up. Other projects Fey and Carlock produced, often written by alums of the *30 Rock* writers' room, included *Cabot College* for Fox, *Family Fortune* for ABC, and *The Kicker* for CBS.

Tina Fey was spending time in these years as a big-screen star, starring in movies from comedy *Sisters* to a more dramatic role in *Whiskey Tango Foxtrot*. She also brought *Mean Girls* to Broadway as a musical, which she's been busy turning back into a musical movie.

In 2020, the COVID-19 pandemic managed to bring the *30 Rock* cast back together one more time. It was a reunion special . . . kind of. Because when you get everybody back together, it's never quite the same. The special was created to serve as a replacement for NBC's annual pitch to advertisers, the upfronts. The *30 Rock* reunion special didn't get much love from the critics, panned for its efforts to promote NBC's lineup—particularly the programs airing on online service Peacock. It felt like the show had finally taken its love of product placement too far, with promos running throughout for NBCUniversal shows, their Olympics coverage, and more. Many NBC affiliate groups refused to run the special due to how it promoted watching Peacock rather than, well, those local stations.

The special's storyline, as far as it goes, features the *TGS* cast trying to reunite for a reboot of the show on streaming platform Peacock, at NBC head Kenneth's request. But Kenneth shoots down the pitch for a new *TGS*—it was all just a sham to get everyone back together for a private Zoom video reunion, as Kenneth missed them. The cast and writers try to get their revenge, ruining Kenneth's pitch to advertisers. But they finally come together to actually help Kenneth with the presentation. It closes with Jack taking on management of new streaming service "Peahen"—and Liz writing a new pilot.

> **Alan Sepinwall:** It reminded me, honestly, of when *Arrested Development* came back, and a number of other shows have done reunions. Revivals almost always give me hives, because the shows are an artifact of a specific time in the lives of the people who make it, of the characters, and of the audience. When you start changing any or all of them, it never quite works.

Sepinwall didn't appreciate the cast being used here for such blatant corporate promotion. The way they'd once lovingly mocked product placement while also doing it with Snapple now crossed to another level, with the lengths to which it promoted the corporation making it impossible to see much comedy in the midst of it.

Before the reunion special was announced and filmed during the coronavirus pandemic, Grizz said that he was hoping they would find a way to bring everyone back together.

> **Grizz Chapman:** I know now it's been a few years, so maybe we can get back together at the fifteenth-year mark or something and do something really special together. Maybe a *Saturday Night Live* episode, or something of that nature. But it would be nice to hang out with everybody again.

Grizz didn't get the chance to actually hang out with everyone in the reunion, thanks to the pandemic keeping us all socially distanced, with actors filming from their homes. But here's hoping for that *SNL* episode bringing everyone back together someday.

And while there seems to have been a general disappointment from both critics and fans with the reunion, *30 Rock* was an important part of 2020 in another way: the continued power of a *30 Rock* meme in a terrible year.

> **Alan Sepinwall:** You've seen a million "Lemon, it's Wednesday" memes on the internet in the hellscape year of 2020. There's a lot of good stories, but [what you remember] a lot of the time is really just a joke.

The show created its own language which also lives on, from "blerg" and "what the what" to "nerds" as an exclamation and "ya burnt" as an insult.

There are several shows that recently debuted or are on the way, written and/or executive produced by Fey and Carlock, including one they're showrunning together: NBC's *Mr. Mayor*, which was promoted at the end of the reunion special. It was originally conceived of as a *30 Rock* spinoff with Jack running for mayor of New York City, looked at as potentially one of the reboots of a classic NBC property that went to their new streaming service Peacock. Alec Baldwin was in negotiations for almost a year, but opted not to do the show. With *The Good Place* ending, they reconceived the show for sitcom legend Ted Danson, with the *30 Rock* connections removed—and its location changed to Los Angeles, as Danson wasn't interested in moving to do the show in New York City.

Fey and Carlock are continuing the trend of bringing back people they've worked with before, including using John Riggi as their eyes and ears as the show films in Los Angeles—they spent most of the first season back on the East Coast, watching via video feed, thanks to the difficulties of the COVID-19 pandemic. It's the flip of the standard writers' room, based in Los Angeles, with production often taking place in Vancouver, or Atlanta, or New York.

John Riggi: My job is just to be on the floor and make sure that things get shot the way they're supposed to be shot and stuff like that. They wrote it all in New York.

In early episodes, many of the Los Angeles jokes felt nonspecific, like they were being written by . . . New Yorkers. Of course, that's also the point—while the jokes weren't always on target, much of the show is the New York perspective making fun of the ridiculousness of LA. The writers' room also includes a number of Angelenos, so it's not all one-sided.

There are diverse actors in supporting roles, though their top two big-name stars are white (Danson and Holly Hunter) and showed little Latino representation in early episodes while telling stories of a half-Latino city. But more diverse guest stars started to show up as it continued. Like almost any classic show, early episodes don't come fully formed, needing time to grow into their greatness. By episode 3, "Brentwood Trash," the show's jokes start to land hard as it mocks LA celebrity culture, with David Spade, Andie MacDowell, and Chrissy Teigen all playing exaggerated versions of themselves at local town hall meetings. It's another example of their ability to get great guest stars and write to their strengths. Fey and Carlock have also worked to diversify their writing staffs.

Daisy Gardner: Rob and Tina have heard the critiques and made an effort. Tina's very much conscious of trying to do the right thing when it comes to boosting women and POC writers.

And Fey and Carlock are as rapid-fire behind the scenes as ever.

> **Vella Lovell (actress, *Mr. Mayor*):** Especially with the pilot, there were multiple drafts, and it felt like every single draft that would come out had thirty new jokes in it. I don't know what their brains are like, but it's just a never-ending fountain of jokes.

Tina also worked on *Girls5Eva* with *Kimmy Schmidt* writer Meredith Scardino (no relation to Don that they know of, though they checked out maps of Italy found that their grandfathers' towns were only miles apart), with Robert Carlock on as an executive producer. The show features a Spice Girls–esque 1990s group reuniting to stage a middle-aged comeback. It ended up being one of the post-*30 Rock* shows that most recaptures that *30 Rock* energy, just in a new setting. Sara Bareilles's Dawn plays like a more grounded Liz Lemon, now into middle age. And while Fey wasn't a showrunner here, she had a big hand in the show—from a cameo in a hallucinatory vision as Dolly Parton to being credited as a songwriter on the show's "Dream Girlfriends."

30 Rock was one of those shows that had just as much of an influence over the next generation of writers as it did on the shows themselves. It created this feedback loop, with the show's own writers not only going on to other major projects, but inspiring those who watched it with its unique brand of humor.

30 Rock and *Unbreakable Kimmy Schmidt* also defined a comedic style known for rapid-fire jokes and quick cutaways.

> **Robert Carlock:** I don't know why we like it. An eagerness to please, I guess—and overdo what the audience might actually be wanting, because there is a density that can be exhausting, for us and probably the viewer.

> **Alan Sepinwall:** The density of the jokes, when they're working, is great. The problem is when they're not working, they can be a little bit exhausting, which is how I started to feel about *Kimmy Schmidt* toward the end.

> **Robert Carlock:** But it's like, we pitch a lot of jokes, naturally, and it's hard to let them go. It's hard to not try to put them all in—we want to give everyone a little something, until they get sick of it.

> **Tina Fey:** It's a sardine can full of jokes. It's just densely packed with salty, oily jokes that many people around the world find off-putting, but a few smart people find delicious.

> **Scott Adsit:** What was new about the show was its taste, and the fact that you would be laughing and miss two jokes while you were laughing. We were ahead of the curve in that way.

Tracy Morgan: I like *30 Rock*, because *30 Rock* is like an HBO show, but on network television. We really, really push the envelope.

Vali Chandrasekaran: There was a really high premium on doing something new. And I have been very fortunate in that I have gotten to work in good places where that is the case. But it really was so part of the DNA, and what we did there, that it makes you think that if you have something, an idea that may work, but you've seen it before—it makes you sit on it for a while until you can find what the *30 Rock* version of that idea is. It's a really good way to train yourself to write.

Don Scardino: My son, who's twenty-two now, was seven [during the show]—he came to set, he knew Alec, and he knew Tina. But it wasn't until he went to college and would watch *30 Rock* with his friends that he realized what it was and what an impact it had.

Matthew Broderick: I love that show. My son loves that show—even when he was eight, nine years old. They'll take more from it in college, and then you get a whole other level. It's like Monty Python: You love it when you're little, then you get older and you realize what they're talking about and it's funny *again*.

John Riggi: [*30 Rock* is] like a little glass ornament in my life that I really am protective of, because to this day, I still think—I know—it's one of the highlights of my career. When I went to my next job after *Larry Sanders*, I was like "Oh shit, all shows aren't like *Larry Sanders*." But then when I got to *30 Rock*, I thought, I landed in *Larry Sanders*-ville again, which I was so lucky to do. And those people and that time is like magic to me.

Teresa Mastropierro: I feel like I'm actually helping spread some positive energy into the world. There's a positive thrust behind everything that Tina puts her name on, and Robert, too.

John Riggi: There was a period about ten years ago, I called my sister's kids—they're both nurses. I was having a bad day in show business, and I said, "Do you think if I went back and actually went to med school, by the time I got out, would I be too old to be a doctor?" Because I was [having] this moment of like, this is bullshit. What am I doing? I'm writing jokes and I'm writing scripts, people are acting like clowns, and so what?

But I have come to believe that if you do this job correctly, and with some integrity, you can actually help people—not in any sort of earth-shattering way, but maybe you make their day a little easier to take, especially now in the times we're living in. Maybe you make them not feel so bad, and maybe they're just able to go on. And that's something.

Don Scardino: We tried to make a comedy movie every week, and we really wanted it to have texture, and depth, and resonate culturally and politically. I wanted them to have style, and visual bang, and great performances.

John Riggi: The people that made that show—they put their heart and soul into it. And we didn't do everything perfectly, and we know that, but we tried really, really hard, and everything was done with the intention of making people laugh and enjoying themselves.

Scott Adsit: I learned that TV is hard for the people who make it. For the producers, and writers, and the directors. It's easier on the actors. But the people who are doing the grunt work, the crew, and the creatives are working so hard and spending all their hours there—they're there all day and all night. It was eye-opening and inspiring.

The legacy of *30 Rock* has left a lot for Tina Fey to live up to. It's hard to go from a long-running, critically beloved show, then have to continue doing it all over again for an entire career. *Kimmy Schmidt* was successful, but shorter lived, and received a closer critique of its messages as society continued to evolve. Her most successful project since *30 Rock* could arguably be turning *Mean Girls* into a musical, yet it was part of our reboot culture in that it was an adaptation of a previous property, and it also hit the stage in 2017—a time when the theatrical world was still obsessed with Lin-Manuel Miranda and *Hamilton*, including that show's complete originality.

Don Scardino: It's hard when you have a great success like *30 Rock*, which she'd been in training for her whole career really, working with Lorne on *SNL* and all the rest of it. We all emerge from the shadow of *30 Rock* at different times in our careers, and it becomes part of our history, part of our arc. But for Tina, it's harder to step out of the shadow of *30 Rock*, because it was all her. But that's happening. She's doing incredible things, and I think probably her best work is ahead of her.

Paul Reubens: It's an important show for a whole bunch of reasons. Not only in the development of Tina Fey, but I think the most classic, best things in many categories, within television and in life, are the things that are innovative, and new, and we haven't seen before. That show contains so many elements that were novel, new, extreme, stupid, silly, exciting. When that show was really humming, it was a joy—just pure brilliance.

Beth McCarthy-Miller: I grew up, when I was really young, loving *The Mary Tyler Moore Show* and *Cheers* and *M*A*S*H* and all these shows that are so iconic, and they've really shaped what television is today. And I think *30 Rock*'s one of those shows.

Chris George: There's something about the characters, the dynamics of the relationships, the lines, the humor that's timeless in a way. People are going to be watching it for decades.

Of course, there are also elements of the show that were of their time, especially when it comes to pop culture references—and problematic elements that probably shouldn't have been part of the show even then.

Ira Madison III: There's a reason why *30 Rock* isn't rewatchable in a way that *The Office,* and *Parks and Rec,* or *How I Met Your Mother* is for Gen Z. They're watching those shows all the time. I don't think people are really watching *30 Rock*, just because if you weren't around when a certain *30 Rock* episode aired, you probably don't understand seventy percent of it.

Jesse Thorn: There are people who love *The Office* or *Friends* more than anything else, because they love the relationships. While the relationships are well managed in *30 Rock*, the reason that you watch *30 Rock* is to see a thousand perfect jokes. And for people who don't value that, they probably have their priorities in the right place, but I don't necessarily want to hang out with them.

Emily VanDerWerff: It's a little frozen in its era. Beyond certain types of jokes that we probably wouldn't have white people, or straight people, or just people telling today, it has references and cultural points that I think will probably cause it to be more of a curiosity as time goes on. But [*30 Rock* is] pound for pound one of the funniest shows that TV's ever made, and that's always going to have value.

30 Rock was never as popular a show as *Friends* or *The Office*. People will be like "Why isn't *30 Rock* getting this boost? Why isn't *Community* getting this boost?" The shows were ultra-specific and aimed at an audience that had a hyper knowledge of cultural reference points.

Jesse Thorn: The really special thing about *30 Rock*, besides the volume of the great jokes, is that in contrast to, say, *The Simpsons*, which is probably the other most-great-jokes show ever, it's not about writing a joke on a sign in the background. It's not about making meta-jokes about the structure of the show, like it is on, say, *Arrested Development*, that ultimately end up taking away from the characters and their arc. Every one of those twelve thousand jokes is funny because of whose mouth it's coming out of, how it's coming out of their mouth, and how perfectly it's written.

Could there ever be a full-blown, ongoing reunion of the show? Fey has seemed to be happy spending her time behind the scenes, writing and producing.

Vali Chandrasekaran: I think we know, if we went back in some other form, it wouldn't quite be the same. But it was amazing.

Scott Adsit: It would be different, because everything is different now. The nature of TV is so different now, and the different media we have now would change the way we look at a TV show.

John Riggi: I miss them all so much. Whenever I talk to Tina, we talk about, it was so special. And a couple years ago, there was talk about rebooting it, and I was like, I don't . . . I don't think I want to do that. I would love for it to come back again. But I also have been in TV long enough to know that things happen at a particular time in a particular way, and if you go back and try to re-create them, they're not that anymore.

You can't just drop yourself back into something that happened ten years ago or twelve years ago, and think that it's going to be the same. It won't—by definition, it won't be the same thing. And maybe it'll be better. But it won't be *30 Rock* again.

But never say never—there are certainly those who would welcome a return.

Grizz Chapman: Keep watching. Fight for it to get back on some sort of prime-time TV.

It's the dilemma of the fan, and the people who are part of creating television: We always know that it won't be the same. But we want it. We want to feel the way a show made us felt again. *30 Rock* was a show that, while giving a sometimes jaded view of the world, was also incredibly hopeful. It's a show whose heroes end up getting everything they ever wanted—they literally do a Charlie and the Chocolate Factory metaphor for the second-to-last episode, with the good-hearted Kenneth rewarded. And its last shot shows Kenneth continuing on into the future, with *30 Rock* as the show that never dies being presented by Liz's great-granddaughter, the Lemon legacy also continuing on for generations.

That's the continued power of Tina Fey's voice. She's been an outspoken trail-blazer and advocate for women from the moment she broke out as *Weekend Update* anchor. Her biggest shows featured diverse casts, and her writers' rooms have started to reflect a reality outside of white Harvard grads and white improv performers.

She, along with collaborators including Robert Carlock and others, have fallen down along the way. They've written jokes and characters that were misguided, and they didn't always take responsibility for the people they hurt. They've had such a deep faith in their own comedy that they haven't always been able to see it from the perspective of people who don't look like them, who don't come from their backgrounds. That's not something that can be excused or ignored.

But that doesn't mean their work doesn't have value. Like John Riggi said, it gives people hope. That's what has kept this book's author on board with Fey/Carlock shows, even when disappointed with certain choices, blind spots, and who's being left out. Because despite all that, Fey writes shows from the perspective of that young Second City improviser who felt left out. She's been a voice for those who felt like they don't fit in, always prizing intelligence and a sense of humor over being cool. She still brings that underdog mindset, even now that she's become one of the most powerful people in Hollywood.

Here's hoping that she keeps telling smart stories about today's underdogs, lifting up a new generation that can help to keep her away from the pitfalls she's sometimes pratfalled into. When her shows are doing that, I can guarantee that we'll all want to go to there.

ACKNOWLEDGMENTS

Thank you to everyone who agreed to speak with me for the book, especially director/producer Don Scardino, who offered encouragement and guidance as I sought to create something memorable and special. Thanks to everyone else who generously shared their stories, time, documents, and more, including Doug Abel, Scott Adsit, Peter Agliata, Alan Alda, Adam Bernstein, Matthew Broderick, Todd Buonopane, Vanja Černjul, Vali Chandrasekaran, Grizz Chapman, Margaret Cho, Nate Corddry, Ken Eluto, Josh Fadem, Paul Feig, Bellamy Forrest, Daisy Gardner, Chris George, Dennie Gordon, Andrew Guest, Jon Haller, Tom Houghton, Marceline Hugot, Cheyenne Jackson, Norah Jones, Kevin Ladson, Nathan Lane, Paula Leggett Chase, Patti LuPone, Ira Madison III, Teresa Mastropierro, Beth McCarthy-Miller, Linda Mendoza, Paul Reubens, Simon Rich, John Riggi, Lonny Ross, Susan Schectar, Alan Sepinwall, Jesse Thorn, Michael Trim, Emily VanDerWerff, Jovan Vitagliano, Bradley Whitford, and Tracy Morgan's former assistant. I am grateful for the long conversations we got to have about how this show was created, and why it still means so much to us. Thanks also to the publicity people, agents, managers, and everyone else who helped to connect us. I hope this book makes us all smile, think, and feel inspired to make something new.

I owe gratitude to everyone who's spoken to me for other stories in the past that were of use in this book, everyone who spoke with me on background for the book, as well as those who considered speaking with me but were ultimately unavailable.

Thank you to my wife, Kristiana—a *30 Rock* fan originally hailing from the heartland—who was there with me all along the way. She provided moral and practical support, as well as the sounding board of a spouse who loves writing and language. Thanks to my fellow authors who provided me with encouragement and guidance on this project, including Andy Greene, John Moe, and Shea Serrano. And thank you to agent Chris Schmidt, who also offered advice along the way.

This book draws from my passion and my experience up to now. Thank you to my writing groups for keeping me motivated as I worked to turn dreams into reality and to my comedy teachers who made me love the way a joke is crafted. Thank you to my colleagues who first encouraged me to write an oral history of "Werewolf Bar Mitzvah" without knowing what it would one day become, as well as those who supported and guided me as I wrote this book.

I would like to thank everyone at Abrams, especially my fantastic editors, Jamison Stolz and Sarah Robbins, as well as the designers, copy editor Margaret Moore, proofreader Christopher Cerasi, and managing editor Annalea Manalili, who all helped to make this book both joyful and meaningful. Jamison, thank you for reaching out to me and seeing all that this book could be. Sarah, thank you for getting in the trenches with me and guiding me through the process of writing this book. It's been a delight to spend the last two years revisiting one of my favorite shows of all time and sharing that deep pleasure with people who finally get all of my references.

Thank you to Aaron Sorkin for creating *Studio 60*. As someone who truly does believe that there is power in the arts, and in comedy, I was always on board and would have watched another six seasons. Despite any critiques, I'll be patiently awaiting the reboot/revival—or whatever your next show is that's filled with dialogue and drama that leaves me inspired and thinking there's hope for making things better after all.

And thank you to Tina Fey and Robert Carlock for creating the series that makes any of this celebration and discussion possible. You wrote something that made the lives of the people who watched it better and lit up our brains with the power of a million perfect jokes. Thanks also to the cast, crew, guest stars, and everyone else who gave us the fully realized world of *30 Rock*. That world lives on whenever we screw up and think "aw, blerg" or have such a grand success that we feel like high-fiving a million angels.

SOURCES

Creating the *30 Rock* Pilot

Author interviews with Doug Abel, Scott Adsit, Peter Agliata, Adam Bernstein, Matthew Broderick, Grizz Chapman, Nate Corddry, Paul Feig, Daisy Gardner, Chris George, Andrew Guest, Jon Haller, Tom Houghton, Kevin Ladson, Nathan Lane, Linda Mendoza, John Riggi, Don Scardino, Alan Sepinwall, Jesse Thorn, Michael Trim, Emily VanDerWerff, Bradley Whitford, and Tracy Morgan's former assistant.

30 Rock writers' room. "Series and Character Notes," July 5, 2006.

Quotes from Aaron Sorkin: DVD commentary. *30 Rock*. Season 5, episode 20, "100." Universal Pictures Home Entertainment, 2011.

Adalian, Josef. "Peacock on 'Studio' Beat." *Variety*, October 15, 2005.

Adalian, Josef. "Scribe Inks NBC U Pact." *Variety*, June 28, 2006.

Adalian, Josef, and Schneider, Michael. "Peacock Promises to Rock the Boat." *Variety*, July 24, 2006.

Adalian, Josef, and Schneider, Michael. "Nets Drive Pickups." *Variety*, May 15, 2006.

Quotes from Alec Baldwin: DVD commentary. *30 Rock*. Season 4, episode 4, "Audition Day." Universal Pictures Home Entertainment, 2010.

Quotes from Tina Fey: Armstrong, Jennifer. "Tina Fey and Jon Hamm Talk About Coupling Up on '30 Rock.'" *Entertainment Weekly*, January 21, 2009.

Quotes from Rachel Dratch: Dratch, Rachel. *Girl Walks into a Bar . . . : Comedy Calamities, Dating Disasters, and a Midlife Miracle*. New York: Penguin Publishing Group, 2012.

Quotes from Tina Fey: Fey, Tina. *Bossypants*. New York: Little, Brown and Company, 2011.

Quotes from Alec Baldwin, Lorne Michaels, Kevin Reilly: Friend, Tad. "Shows About Shows." *New Yorker*, April 17, 2006.

Quotes from Robert Carlock: Heisler, Steve. "Robert Carlock Walks Us Through High-lights from *30 Rock*'s Six Seasons So Far (Part 1 of 4)." *A.V. Club,* May 21, 2012.

Quotes from Jack McBrayer: DVD commentary. *30 Rock.* Season 1, episode 18, "Fire-works." Universal Pictures Home Entertainment, 2007.

Quotes from Judah Friedlander: DVD commentary. *30 Rock.* Season 6, episode 10, "Alexis Goodlooking and the Case of the Missing Whisky." Universal Pictures Home Entertainment, 2012.

Quotes from Judah Friedlander: DVD commentary. *30 Rock.* Season 2, episode 7, "Cougars." Universal Pictures Home Entertainment, 2008.

Quotes from Judah Friedlander: DVD commentary. *30 Rock.* Season 5, episode 15, "It's Never Too Late for Now." Universal Pictures Home Entertainment, 2011.

Lowry, Brian. "30 Rock." *Variety,* October 8, 2006.

Quotes from Tina Fey: Moore, Frazier. "On '30 Rock,' Tina Fey Draws from Her Past at 'SNL.'" Associated Press, October 10, 2006.

NBC Entertainment. (@nbc). "14 years ago, @nbc30rock was still 'Untitled Tina Fey Pilot.'" Twitter, March 29, 2020. https://twitter.com/nbc/status/12443513444392 55040/photo/2.

Quotes from Lorne Michaels: *The Academy of Television Arts and Sciences Presents: An Evening with* 30 Rock. Via *30 Rock* Blu-Ray collection, Season 2, Disc 3. The Academy of Television Arts and Sciences.

Quotes from Lorne Michaels: Schneider, Michael. "Inside Move: Dratch Latched to Multiple 'Rock' Roles." *Variety,* August 15, 2006.

Schneider, Michael. "Sorkin Skein Finds a Friend." *Variety,* January 27, 2006.

Quotes from Tina Fey: DVD commentary. *30 Rock.* Season 5, episode 18, "Plan B." Universal Pictures Home Entertainment, 2007.

Quotes from Tina Fey: DVD commentary. *30 Rock.* Season 4, episode 12, "Verna." Universal Pictures Home Entertainment, 2010.

Quotes from Tina Fey: Topel, Fred. "*30 Rock* Strikes a Chord." *Wave,* January 16–29, 2008.

Quotes from Tracy Morgan: DVD commentary. *30 Rock.* Season 1, episode 12, "Tracy Does Conan." Universal Pictures Home Entertainment, 2007.

Quotes from Jeff Zucker: Jeff Zucker Archive interview. By Dan Pasternack and Rachel Herman. *The Interviews: An Oral History of Television.* Television Academy Foundation, June 22, 2009, and August 11, 2009.

Season 1 (2006–07): *30 Rock* vs. *Studio 60*

Author interviews with Doug Abel, Scott Adsit, Peter Agliata, Adam Bernstein, Mat-thew Broderick, Grizz Chapman, Nate Corddry, Ken Eluto, Paul Feig, Daisy Gardner,

Chris George, Dennie Gordon, Andrew Guest, Jon Haller, Tom Houghton, Kevin Ladson, Nathan Lane, Ira Madison III, Teresa Mastropierro, Beth McCarthy-Miller, Paul Reubens, John Riggi, Lonny Ross, Don Scardino, Alan Sepinwall, Jesse Thorn, Emily VanDerWerff, Bradley Whitford, and Tracy Morgan's former assistant.

Archival author interview with Keith Powell (2020). "How to Make a Sitcom Safely During Coronavirus: Have the Cast Be the Crew." LAist/KPCC.

Quotes from Aaron Sorkin: DVD commentary. *30 Rock*. Season 5, episode 20, "100." Universal Pictures Home Entertainment, 2011.

Adalian, Josef. "NBC Orders Full Season of '30 Rock.'" *Variety*, December 1, 2006.

Adalian, Josef. "NBC Renews '30 Rock.'" *Variety*, April 4, 2007.

Quotes from Alec Baldwin: Baldwin, Alec. "Alec Baldwin on Fatherhood, '30 Rock,' Politics and More." *Washington Post*, December 15, 2008.

Quotes from Alec Baldwin: DVD commentary. *30 Rock*. Season 1, episode 21, "Hiatus." Universal Pictures Home Entertainment, 2007.

Associated Press. "Alec Baldwin's Request to Quit '30 Rock' Denied." April 25, 2007.

Andreeva, Nellie. "NBC Picks Up '30 Rock' for Full Season." Associated Press, December 2, 2006.

Associated Press. "NBC's 'Studio 60' Gets Full Season." November 10, 2006.

Quotes from Steven Weber: Ray-Harris, Ashley. "Steven Weber on Wings, Party Down, and Why 'Studio 60 on the Sunset Strip' Bombed." *A.V. Club,* December 6, 2016.

Quotes from Alec Baldwin: Baldwin, Alec. *Nevertheless: A Memoir*. New York: HarperCollins, 2017.

Quotes from Robert Carlock: Berkshire, Geoff. "Q&A: Robert Carlock and Mike Schur on 'SNL,' Emmys and Making Broad Comedy." *Variety*, August 19, 2015.

Brown, Scott. "'30 Rock' vs. 'Studio 60': The Sketch-Off." *Entertainment Weekly*, updated August 3, 2020.

Quotes from Jane Krakowski: Crook, John. "'30 Rock' Returns for Its Fourth Season." *Zap2it/Newsday*, October 8, 2009.

Quotes from Don Scardino, Aaron Sorkin: DVD commentary. *30 Rock*. Season 5, episode 20, "100." Universal Pictures Home Entertainment, 2011.

Quotes from Donald Glover, Gillian Jacobs: DVD commentary. *30 Rock*. Season 4, episode 3, "Stone Mountain." Universal Pictures Home Entertainment, 2010.

Quotes from Emily Mortimer: "Emily Mortimer on Her *Scream 3* Death, *Notting Hill*, & More." Interview by Lola Ogunnaike. "Couch Surfing," PeopleTV, *People/Entertainment Weekly*, August 17, 2018.

Quotes from Tina Fey: *The Howard Stern Show*. SiriusXM, December 14, 2015.

Friedman, Roger. "'Studio 60' Cancellation Imminent." FoxNews.com, November 3, 2006.

Quotes from Lorne Michaels: Friend, Tad. "Shows About Shows." *New Yorker*, April 17, 2006.

Goetzl, David. "FoxNews.com Columnist Gets It Wrong, NBC Says 'Studio 60' Stays Onboard." MediaPost Publications, October 31, 2006.

Heisler, Steve. "Jack McBrayer | Interview." *Time Out Chicago,* November 20, 2007.

Quotes from Emily Mortimer: Gensler, Howard. "Emily Mortimer Enjoys Her Work in 'Lars and the Real Girl.'" *Philadelphia Inquirer*, October 19, 2007.

Quotes from John Lutz: DVD commentary. *30 Rock.* Season 3, episode 13, "Goodbye, My Friend." Universal Pictures Home Entertainment, 2009.

Quotes from Judah Friedlander: DVD commentary. *30 Rock.* Season 2, episode 7, "Cougars." Universal Pictures Home Entertainment, 2008.

Quotes from Judah Friedlander: DVD commentary. *30 Rock.* Season 5, episode 15, "It's Never Too Late for Now." Universal Pictures Home Entertainment, 2011.

Kaplan, Don. "Stumbling 'Studio' Skips a Beat." *New York Post*, October 29, 2006.

Kissell, Rick. "NBC's 'Rock' Solid in Premiere." *Variety*, October 12, 2006.

Kissell, Rick. "Peacock's Not Laffing." *Variety*, October 20, 2006.

Kois, Dan. "Studio 60's Sermonizing Sketch Comedy." *Slate,* October 23, 2006.

Quotes from Tina Fey: Baldwin, Kristen. "One Fine Fey." *Entertainment Weekly*, April 15, 2007.

Quotes from Tina Fey: Moore, Frazier. "NBC's '30 Rock': Chockablock with Laughs." Associated Press, January 16, 2007.

Netburn, Deborah. "Comedy Writers Aren't Laughing About '60.'" *Los Angeles Times*, December 25, 2006.

Quotes from Alec Baldwin: Parker, Ian. "Why Me?" *New Yorker*, September 8, 2008.

Popkin, Jeremy. "Talking to Nate Corddry About 'Mom,' 'The Heat,' and Why Boston Stereotypes Will Always Be Funny." Vulture, September 23, 2013.

Quotes from Donald Glover: "Donald Glover of 'Community' and Derrick Comedy's Mystery Team." *The Sound of Young America*, December 10, 2009.

Quotes from Robert Carlock, Tina Fey, Lorne Michaels: *The Academy of Television Arts and Sciences Presents: An Evening with* 30 Rock. Via *30 Rock* Blu-Ray collection, Season 2, Disc 3. The Academy of Television Arts and Sciences.

Quotes from Keith Raywood: Keith Raywood Archive interview. By Jenni Matz. *The Interviews: An Oral History of Television*. Television Academy Foundation, May 19, 2017.

Quotes from Robert Carlock: DVD commentary. *30 Rock.* Season 7, episodes 12/13, "Hogcock!/Last Lunch." Universal Pictures Home Entertainment, 2013.

Quotes from Robert Carlock, John Riggi: DVD commentary. *30 Rock.* Season 2, episode 13, "Succession." Universal Pictures Home Entertainment, 2008.

Quotes from Scott Adsit: DVD commentary. *30 Rock*. Season 2, episode 11, "MILF Island." Universal Pictures Home Entertainment, 2008.

Sepinwall, Alan. "Studio 60: Really, I Ask You, Is That All There Is?" *What's Alan Watching?* (blog), October 2, 2006.

"The Lazy Journalist." "The TV Ratings Guide: 2006–07 Ratings History." TV Ratings Guide, retrieved March 21, 2021.

"The Lazy Journalist." "The TV Ratings Guide: 2019–20 Ratings History." TV Ratings Guide, June 19, 2020.

Quotes from Tina Fey: DVD commentary. *30 Rock*. Season 1, episode 12, "Black Tie." Universal Pictures Home Entertainment, 2007.

Quotes from Tina Fey: DVD commentary. *30 Rock*. Season 4, episode 12, "Verna." Universal Pictures Home Entertainment, 2010.

Quotes from Tina Fey: Topel, Fred. "*30 Rock* Strikes a Chord." *Wave*, January 16–29, 2008.

Quotes from Tracey Wigfield: DVD commentary. *30 Rock*. Season 5, episode 17, "Queen of Jordan." Universal Pictures Home Entertainment, 2011.

Quotes from Tracy Morgan: DVD commentary. *30 Rock*. Season 5, episode 7, "Brooklyn Without Limits." Universal Pictures Home Entertainment, 2011.

Quotes from Tracy Morgan: DVD commentary. *30 Rock*. Season 1, episode 12, "Tracy Does Conan." Universal Pictures Home Entertainment, 2007.

Voss, Erik. "The Day Comedy Won: How *30 Rock* Beat *Studio 60 on the Sunset Strip*." Vulture, December 17, 2010.

Quotes from Tina Fey: West, Kelly. "Interview: Tina Fey Talks About *30 Rock*." CinemaBlend, April 1, 2008.

Quotes from Jeff Zucker: Jeff Zucker Archive interview. By Dan Pasternack and Rachel Herman. *The Interviews: An Oral History of Television*. Television Academy Foundation, June 22, 2009, and August 11, 2009.

Season 2 (2007–08): The Strike

Author interviews with Scott Adsit, Adam Bernstein, Matthew Broderick, Todd Buonopane, Vanja Černjul, Grizz Chapman, Bellamy Forrest, Daisy Gardner, Andrew Guest, Jon Haller, Marceline Hugot, Kevin Ladson, Teresa Mastropierro, John Riggi, Don Scardino, Alan Sepinwall, Emily VanDerWerff, and Bradley Whitford.

Archival author interviews with Robert Carlock, Tami Sagher (2018): "'Werewolf Bar Mitzvah' From '30 Rock': An Oral History." LAist/KPCC.

Quotes from Tina Fey: "Tina Fey Dishes Details on Seinfeld's '30 Rock' Guest Slot." *Access Hollywood*, September 17, 2007.

Adalian, Josef. "NBC Rolls '30 Rock' into Hot Time Slot." *Variety*, April 22, 2008.

Quotes from Alec Baldwin: Baldwin, Alec. "Alec Baldwin on Fatherhood, '30 Rock,' Politics and More." *Washington Post*, December 15, 2008.

Quotes from Alec Baldwin: DVD commentary. *30 Rock*. Season 4, episode 4, "Audition Day." Universal Pictures Home Entertainment, 2010.

Quotes from Edie Falco: Edie Falco Archive interview. By Adrienne Faillace. *The Interviews: An Oral History of Television*. Television Academy Foundation, November 15, 2016.

Fleming, Michael. "Pair Will Carry U's 'Baby.'" *Variety*, September 27, 2006.

Ford, Rebecca, and Rose, Lacey. "100 Days That Changed Hollywood: The Writers Strike, 10 Years Later." *Hollywood Reporter*, May 17, 2018.

Quotes from Robert Carlock: Heisler, Steve. Robert Carlock Walks Us Through Highlights from *30 Rock*'s Six Seasons So Far (Part 1 of 4)." *A.V. Club,* May 21, 2012.

Heisler, Steve. "Robert Carlock Walks Us Through Some Series Highlights (Part 2 of 4)." *A.V. Club,* May 22, 2012.

Quotes from Tina Fey: "'30 Rock' Invites a Master to Its Domain.'" Hollywood.com, October 4, 2007.

Quotes from Jack McBrayer, Jane Krakowski: DVD commentary. *30 Rock*. Season 2, episode 15, "Cooter." Universal Pictures Home Entertainment, 2008.

Quotes from Jane Krakowski: DVD commentary. *30 Rock*. Season 2, episode 2, "The Collection." Universal Pictures Home Entertainment, 2008.

Quotes from Judah Friedlander: DVD commentary. *30 Rock*. Season 6, episode 10, "Alexis Goodlooking and the Case of the Missing Whisky." Universal Pictures Home Entertainment, 2012.

Quotes from Judah Friedlander: DVD commentary. *30 Rock*. Season 2, episode 7, "Cougars." Universal Pictures Home Entertainment, 2008.

Mojica, Yvonne. "Yvonne Mojica - Television Graphics." Accessed January 30, 2021, from yvonnemojica.com/Television_30ROCK.html.

Quotes from Tina Fey: DVD commentary. *30 Rock*. Season 2, episode 10, "Episode 210." Universal Pictures Home Entertainment, 2008.

Quotes from Keith Raywood: Keith Raywood Archive interview. By Jenni Matz. *The Interviews: An Oral History of Television*. Television Academy Foundation, May 17, 2017.

Quotes from Robert Carlock, John Riggi: DVD commentary. *30 Rock*. Season 2, episode 13, "Succession." Universal Pictures Home Entertainment, 2008.

Quotes from Tracy Morgan: Rosenblum, Emma. "How Tracy Morgan Differs from His '30 Rock' Character." *New York,* October 23, 2008.

Sepinwall, Alan. "Dispatches from the TCA Awards: Tom Hanks' Shame, Tina Fey's Pockets, Paul Giamatti's Habit and a Whole Lotta 'Mad Men.'" *What's Alan Watching?* (blog), July 20, 2008.

Quotes from Tina Fey: Spitznagel, Eric. "An Interview with Tina Fey." *Believer,* November 1, 2003.

Quotes from Tina Fey: DVD commentary. *30 Rock.* Season 4, episode 19, "Argus." Universal Pictures Home Entertainment, 2010.

Quotes from Tina Fey: DVD commentary. *30 Rock.* Season 1, episode 12, "Black Tie." Universal Pictures Home Entertainment, 2007.

Quotes from Tina Fey: DVD commentary. *30 Rock.* Season 2, episode 14, "Sandwich Day." Universal Pictures Home Entertainment, 2008.

Quotes from Tracy Morgan: DVD commentary. *30 Rock.* Season 1, episode 12, "Tracy Does Conan." Universal Pictures Home Entertainment, 2007.

Quotes from Tina Fey: West, Kelly. "Interview: Tina Fey Talks About *30 Rock.*" CinemaBlend, April 1, 2008.

Season 3 (2008–09): Tina's Doppelgänger Celebrity

Author interviews with Peter Agliata, Alan Alda, Todd Buonopane, Vali Chandrasekaran, Grizz Chapman, Nate Corddry, Ken Eluto, Paul Feig, Bellamy Forrest, Chris George, Jon Haller, Marceline Hugot, Norah Jones, Kevin Ladson, Patti LuPone, Ira Madison III, Beth McCarthy-Miller, John Riggi, Don Scardino, Alan Sepinwall, Jesse Thorn, Emily VanDerWerff, and Jovan Vitagliano.

Archival author interviews with Robert Carlock, Tami Sagher (2018): "'Werewolf Bar Mitzvah' From '30 Rock': An Oral History." LAist/KPCC.

Adalian, Josef. "*30 Rock* Is Pulling Blackface Episodes from Streaming Platforms and TV Reruns." Vulture, June 22, 2020.

Quotes from Alec Baldwin: Baldwin, Alec. "Alec Baldwin on Fatherhood, '30 Rock,' Politics and More." *Washington Post*, December 15, 2008.

Alter, Rebecca. "Every Blackface Episode and Scene That's Been Removed from Streaming So Far." Vulture, June 29, 2020.

Quotes from Tina Fey: Armstrong, Jennifer. "Tina Fey and Jon Hamm Talk About Coupling Up on '30 Rock.'" *Entertainment Weekly*, January 21, 2009.

Quotes from Tom Ceraulo: Ceraulo, Tom. "Behind the Scenes at the Final Days of '30 Rock.'" BuzzFeed, January 30, 2013.

Coyle, Jake. "Tina Fey 'Likely' to Play Sarah Palin on 'SNL.'" Associated Press, September 16, 2008.

Quotes from Donald Glover, Gillian Jacobs: DVD commentary. *30 Rock.* Season 4, episode 3, "Stone Mountain." Universal Pictures Home Entertainment, 2010.

Framke, Caroline. "Why Removing Blackface Episodes Is 'Just Trying to Band-Aid Over History.'" *Variety*, July 1, 2020.

Quotes from Robert Carlock: Hanel, Marnie. "Q&A: *30 Rock*'s Robert Carlock." *Vanity Fair*, November 6, 2008.

Quotes from Jeff Richmond: Heisler, Steve. "*30 Rock*'s Five Top Musical Moments, Picked by the Show's Composer, Jeff Richmond." Vulture, March 6, 2013.

Quotes from Jack McBrayer: DVD commentary. *30 Rock*. Season 2, episode 2, "The Collection." Universal Pictures Home Entertainment, 2008.

Quotes from Tina Fey: Jacobs, A. J. "Tina Fey, Make Us Laugh." *Esquire*, May 1, 2008.

Quotes from John Lutz: DVD commentary. *30 Rock*. Season 3, episode 13, "Goodbye, My Friend." Universal Pictures Home Entertainment, 2009.

Quotes from Jon Hamm: Jon Hamm Archive interview. By Jenni Matz. *The Interviews: An Oral History of Television*. Television Academy Foundation, June 25, 2015.

Quotes from Judah Friedlander: DVD commentary. *30 Rock*. Season 3, episode 13, "Goodbye, My Friend." Universal Pictures Home Entertainment, 2009.

Quotes from Alec Baldwin, Tina Fey: Levin, Gary. "Critics, Emmys Love '30 Rock'; When Will the Viewers?" *USA Today*, October 14, 2009.

Maas, Jennifer. "'The Office' Christmas Episode Edited to Remove Blackface Scene." *TheWrap,* June 26, 2020.

Quotes from Elaine Stritch: O'Connor, Mickey. "Have Yourself a Merry Little *30 Rock* Christmas!" TVGuide.com, December 11, 2008.

Quotes from Alan Alda: DVD commentary. *30 Rock*. Season 3, episode 21, "Mamma Mia." Universal Pictures Home Entertainment, 2009.

Quotes from Robert Carlock: Ryan, Mike. "'30 Rock' Showrunner: That 2009 Callout of Bill Cosby Was Intentional and Actually Had to Be Dialed Back." Uproxx, February 19, 2016.

Spitznagel, Eric. "Playboy Interview: Tina Fey." *Playboy*, January 2008.

Quotes from Tina Fey: DVD commentary. *30 Rock*. Season 3, episode 22, "Kidney Now!" Universal Pictures Home Entertainment, 2009.

Quotes from Tina Fey, Jeff Richmond: DVD commentary. *30 Rock*. Season 3, episode 8, "Flu Shot." Universal Pictures Home Entertainment, 2009.

Season 4 (2009–10): Selling NBC, a New Cast Member, and the Quest for the EGOT

Author interviews with Scott Adsit, Peter Agliata, Vali Chandrasekaran, Grizz Chapman, Nate Corddry, Josh Fadem, Daisy Gardner, Andrew Guest, Jon Haller, Marceline Hugot, Cheyenne Jackson, Patti LuPone, Beth McCarthy-Miller, Simon Rich, John Riggi, Lonny Ross, Don Scardino, Susan Schectar, Alan Sepinwall, Jesse Thorn, Michael Trim, and Emily VanDerWerff.

Quotes from Alec Baldwin: DVD commentary. *30 Rock*. Season 4, episode 4, "Audition Day." Universal Pictures Home Entertainment, 2010.

Quotes from Elizabeth Banks: Ausiello, Michael. "'30 Rock' Scoop: Elizabeth Banks Channels Sean Hannity, Romances Alec Baldwin." *Entertainment Weekly*, January 4, 2010.

Quotes from Tracy Morgan: Bereznak, Alyssa, and Surrey, Miles. "'Who's an EGOT?' How '30 Rock' Made a Fake Award into a Real-Life Goal." Ringer, February 21, 2019.

Quotes from Melissa Francis: Brissey, Breia. "Is This the Real Avery Jessup?" *Entertainment Weekly*, February 13, 2012.

Quotes from Robert Carlock: Crook, John. "'30 Rock' Returns for Its Fourth Season." Zap2it, October 8, 2009.

Quotes from Donald Glover, Gillian Jacobs: DVD commentary. *30 Rock*. Season 4, episode 3, "Stone Mountain." Universal Pictures Home Entertainment, 2010.

Quotes from Buzz Aldrin: Eng, Joyce. "Buzz Aldrin Dancing for Space—and Beyond." TVGuide.com, March 28, 2010.

Gilbert, Sophie. "The Strange, True, Tragicomic History of EGOT." *Atlantic*, June 9, 2016.

Hely, Steve, and Vali Chandrasekaran. *The Ridiculous Race: 26,000 Miles, 2 Guys, 1 Globe, No Airplanes*. New York: Holt Paperbacks, 2008.

Quotes from Jon Hamm: Hochberg, Mina. "Jon Hamm on Stolen and Playing a Single Don Draper: 'He Has a Monkey Off His Back.'" Vulture, March 11, 2010.

Quotes from Jack McBrayer: DVD commentary. *30 Rock*. Season 4, episode 21, "Emanuelle Goes to Dinosaur Land." Universal Pictures Home Entertainment, 2010.

Quotes from Jane Krakowski, Jack McBrayer: DVD commentary. *30 Rock*. Season 4, episode 5, "The Problem Solvers." Universal Pictures Home Entertainment, 2010.

Quotes from John Lutz: DVD commentary. *30 Rock*. Season 3, episode 13, "Goodbye, My Friend." Universal Pictures Home Entertainment, 2009.

Quotes from Alec Baldwin, Tina Fey: Levin, Gary. "Critics Love '30 Rock'; When Will the Viewers?" *USA Today*, October 15, 2009.

Quotes from Elizabeth Banks: Lisotta, Christopher. "Emmy-Worthy Guest Performers Deliver under Pressure." Associated Press, June 8, 2010.

Quotes from Dean Winters: Miller, Gerri. "Dean Winters Survived 17 Surgeries and 9 Amputations, Who Knew?" Made Man, February 27, 2015.

"Dean Winters' Amazing Journey Back from Death." *Page Six*, June 18, 2010.

Quotes from Robert Carlock: Heisler, Steve. "Robert Carlock Walks Us Through Some Series Highlights (Part 3 of 4)." *A.V. Club*, May 22, 2012.

Schneider, Michael. "NBC Renews Entire Thursday Night Comedy Block for next Season." *Variety*, March 5, 2010.

Quotes from Sue Galloway, John Lutz: DVD commentary. *30 Rock*. Season 4, episode 10, "Black Light Attack!" Universal Pictures Home Entertainment, 2010.

Quotes from Tina Fey: DVD commentary. *30 Rock*. Season 4, episode 12, "Verna." Universal Pictures Home Entertainment, 2010.

Quotes from Tina Fey, Jeff Richmond: DVD commentary. *30 Rock*. Season 4, episode 19, "Argus." Universal Pictures Home Entertainment, 2010.

Quotes from Keith Powell: Wieselman, Jarett. "'30 Rock' Star Keith Powell: Cakes for Everybody!" *Page Six*, September 23, 2010.

Season 5 (2010–11): Breaking the Format

Author interviews with Scott Adsit, Peter Agliata, Todd Buonopane, Vali Chandrasekaran, Grizz Chapman, Margaret Cho, Josh Fadem, Paul Feig, Daisy Gardner, Chris George, Dennie Gordon, Jon Haller, Cheyenne Jackson, Kevin Ladson, Nathan Lane, Paula Leggett Chase, Beth McCarthy-Miller, John Riggi, Alan Sepinwall, Jesse Thorn, and Emily VanDerWerff.

Archival author interview with Tracey Wigfield (2020). "Only in 2020 Would 'Saved by the Bell' Be a Guiding Light for Humanity—The New Class Takes Down White Privilege with Precision and Jokes." LAist/KPCC.

Quotes from Tracy Morgan: Bereznak, Alyssa, and Miles Surrey. "'Who's an EGOT?' How '30 Rock' Made a Fake Award into a Real-Life Goal." Ringer, February 21, 2019.

Cerasaro, Pat. "InDepth InterView: Reality Bites? Janeane Garofalo on RUSSIAN TRANSPORT, GENERAL EDUCATION, BAD PARENTS & More!" BroadwayWorld .com, February 25, 2012.

Quotes from Robert Carlock: Heisler, Steve. "*30 Rock* Showrunner Robert Carlock Walks Us Through Some Recent Series Highlights." *A.V. Club,* May 24, 2012.

Madison III, Ira. "Tina Fey Is As Bad at Clapbacks As Aaron Sorkin." MTV News, April 28, 2016.

Quotes from Jon Hamm: Jon Hamm Archive interview. By Jenni Matz. *The Interviews: An Oral History of Television.* Television Academy Foundation, June 25, 2015.

Quotes from Judah Friedlander: DVD commentary. *30 Rock*. Season 5, episode 15, "It's Never Too Late for Now." Universal Pictures Home Entertainment, 2011.

Ng, Philiana. "'30 Rock's' Tracy Morgan Undergoes Kidney Transplant." *Hollywood Reporter*, December 20, 2010.

Quotes from Lorne Michaels: Parker, Ian. "Why Me?" *New Yorker*, September 1, 2008.

Quotes from Tina Fey: "'30 Rock' Star and Creator Moves On." *Fresh Air*, NPR, April 13, 2011.

Smith, Chris. "How 'Saturday Night Live' Became a Grim Joke." *New York,* March 13, 1995.

Quotes from Sue Galloway, John Lutz: DVD commentary. *30 Rock.* Season 5, episode 12, "Operation Righteous Cowboy Lightning." Universal Pictures Home Entertainment, 2011.

"Alec Baldwin Says NBC's '30 Rock' Is Ending Next Year." *Hollywood Reporter*, April 6, 2011.

"Thursday Finals: *The Big Bang Theory, $#*!, 30 Rock, The Office, Outsourced, Grey's Anatomy, Fringe* All Adjusted Up." TV by the Numbers, October 17, 2010.

Quotes from Tina Fey: DVD commentary. *30 Rock.* Season 5, episode 4, "Live Show (West Coast Version)." Universal Pictures Home Entertainment, 2011.

Quotes from Tina Fey, Jeff Richmond: DVD commentary. *30 Rock.* Season 5, episode 18, "Plan B." Universal Pictures Home Entertainment, 2011.

Quotes from Tom Ceraulo, Tracey Wigfield: DVD commentary. *30 Rock.* Season 5, episode 17, "Queen of Jordan." Universal Pictures Home Entertainment, 2011.

Quotes from Tracy Morgan: DVD commentary. *30 Rock.* Season 5, episode 7, "Brooklyn Without Limits." Universal Pictures Home Entertainment, 2011.

Season 6 (2012): Jack vs. North Korea

Author interviews with Scott Adsit, Vali Chandrasekaran, Chris George, Cheyenne Jackson, Kevin Ladson, Paula Leggett Chase, Patti LuPone, Teresa Mastropierro, Beth McCarthy-Miller, Linda Mendoza, John Riggi, and Alan Sepinwall.

Brissey, Breia. "'30 Rock': Anyone Else Tired of Hazel Wassername?" *Entertainment Weekly*, March 30, 2012.

Quotes from Robert Carlock: Harmanci, Reyhan. "'30 Rock' Co-Creator Tells the Story Behind Leap Day William." Atlas Obscura, February 29, 2016.

Quotes from Luke Del Tredici: Ivie, Devon. "The Story Behind *30 Rock*'s Magnificently Silly Leap Day Episode." Vulture, February 28, 2020.

Quotes from Jane Krakowski, Colleen McGuinness: DVD commentary. *30 Rock.* Season 7, episode 8, "My Whole Life Is Thunder." Universal Pictures Home Entertainment, 2013.

Quotes from Jane Krakowski: DVD commentary. *30 Rock.* Season 6, episode 19, "Live from Studio 6H." Universal Pictures Home Entertainment, 2013.

Quotes from Judah Friedlander: DVD commentary. *30 Rock.* Season 6, episode 10, "Alexis Goodlooking and the Case of the Missing Whisky." Universal Pictures Home Entertainment, 2012.

Quotes from Tina Fey: Karasawa, Chiemi. *"Elaine Stritch: Shoot Me."* Isotope Films/ Sundance Selects, 2013.

Quotes from Tracy Morgan: Sytsma, Alan. "Tracy Morgan Really, Really Likes the New Benihana." *Grub Street,* February 24, 2012.

"Tracy Morgan: I'll Kill My Son If He Acts Gay." TMZ, June 10, 2011.

Quotes from Tom Ceraulo, Tracey Wigfield: DVD commentary. *30 Rock.* Season 6, episode 1, "Dance Like Nobody's Watching." Universal Pictures Home Entertainment, 2012.

Quotes from Tracey Wigfield: DVD commentary. *30 Rock.* Season 7, episode 7, "Mazel Tov, Dummies!" Universal Pictures Home Entertainment, 2013.

Season 7 (2012–13): Happy-ish Endings

Author interviews with Scott Adsit, Matthew Broderick, Todd Buonopane, Vali Chandrasekaran, Grizz Chapman, Daisy Gardner, Andrew Guest, Jon Haller, Marceline Hugot, Kevin Ladson, Beth McCarthy-Miller, Linda Mendoza, John Riggi, Don Scardino, Alan Sepinwall, and Emily VanDerWerff.

Quotes from Alec Baldwin: Baldwin, Alec. *Nevertheless: A Memoir.* New York: Harper-Collins, 2017.

Quotes from Tom Ceraulo: Ceraulo, Tom. "Behind the Scenes at the Final Days of '30 Rock.'" BuzzFeed, January 30, 2013.

Eum, Jennifer. "Goodbye *30 Rock*: Low Ratings, but Plenty of Awards." *Forbes*, January 31, 2013.

Quotes from Jane Krakowski, Colleen McGuinness: DVD commentary. *30 Rock.* Season 7, episode 8, "My Whole Life Is Thunder." Universal Pictures Home Entertainment, 2013.

Quotes from Jane Krakowski, Jeff Richmond: DVD commentary. *30 Rock.* Season 7, episode 11, "A Goon's Deed in a Weary World." Universal Pictures Home Entertainment, 2013.

Quotes from Robert Carlock, Tina Fey: DVD commentary. *30 Rock.* Season 7, episodes 12/13, "Hogcock!/Last Lunch." Universal Pictures Home Entertainment, 2013.

Quotes from Tom Ceraulo, Tracey Wigfield: DVD commentary. *30 Rock.* Season 7, episode 7, "Mazel Tov, Dummies!" Universal Pictures Home Entertainment, 2013.

30 Rock's Legacy: From *Unbreakable Kimmy Schmidt* to *Mr. Mayor*

Author interviews with Scott Adsit, Matthew Broderick, Vali Chandrasekaran, Grizz Chapman, Josh Fadem, Bellamy Forrest, Daisy Gardner, Chris George, Nathan Lane, Ira Madison III, Teresa Mastropierro, Beth McCarthy-Miller, Paul Reubens,

John Riggi, Don Scardino, Susan Schectar, Alan Sepinwall, Jesse Thorn, Emily VanDerWerff, and Bradley Whitford.

Archival author interview with Robert Carlock (2018): "'Werewolf Bar Mitzvah' from '30 Rock': An Oral History." LAist/KPCC.

Archival author interview with Vella Lovell (2021).

D'Alessandro, Anthony. "'Unbreakable Kimmy Schmidt's Tina Fey & Robert Carlock on Netflix and Their Modern Princess Tale." *Deadline*, May 13, 2015.

Quotes from Jeff Richmond: Dowd, Maureen. "What Tina Fey Wants." *Vanity Fair*, December 1, 2008.

Ferguson, LaToya. "*30 Rock* Returns (Sort of) to Shill NBC Universal and Demolish Any Remaining Fourth Wall." *A.V. Club,* July 17, 2020.

Lloyd, Robert. "'Mr. Mayor' Is an Outsider's Comedy About L.A. But Don't Give Up on It Just Yet." *Los Angeles Times*, January 7, 2021.

Hubbard, Matt. (@mrhubbard00). "For ten seconds in 2012 I convinced a room full of writers that the last scene in the 30 Rock finale should end with Kenneth Parcell Quantum Leaping into another body. I consider this my greatest creative achievement." Twitter, January 30, 2021. https://twitter.com/mrhubbard00/status/1355354615055671297.

Porter, Rick. "'30 Rock' Special, 'Holey Moley': TV Ratings Thursday, July 16, 2020." *Hollywood Reporter*, July 17, 2020.

Sepinwall, Alan. "'Mr. Mayor': Ted Danson Goes to City Hall." *Rolling Stone*, January 6, 2021.

Quotes from Tina Fey: DVD commentary. *30 Rock*. Season 4, episode 12, "Verna." Universal Pictures Home Entertainment, 2010.

Wallenstein, Andrew. "Tina Fey Inks 4-Year Pact with Universal TV." *Variety*, September 25, 2012.

SELECTED BIBLIOGRAPHY

30 Rock. 2006–13. DVD & Blu-Ray.

30 Rock scripts

Additional background interviews, emails, written materials/notes

Deadline Hollywood

Fey, Tina. *Bossypants*. New York: Little, Brown and Company, 2011.

Hollywood Reporter

Saturday Night Live

Studio 60 on the Sunset Strip. 2006–07.

Variety